Mastering Mechanical Desktop: Parametric Design

Mastering Mechanical Desktop: Parametric Design

RON K. C. CHENG
The Hong Kong Polytechnic University

Autodesk.
Press

I(T)P   An International Thomson Publishing Company

Albany • Bonn • Boston • Cincinnati • Detroit • London • Madrid
Melbourne • Mexico City • New York • Pacific Grove • Paris • San Francisco
Singapore • Tokyo • Toronto • Washington

Trademarks

AutoCAD, Mechanical Desktop, AutoCAD Designer and AutoSurf are registered trademarks of Autodesk, Inc.
DOS and Windows are a registered trademark of Microsoft Corporation.
The ITP logo is a trademark under license.

Copyright ©1998
PWS Publishing Company
Autodesk Press imprint
an International Thomson Publishing Company

Printed and bound in the United States of America.
1 2 3 4 5 6 7 8 9 10 — 01 00 99 98 97

For more information contact:

Autodesk Press
3 Columbia Circle, Box 15-015
Albany, New York 12212-5015

International Thomson Publishing Europe
Berkshire House
168–173 High Holborn
London WC1V 7AA
England

Thomas Nelson Australia
102 Dodds Street
South Melbourne, 3205
Victoria, Australia

Nelson Canada
1120 Birchmont Road
Scarborough, Ontario
Canada M1K 5G4

International Thomson Publishing Southern Africa
Building 18, Constantia Park
240 Old Pretoria Road
P.O. Box 2459
Halfway House, 1685 South Africa

International Thomson Editores
Campos Eliseos 385, Piso 7
Col. Polanco
11560 Mexico D.F., Mexico

International Thomson Publishing GmbH
Königswinterer Strasse 418
53227 Bonn, Germany

International Thomson Publishing France
Tour Maine-Montparnasse
33, Avenue du Maine
75755 Paris Cedex 15, France

International Thomson Publishing Asia
221 Henderson Road
#05-10 Henderson Building
Singapore 0315

International Thomson Publishing Japan
Hirakawacho Kyowa Building, 31
2-2-1 Hirakawacho
Chiyoda-ku, Tokyo 102
Japan

Assistant Editor: Suzanne Jeans
Production Editor: Andrea Goldman
Manufacturing Buyer: Andrew Christensen
Marketing Manager: Nathan Wilbur
Interior Design/Cover Image: Ron C. K. Cheng
Cover Design: Autodesk, Inc.
Cover Printer: Phoenix Color Corp.
Printer & Binder: Courier–Westford

Library of Congress Cataloging-in-Publication Data

Cheng, Ron.
    Mastering Mechanical Desktop: parametric design / Ron K. C. Cheng.
        p.   cm.
    Includes index.
    ISBN 0–534–95109–0
    1. Engineering graphics. 2. Autodesk Mechanical desktop. 3. Engineering design--Data processing.
    4. AutoCAD Designer. I. Title.
T353.C518 1997   97–29788
620'.0042'02855369--dc21   CIP

Contents

Preface

This book is intended for people who would like to use AutoCAD Designer to produce engineering designs effectively. AutoCAD Designer is a component of Mechanical Desktop. (The other component is AutoSurf, which is covered in another book in this series.) Because it is a parametric feature-based solid modeling system, AutoCAD Designer enables you to produce dimension-driven three-dimensional solid models and to create virtual assemblies of the solid models.

Within the framework of the AutoCAD CAD system, there are two kinds of solids: AutoCAD Designer solids and AutoCAD native solids. Both are three-dimensional solid models, and they are fully compatible with each other. You may convert a native solid to a static parametric solid part or convert a parametric solid to a native solid. AutoCAD Designer is also compatible with AutoSurf objects. You may use AutoSurf to create a NURBS surface to cut an AutoCAD Designer solid. Thus you can have a free-form surface incorporated into a solid model. You may also convert a parametric solid model to a set of NURBS surfaces.

This book will guide you in using AutoCAD Designer to produce a number of parametric solid parts, virtual assemblies, and engineering documents. In addition, you will learn how to integrate AutoCAD Designer with AutoSurf and AutoCAD native solids. There are six chapters and an appendix in this book. Chapter 1 is an introduction to the AutoCAD Designer application. Chapter 2 guides you through the steps required to produce a dimension-driven parametric solid by extruding. In Chapter 3, you will learn how to create solid features by sweeping and revolving. After learning how to make solid models, you will learn how to assemble the solid parts together to form virtual assemblies in Chapter 4. Documentation is sometimes necessary. Chapter 5 shows you how to produce two-dimensional engineering drawings from solid parts and assemblies. AutoCAD Designer is fully compatible with native solids and AutoSurf surfaces. Chapter 6 takes you through the steps to inter-operate the three types of objects. The AutoCAD Designer commands and variables used are summarized in the appendix. After working through the projects in this book, you should be able to apply the techniques to use AutoCAD Designer in engineering designs.

Acknowledgments

This book never would have been realized without the contributions of many individuals.
    I am grateful to the following reviewers for their thoughtful suggestions and help:
* Robert A. Chin, Department of Industrial Technology, East Carolina University

- Hollis Driskell, Department of Drafting and Design, Trinity Valley Community College
- Michael Stewart, Department of Engineering Technology, University of Arkansas
- Ed Wheeler, Engineering Department, University of Tennessee at Martin

Several people at PWS Publishing also deserve special mention, particularly Bill Barter, Jonathan Plant, Suzanne Jeans, Andrea Goldman, Tricia Kelly, and Monica Block.

Chapter 1

Introduction

AutoCAD Designer is a parametric feature-based solid modeling system for creating, and subsequent editing, of a dimension-driven three-dimensional solid model in a computer. It enables you to create a parametric solid model from rough sketches, to assemble solid models, to output two-dimensional engineering drawings, and to generate exploded views from an assembly.

Using AutoCAD Designer to create a design, you will start from a rough sketch that need not be precise at all. Horizontal lines need not be absolutely horizontal. Vertical lines need not be perfectly vertical. End points do not have to coincide with each other. After you make a sketch, AutoCAD Designer will, according to a set of rules, resolve the sketch to a profile, a path, or a cutting line.

To create a parametric solid feature, you may extrude a profile linearly, or revolve a profile about an axis, or sweep a profile along a path. With a cutting line, you may use it to create an offset section while preparing a two-dimensional engineering drawing from the solid model. See Figure 1.1.

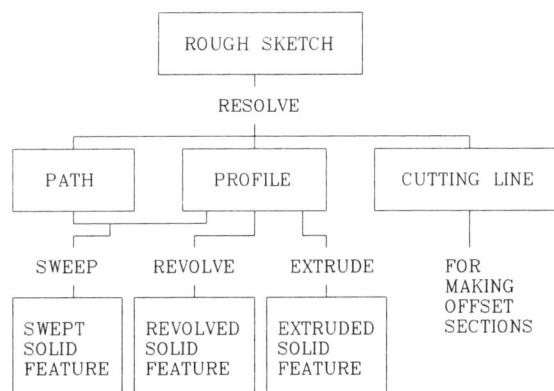

Figure 1.1 From rough sketch to solid feature

In regard to two-dimensional drawing, AutoCAD Designer can automatically generate a detailed drawing with multiple views from a solid part. The solid part and the engineering drawing have bidirectional associativity. If you change a solid part, the detailed drawing changes. If you modify the detailed drawing, the solid part changes as well.

1

A design usually consists of several components. You may make use of AutoCAD Designer to assemble the components together, to check interference, to generate a bill of materials, and to output an exploded view. Furthermore, AutoCAD Designer provides facilities to output mass property information.

1.1   Sketching Approach

When you begin to design, you normally concentrate on shapes rather than on dimensions. However, many computer-aided design systems require you to input precise lengths and orientations of entities from the onset. In the preliminary design stage, such data are not available.

With AutoCAD Designer, you may use the computer as an electronic sketching pad to record your design idea. You may start from rough sketches and determine the dimensions later. The starting point for the creation of a parametric feature-based solid model is to make a sketch, which is not an accurate drawing.

In the sketch, dimensions are not important, lines need not be absolutely horizontal or vertical, and objects need not be joined precisely together at their ends. In fact, you should concentrate only on forms and shapes. You will focus on the dimensions at a later design stage.

After you have produced a rough sketch, you should let AutoCAD Designer resolve it to a profile, a path, or a cutting line (see Figure 1.2). In the process of resolving a sketch, AutoCAD Designer applies, unless otherwise determined, the following logical geometric constraints:

- Objects will join together at their end points if they are close enough.
- Lines, arcs, and circles will become tangential if they are nearly tangential to each other.
- Arcs and circles will become concentric if they are nearly concentric.
- Arcs and circles will have the same radius if they have nearly the same radius.
- Lines will become horizontal if they are nearly horizontal.
- Lines will become vertical if they are nearly vertical.
- Lines will become parallel if they are nearly parallel to each other.
- Lines will become perpendicular if they are nearly perpendicular to each other.
- Lines will become collinear if they lie nearly on the same straight line.

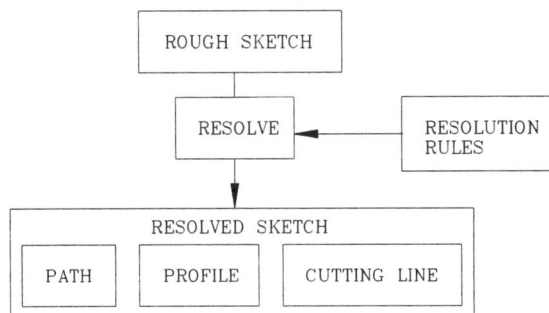

Figure 1.2 Resolution of rough sketch

1.2   Geometric Constraints and Parametric Dimensions

You may resolve a sketch to a profile, a path, or a cutting line (see Figure 1.3). Before you may use it for subsequent operation, you should fully constrain it. Otherwise, you may have unpredictable result later when you modify your solid. Fully constraining a profile, a path, or a cutting line involves two stages. First, you will make necessary adjustments to the geometric constraints that AutoCAD Designer automatically applies to the sketch. You should delete those constraints that you do not want, and you have to add those constraints that AutoCAD Designer does not apply for you. For example, AutoCAD Designer will not apply a horizontal constraint to a line that deviates largely from being horizontal.

Besides geometric constraints, you need to add parametric dimensions to complete the constraint requirement. To add dimensions, you may supply a numeric value or an expression as an equation. For example, you may set the width of a rectangle to be in a certain proportion to its length. You can establish a set of global parameters that control the dimensions of a number of solid parts in a file or across many files.

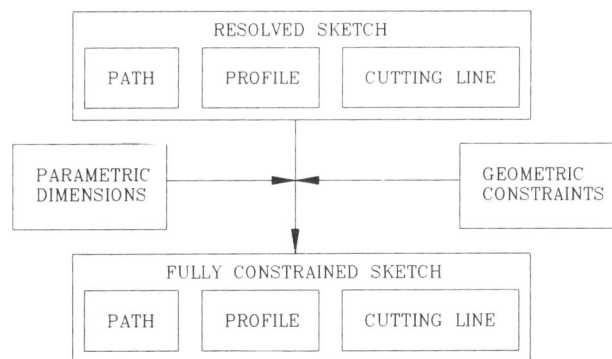

Figure 1.3 Creation of sketched solid features

In the process of adding geometric constraints and parametric dimensions, you will note the instantaneous change in the form and shape of the profile, path or cutting line. The dimensions drive the form and shape.

1.3   Parametric Feature-Based Approach

AutoCAD Designer operates on the building-block principle. To make a three-dimensional solid model, you have to analyze your design to break it down into a number of simple solid features and then create these solid features one by one. The first solid feature of a model is called the base feature; subsequent solid features may unite to, subtract from, or form an intersection with the existing solid feature.

AutoCAD Designer has two kinds of solid features, the sketched solid features and the placed solid features. The sketched solid features are solids that you create from a sketch by extruding, revolving, or sweeping. The placed solid features are the chamfer feature, fillet feature, and hole feature. A placed solid feature differs from a sketched solid feature in that it does not derive from a sketch. You do not have to sketch a chamfer, a fillet, or a hole. You simply add them to the existing feature by specifying their parameters. See Figure 1.4.

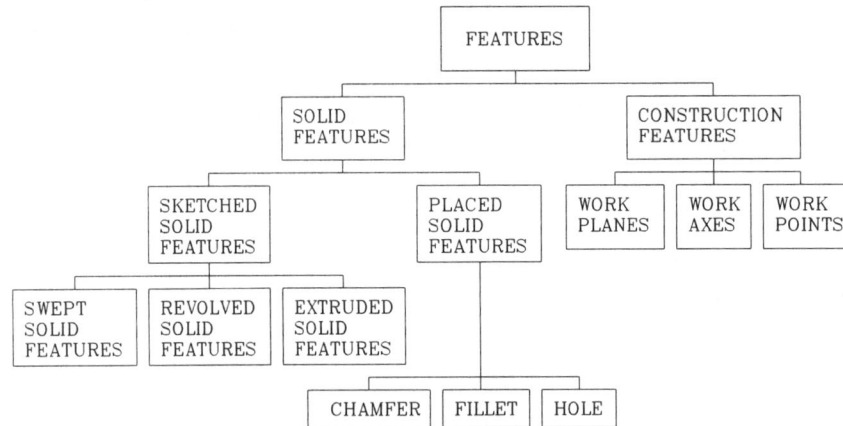

Figure 1.4 Types of solid features

AutoCAD Designer is a feature-based design tool. See Figure 1.5. You may define and maintain parametric relationships between the solid features by prior establishment of parametric work axes, work planes, and work points. Collectively speaking, the work axes, the work planes, and the work points are called construction features. They form an integral part of the parametric solid part.

Figure 1.5 Building-block principle

1.4 Assembly and Documentation

With two or more solid parts, you may set up an assembly. The solid parts that make up the assembly may come from a single drawing file or from a set of drawing files. To create an assembly, you will express the solid parts as component definitions. Then you will insert the component definitions as instances. Finally, you will apply assembly constraints to control the relationship between the instances. The assembly constraints concern six degrees of freedom — translational freedom in three directions and rotational freedom about three axes.

```
┌──────────┐      ┌──────────────┐
│  SOLID   │─────▶│  COMPONENT   │
│  PARTS   │      │ DEFINITIONS  │
└──────────┘      └──────────────┘
                          │
                          ▼
                  ┌──────────────┐
                  │  INSTANCES   │
                  └──────────────┘      ┌──────────────┐
                          │        ◀────│  ASSEMBLY    │
                          ▼             │ CONSTRAINTS  │
                  ┌──────────────┐      └──────────────┘
                  │   ASSEMBLY   │
                  └──────────────┘
```

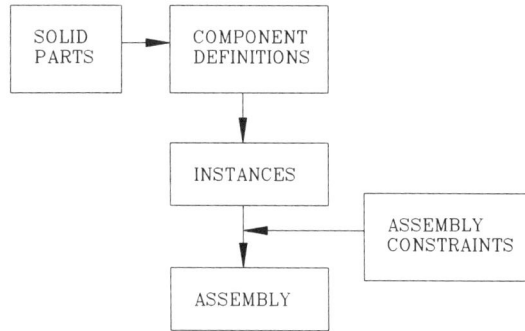

Figure 1.6 From solid parts to assembly

You may generate a two-dimensional engineering drawing from a three-dimensional solid part and an exploded view from an assembly. The engineering drawing and the solid parts are associated bidirectionally. If you edit a solid part, the document is updated automatically. If you change a parametric dimension of a document, the solid part is also modified.

1.5   Compatibility and Inter-operation

AutoCAD Designer solids are fully compatible with AutoCAD native solid models and AutoSurf NURBS surface models.

You may inter-operate them. You may change an AutoCAD designer solid to a native solid or convert a native solid into a static AutoCAD Designer base feature. You may use an AutoSurf NURBS surface as a surface feature to cut a parametric solid, or to convert a parametric solid to a set of NURBS surfaces. See Figure 1.7.

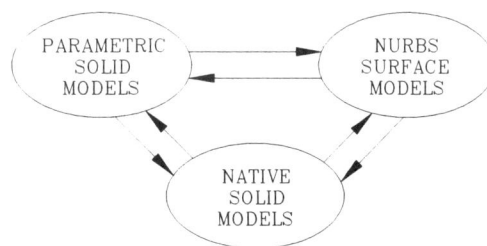

Figure 1.7 Inter-operation

1.6   About This Book

This book is designed to give you an opportunity to practice applying AutoCAD Designer to produce three-dimensional parametric engineering designs, to create an assembly from a set of solid parts, to output two-dimensional engineering drawings, and to become familiar with the utilities provided. It is presumed that you have installed the AutoCAD Designer application properly in the computer. There are six chapters and an appendix in this book. This chapter has offered a brief introduction to the AutoCAD Designer application.

In Chapter 2, you will create two solid parts. Each of them consists of several sketched solid features and placed solid features. You will make rough sketches, resolve the sketches, constrain the sketches fully, and extrude the sketches to form solid features. To maintain parametric relationships between the sketched solid features, you will establish parametric construction features, on which you will set up sketch planes for making sketches. In addition to sketched solid features, you will also add placed solid features to the solid parts. In order to experience the flexibility of solid model making with dimension-driven parametric approach, you will edit the solid part by altering the parametric dimensions and geometric constraints of the features. You will also work on display control of three-dimensional objects.

After learning how to extrude a profile to form a solid feature in Chapter 2, you will learn, in Chapter 3, how to make a solid feature by sweeping a profile along a path and by revolving a profile about an axis. You will work on two sets of solid parts. You will create four solid parts of an universal joint in a single file and will create three solid parts of an electric motor casing in separate files. To maintain a relationship between the parametric dimensions of the solid parts within a single file, and across a set of files, you will set up global parameters. Then you will learn how to modify a set of solid parts by altering the values of the global parameters. In addition, you will work on solid-part utilities.

Having made two sets of solid parts in Chapter 3, you will put them together to form two assemblies in Chapter 4. You will create local and external component definitions from the solid parts. From the component definitions, you will create instances of the definitions. Then you will apply assembly constraints to the instances to assemble them together to form sub-assembly and assembly. As in the case of solid parts, there are assembly utilities for you to work on.

Upon completion of Chapters 2, 3, and 4, you should be able to create dimension-driven parametric solid models, create component definitions, and assemble the instances together. In Chapter 5, you will create two-dimensional engineering drawings from a solid part and create exploded drawings from an assembly. The two-dimensional drawings and the three-dimensional models are associated bidirectionally. Changes in the parametric dimensions will cause changes to both the three-dimensional model and the two-dimensional drawing.

In Chapter 6, you will inter-operate three types of AutoCAD 3D models: the native solid models, the NURBS surface models, and the parametric solid models. To work on this chapter, you need to have access to the AutoSurf application.

Finally, the appendix offers a brief explanation of all the commands and variables provided by AutoCAD Designer. To facilitate application, the commands are arranged in logical groups rather than in alphabetical order.

1.7 Command Execution

After you have installed AutoCAD Designer properly and used the default Designer menu, you should have four additional pull-down menu items that are specific to AutoCAD Designer — Parts, Assemblies, Drawings, and Mtools. If you do not find these pull-down menu items, you may use the MENULOAD command (Windows version) to add them to the Windows menu bar. See Figure 1.8.

When the dialog box appears, pick the Menu Bar page. Then select the respective items for insertion.

Command: **MENULOAD**

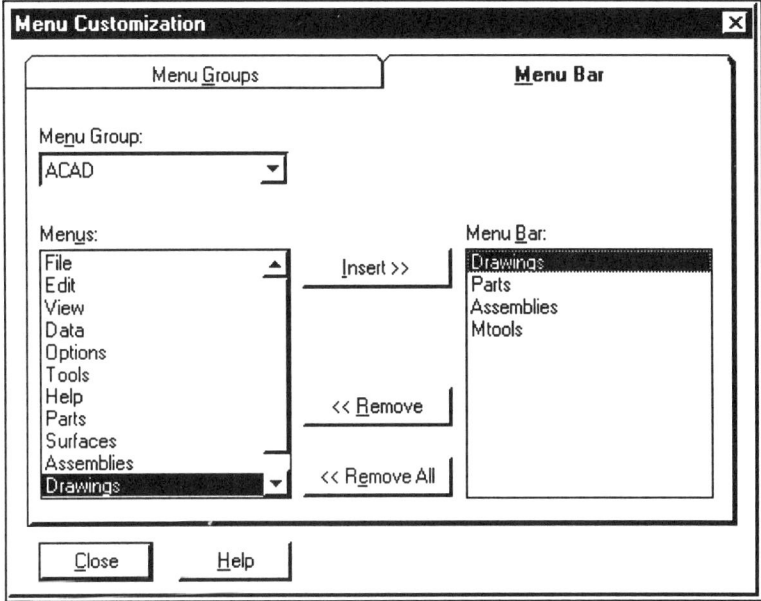

Figure 1.8 Loading AutoCAD Designer pull-down menu items

In Windows version, you may have five additional toolbars related to AutoCAD Designer –– Part Create, Part Edit, Assembly, Drawing, and View. If you do not find these toolbars, you may pick the Mtools pull-down menu, then click the Mechanical Toolbars item, and then select an item there.

Suppose that you want to use the Part Create toolbar. You should select the Mtools pull-down menu, then click the Mechanical Toolbars item, and then click the Part Create item. See Figure 1.9 and Figure 1.10.

<Mtools>   <Mechanical Toolbars>   <Part Create>

> **Note**:
> In the delineation that follows, <AAA> <BBB> will mean picking the <AAA> pull-down menu and then clicking the <BBB> item.

Command: **TOOLBAR**
Toolbar name (or ALL): ACAD.PART_CREATE
Show/Hide/Left/Right/Top/Bottom/Float: <Show>: _show

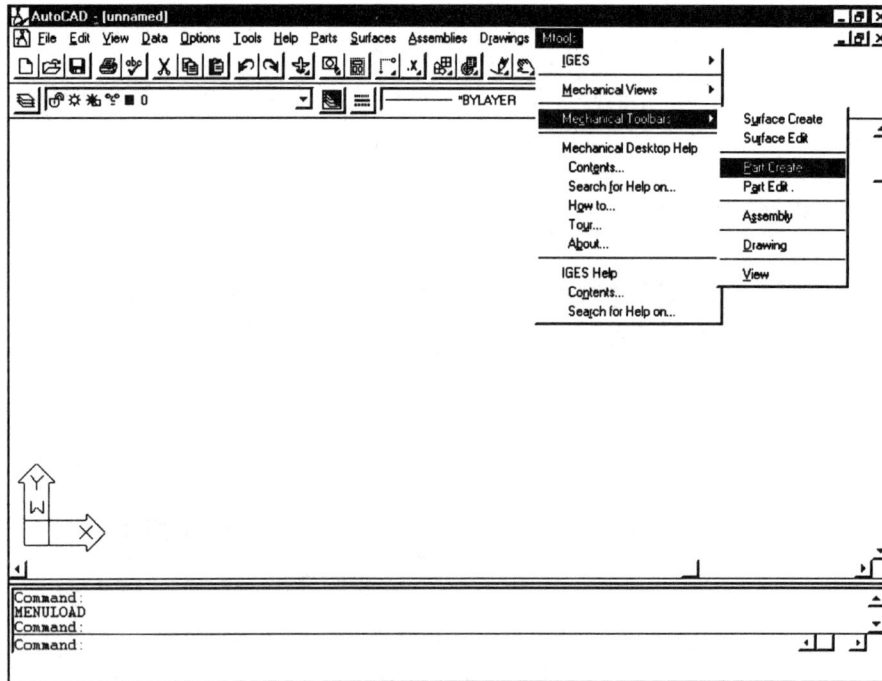

Figure 1.9 Bringing up the Part Create toolbar

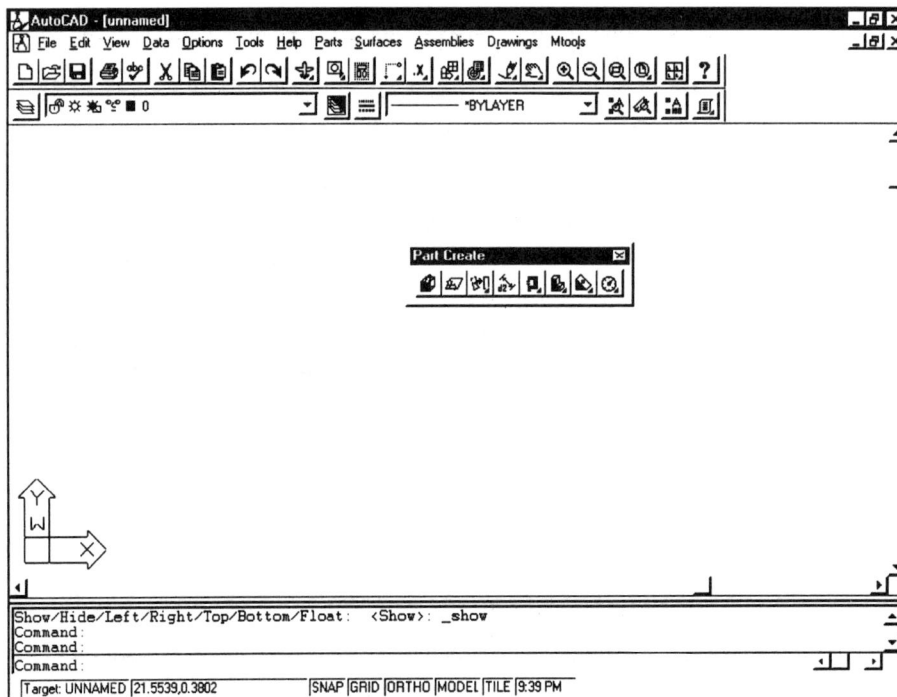

Figure 1.10 The Part Create toolbar shown up

With the pull-down menu and toolbars in position, you may execute an AutoCAD Designer command in several ways. You may use the pointing device to pick an item from the pull-down menu or the cascading menu from the pull-down menu. You may also use the pointing device to click an icon from the toolbars (Windows version). Finally, you may directly key in the command at the command window (Windows version) or the command prompt area (DOS version).

1.8 Registered Trademarks

The followings are registered trademarks of AutoDesk, Inc.:
AutoCAD
AutoCAD Designer
AutoSurf

Chapter 2
Parametric Approach

AutoCAD Designer is a flexible parametric solid modeling tool. In line with general design procedure, you need to decide the final form and shape of the model. Unlike the conventional approach, however, you need not concern yourself with the exact shape and dimension from the onset. After you are satisfied with the form and shape, you may then change the size and edit the features.

In this chapter, to appreciate the use of AutoCAD Designer as a tool in mechanical engineering design, you will create the solid models of two engineering components. See Figure 2.1.

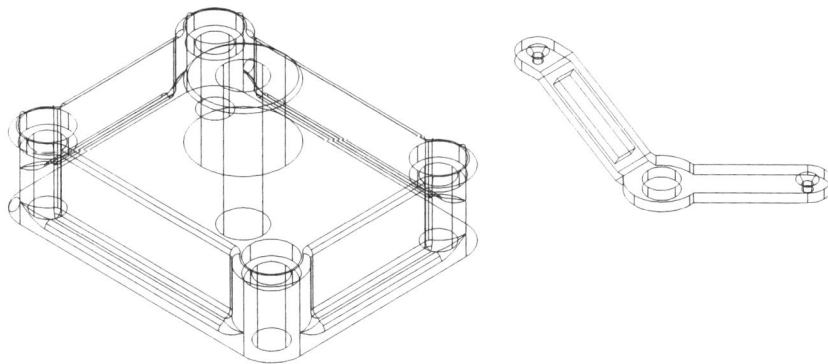

Figure 2.1 Two engineering components

2.1 Analyzing the First Component

Given a solid model to create, you should take some time to analyze its constituents. This analysis process will help you to break down the model into a number of simple solid features.

In AutoCAD Designer terms, there are two types of solid features, the sketched solid features and the placed solid features. The first sketched solid feature of a solid part is called the base feature. You may add sketched solid features to a solid part by cutting, joining, or intersecting. The second type of solid feature is the placed solid feature. The distinction between a sketched solid feature and a placed solid feature is that a sketched solid feature starts from a rough sketch, whereas a placed solid feature is added to the solid part directly.

Figure 2.2 shows a breakdown of sketched solid features of the first model.

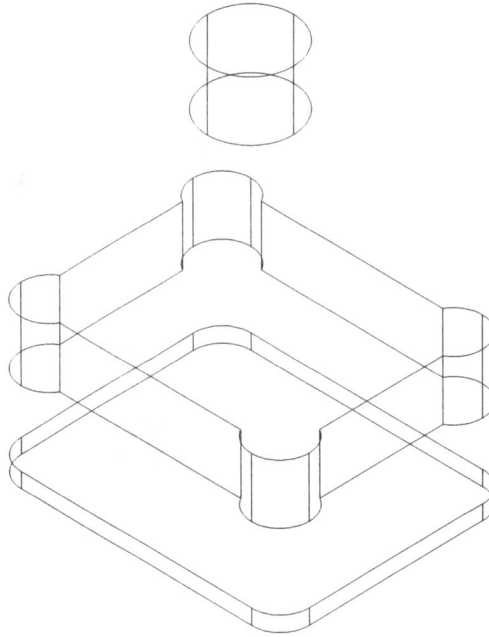

Figure 2.2 Sketched solid features of the first component

There are three sketched solid features in this model. You will build them from rough sketches. First you will sketch, resolve, and extrude the base feature. Then you will make the second feature and join it to the base feature. Next you will follow a similar procedure to make the third feature. Finally, you will place the chamfer feature, the fillet features, and the hole features to the solid part.

2.2   Sketching, Resolving, and Extruding

AutoCAD allows you to choose dialog box interaction or purely command prompt line interaction. To use dialog box display, you have to ensure that the system variable CMDDIA is set to 1.

Command: **CMDDIA**
New value for CMDDIA: **1**

To begin, let us take a look at the version number of the AutoCAD Designer that you have installed in your computer. Run the AMABOUT command. This command tells you the version number as well as the release notes. You may need this information. Click the [OK] button afterwards.

Command: **AMABOUT**

```
┌─────────────────────────────────────────────────────────────────┐
│ Autodesk Mechanical Desktop(R) R1                                 │
│  ╱◥◣   AutoCAD(R) Designer      R2        Current Version         │
│ ╱◢◥◣   AutoSurf(R)             R3        Current Version         │
│╱◢◥◣◥◣  Assembly Module         R1        Current Version         │
│        Drawing Manager Module  R2        Current Version         │
│ ┌───────────────────────────────────────────────────────────┬─┐ │
│ │ Thank you for choosing the Autodesk Mechanical Desktop(R)! │▲│ │
│ │                                                           │ │ │
│ │ Whether you're new to the Autodesk Mechanical Desktop or a│ │ │
│ │  veteran user, please look first at the Getting Started   │ │ │
│ │ manual. It explains how to navigate printed and on-line   │ │ │
│ │ documentation.                                            │ │ │
│ │                                                           │ │ │
│ │ For additional important information and details on any   │ │ │
│ │ last-minute software changes not included in the          │ │ │
│ │ documentation, please refer to the README files.          │ │ │
│ │                                                           │ │ │
│ │ Be sure to return the Registration Card if you haven't    │▼│ │
│ │ already                                                   │ │ │
│ └───────────────────────────────────────────────────────────┴─┘ │
│                        ┌─────────┐                                │
│                        │   OK    │                                │
│                        └─────────┘                                │
└─────────────────────────────────────────────────────────────────┘
```

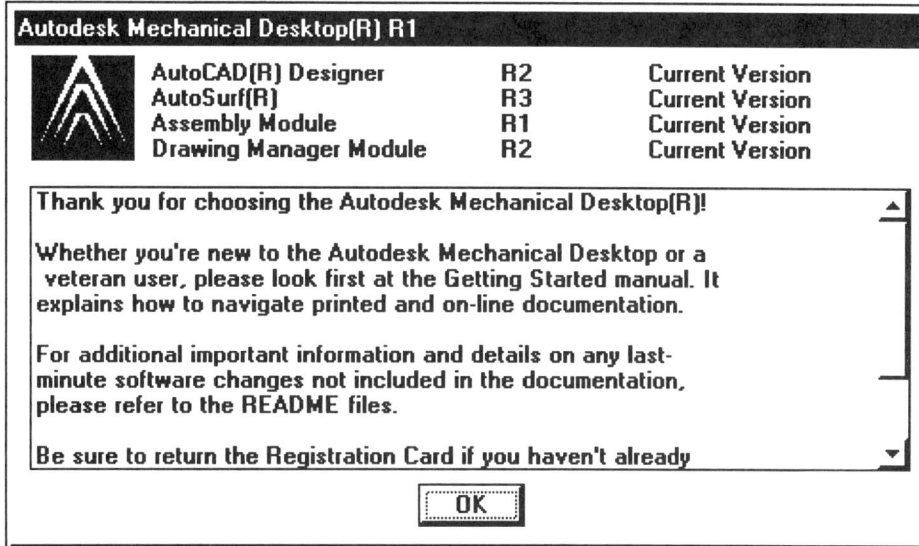

Start a new drawing with the NEW command.

<File>   <New...>

Command: **NEW**

To organize better the entities in your drawing, you will need two additional layers, one for holding the rough sketches and the other for placing the parametric solids. Run the LAYER command or the DDLMODES command to create two layers, and set the current layer to SKETCH.

<Data>   <Layers...>

Command: **DDLMODES**

Layer name	Color
SKETCH	**cyan**
SOLID	**yellow**

Current layer: **SKETCH**

While you execute the DDLMODES command, you may find that there are a number of layers prefixed by the letters "AM." AutoCAD Designer uses these layers for specific reasons. Do not make any change to these layers or manipulate the entities residing on these layers. Just leave them alone.

Before starting to create a sketch, you should zoom your screen display to an appropriate known size. This will give you a better perception of the size of the sketch that you are going to make. Run the LIMITS command to set the limits to 297 units times 210 units.

<Data>   <Drawing Limits>

Command: **LIMITS**

ON/OFF/<Lower left corner>: **0,0**
Upper right corner: **297,210**

Then select the Zoom All icon from the Standard toolbar to issue the ZOOM command to zoom to all.

[Standard Toolbar]   [Zoom All]

> **Note:**
> In the delineation that follows, [AAA] [BBB] will mean to use the [AAA] toolbar and to select the [BBB] icon.

Command: **ZOOM**
All/Center/Dynamic/Extents/Left/Previous/Vmax/Window/<Scale(X/XP)>: **ALL**

Also turn on grid mesh display of 10 units times 10 units with the GRID command.

Command: **GRID**
Grid spacing(X) or ON/OFF/Snap/Aspect: **10**

Now your screen should display an area of around 297 units times 210 units. You will create a rough sketch within this area. Subsequently, you will resolve the sketch and extrude it to form a solid feature.

To work in three-dimensional space, you should always keep track of the location of the current XY plane and origin. Placing the UCS icon at the origin position would surely help. Issue the UCSICON command to set the icon at the origin position.

<Options>   <UCS>   <Icon Origin>

Command: **UCSICON**
ON/OFF/All/Noorigin/ORigin: **OR**

Before creating the first solid feature, let us briefly review the procedure of creating an extruded solid feature. To create an extruded feature, you will make a rough sketch. From the sketch, you will resolve it to form a profile. Finally, you will extrude the profile to form a solid feature. The first sketched solid feature then becomes the base feature.

To create a sketch with AutoCAD Designer, you need a sketch plane. The sketch plane for the base feature can simply be the XY plane of the current UCS. For subsequent sketches, you need to specify a sketch plane explicitly. You will learn more about sketch plane and related construction features when you proceed to the second feature of this solid.

As shown in Figure 2.3, run the PLINE command to prepare a rough sketch. Although the following delineation specifies the coordinates of the endpoints, they only serve as a guide. You should make use of the coordinate display of AutoCAD to position the cursor to an approximate location. Issue the PLINE command.

[Draw]   [Polyline]

Command: **PLINE**
From point: **[Select a point near (70,70).]**
Arc/Close/Halfwidth/Length/Undo/Width/
<Endpoint of line>: **[Select a point near (70,150).]**
Arc/Close/Halfwidth/Length/Undo/Width/<Endpoint of line>: **A**
Angle/CEnter/CLose/Direction/Halfwidth/Line/Radius/Second pt/Undo/Width/
<Endpoint of arc>: **[Select a point near (90,170).]**
Angle/CEnter/CLose/Direction/Halfwidth/Line/Radius/Second pt/Undo/Width/
<Endpoint of arc>: **L**
Arc/Close/Halfwidth/Length/Undo/Width/
<Endpoint of line>: **[Select a point near (210,170).]**
Arc/Close/Halfwidth/Length/Undo/Width/<Endpoint of line>: **A**
Angle/CEnter/CLose/Direction/Halfwidth/Line/Radius/Second pt/Undo/Width/
<Endpoint of arc>: **[Select a point near (230,150).]**
Angle/CEnter/CLose/Direction/Halfwidth/Line/Radius/Second pt/Undo/Width/
<Endpoint of arc>: **L**
Arc/Close/Halfwidth/Length/Undo/Width/
<Endpoint of line>: **[Select a point near (230,70).]**
Arc/Close/Halfwidth/Length/Undo/Width/<Endpoint of line>: **A**
Angle/CEnter/CLose/Direction/Halfwidth/Line/Radius/Second pt/Undo/Width/
<Endpoint of arc>: **[Select a point near (210,50).]**
Angle/CEnter/CLose/Direction/Halfwidth/Line/Radius/Second pt/Undo/Width/
<Endpoint of arc>: **L**
Arc/Close/Halfwidth/Length/Undo/Width/<Endpoint of line>: **[Select a point near (90,50).]**
Arc/Close/Halfwidth/Length/Undo/Width/<Endpoint of line>: **A**
Angle/CEnter/CLose/Direction/Halfwidth/Line/Radius/Second pt/Undo/Width/
<Endpoint of arc>: **[Select a point near (70,70).]**
Angle/CEnter/CLose/Direction/Halfwidth/Line/Radius/Second pt/Undo/Width/
<Endpoint of arc>: **[Enter]**

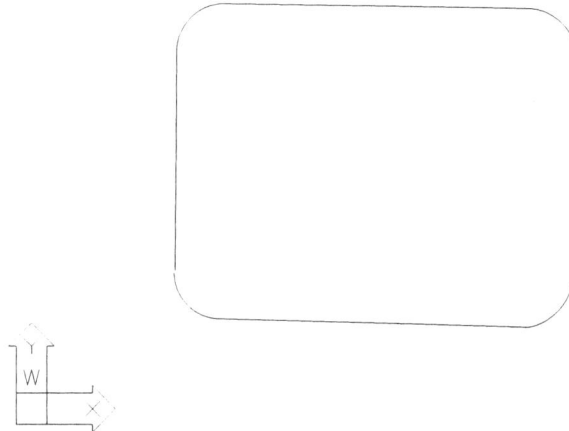

Figure 2.3 A rough sketch created

To reiterate, the sketch need not be precise at all. You do not have to use the snap object tool to locate the endpoints. Now, you may ask how rough can a sketch be, and how AutoCAD Designer interprets your sketch. Of course, there are rules. You may classify the rules into two categories.

The first set is the rules of geometric constraint:

- Lines that are nearly horizontal are treated as horizontal.
- Lines that are nearly vertical are treated as vertical.
- Lines, arcs, and circles that are nearly tangential to each other are treated as tangential.
- Arcs and circles that are nearly concentric are treated as concentric.
- Arcs and circles that have nearly the same radius are treated as having the same radius.
- Lines that are close to lying on a same straight line are treated as collinear.
- Lines that are nearly perpendicular to each other are treated as perpendicular.
- Lines that are nearly parallel are treated as parallel.

The second set of rules joins objects together or attaches objects to another object:

- Endpoints that are close together are treated as a single vertex.
- Endpoints that are near to a line, an arc, or a circle are treated as attached to the line, arc, or circle.

There are times when you do not want to apply the first set of geometric constraint rules to your sketch during resolution. You may want to attach only the endpoints. If such is the case, you should set the AMRULEMODE variable to 0. To apply the rules to your sketch, set it to 1.

> Command: **AMRULEMODE**
> New value for AMRULEMODE: **1**

There may be two more questions that you would ask. How close to horizontal must a line be for it to be treated as horizontal? How close together must two endpoints be for them to be treated as a single vertex?

The answer to the first question is that you may use the AMSKANGTOL variable to set the angular tolerance. Set its value to 5 degrees.

> Command: **AMSKANGTOL**
> New value for AMSKANGTOL: **5**

The answer to the second question is that the PICKBOX variable determines the tolerance. Set its value to 5 pixels.

> Command: **PICKBOX**
> New value for PICKBOX: **5**

Unlike the AMSKANGTOL variable, which specifies the angular tolerance in degrees, the PICKBOX variable specifies a pickbox size in terms of screen pixel size. If the pickbox size is five pixels, two endpoints will join together if you zoom the screen display such that the gap between them is smaller than five screen pixels. In other words, a gap that appears to be larger if you zoom close enough will not join together simply because the gap is larger than the pickbox size. At the other end of the spectrum, if you zoom very far away, a number of vertexes that are close together within the specified pickbox size will join together as a single vertex. As a result, you may lose some line segments. Therefore, you should set the pickbox neither too large nor too small.

Sometimes you may want to resolve a line as inclining at precisely 4 degrees, despite setting the angular tolerance to 5 degrees. To override the angular tolerance, and treat the sketch as precise, you may manipulate the AMSKMODE variable. Setting it to 0 will treat your sketch as precise. Lines will be constrained as horizontal only if you draw them as horizontal lines. For the sketch you have made, set the variable to 1 so that the angular tolerance is applied.

Command: **AMSKMODE**
New value for AMSKMODE: **1**

To set the variables that affect parts creation, you may use the AMPARTVARS command.

<Parts>   <Preferences...>

Command: **AMPARTVARS**

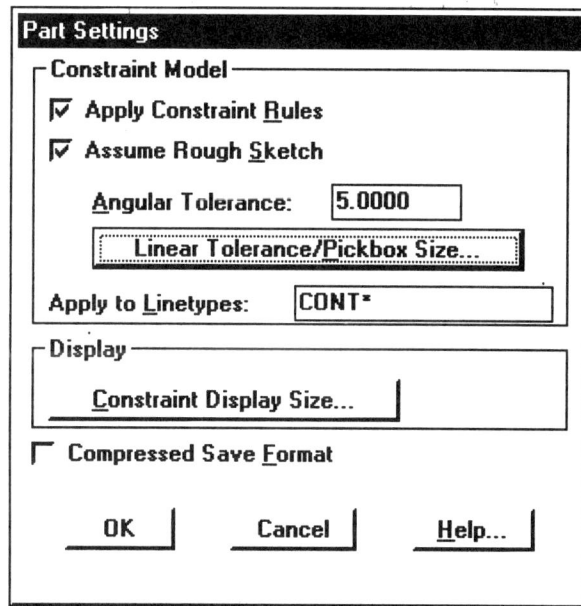

```
Part Settings
┌ Constraint Model ─────────────────────┐
  ☑ Apply Constraint Rules
  ☑ Assume Rough Sketch

    Angular Tolerance:    5.0000

         Linear Tolerance/Pickbox Size...

  Apply to Linetypes:     CONT*
└───────────────────────────────────────┘
┌ Display ──────────────────────────────┐
         Constraint Display Size...
└───────────────────────────────────────┘
  ☐ Compressed Save Format

       OK        Cancel        Help...
```

Once you know the rules and have set the related variables, you may resolve the rough sketch. Run the AMPROFILE command and select the objects that you have created. See Figure 2.4.

<Parts>   <Sketch>   <Profile>

Command: **AMPROFILE**
Select objects for sketch:
Select objects: **LAST**
Select objects: **[Enter]**
Solved under constrained sketch requiring 7 dimensions or constraints.

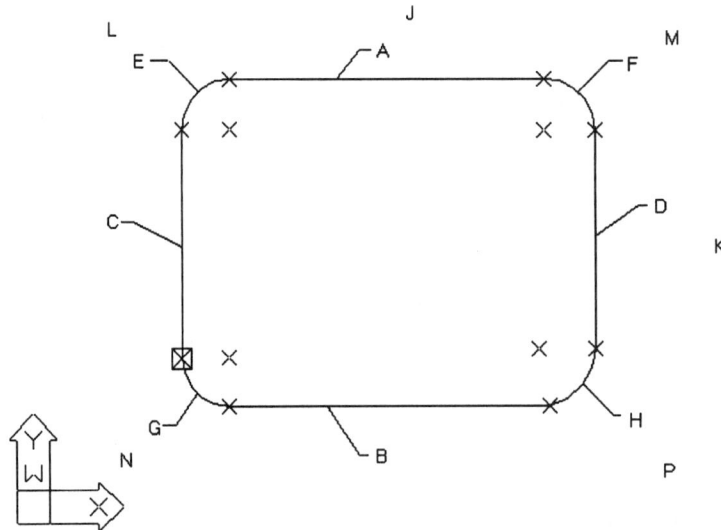

Figure 2.4 Rough sketch resolved to a profile

Because the rough sketch shown in Figure 2.3 may not be exactly the same as yours, the geometric constraints that AutoCAD Designer automatically applies to your profile may be different. Consequently, the number of geometric constraints and parametric dimensions that you need to add in order to constrain the profile fully may be different from the illustration above. Anyway, take a look at the geometric constraints applied to your drawing by using the AMSHOWCON command. See Figure 2.5.

<Parts>   **<Sketch>**   **<Constraints>**   **<Show>**

Command: **AMSHOWCON**
All/Select/Next/<eXit>:**ALL**

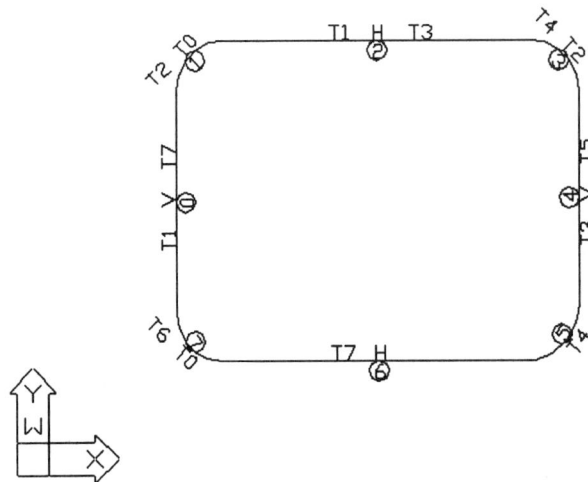

Figure 2.5 Geometric constraint symbols shown

All/Select/Next/<eXit>: **[Enter]**

In the constraint diagram, there are numeric and alphabetic symbols. The numbers denote the entity names. The alphabets denote the geometric constraints. The following list gives the meanings of the alphabetic constraint symbols:

H	Horizontal constraint
V	Vertical constraint
L	Perpendicular constraint
P	Parallelism constraint
X	X values constraint for center points
Y	Y values constraint for center points
C	Collinear constraint
N	Concentric constraint
J	Projected constraint
R	Same radius constraint
T	Tangential constraint

In your screen display, the constraint symbols may appear too large or too small. To adjust their display size, you may manipulate the AMCONDSPSZ variable.

Command: **AMCONDSPSZ**
New value for AMCONDSPSZ: **6**

Besides setting the AMCONDSPSZ variable directly, you may click and drag the slider bar from the sub-dialog box of the AMPARTVARS command to set the constraint symbol size.

<Parts>   <Preferences...>

Command: **AMPARTVARS**

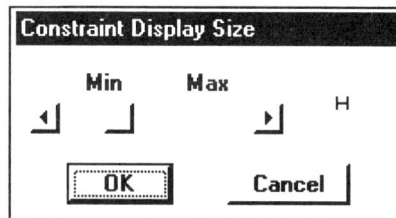

To fulfill the constraint requirement, you may have to add geometric constraints and parametric dimensions to your profile. Issue the AMADDCON command. Click the check box next to the item Display. This will cause the constraint symbols to display while you are adding constraints to the profile.

<Parts>   <Sketch>   <Constraints>   <Add>

Command: **AMADDCON**

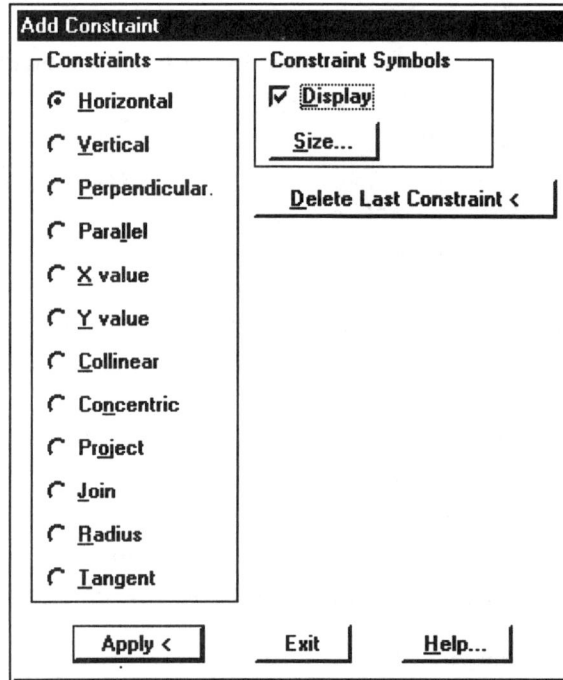

```
[Constraints:Horizontal          Constraint Symbols: Display
Apply                                                           ]
```

```
Select line: [Select A (Figure 2.4).]
This constraint already exists.
```

While you are adding the geometric constraints to your profile, it is likely that AutoCAD Designer may prompt you that a particular constraint already exists. You may ignore this prompt.

```
Select line: [Select B (Figure 2.4).]
Select line: [Enter]
```

```
[Constraints: Vertical          Constraint Symbols: Display
Apply                                                           ]
```

```
Select line: [Select C (Figure 2.4).]
Select line: [Select D (Figure 2.4).]
Select line: [Enter]
```

```
[Constraints: Tangent          Constraint Symbols: Display
Apply                                                           ]
```

```
Select line, circle, arc, or ellipse: [Select E (Figure 2.4).]
Select line, circle, arc, or ellipse: [Select A (Figure 2.4).]
Select line, circle, arc, or ellipse: [Select E (Figure 2.4).]
Select line, circle, arc, or ellipse: [Select C (Figure 2.4).]
Select line, circle, arc, or ellipse: [Select F (Figure 2.4).]
Select line, circle, arc, or ellipse: [Select A (Figure 2.4).]
Select line, circle, arc, or ellipse: [Select F (Figure 2.4).]
Select line, circle, arc, or ellipse: [Select D (Figure 2.4).]
Select line, circle, arc, or ellipse: [Select G (Figure 2.4).]
```

Select line, circle, arc, or ellipse: **[Select B (Figure 2.4).]**
Select line, circle, arc, or ellipse: **[Select G (Figure 2.4).]**
Select line, circle, arc, or ellipse: **[Select C (Figure 2.4).]**
Select line, circle, arc, or ellipse: **[Select H (Figure 2.4).]**
Select line, circle, arc, or ellipse: **[Select B (Figure 2.4).]**
Select line, circle, arc, or ellipse: **[Select H (Figure 2.4).]**
Select line, circle, arc, or ellipse: **[Select D (Figure 2.4).]**
Select line, circle, arc, or ellipse: **[Enter]**

[Exit   ]

The command opposite to the AMADDCON command is the AMDELCON command. If you want to remove a geometric constraint, you may apply this command.

<Parts>   **<Sketch>**   **<Constraints>**   **<Delete>**

Command: **AMDELCON**
Size/All/<Select>: **[Select a constraint that you want to delete, or enter to exit.]**

After adding the geometric constraints, you will add parametric dimensions to your profile. AutoCAD dimension variables also govern the format of display of the parametric dimensions. You may directly set the variable values or use the DDIM command to make the appropriate changes. Assuming that you have a basic knowledge of AutoCAD, you should do the setting of dimension variables by yourself.

You may choose to display the parametric dimension value in one of the three methods provided: numeric display, parameter display, or equation display. Numeric display will merely tell you the exact dimension value. Parameter display will tell you the parameter name assigned to the dimension. The first dimension is D0, the second D1, and so on. Depending on the sequence of dimensioning, the parameter names that display on your screen may not be the same as those shown in the illustration in this book. Because of this, you may want to note down the parameter names of your drawing on a separate piece of paper while you are working, if they are different from the illustration. The third type of display is the equation display. The dimension value is expressed as an equation with the parameter name equal to an expression. Run the AMDIMDSP command, and choose the equation display.

<Parts>   **<Display>**   **<Dim Display>**

Command: **AMDIMDSP**
Parameters/Equations/<Numeric>: **E**

Issue the AMPARDIM command to add parametric dimensions to control the size of the resolved sketch. While you add parametric dimensions, you may express a dimension value as an equation to maintain a relationship between several dimensions of a resolved sketch. In this case, the width is 3/4 of the length, the four rounded corners are identical, and they have a common radius equal to 1/10 of the length. See Figure 2.6.

To remind you again, the parameter names D? in the following command prompt may differ slightly from your screen. In the illustration, D0 refers to the length in the X axis direction. D1 refers to the width in the Y axis direction. D2 refers to the radius of the upper left arc.

<Parts>   <Sketch>   <Add Dimension>

Command: **AMPARDIM**
Select first object: **[Select C (Figure 2.4).]**
Select second object or place dimension: **[Select D (Figure 2.4).]**
Specify dimension placement: **[Select J (Figure 2.4).]**
Undo/Hor/Ver/Align/Par/Enter Dimension value: **[Enter]**

Then you should see D0 appearing on the screen as the parameter name.

Select first object: **[Select A (Figure 2.4).]**
Select second object or place dimension: **[Select B (Figure 2.4).]**
Specify dimension placement: **[Select K (Figure 2.4).]**
Undo/Hor/Ver/Align/Par/Enter Dimension value: **D0*3/4 [or D?*3/4, where D? is the parameter name of the last dimension.]**

Select first object: **[Select E (Figure 2.4).]**
Select second object or place dimension: **[Select L (Figure 2.4).]**
Undo/Enter Dimension value: **D0/10 [or D?/10, where D? is the same as the last D?.]**

Select first object: **[Select F (Figure 2.4).]**
Select second object or place dimension: **[Select M (Figure 2.4).]**
Undo/Enter Dimension value: **D2 [or the parameter name of the last radius dimension.]**

Select first object: **[Select G (Figure 2.4).]**
Select second object or place dimension: **[Select N (Figure 2.4).]**
Undo/Enter Dimension value: **D2 [or the same parameter name of the last dimension.]**

Select first object: **[Select H (Figure 2.4).]**
Select second object or place dimension: **[Select P (Figure 2.4).]**
Undo/Enter Dimension value: **D2 [or the same parameter name of the last dimension.]**
Solved fully constrained sketch
Select first object: **[Enter]**

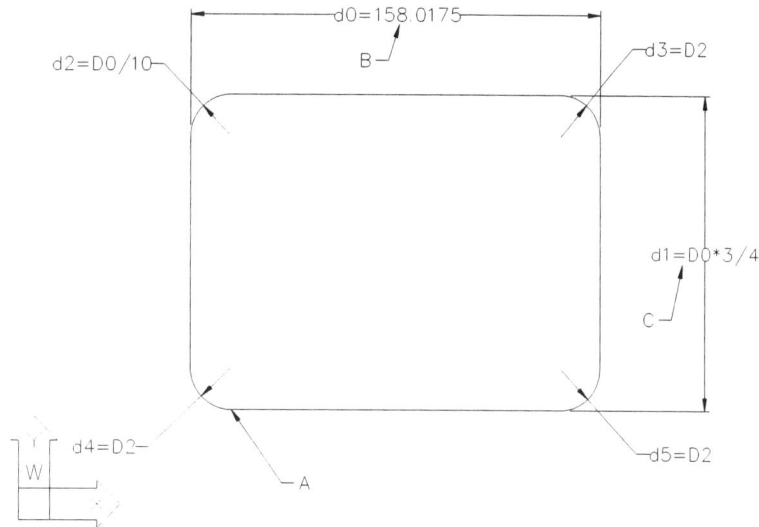

Figure 2.6 Fully constrained profile

You have finished adding parametric dimensions to the resolved sketch. If, in the process of adding dimensions, you have wrongly specify a dimension, you may remove it with the ERASE command.

Compare your screen with Figure 2.6. The parameter names may not be the same. If they differ, note down your parameter names on a piece of paper.

If you find the general scaling of the dimensions too large or too small, you should change the dimension variables using the DDIM command. Then apply the DIMSTYLE command to update the changes.

Command: **DDIM**
[**Make appropriate changes.**]

Command: **DIMSTYLE**
Dimension Style Edit (Save/Restore/STatus/Variables/Apply/?) <Restore>: **A**
Select objects: **ALL**
Select objects: **[Enter]**

Now the profile is fully constrained. It is parametric. If you change a dimension, its size, and probably its shape, will change as well. When the profile changes in size, there is one point that will not move. It is called the fix point. To manipulate the fix point, run the AMFIXPT command. You may choose any point on the profile to be fixed.

<Parts>   **<Sketch>**   **<Fix Point>**

Command: **AMFIXPT**
Specify new fixed point for sketch: **END** of **[Select A (Figure 2.6).]**

After fixing a point to be immovable, alter the parametric dimension of your profile with the AMMODDIM command, and watch your screen carefully for any change. You may notice that the fix point remains stationary while the size of the profile changes.

<Parts>   **<Change Dimension>**

Command: **AMMODDIM**
Select dimension to change: **[Select B (Figure 2.6).]**
New value for dimension: **150**
Solved fully constrained sketch.
Select dimension to change: **[Select B (Figure 2.6).]**
New value for dimension: **200**
Solved fully constrained sketch.
Select dimension to change: **[Enter]**

The profile is completed. Before making the solid, set the current layer to SOLID.

<Data>   **<Layers...>**

Command: **DDLMODES**
Current layer: **SOLID**

Use the short cut key [8] to set to an isometric viewing position.

Command: **8**

There are other short cut keys that you may find useful:

F	Fits all the objects to the screen.
W	Toggles between drawing and model mode with the AMMODE command.
QQ	Edits the drawing views with the AMEDITVIEW command.
UU	Sets the UCS to the view with the UCS command.
1	Sets the display to a single viewport.
2	Sets the display to two viewports.
3	Sets the display to three viewports.
4	Sets the display to four viewports.
5	Sets the display to the top view.
6	Sets the display to the front view.
7	Sets the display to the right side view.
8	Sets the display to the isometric view.
9	Sets the display to the current UCS, i.e., perpendicular to the sketch plane.
0	Performs the HIDE command.
[	Rotates the view to the left.
]	Rotates the view to the right.
=	Rotates the view upward.
-	Rotates the view downward.

To find out more about the short cut keys available, you may open the text file ACAD.PGP that is located in the SUPPORT directory.

With the resolved profile ready, apply the AMEXTRUDE command to extrude it to form a parametric solid feature. See Figure 2.7. The distance of extrusion is 1/10 of the length, D0. If the parameter name of the length dimension is D?, replace D0 with D?.

<Parts>   **<Feature>**   **<Extrude...>**

Command: **AMEXTRUDE**

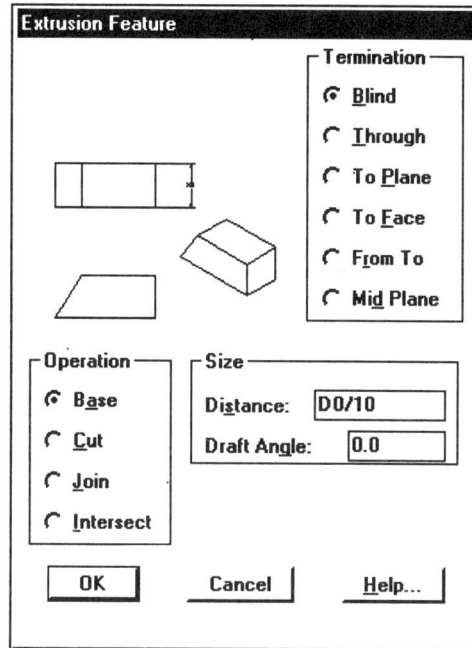

```
[Termination:        Blind
 Operation:          Base
 Size:
    Distance:        D0/10
    Draft angle:     0
 OK                                ]
```

Direction Flip/<Accept>: **[Accept, if the arrow is pointing upward. Otherwise, flip.]**

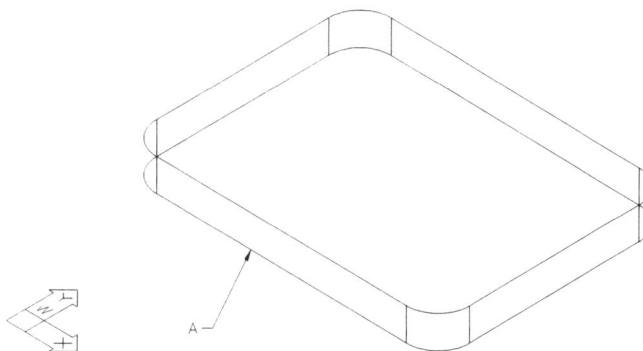

Figure 2.7 The sketched solid feature

You have extruded the resolved profile to form a parametric solid feature. Because this is the first feature of a parametric solid part, it is the base feature.

Earlier, you saw that the AMMODDIM command may modify the dimension value of a sketch. To edit a feature, you may run the AMEDITFEAT command.

<Parts>   **<Edit Feature>**

Command: **AMEDITFEAT**
Sketch/surfCut/<select Feature>: **[Select A (Figure 2.7).]**

After you select a feature, the parametric dimensions appear again.

Select object: **[Select the dimension that controls the thickness.]**
Enter new value for dimension: **D0/20**
Select object: **[Enter]**

After editing a feature, you have to issue the AMUPDATE command to update the change. See Figure 2.8.

<Parts>   **<Update>**

Command: **AMUPDATE**

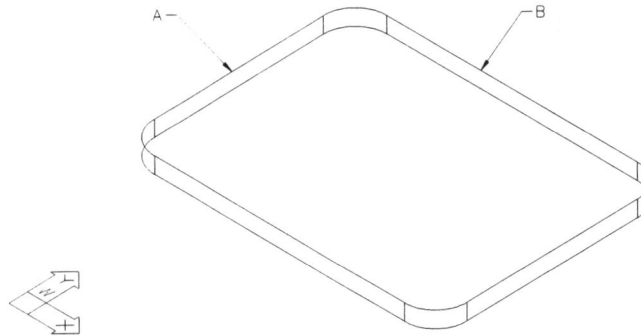

Figure 2.8 The base feature edited and updated

You have edited and updated the base feature.

2.3   Construction Features and Additional Sketched Features

Figure 2.2 shows that this solid part consists of two more sketched solid features in addition to the base feature. To reiterate, you need a sketch for each sketched solid feature. Unlike the first sketched solid feature, which you may sketch on the XY plane of the current UCS, you should specify a sketch plane.

Simply speaking, the sketch plane is a XY plane where you create the sketch. Therefore, you may think of a sketch plane as being the XY plane of an UCS. However, a sketch plane is more than that. If you simply use an UCS as a sketch plane, the position of the sketch, and the solid feature created from the sketch, will be fixed relative to the UCS but not to the other sketched solid features. As a result, there will be no parametric relationship between the solid features. When you edit and update a solid part having solid features that are not parametrically related, the outcome may be unpredictable.

In order to establish a parametric relationship between the solid features of a solid part, you need to set up work plane, work axis, and work point. Collectively, these are called construction features. On the bases of these objects that are parametrically linked to an existing feature, you may set the sketch plane. Besides parametric construction features, an existing face and edge of a solid feature are also parametric. Therefore, you may set the sketch plane to them as well.

To appreciate how to make a parametric work plane on the upper face of the base feature and set the sketch plane on it, run the AMWORKPLN command. This command allows you to define a work plane according to two modifiers. See Figure 2.9.

<Parts>   **<Feature>**   **<Work Plane...>**

Command: **AMWORKPLN**

```
Work Plane Feature
┌─1st Modifier──────────┐  ┌─2nd Modifier──────────┐
│  ○ On Edge/Axis       │  │  ⊙ On Edge/Axis        │
│  ○ On Vertex          │  │  ○ On Vertex           │
│  ○ Tangent            │  │  ○ Tangent             │
│  ⊙ Planar Parallel    │  │  ○ Planar Parallel     │
│  ○ Planar Normal      │  │  ○ Planar Normal       │
│  ○ Sweep Profile      │  │  ○ Planar Angle        │
│                       │  │  ○ On 3 Vertices       │
│  ○ On UCS             │  │  ○ Offset              │
│  ○ World XY           │  └────────────────────────┘
│  ○ World YZ           │  ┌────────────────────────┐
│  ○ World XZ           │  │  Offset: [1        ]    │
│  ☑ Create Sketch Plane│  │  Angle:  [45       ]    │
│                       │  └────────────────────────┘
│    [ OK ]   [ Cancel ]   [ Help... ]
```

[1st modifier: **Planar Parallel**
 2nd modifier: **On Edge/Axis**
 Create Sketch Plane: **YES**
 OK   ]

worldX/worldY/worldZ/<Select work axis or straight edge>: **[Select A (Figure 2.8).]**
worldXy/worldYz/worldZx/Ucs/<Select work plane or planar face>: **[Select A (Figure 2.8).]**
Next/<Accept>: **[Accept, if the upper face is highlighted. Otherwise, Next.]**

At this stage, a parametric work plane is created on the upper face of the base solid. The following prompts enable you to specify the orientation of the XY plane of the sketch plane on this work plane.

worldX/worldY/worldZ/<Select work axis or straight edge>: **[Select B (Figure 2.8).]**
Rotate/Z-flip/<Accept>: **[R, if the Y axis direction is not the same as Figure 2.9.]**
Rotate/Z-flip/<Accept>: **[Z, if the X axis direction is not the same as Figure 2.9.]**
Rotate/Z-flip/<Accept>: **[Enter, if Y axis and X axis direction are the same as Figure 2.9.]**

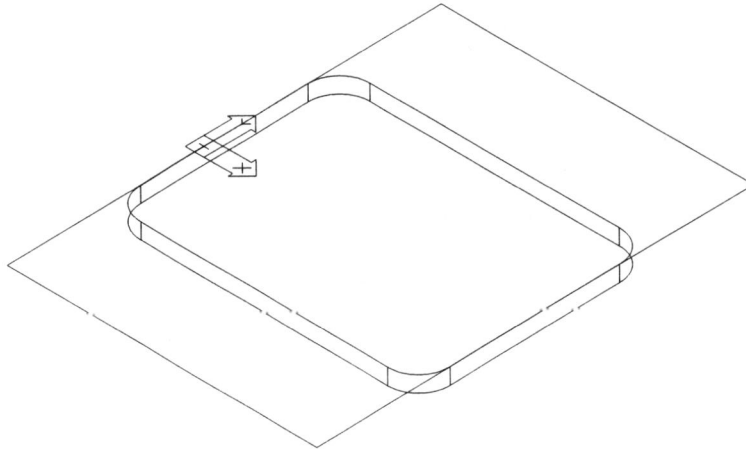

Figure 2.9 A sketch plane set to the new work plane

Because you have already located the UCS icon at the origin position, you may find the change of UCS and UCS origin in Figure 2.9.

As mentioned earlier, you need to sketch on a sketch plane. To find out which is the active sketch plane, you may run the AMSHOWACT command.

<Parts>   **<Utilities>**   **<Show Active>**

Command: **AMSHOWACT**
Sketchplane/<Part>: **S**
Press <ENTER> to continue:

To continue, set the display to a view perpendicular to the sketch plane with the short cut key [9].

Command: **9**

Before making another sketch on the new sketch plane, set the current layer to SKETCH with the DDLMODES command.

<Data>   **<Layers...>**

Command: **DDLMODES**
Current Layer: **SKETCH**

As shown in Figure 2.10, use the ARC command and the LINE command to create a rough sketch.

[Draw]   **[Arc Start End Angle]**

Command: **ARC**

[Draw]   **[Line]**

Command: **LINE**

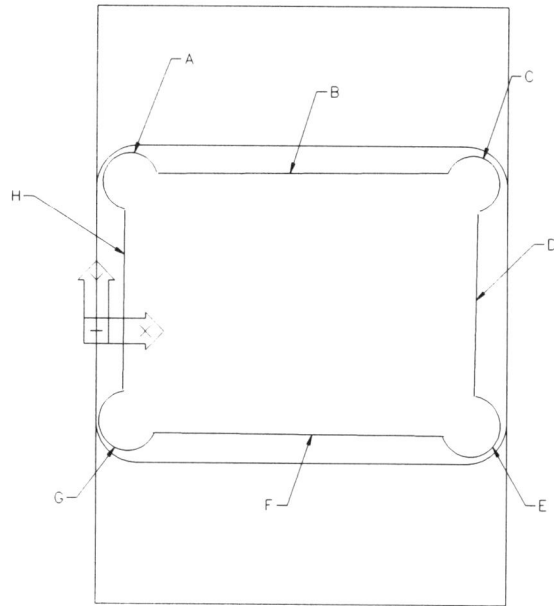

Figure 2.10 A rough sketch created on the new sketch plane

As for the first sketch, apply the AMPROFILE command to resolve the rough sketch to a profile. See Figure 2.11.

<Parts>   **<Sketch>**   **<Profile>**

Command: **AMPROFILE**
Select objects for sketch:
Select objects: **[Select A, B, C, D, E, F, G, and H (Figure 2.10).]**
Select objects: **[Enter]**

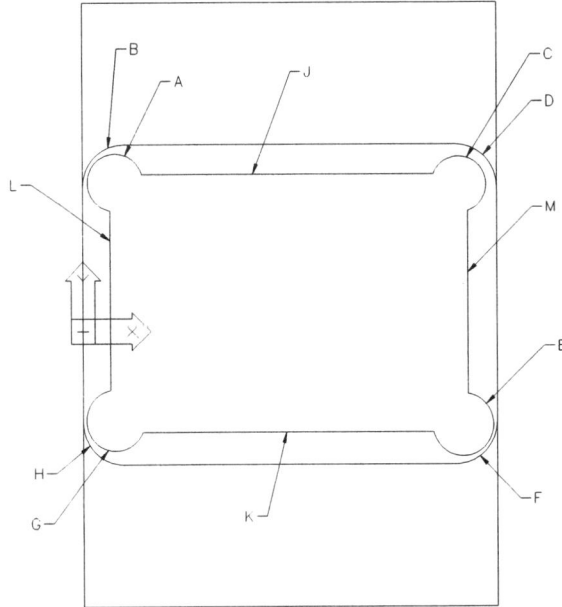

Figure 2.11 The second rough sketch resolved

Because no two rough sketches are the same, the outcome of each resolution is unique. To find out what geometric constraints AutoCAD Designer has applied to the sketch, you may issue the AMSHOWCON command.

Before you may extrude this profile to form a solid feature, you should, as before, add geometric constraints and parametric dimensions.

To add geometric constraints, apply the AMADDCON command. See Figure 2.12.

<Parts>   **<Sketch>**   **<Constraints>**   **<Add>**

Command: **AMADDCON**

[Constraints: **Radius**   Constraint Symbols: **Display**
Apply   ]

Select first arc or circle: **[Select A (Figure 2.11).]**
Select second arc or circle: **[Select B (Figure 2.11).]**
Select first arc or circle: **[Select C (Figure 2.11).]**
Select second arc or circle: **[Select D (Figure 2.11).]**
Select first arc or circle: **[Select E (Figure 2.11).]**
Select second arc or circle: **[Select F (Figure 2.11).]**
Select first arc or circle: **[Select G (Figure 2.11).]**
Select second arc or circle: **[Select H (Figure 2.11).]**
Select first arc or circle: **[Enter]**

[Constraints: **Concentric**   Constraint Symbols: **Display**
Apply   ]

Select first arc or circle: **[Select A (Figure 2.11).]**
Select second arc or circle: **[Select B (Figure 2.11).]**
Select first arc or circle: **[Select C (Figure 2.11).]**

Select second arc or circle: **[Select D (Figure 2.11).]**
Select first arc or circle: **[Select E (Figure 2.11).]**
Select second arc or circle: **[Select F (Figure 2.11).]**
Select first arc or circle: **[Select G (Figure 2.11).]**
Select second arc or circle: **[Select H (Figure 2.11).]**
Select first arc or circle: **[Enter]**

[Constraints: **Horizontal**   Constraint Symbols:**Display**
Apply   ]

Select line: **[Select J (Figure 2.11).]**
Select line: **[Select K (Figure 2.11).]**
Select line: **[Enter]**

[Constraints: **Vertical**   Constraint Symbols:**Display**
Apply   ]

Select line: **[Select L (Figure 2.11).]**
Select line: **[Select M (Figure 2.11).]**
Select line: **[Enter]**

[**Exit**   ]

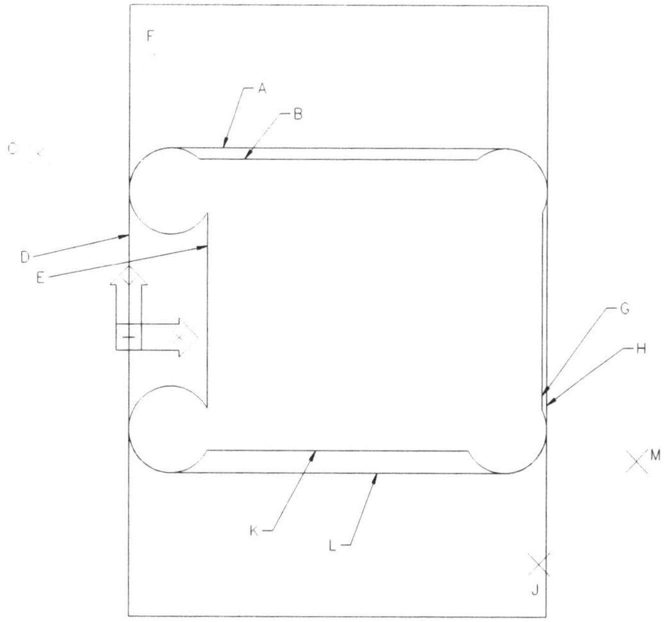

Figure 2.12 Geometric constraints added

After constraining the profile geometrically, you should add parametric dimensions. Execute the AMPARDIM command. See Figure 2.13.

<Parts>   **<Sketch>**   **<Add Dimension>**

Command: **AMPARDIM**
Select first object: **[Select A (Figure 2.12).]**

Select second object or place dimension: **[Select B (Figure 2.12).]**
Specify dimension placement: **[Select C (Figure 2.12).]**

> **Note:**
> In the following delineation, the parameter names refer to the names specified in the illustrations earlier in this chapter. It is possible that the parameter names may be different from yours. If that is the case, you should replace D2 by the parameter name of the dimensions used to set the D2 dimension in Figure 2.6, the radius of the upper left arc, and so on.

Undo/Hor/Ver/Align/Par/Enter Dimension value: **D2/2 [or D?/2, where D? is the parameter name of the dimension of the upper left radius shown in Figure 2.6.]**

Select first object: **[Select D (Figure 2.12).]**
Select second object or place dimension: **[Select E (Figure 2.12).]**
Specify dimension placement: **[Select F (Figure 2.12).]**
Undo/Hor/Ver/Align/Par/Enter Dimension value: **D2/2**

Select first object: **[Select G (Figure 2.12).]**
Select second object or place dimension: **[Select H (Figure 2.12).]**
Specify dimension placement: **[Select J (Figure 2.12).]**
Undo/Hor/Ver/Align/Par/Enter Dimension value: **D2/2**

Select first object: **[Select K (Figure 2.12).]**
Select second object or place dimension: **[Select L (Figure 2.12).]**
Specify dimension placement: **[Select M (Figure 2.12).]**
Undo/Hor/Ver/Align/Par/Enter Dimension value: **D2/2**
Solved fully constrained sketch.
Select first object: **[Enter]**

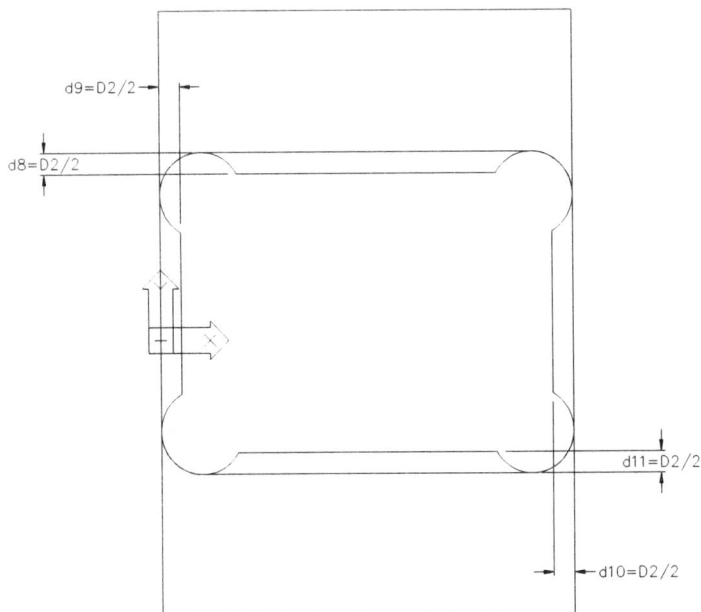

Figure 2.13 Second profile fully constrained

Check your profile carefully. Make sure that you have applied the geometric constraints and the parametric dimensions properly. Next, you will extrude the second profile to form a solid feature.

Before proceeding, set the display to an isometric view with the short cut key [8]. Then execute the AMEXTRUDE command to extrude the second profile and to join it to the last feature. The distance of extrusion is 1/5 of the length, D0. If the parameter name of the length dimension is D?, replace D0 with D?. See Figure 2.14.

Command: **8**

<Parts>   **<Feature>**   **<Extrude...>**

Command: **AMEXTRUDE**

[Termination: **Blind**
 Operation: **Join**
 Size:
   Distance: **D0/5**
   Draft angle: **0**
OK   ]

Direction Flip/<Accept>: **[Accept, if the arrow is pointing upward. Otherwise, flip.]**

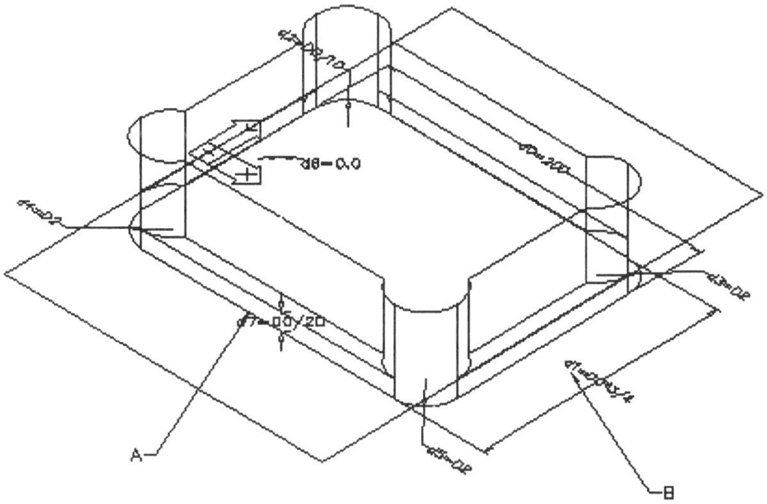

Figure 2.14 Second sketched solid feature joined to the base feature

Now your solid part has two sketched solid features. To demonstrate how to edit a solid part with more than one solid feature, apply the AMEDITFEAT command.

After running the AMEDITFEAT command, select the base feature, and then select the dimension that represents the width. The original dimension is 3/4 of the length. Change it to 0.8 of the length. In the delineation below, D0 is the length. You should change D0 to the parameter name that represents the length of the solid in your drawing. After editing, issue the AMUPDATE command to update the change.

<Parts>   <Edit Feature>

Command: **AMEDITFEAT**
Sketch/surfCut/<select Feature>: **[Select A (Figure 2.14).]**
Next/<Accept>: **[Accept, if the base feature is highlighted. Otherwise, Next.]**

The parametric dimensions of the base feature will show up.

Select object: **[Select B (Figure 2.14).]**
Enter new value for dimension: **D0*0.8 [or D?*0.8, where D? is the width of the base.]**
Solved fully constrained sketch.
Select object: **[Enter]**

Do you still remember where the fix point is? If not, refer to Figure 2.6. The fix point is a point where the parametric solid is anchored. Note down where is it before you apply the AMUPDATE command. See Figure 2.15.

<Parts>   <Update>

Command: **AMUPDATE**

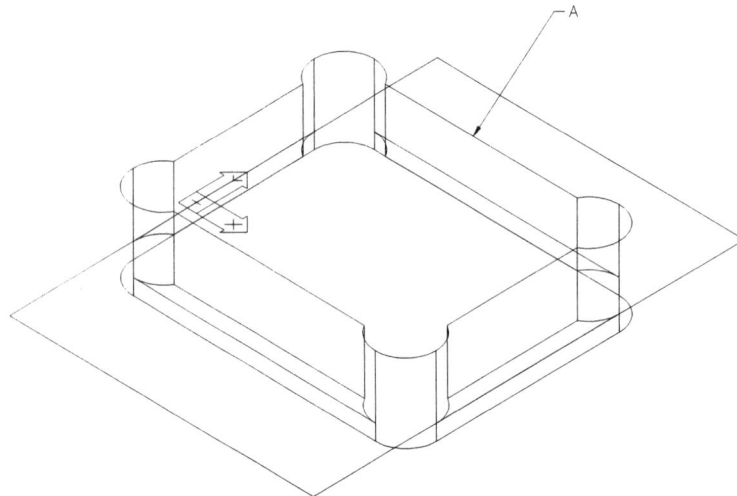

Figure 2.15 The base feature edited and the model updated

You should have found that the fix point did not move at all while all other features were updating.

Next, you will edit the general shape of the second sketched solid feature. Before you do that, run the QSAVE command to save your work.

<File>   <Save...>

Command: **QSAVE**

[File name: **PLATE1**
OK   ]

If you compare a parametric solid with a native solid of similar shape in terms of file size, you may find that the AutoCAD Designer file is larger. The reason is that there are parametric information and parts history to store in the file. If file storage space is your main concern, you may save your AutoCAD Designer file in a compressed format. To save to a compressed format, you need to manipulate the AMCOMPSV variable.

Command: **AMCOMPSV**
New value for AMCOMPSV: **1**

To set this variable, you may use the AMPARTVAR command.

<Parts>   <Preferences...>

Command: **AMPARTVARS**

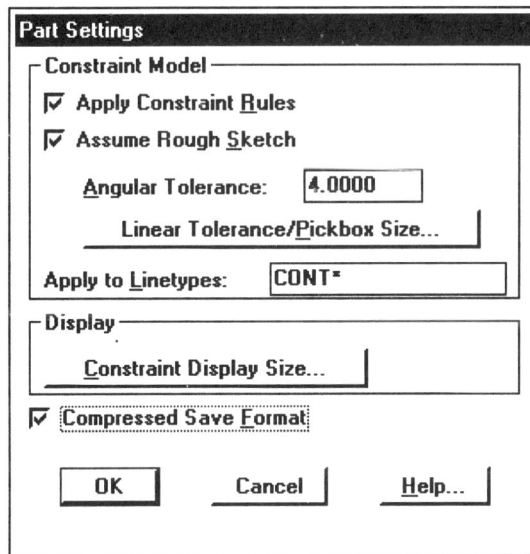

After setting the AMCOMPSV variable, save your file to another name using the SAVEAS command.

<File>   <Save As...>

Command: **SAVEAS**

[File name: **PLATE2**
OK   ]

Now you may compare the sizes of the two files. The file that was saved after setting the AMCOMPSV variable to 1 is much smaller. Besides giving you a smaller file size, opening a compressed file takes less time. However, you will have to wait for some time for AutoCAD Designer to reconstruct the parts history if you update the part of a compressed file.

Earlier, you have used the AMEDITFEAT command to change the parametric dimensions of a feature. Now you will run this command to change the sketch that was used to create the feature.

<Parts>   **<Edit Feature>**

Command: **AMEDITFEAT**
Sketch/surfCut/<select Feature>: **S**
Select sketched feature: **[Select A (Figure 2.15).]**

After you choose the sketch option and select a sketched feature, the feature disappears temporarily from the screen. The original sketch shows up. See Figure 2.16. You may edit the sketch.

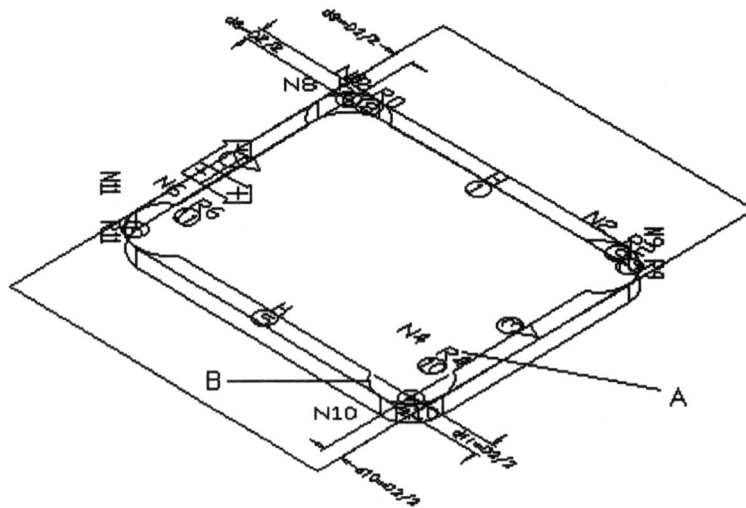

Figure 2.16 The solid part caused to disappear and a sketch displayed

Run the AMDELCON command to delete a constraint.

Command: **AMDELCON**
Size/All/<select>: **[Select A, the constraint governing the radius of the lower right corner (Figure 2.16).]**
Solved under constrained sketch requiring 1 dimensions or constraints.
Size/All/<select>: **[Enter]**

Now the sketch is underconstrained. It needs one parametric dimension or geometric constraint. Run the AMPARDIM command to add a parametric dimension to the radius of the lower right corner.

\<Parts\>   **\<Sketch\>**   **\<Add Dimension\>**

Command: **AMPARDIM**
Select first object: **[Select B (Figure 2.16).]**
Select second object or place dimension: **[Select a point near B (Figure 2.16).]**
Undo/Enter Dimension value: **D2*2 [or D?, where D? is the radius of the upper left arc.]**
Solved fully constrained sketch.
Select first object: **[Enter]**

Once again, the sketch is fully constrained. Apply the AMUPDATE command to update the change. See Figure 2.17.

\<Parts\>   **\<Update\>**

Command: **AMUPDATE**

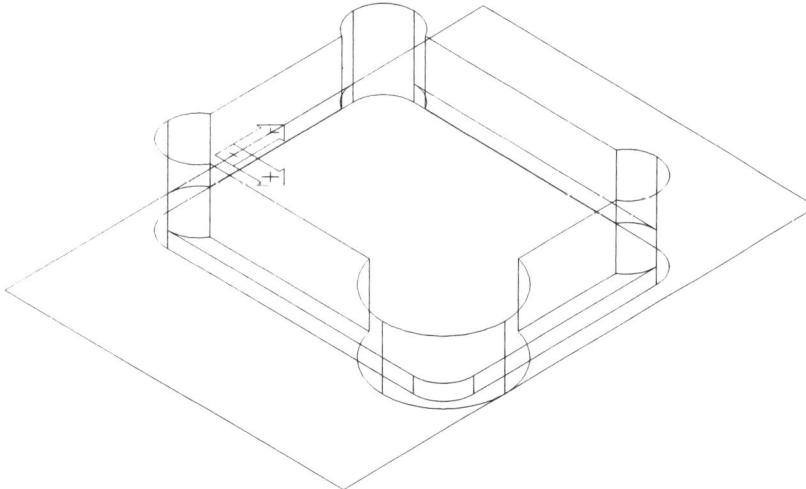

Figure 2.17 The parametric solid edited and updated

Now that you know how to edit the sketch of a solid feature, discard the changes and open the same file again.

\<File\>   **\<Open...\>**

Command: **OPEN**

[File name: **PLATE1**
OK   ]

Your drawing should resemble Figure 2.15. You will add the third sketched solid feature to the parametric solid part. Before you do that, you need to set a new sketch plane. Run the AMWORKPLN command. See Figure 2.18.

<Parts>   **<Feature>**   **<Work Plane...>**

Command: **AMWORKPLN**

[1st modifier: **Planar Parallel**
 2nd modifier: **On Edge/Axis**
Create Sketch Plane: **YES**
OK   ]

worldX/worldY/worldZ/<Select work axis or straight edge>: **[Select A (Figure 2.15).]**
worldXy/worldYz/worldZx/Ucs/<Select work plane or planar face>: **[Select A (Figure 2.15).]**
Next/<Accept>: **[Accept, if the upper plane is highlighted. Otherwise, Next.]**
worldX/worldY/worldZ/<Select work axis or straight edge>: **[Select A (Figure 2.15).]**
Rotate/Z-flip/<Accept>: **[R, if the Y axis direction is not the same as Figure 2.18.]**
Rotate/Z-flip/<Accept>: **[Z, if the X axis direction is not the same as Figure 2.18.]**
Rotate/Z-flip/<Accept>: **[Enter, if Y axis and X axis direction are the same as in Figure 2.18.]**

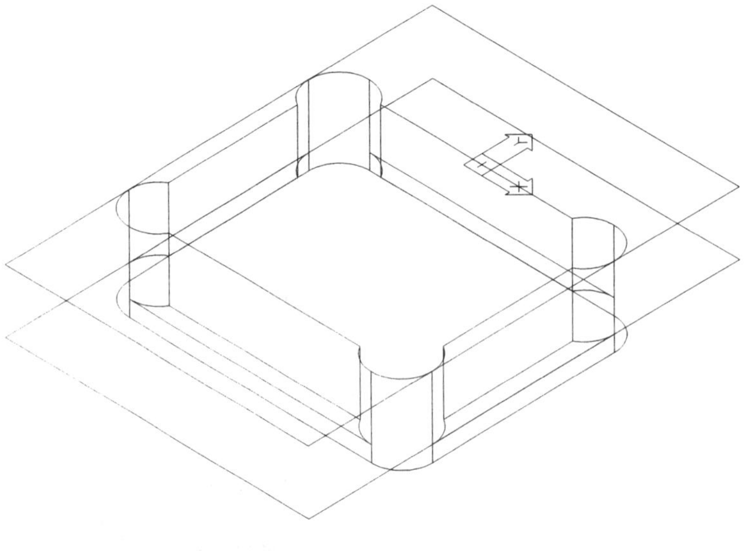

Figure 2.18 A new work plane created

Use the CIRCLE command to draw a circle on the new sketch plane.

[Draw]   **[Circle Center Radius]**

Command: **CIRCLE**

Apply the AMPROFILE command to resolve the circle to a profile for subsequent extrusion. See Figure 2.19.

<Parts>   **<Sketch>**   **<Profile>**

Command: **AMPROFILE**

Select objects for sketch:
Select objects: **LAST**
Select objects: **[Enter]**
Solved under constrained sketch requiring 3 dimensions or constraints.

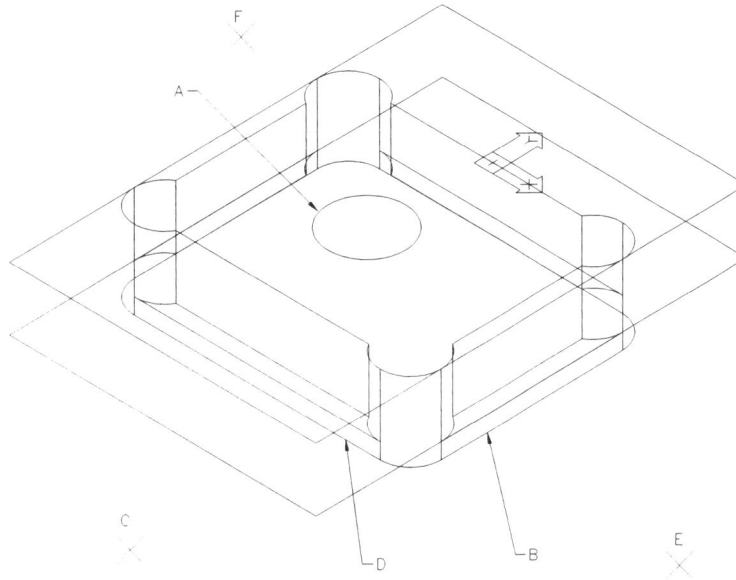

Figure 2.19 A circle drawn and resolved

The resolved profile needs three dimensions or constraints. Run the AMPARDIM command to complete the constraint. See Figure 2.20.

<Parts>   **<Sketch>**   **<Add Dimension>**

Command: **AMPARDIM**
Select first object: **[Select A (Figure 2.19).]**
Select second object or place dimension: **[Select B (Figure 2.19).]**
Specify dimension placement: **[Select C (Figure 2.19).]**
Undo/Hor/Ver/Align/Par/Enter Dimension value: **D0/2 [D0 is the length of the base feature.]**

Select first object: **[Select A (Figure 2.19).]**
Select second object or place dimension: **[Select D (Figure 2.19).]**
Specify dimension placement: **[Select E (Figure 2.19).]**
Undo/Hor/Ver/Align/Par/Enter Dimension value: **D1/2 [D1 is the width of the base feature.]**

Select first object: **[Select A (Figure 2.19).]**
Select second object or place dimension: **[Select F (Figure 2.19).]**
Undo/Enter Dimension value: **D2*3 [D2 is the radius of the corner of the base feature.]**
Solved fully constrained sketch.
Select first object: **[Enter]**

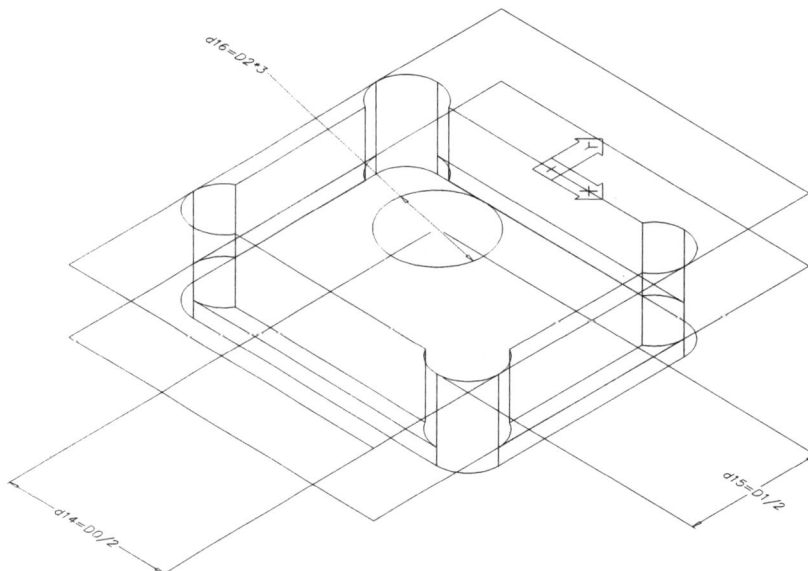

Figure 2.20 Fully constrained profile

Displaying the work planes is helpful while you are creating a sketch. However, you might want to turn them off if you do not need them anymore. Run the AMPLNDSP command to turn off the display of the work planes.

<Parts>   **<Display>**   **<Work Plane>**   **<Off>**

Command: **AMPLNDSP**
Display/ON/<OFf>: **OFF**
Select/<All>: **ALL**

To build the third feature, run the AMEXTRUDE command. The distance of extrusion is 1/5 of the length of the base. Replace D0 with the parameter name of your drawing if necessary. See Figure 2.21.

<Parts>   **<Feature>**   **<Extrude...>**

Command: **AMEXTRUDE**

[Termination: **Blind**
Operation: **Join**
Size:
   Distance: **D0/5**
   Draft angle: **0**
OK   ]

Direction Flip/<Accept>: **[Accept, if the arrow is pointing upward. Otherwise, Flip.]**

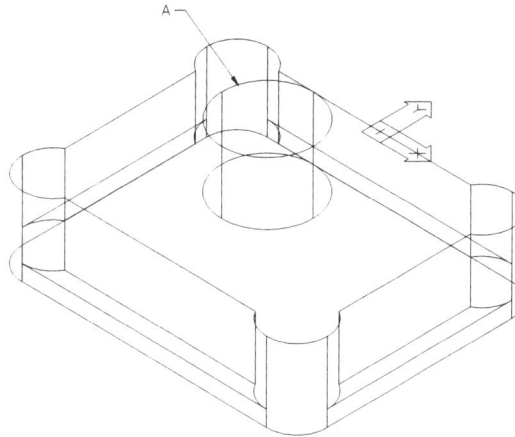

Figure 2.21 Third sketched solid feature joined

You have created a parametric solid model with three sketched solid features.

2.4   Placed Features

To complete the solid model, you will add chamfered edges, filleted edges, and holes to the solid part. These features are called placed features. In AutoCAD Designer terms, they are called chamfer feature, fillet feature, and hole feature, respectively. They are distinguished from the sketched solid features in that they do not need a sketch. All you have to do is specify a location.

Run the AMCHAMFER command to chamfer the upper edge of the second sketched solid feature. See Figure 2.22.

\<Parts\>   **\<Feature\>**   **\<Chamfer...\>**

Command: **AMCHAMFER**

[Operation: **Equal Distance**
Parameters: Distance1: **D2/10 [1/10 of the upper left radius]**
OK   ]

Pick the edge to chamfer: **[Select A (Figure 2.21).]**
Pick the edge to chamfer: **[Enter]**

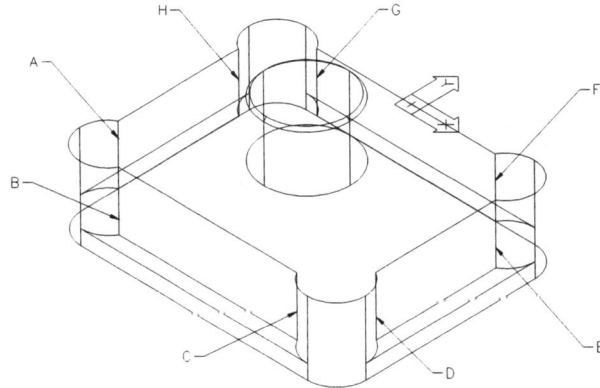

Figure 2.22 A chamfer feature added

Run the AMFILLET command to fillet eight vertical edges. See Figure 2.23.

<Parts>   **<Feature>**   **<Fillet>**

Command: **AMFILLET**
Pick the edge to fillet: **[Select A, B, C, D, E, F, G, and H (Figure 2.22).]**
Pick the edge to fillet: **[Enter]**
Fillet radius: **D2/5 [1/5 of the upper left radius]**

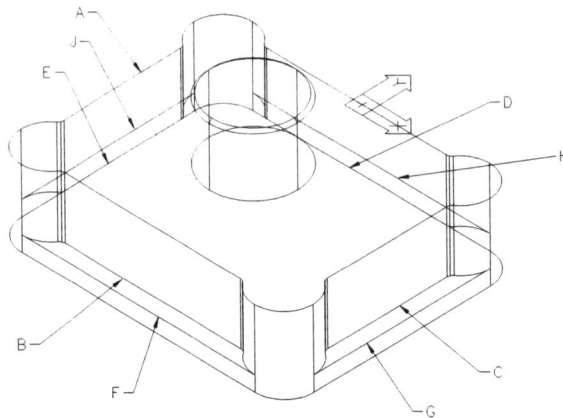

Figure 2.23 Eight vertical edges filleted

Repeat the AMFILLET command to fillet the edge of the upper face and four edges.

<Parts>   **<Feature>**   **<Fillet>**

Command: **AMFILLET**
Pick the edge to fillet: **[Select A, B, C, D, and E (Figure 2.23).]**
Pick the edge to fillet: **[Enter]**
Fillet radius: **D2/5 [1/5 of the upper left radius]**

Run the AMFILLET again to fillet four more edges. See Figure 2.24.

\<Parts\> **\<Feature\>** **\<Fillet\>**

Command: **AMFILLET**
Pick the edge to fillet: **[Select F, G, H, and J (Figure 2.23).]**
Pick the edge to fillet: **[Enter]**
Fillet radius: **D2/5 [1/5 of the upper left radius]**

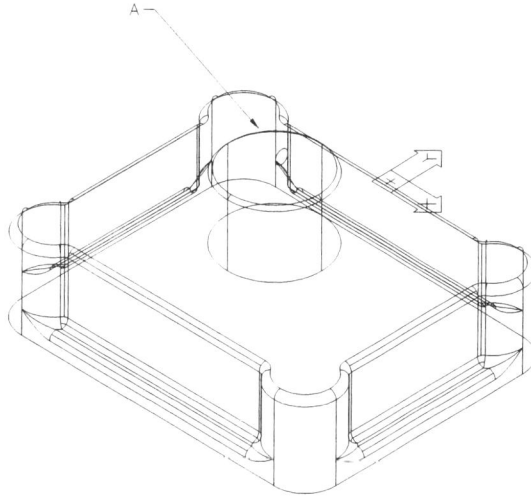

Figure 2.24 Edges filleted

The third type of placed solid feature is the hole feature. Run the AMHOLE command to create a tapped through hole. See Figure 2.25. Note that the display on the screen does not show the screw threads. The thread will display only in a two-dimensional drawing that is generated from the solid part.

\<Parts\> **\<Feature\>** **\<Hole...\>**

Command: **AMHOLE**

Hole Feature

Operation
- Drilled
- C'Bore
- C'Sink

Termination
- Through
- Blind

Tapped...

Placement
- Concentric
- 2 Edges
- On Point
- From Hole

Drill Size
- Depth: 1.5
- Dia: D2*1.5-2
- PT Angle: 118.0

C' Bore/Sunk Size
- C' Depth: 0.375
- C' Dia: 0.88
- C' Angle: 45

OK   Cancel   Help...

Thread Dimensions

☑ Tapped   Thread Options
- Major Dia: D2*1.5
- Thread Depth
  - ☐ Full Depth
  - Depth: 20

OK   Cancel   Help...

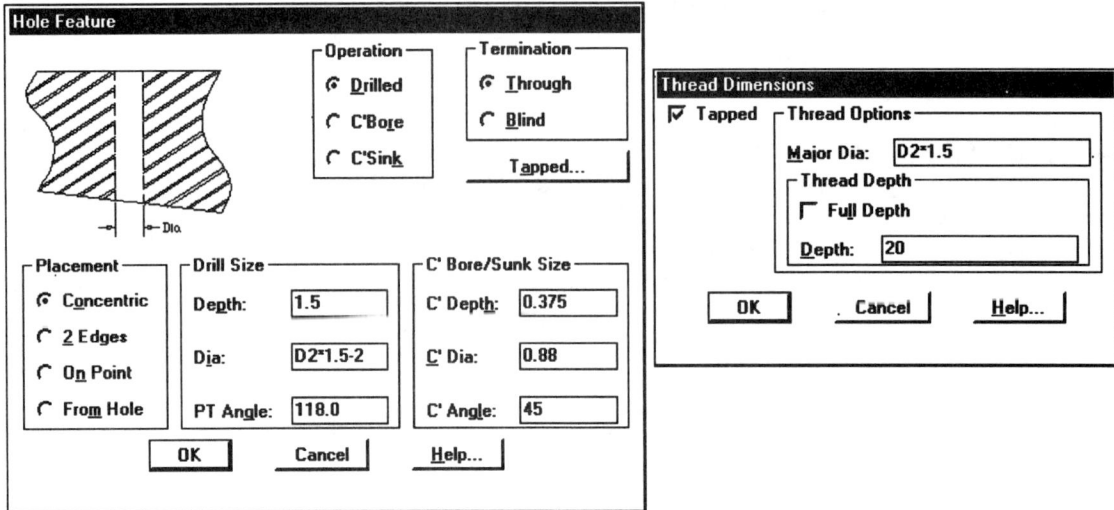

[Operation: **Drilled**
 Termination: **Through**
 Placement: **Concentric**

   [Tapped...:
       Thread Dimensions:
           Tapped: **YES**
       Thread Options:
           Major Dia: **D2*1.5**
       Thread Depth:
           Full Depth: **NO**
           Depth: **20**
     OK   ]

 Drill Size:
     Dia: **D2*1.5-2**
 OK   ]

worldXy/worldYz/worldZx/Ucs/<Select work plane or planar face>: **[Select A (Figure 2.24).]**
Select concentric edge: **[Select A (Figure 2.24).]**

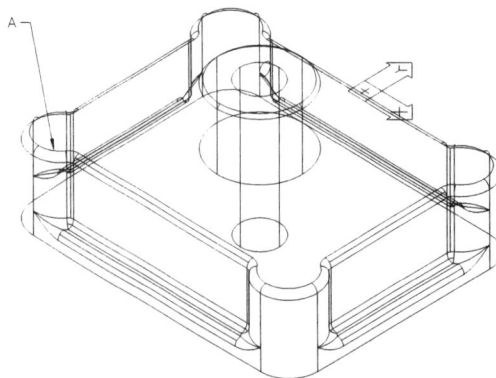

Figure 2.25 A tapped hole added (thread not shown)

Issue the AMHOLE command again. This time, create a counterbored hole. See Figure 2.26.

<Parts>   **<Feature>**   **<Hole...>**

Command: **AMHOLE**

[Operation: **C'Bore**
 Termination: **Through**
 Placement: **Concentric**
 Drill Size:
     Dia: **D2 [same as the upper left radius]**
 C'Bore/Sunk Size
     C'Depth: **D2/2 [1/2 of the upper left radius]**
     C'Dia: **D2*1.5 [1.5 times the upper left radius]**
OK   ]

worldXy/worldYz/worldZx/Ucs/<Select work plane or planar face>: **[Select A (Figure 2.25).]**
Select concentric edge: **[Select A (Figure 2.25).]**

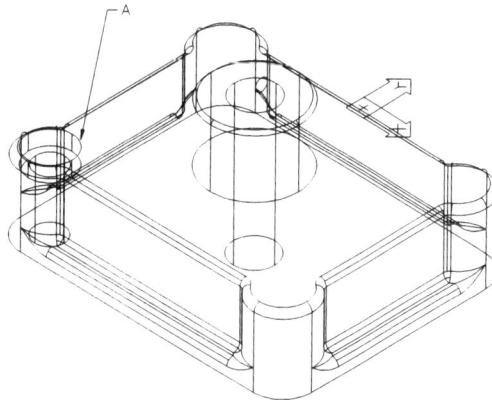

Figure 2.26 A counterbored hole added

Features can be arrayed, thus saving time in creation. Execute the AMARRAY command to create a rectangular array of the counterbored hole. See Figure 2.27.

<Parts>   **<Feature>**   **<Array...>**

Command: **AMARRAY**

Select feature: **[Select A (Figure 2.26).]**
Next/<Accept>: **[Accept, if the hole is highlighted. Otherwise, Next.]**

[Array Type: **Rectangular**
 Columns along X axis
     Number: **2**
     Spacing: **D0-2*D2**
                           [Overall length, D0, minus 2 times the upper left radius]

Rows along Y axis
    Number: **2**
    Spacing: **D1-2*D2**
                              [Overall width, D1, minus 2 times the upper left radius]
OK   ]

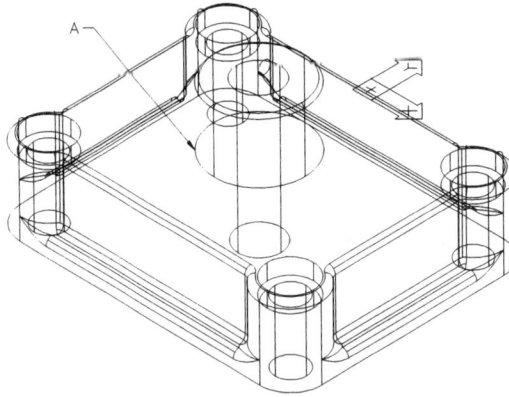

Figure 2.27 The counterbored hole arrayed

You have completed the solid model of the first engineering component. In the process of making this model, you have established a parts history. First, you created a sketched solid feature on the default sketch plane. The default sketch plane lies on the XY plane of the current UCS. It is not necessary for you to define a work plane explicitly or to set a sketch plane for the first sketch. The first sketched solid feature became the base feature. Then you created a work plane and set the sketch plane to this work plane. On this sketch plane, you created the second sketched solid feature to join to the base feature. After making the second feature, you built another work plane. You set the sketch plane to this work plane. Then you created the third sketched solid feature and joined it to the second solid feature. Next you chamfered and filleted the edges. Finally, you placed five holes on the solid.

You may replay everything that you have done by running the AMREPLAY command. Before you do that, save your work to a file.

        <File>   **<Save As...>**

        Command: **SAVEAS**

        [File name: **PLATE3**
        OK   ]

To replay the parts history, run the AMREPLAY command.

        <Parts>   **<Utilities>**   **<Replay>**

        Command: **AMREPLAY**

Once you issued this command, the screen display returns to the initial stage of the parts history. The sketch for the base feature appears. The display shows the profile with the geometric constraints and parametric dimensions, including the parameter name if you have chosen equation display. The display will resemble Figure 2.6.

> Display/Size/Truncate/eXit/<Next>: **D**

With the "Display" option, you may take a look at the geometric constraints as well as the parametric dimensions.

> Display/Size/Truncate/eXit/<Next>: **S**

Using the "Size" option, you may change the display size of the geometric constraint symbols.

> Display/Size/Truncate/eXit/<Next>: **[Enter]**

If you press the [Enter] key, the next stage of the parts history will appear. Refer to Figure 2.8.

> Extrusion Blind
> Truncate/eXit/<Next>: **[Enter]**

Pressing the [Enter] key again will elicit the next object, which is the work plane.

> Work plane On axis/edge, Planar parallel
> Truncate/eXit/<Next>: **TRUNCATE**

To truncate means to chop off the remaining operations in the parts history. As a result, you will remove the parts history that follows the last displayed operation. See Figure 2.28.

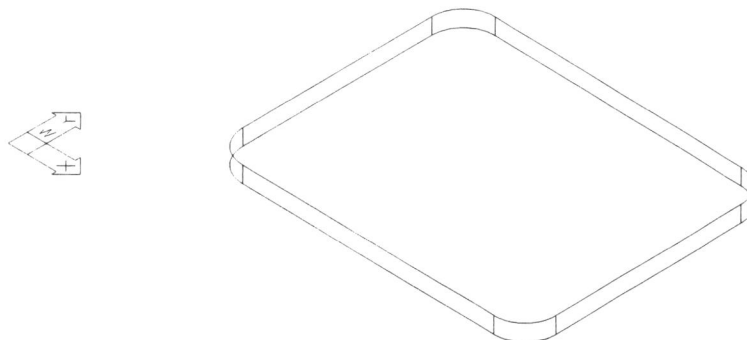

Figure 2.28 Parametric solid truncated to an early stage of creation

Do not save the drawing. Open it again with the OPEN command.

<File>   **<Open...>**

Command: **OPEN**

[**Discharge changes**   ]

[File name: **PLATE3**
OK   ]

As demonstrated above, the AMREPLAY command can replay the parts history and truncate a parametric solid to one of the intermediate stages in its history.

Besides truncating, there is another way to remove a certain portion of the model. Execute the AMDELFEAT command to delete the third sketched solid feature. In so doing, you will remove its dependent features, the chamfered edge, and the hole as well. See Figure 2.29.

<Parts>   **<Feature>**   **<Delete>**

Command: **AMDELFEAT**
Select feature: **[Select A (Figure 2.27).]**
Next/<Accept>: **[Accept, if the third sketched feature is highlighted. Otherwise, Next.]**
Highlighted features will be deleted. Continue ? No/<Yes>: **[Enter]**

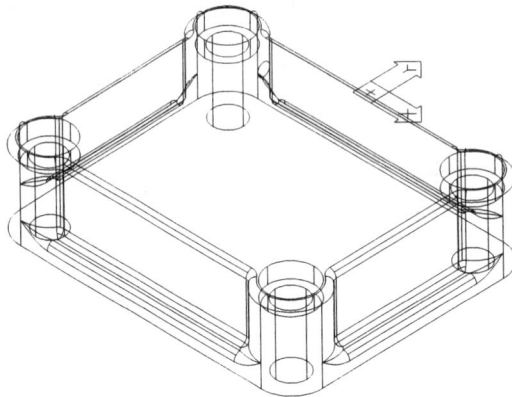

Figure 2.29 A solid feature and its dependent solid features deleted

Do not save the drawing. Start another drawing with the NEW command.

<File>   **<New...>**

Command: **NEW**

[**Discard changes**   ]

2.5   The Second Component

You will now start to build a parametric solid model for the second component shown in Figure 2.1.

First of all, you have to analyze the component. Obviously, you find three placed solid features — the three holes. Without careful thought, it is difficult to find that there are three sketched solid features as well.

The main body of the component is the intersection of two sketched solid features. You may select one of the two solid features as the base feature and then build the second solid feature to intersect with it. The third sketched solid feature is a slot that you will cut into the intersection. Figure 2.30 shows a breakdown of the sketched solid features.

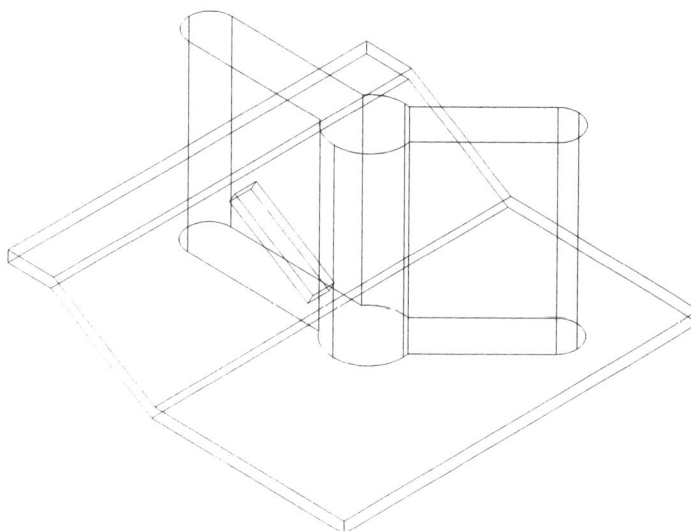

Figure 2.30 Sketched solid features of the second model

2.6   Construction Lines and Sketching

To prepare the drawing, set the drawing limits with the LIMITS command, use the ZOOM command to zoom to limits, apply the DDLMODES command to create two additional layers, and set the UCS icon to display at the origin position with the UCSICON command.

<Data>	<Drawing Limits>

Command: **LIMITS**
Reset Model space limits:
ON/OFF/<Lower left corner>: **0,0**
Upper right corner: **297,210**

[Standard Toolbar]   [Zoom All]

Command: **ZOOM**

All/Center/Dynamic/Extents/Left/Previous/Vmax/Window/<Scale(X/XP)>: **ALL**

<Data>   <Layers...>

Command: **DDLMODES**

Layer name	Color
SKETCH	**cyan**
SOLID	**yellow**

Current layer: **SKETCH**

Command: **UCSICON**
ON/OFF/All/Noorigin/ORigin: **OR**

To draw the first sketch of a component, you do not need to create any work plane or to set a sketch plane. The XY plane of the current UCS is the default sketch plane. As shown in Figure 2.31, use the LINE command and the ARC command to create a rough sketch.

[**Draw**]   [**Line**]

Command: **LINE**

[**Draw**]   [**Arc Start End Angle**]

Command: **ARC**

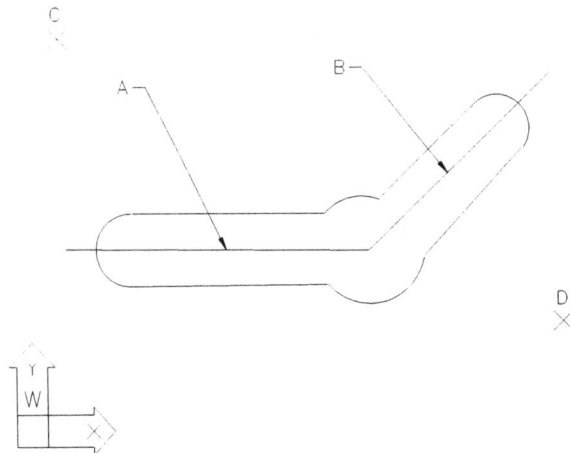

Figure 2.31 A rough sketch with construction lines

When you make a sketch, you may include construction lines. AutoCAD Designer recognizes the line type that the AMSKSTYLE variable specifies as sketching lines and regards any other line type as construction lines. Check the setting of the AMSKSTYLE variable.

Command: **AMSKSTYLE**
New values for AMSKSTYLE <CONTINUOUS>: **[Enter]**

To set the sketching lines line type, you may use the AMPARTVARS command.

<Parts>   **<Preferences...>**

Command: **AMPARTVARS**

You have used the AMPARTVARS command a number of times. To sum up, this command sets the following variables:

- AMRULEMODE: Apply Constraint Rules
- AMSKMODE: Assume Rough Sketch
- AMSKANGTOL: Angular Tolerance
- PICKBOX: Linear Tolerance/PickBox Size
- AMSKSTYLE: Apply to Linetype
- AMCONDSPSZ: Constraint Display Size
- AMCOMPSV: Compressed Save Format

With such setting, AutoCAD Designer will regard any line type that is not CONTINUOUS as construction lines.

Change the line type of two line segments to HIDDEN.

<Edit>   **<Properties...>**

Select objects: **[Select A and B (Figure 2.31).]**
Select objects: **[Enter]**

[Properties
Linetype...   HIDDEN
OK   ]

The default AutoCAD settings are in English units. The drawing produced here is in metric units. In order to have a better visual appearance of the lines, set the line type scale to 25 with the LTSCALE command.

Command: **LTSCALE**
New scale factor: **25**

When you resolve a set of entities, those having line type other than that which the AMSKSTYLE variable specifies will become construction lines. The construction lines are part of the profile. Although AutoCAD Designer will not include the construction lines for subsequent operation, the construction lines play a vital part in constraining the profile. You may apply geometric constraints and parametric dimensions on the construction lines together with the other sketching lines.

Run the AMPROFILE command. Include the construction lines in your object selection set. See Figure 2.32.

<Parts>   **<Sketch>**   **<Profile>**

Command: **AMPROFILE**
Select objects for sketch:
Select objects: **[Select C (Figure 2.31).]**
Other corner: **[Select D (Figure 2.31).]**
Select objects: **[Enter]**

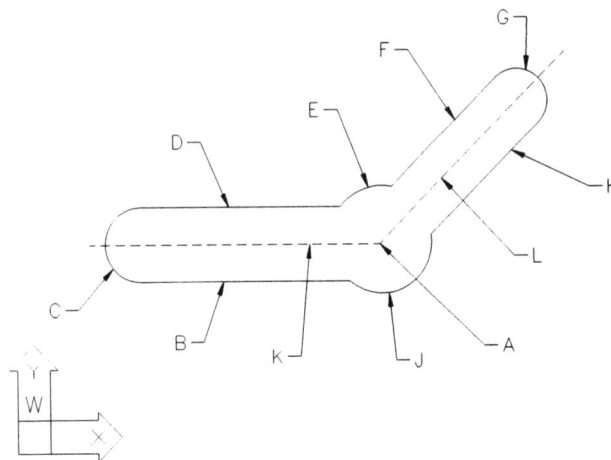

Figure 2.32 Rough sketch resolved to a profile

Manipulate the AMFIXPT command to set the intersecting point of the two construction lines to be the immovable point on the profile.

<Parts>   **<Sketch>**   **<Fix Point>**

Command: **AMFIXPT**
Specify new fixed point for sketch: **[Select A (Figure 2.32).]**

After setting the fixed point, issue the AMSHOWCON command to display the geometric constraint that AutoCAD Designer applies to your sketch.

    <Parts>   **<Sketch>**   **<Constraints>**   **<Show>**

Command: **AMSHOWCON**
All/Select/Next/<eXit>: **ALL**
All/Select/Next/<eXit>: **[Enter]**

Because every sketch is unique, the type of constraint that AutoCAD Designer applies to each profile is different.

In order to remove some irrelevant constraints, use the AMDELCON command to delete all other constraints except the tangential constraints.

    <Parts>   **<Sketch>**   **<Constraints>**   **<Delete>**

Command: **AMDELCON**
Size/All/<select>: **[Select all constraints except those with a T symbol.]**
Size/All/<select>: **[Enter]**

After removing the irrelevant constraints, run the AMADDCON command to add the required geometric constraints. See Figure 2.33.

Observe the change in the profile as you add constraints to it.

    <Parts>   **<Sketch>**   **<Constraints>**   **<Add>**

Command: **AMADDCON**

[Constraints: **Tangent**   Constraint Symbols: **Display**
Apply   ]

Select line, circle, arc, or ellipse: **[Select B (Figure 2.32).]**
Select circle, arc, or ellipse: **[Select C (Figure 2.32).]**
Select line, circle, arc, or ellipse: **[Select C (Figure 2.32).]**
Select circle, arc, or ellipse: **[Select D (Figure 2.32).]**
Select line, circle, arc, or ellipse: **[Select F (Figure 2.32).]**
Select circle, arc, or ellipse: **[Select G (Figure 2.32).]**
Select line, circle, arc, or ellipse: **[Select G (Figure 2.32).]**
Select circle, arc, or ellipse: **[Select H (Figure 2.32).]**
Select line, circle, arc, or ellipse: **[Enter]**

[Constraints: **Radius**   Constraint Symbols: **Display**
Apply   ]

Select first arc or circle: **[Select C (Figure 2.32).]**
Select second arc or circle: **[Select G (Figure 2.32).]**
Select first arc or circle: **[Select E (Figure 2.32).]**
Select second arc or circle: **[Select J (Figure 2.32).]**
Select first arc or circle: **[Enter]**

[Constraints: **Concentric**   Constraint Symbols: **Display**
Apply   ]

Select first arc, circle, or ellipse: **[Select E (Figure 2.32).]**
Select second arc, circle, or ellipse: **[Select J (Figure 2.32).]**
Select first arc, circle, or ellipse: [Enter]

[Constraints: **Project**   Constraint Symbols: **Display**
Apply   ]

Specify point to project (use a snap mode): **CEN** of **[Select C (Figure 2.32).]**
Select line, circle, arc, ellipse, or spline: **[Select K (Figure 2.32).]**
Specify point to project (use a snap mode): **CEN** of **[Select G (Figure 2.32).]**
Select line, circle, arc, ellipse, or spline: **[Select L (Figure 2.32).]**
Specify point to project (use a snap mode): **[Enter]**

[Constraints: **Join**   Constraint Symbols: **Display**
Apply   ]

Specify first point to join (use a snap mode): **CEN** of **[Select E (Figure 2.32).]**
Specify the second point to join (use a snap mode): **END** of **[Select K (Figure 2.32).]**
Specify first point to join (use a snap mode): **[Enter]**

[Constraints: **Parallel**   Constraint Symbols: **Display**
Apply   ]

Select first line: **[Select B (Figure 2.32).]**
Select second line: **[Select D (Figure 2.32).]**
Select first line: **[Select B (Figure 2.32).]**
Select second line: **[Select K (Figure 2.32).]**
Select first line: **[Select F (Figure 2.32).]**
Select second line: **[Select H (Figure 2.32).]**
Select first line: **[Select F (Figure 2.32).]**
Select second line: **[Select L (Figure 2.32).]**
Select first line: **[Enter]**

[Constraints: **Horizontal**   Constraint Symbols: **Display**
Apply   ]

Select line: **[Select K (Figure 2.32).]**
Select line: **[Enter]**

[**Exit**   ]

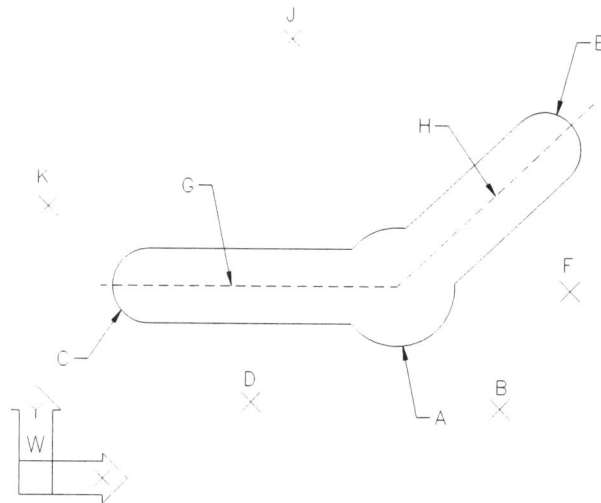

Figure 2.33 Geometric constraints applied

Before adding parametric dimensions, set the dimension display to show the equation by running the AMDIMDSP command.

    <Parts>   **<Display>**   **<Dim Display>**

Command: **AMDIMDSP**
Parameters/<Equations>/Numeric: **E**

With equation display, issue the AMPARDIM command to add parametric dimensions to the profile interactively. See Figure 2.34.

    <Parts>   **<Sketch>**   **<Add Dimension>**

Command: **AMPARDIM**
Select first object: **[Select A (Figure 2.32).]**
Select second object or place dimension: **[Select B (Figure 2.33).]**
Undo/Enter Dimension value: **20**

Select first object: **[Select A (Figure 2.33).]**
Select second object or place dimension: **[Select C (Figure 2.33).]**
Specify dimension placement: **[Select D (Figure 2.33).]**
Undo/Hor/Ver/Align/Par/Enter Dimension value: **90**

Select first object: **[Select A (Figure 2.33).]**
Select second object or place dimension: **[Select E (Figure 2.33).]**
Specify dimension placement: **[Select F (Figure 2.33).]**
Undo/Hor/Ver/Align/Par/Enter Dimension value: **ALIGN**
Undo/Hor/Ver/Align/Par/Enter Dimension value: **75**

Select first object: **[Select G (Figure 2.33).]**
Select second object or place dimension: **[Select H (Figure 2.33).]**
Specify dimension placement: **[Select J (Figure 2.33).]**
Undo/Enter Dimension value: **130**

Select first object: **[Select C (Figure 2.33).]**
Select second object or place dimension: **[Select K (Figure 2.33).]**
Undo/Enter Dimension value: **12**
Solved fully constrained sketch.
Select first object: **[Enter]**

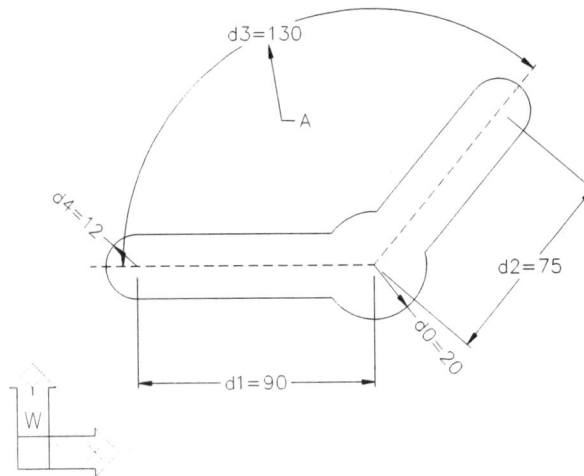

Figure 2.34 Fully constrained sketch

If you compare your screen with Figure 2.34, you may find that the parameter names are different. Here D0 is the radius of the central arc; D1 is the distance between the center of the left arc and the central arc; D2 is the distance between the center of the right arc and the central arc; D3 is the angular measurement; and D4 is the radius of the left arc.

Suppose the angular dimension should be 135° instead of 130°. Run the AMMODDIM command to modify the dimension value of this angular measurement. Note the change.

<Parts>   <Change Dimension>

Command: **AMMODDIM**
Select dimension to change: **[Select A (Figure 2.34).]**
New value for dimension <130>: **135**
Solved fully constrained sketch.
Select dimension to change: **[Enter]**

The profile for the base solid feature is completed. Before extruding it to form a solid feature, apply the short cut key [8] to set to an isometric view, and set the current layer to SOLID.

Command: **8**

**[Object Properties
Layer Control
SOLID   ]**

Execute the AMEXTRUDE command to extrude it to form a base solid feature. See Figure 2.35.

<Parts>   **<Feature>**   **<Extrude...>**

Command: **AMEXTRUDE**

[Termination:	**Blind**
Operation:	**Base**
Size:	
Distance:	**100**
Draft angle:	**0**
OK	]

Direction Flip/<Accept>: **[Accept, if the arrow is pointing upward. Otherwise, Flip.]**

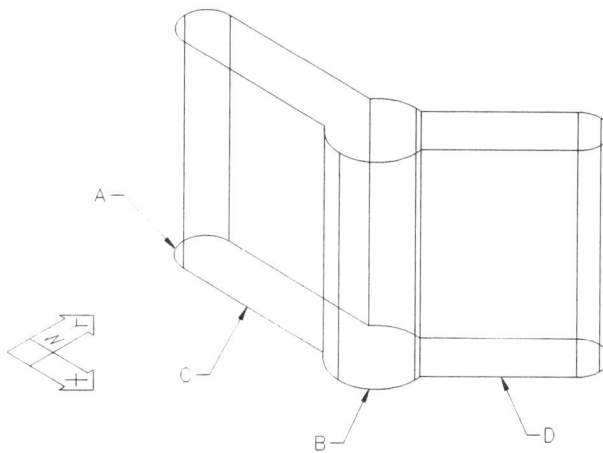

Figure 2.35 Base feature created

You have completed the base solid feature of the second component.

2.7   Extruding and Intersection

The second sketched solid feature of the component is also an extruded feature. This feature will intersect with the base feature. To create the second feature, you will do sketching. Set the current layer to SKETCH.

[Object Properties
Layer Control
SKETCH   ]

There are three kinds of construction features: the work plane, the work axis, and the work point. You have learned how to create a work plane with the AMWORKPLN command. Now you will learn how to create work axes with the AMWORKAXIS command.

A work axis is a parametric axis that links to the axis of a circular feature. You may use a work axis to locate work planes or sketch planes. Execute the AMWORKAXIS command to create two work axes. Then run the AMWORKPLN command to create a work plane to align with the bottom face of the base feature. See Figure 2.36.

\<Parts\>   \<Feature\>   \<Work Axis\>

Command: **AMWORKAXIS**
Select cylinder/cone/torus: **[Select A (Figure 2.35).]**

\<Parts\>   \<Feature\>   \<Work Axis\>

Command: **AMWORKAXIS**
Select cylinder/cone/torus: **[Select B (Figure 2.35).]**

\<Parts\>   \<Feature\>   \<Work Plane...\>

Command: **AMWORKPLN**

[1st Modifier: **On Edge/Axis**
 2nd Modifier: **On Edge/Axis**
 Create Sketch Plane: **NO**
OK   ]

worldX/worldY/worldZ/\<Select work axis or straight edge\>: **[Select C (Figure 2.35).]**
worldX/worldY/worldZ/\<Select work axis or straight edge\>: **[Select D (Figure 2.35).]**

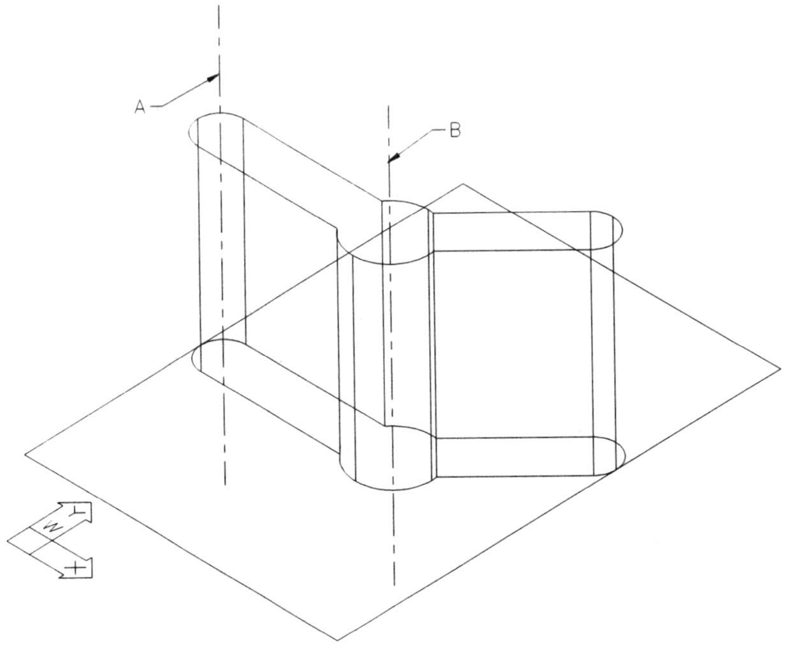

Figure 2.36 Work axes, and work plane created

Repeat the AMWORKPLN command to create another work plane that is parallel to the two newly created work axes. See Figure 2.37.

<Parts>   **<Feature>**   **<Work Plane...>**

Command: **AMWORKPLN**

[1st Modifier: **On Edge/Axis**
 2nd Modifier: **On Edge/Axis**
 Create Sketch Plane: **NO**
 OK   ]

worldX/worldY/worldZ/<Select work axis or straight edge>: **[Select A (Figure 2.36).]**
worldX/worldY/worldZ/<Select work axis or straight edge>: **[Select B (Figure 2.36).]**

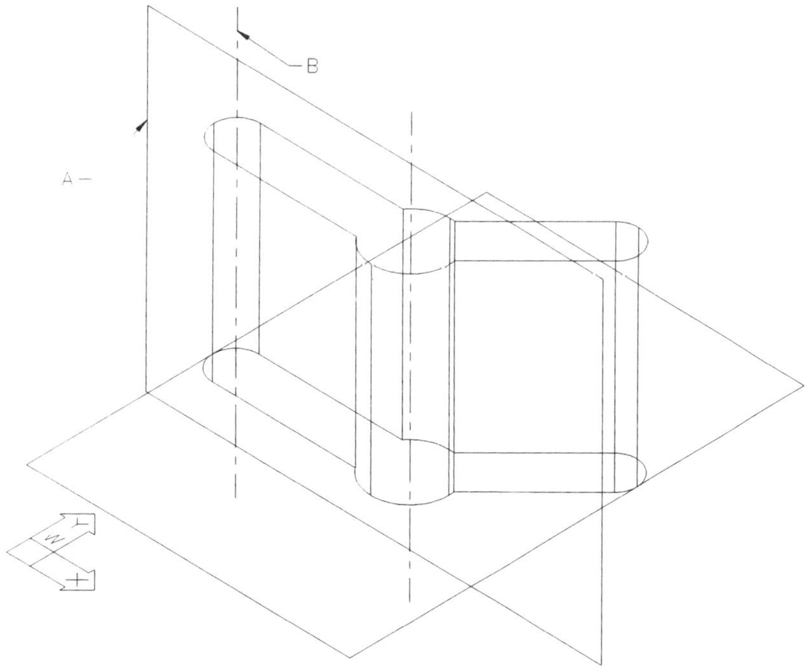

Figure 2.37 Another work plane created

While you are creating a work plane, you may choose to select to set the sketch plane to the new work plane. With two or more work planes created on a solid part, you may explicitly assign a sketch plane. Run the AMSKPLN command to set the sketch plane to the vertical work plane that you have created.

<Parts>   **<Sketch>**   **<Sketch Plane>**

Command: **AMSKPLN**
worldXy/worldYz/worldZx/Ucs/<Select work plane or planar face>: **[Select A (Figure 2.37).]**
worldX/worldY/worldZ/<Select work axis or straight edge>: **[Select B (Figure 2.37).]**
Rotate/Z-flip/<Accept>: **[R, if the Y axis is not pointing upward.]**

Rotate/Z-flip/<Accept>: **[Z, if the X axis is not pointing to the right.]**
Rotate/Z-flip/<Accept>: **[Accept, it the Y axis is pointing upward, and the X axis is pointing to the right.]**

Set the display to the plan view of the current UCS with the short cut key [9]. This key gives a view that is perpendicular to the current sketch plane. The UCS is there on the sketch plane. You should remember that the sketch plane is what you should always be referring to in AutoCAD Designer.

Command: **9**

As shown in Figure 2.38, use the PLINE command to create a polyline.

[Draw]   **[Polyline]**

Command: **PLINE**

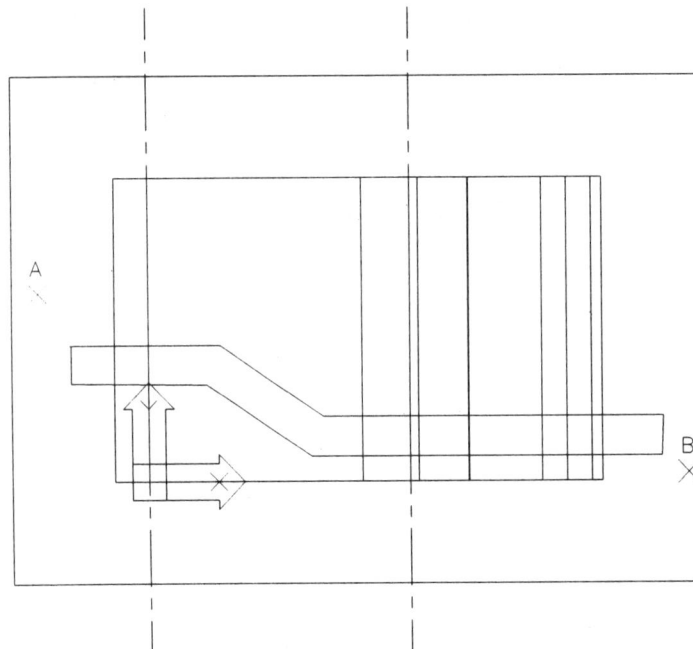

Figure 2.38 A sketch created on the new sketch plane

Issue the AMPROFILE command to resolve the sketch to a profile. See Figure 2.39.

<Parts>   <Sketch>   <Profile>

Command: **AMPROFILE**
Select objects for sketch:
Select objects: **[Select A (Figure 2.38).]**
Other corner: **[Select B (Figure 2.38).]**
Select objects: **[Enter]**

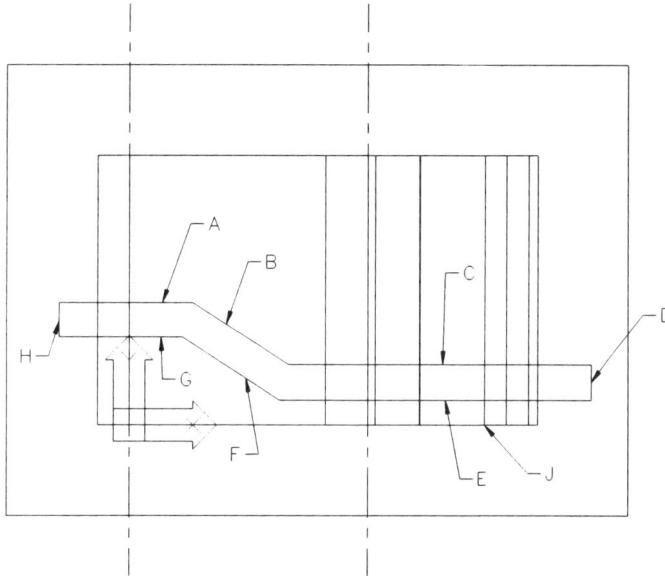

Figure 2.39 The sketch resolved

A profile needs geometric constraints and parametric dimensions. Run the AMADDCON command to add geometric constraints. Note the change to the profile. See Figure 2.40.

<Parts>   <Sketch>   <Constraints>   <Add>

Command: **AMADDCON**

[Constraints: **Horizontal**   Constraint Symbols: **Display**
Apply   ]

Select line: **[Select A, C, E, and G (Figure 2.39).]**
Select line: **[Enter]**

[Constraints: **Vertical**   Constraint Symbols: **Display**
Apply   ]

Select line: **[Select D, and H (Figure 2.39).]**
Select line: **[Enter]**

[Constraints: **Parallel**   Constraint Symbols: **Display**
Apply   ]

Select first line: **[Select B, and F (Figure 2.39).]**
Select first line: **[Enter]**

[Constraints: **Collinear**   Constraint Symbols: **Display**
Apply   ]

Select first line: **[Select E, and J (Figure 2.39).]**
Select first line: **[Enter]**

[**Exit**   ]

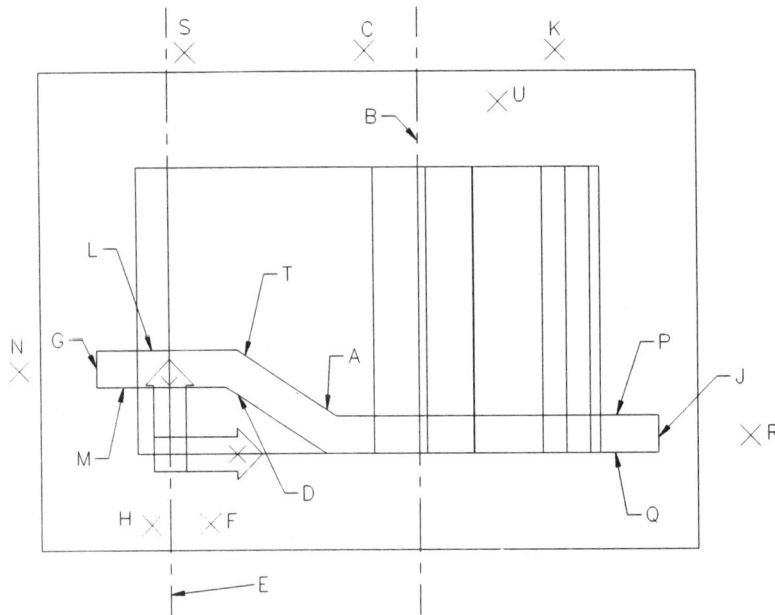

Figure 2.40 Geometric constraints applied

After constraining the profile geometrically, apply the AMPARDIM command to add parametric dimensions. See Figure 2.41.

The parametric dimensions will be expressed as a function of those dimensions in the base feature. Refer to Figure 2.34, and compare the parameter names in the illustration with yours. Make necessary adjustments to the names in the following delineation.

<Parts>   <Sketch>   <Add Dimension>

Command: **AMPARDIM**
Select first object: **[Select A (Figure 2.40).]**
Select second object or place dimension: **[Select B (Figure 2.40).]**
Specify dimension placement: **[Select C (Figure 2.40).]**
Undo/Hor/Ver/Align/Par/Enter Dimension value: **HOR**
Undo/Hor/Ver/Align/Par/Enter Dimension value: **DO [Refer to Figure 2.34.]**

Select first object: **[Select D (Figure 2.40).]**
Select second object or place dimension: **[Select E (Figure 2.40).]**
Specify dimension placement: **[Select F (Figure 2.40).]**
Undo/Hor/Ver/Align/Par/Enter Dimension value: **HOR**
Undo/Hor/Ver/Align/Par/Enter Dimension value: **D4 [Refer to Figure 2.34.]**

Select first object: **[Select G (Figure 2.40).]**
Select second object or place dimension: **[Select E (Figure 2.40).]**
Specify dimension placement: **[Select H (Figure 2.40).]**
Undo/Hor/Ver/Align/Par/Enter Dimension value: **HOR**
Undo/Hor/Ver/Align/Par/Enter Dimension value: **D4 [Refer to Figure 2.34.]**

Select first object: **[Select B (Figure 2.40).]**
Select second object or place dimension: **[Select J (Figure 2.40).]**
Specify dimension placement: **[Select K (Figure 2.40).]**
Undo/Hor/Ver/Align/Par/Enter Dimension value: **HOR**

Undo/Hor/Ver/Align/Par/Enter Dimension value: **D2+D4 [Refer to Figure 2.34.]**

Select first object: **[Select L (Figure 2.40).]**
Select second object or place dimension: **[Select M (Figure 2.40).]**
Specify dimension placement: **[Select N (Figure 2.40).]**
Undo/Hor/Ver/Align/Par/Enter Dimension value: **D4/2 [Refer to Figure 2.34.]**

Select first object: **[Select P (Figure 2.40).]**
Select second object or place dimension: **[Select Q (Figure 2.40).]**
Specify dimension placement: **[Select R (Figure 2.40).]**
Undo/Hor/Ver/Align/Par/Enter Dimension value: **D4/2 [Refer to Figure 2.34.]**

Select first object: **[Select A (Figure 2.40).]**
Select second object or place dimension: **[Select D (Figure 2.40).]**
Specify dimension placement: **[Select S (Figure 2.40).]**
Undo/Hor/Ver/Align/Par/Enter Dimension value: **PAR**
Undo/Hor/Ver/Align/Par/Enter Dimension value: **D4/2 [Refer to Figure 2.34.]**

Select first object:**[Select P (Figure 2.40).]**
Select second object or place dimension: **[Select T (Figure 2.40).]**
Specify dimension placement: **[Select U (Figure 2.40).]**
Undo/Enter Dimension value: **150**
Solved fully constrained sketch.
Select first object: **[Enter]**

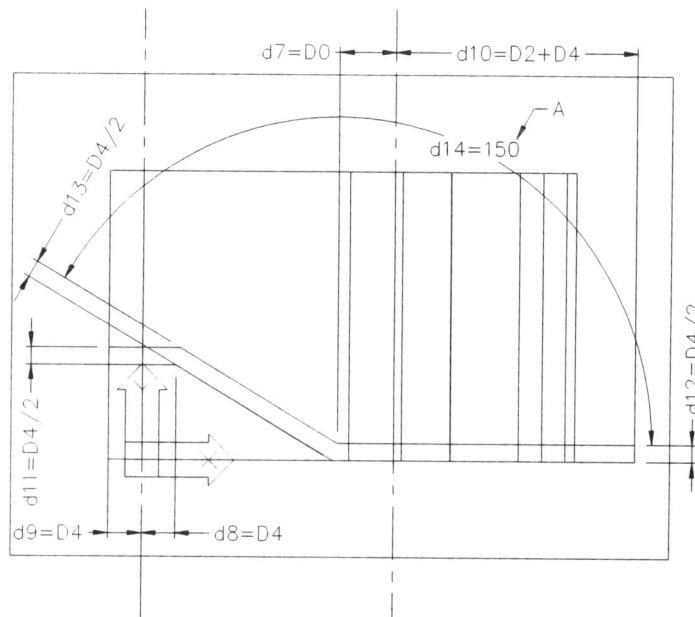

Figure 2.41 Fully constrained profile

Return to an isometric view. Then use the AMEXTRUDE command to extrude and intersect with the base feature. See Figure 2.42. The distance of extrusion is a function of a dimension of the base feature.

Command: **8**

<Parts>   **<Feature>**   **<Extrude...>**

Command: **AMEXTRUDE**

[Termination: **Mid Plane**
Operation: **Intersect**
Size: Distance: **2*D2 [Refer to Figure 2.34.]**
OK   ]

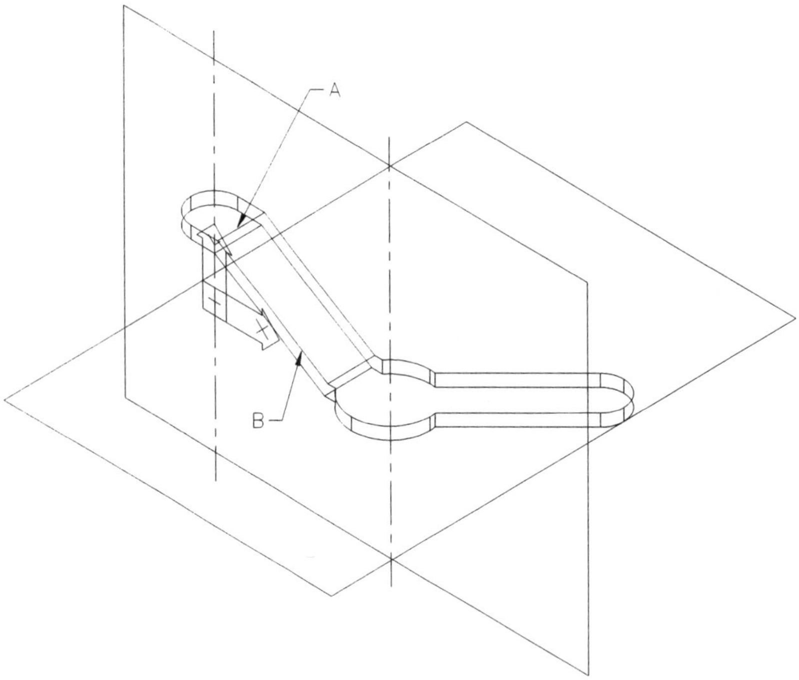

Figure 2.42 Second profile extruded and intersected with the base feature

Apply the AMWORKPLN command to create a work plane on an inclined face. Also set the sketch plane to this work plane. See Figure 2.43.

<Parts>   **<Feature>**   **<Work Plane...>**

Command: **AMWORKPLN**

[1st Modifier: **On Edge/Axis**
 2nd Modifier: **On Edge/Axis**
 Create Sketch Plane: **YES**
OK   ]

worldX/worldY/worldZ/<Select work axis or straight edge>: **[Select A (Figure 2.42).]**
worldX/worldY/worldZ/<Select work axis or straight edge>: **[Select B (Figure 2.42).]**
worldX/worldY/worldZ/<Select work axis or straight edge>: **[Select A (Figure 2.42).]**
Rotate/Z-flip/<Accept>: **[R, if the Y axis direction is not the same as Figure 2.43.]**
Rotate/Z-flip/<Accept>: **[Z, if the X axis direction is not the same as Figure 2.43.]**
Rotate/Z-flip/<Accept>: **[Enter, if Y axis and X axis direction are the same as Figure 2.43.]**

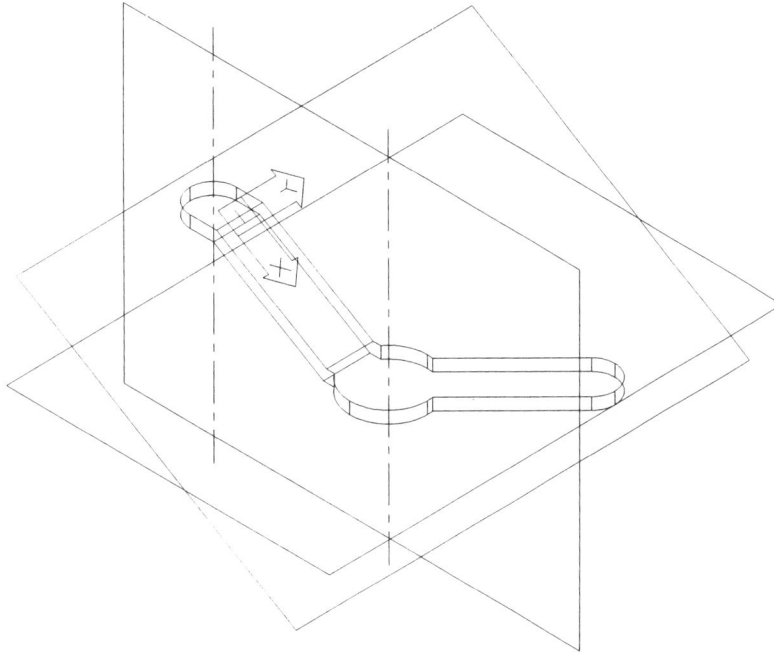

Figure 2.43 A new work plane created and the sketch plane set

Set the display to the plan view of the new sketch plane with the short cut key [9].

Command: **9**

On this sketch plane, use the PLINE command to create a rectangle. Then resolve it to a profile with the AMPROFILE command. See Figure 2.44.

[**Draw**]   [**Polyline**]

Command: **PLINE**

<**Parts**>   <**Sketch**>   <**Profile**>

Command: **AMPROFILE**
Select objects for sketch:
Select objects: **LAST**
Select objects: **[Enter]**

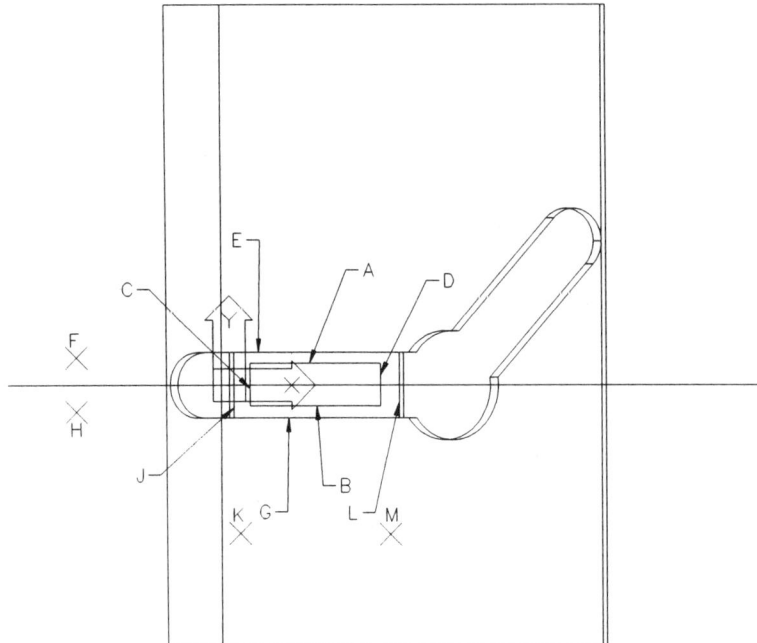

Figure 2.44 Third sketch resolved

Use the AMADDCON command to add horizontal constraint to the two horizontal lines and vertical constraints to the two vertical lines. Then issue the AMPARDIM command to add four parametric dimensions. See Figure 2.45.

\<Parts\>   **\<Sketch\>**   **\<Constraints\>**   **\<Add\>**

Command: **AMADDCON**

\<Parts\>   **\<Sketch\>**   **\<Add Dimension\>**

Command: **AMPARDIM**
Select first object: **[Select A (Figure 2.44).]**
Select second object: **[Select E (Figure 2.44).]**
Specify dimension placement: **[Select F (Figure 2.44).]**
Undo/Hor/Ver/Align/Par/Enter Dimension value: **D4/2 [D4 is the radius of the left arc.]**

Select first object: **[Select B (Figure 2.44).]**
Select second object: **[Select G (Figure 2.44).]**
Specify dimension placement: **[Select H (Figure 2.44).]**
Undo/Hor/Ver/Align/Par/Enter Dimension value: **D4/2 [D4 is the radius of the left arc.]**

Select first object: **[Select C (Figure 2.44).]**
Select second object: **[Select J (Figure 2.44).]**
Specify dimension placement: **[Select K (Figure 2.44).]**
Undo/Hor/Ver/Align/Par/Enter Dimension value: **D4/2 [D4 is the radius of the left arc.]**

Select first object: **[Select D (Figure 2.44).]**
Select second object: **[Select L (Figure 2.44).]**
Specify dimension placement: **[Select M (Figure 2.44).]**

Undo/Hor/Ver/Align/Par/Enter Dimension value: **D4/2 [D4 is the radius of the left arc.]**
Solved fully constrained sketch.
Select first object: **[Enter]**

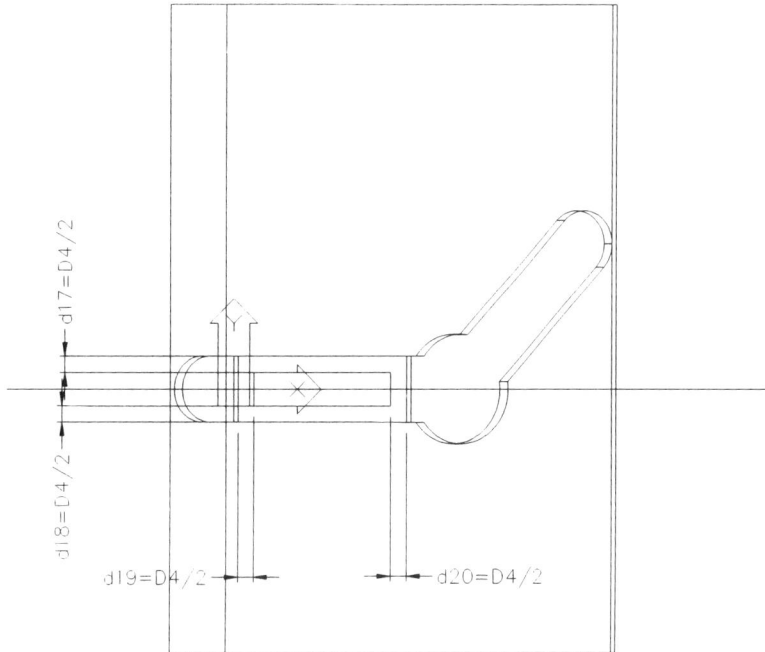

Figure 2.45 Third sketch fully constrained

Once again, return to an isometric view. Then issue the AMEXTRUDE command to extrude the profile, and cut it from the existing feature. After that, turn off the display of the work planes and the work axes by running the AMPLNDSP command and the AMAXISDSP command, respectively. See Figure 2.46.

Command: **8**

<Parts>   <Feature>   <Extrude...>

Command: **AMEXTRUDE**

[Termination: **Through**
 Operation: **Cut**
 Size:
    Draft Angle: **0**
OK   ]

Direction Flip/<Accept>: **[Accept, if the arrow is pointing downward. Otherwise, Flip.]**

<Parts>   <Display>   <Work Plane>   <Off>

Command: **AMPLNDSP**
Display/ON/<OFf>: **OFF**

Select/<All>: **ALL**

<Parts>   **<Display>**   **<Work Axis>**   **<Off>**

Command: **AMAXISDSP**
ON/<OFf>: **OFF**

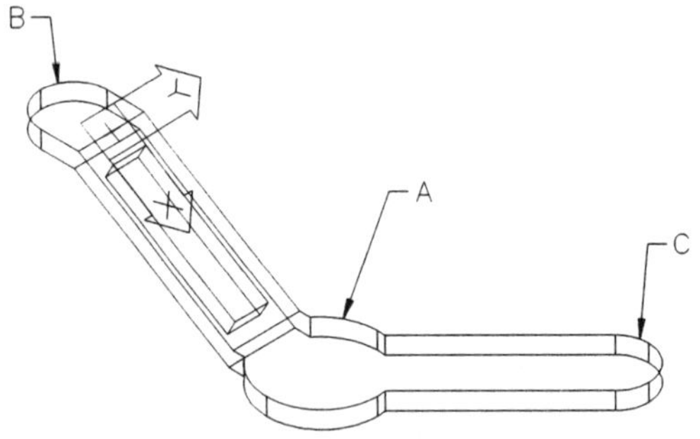

Figure 2.46 Solid part cut by the third sketched solid feature

On the solid part, there should be three placed features — a drilled through hole and two countersunk through holes. Apply the AMHOLE command to complete the model. See Figure 2.47.

<Parts>   **<Feature>**   **<Hole...>**

Command: **AMHOLE**

[Operation: **Drilled**
 Termination: **Through**
 Placement: **Concentric**
 Drill Size: **D0 [Refer to Figure 2.34.]**
OK   ]

worldXy/worldYz/worldZx/Ucs/<Select work plane or planar face>: **[Select A (Figure 2.46).]**
Select concentric edge:**[Select A (Figure 2.46).]**

<Parts>   **<Feature>**   **<Hole...>**

Command: **AMHOLE**

[Operation: **C'Sink**
 Termination: **Through**
 Placement: **Concentric**
 Drill Size: **D4/2 [Refer to Figure 2.34.]**
 C'Bore/Sunk Size:
    C'Dia: **D4**
    C'Angle: **90**
OK   ]

worldXy/worldYz/worldZx/Ucs/<Select work plane or planar face>: **[Select B (Figure 2.46).]**
Select concentric edge:**[Select B (Figure 2.46).]**

<Parts>   **<Feature>**   **<Hole...>**

Command: **AMHOLE**

[Operation: **C'Sink**
 Termination: **Through**
 Placement: **Concentric**
 Drill Size: **D4/2 [Refer to Figure 2.34.]**
 C'Bore/Sunk Size:
     C'Dia: **D4**
     C'Angle: **90**
OK   ]

worldXy/worldYz/worldZx/Ucs/<Select work plane or planar face>: **[Select C (Figure 2.46).]**
Select concentric edge:**[Select C (Figure 2.46).]**

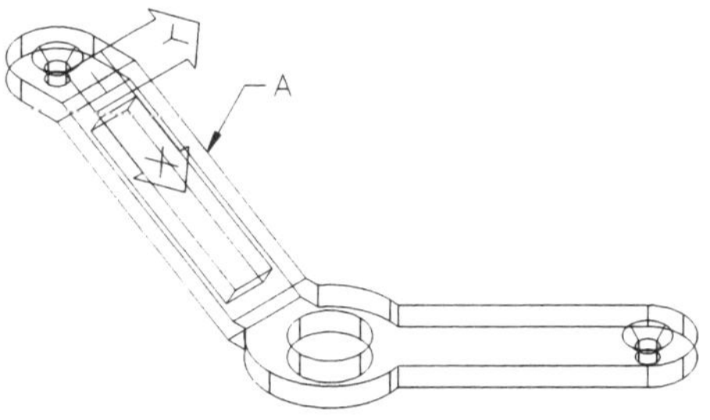

Figure 2.47 Three holes placed

You have completed the solid model of the second engineering component. To appreciate how to modify a complex solid model like this one, run the AMEDITFEAT command to edit two angular measurements; one is on the base feature, and the other one is on the feature that intersects with the base feature.

<Parts>   **<Edit Feature>**

Command: **AMEDITFEAT**
Sketch/surfCut/<select Feature>: **[Select A (Figure 2.47).]**
Next/<Accept>: **[Accept, if the base feature is highlighted. Otherwise, Next.]**
Select object: **[Select A (Figure 2.34).]**
Enter new value for dimension: **210**
Solved fully constrained sketch.
Select object: **[Enter]**

<Parts>   **<Edit Feature>**

Command: **AMEDITFEAT**
Sketch/surfCut/<select Feature>: **[Select A (Figure 2.47).]**

Next/<Accept>: **[Accept, if the second feature is highlighted. Otherwise, Next.]**
Select object: **[Select A (Figure 2.41).]**
Enter new value for dimension: **120**
Solved fully constrained sketch.
Select object: **[Enter]**

Then use the AMUPDATE command to update the change.

<Parts>   **<Update>**

Command: **AMUPDATE**
Update Failed.
Highlighted feature (Work plane On edge/axis, On edge/axis) could not be computed.
Press ENTER to continue..
Use UNDO or AMEDITFEAT to return dimensions to previous values.

Very surprisingly indeed, it cannot be updated. What is the reason?

Refer to Figure 2.35. The height of extrusion of the base feature is 100 units. This value is too small if the angular measurement, A of Figure 2.41, is getting smaller. Therefore, issue the AMEDITFEAT command again to edit the extrusion height of the base feature. Then update the change with the AMUPDATE command. See Figure 2.48.

<Parts>   **<Edit Feature>**

Command: **AMEDITFEAT**
Sketch/surfCut/<select Feature>: **[Select A (Figure 2.47).]**
Next/<Accept>: **[Accept, if the base feature is highlighted. Otherwise, Next.]**
Select object: **[Select the dimension of extrusion of the base feature.]**
Enter new value for dimension: **200**
Solved fully constrained sketch.
Select object: **[Enter]**

<Parts>   **<Update>**

Command: **AMUPDATE**

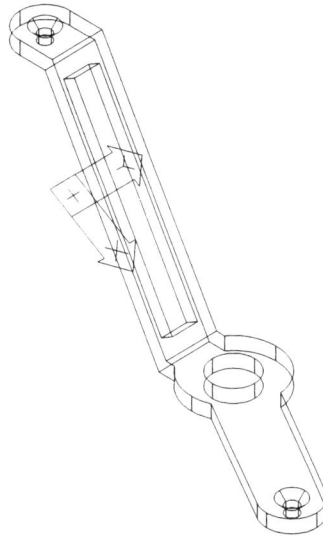

Figure 2.48 Features edited and updated again

You have completed the second model. Save your work.

<File>   **<Save...>**

Command: **QSAVE**

[File name: **LEVER**
OK   ]

If you wish to ensure that a certain dimension of a feature maintains a relationship with another dimension, you have to express the dimension as an equation. To write an equation, you may use the following mathematical operators.

Operation	Description
^	Exponent
+	Add
-	Subtract
*	Multiply
/	Divide
%	Modulus (remainder)
sqrt	Square root
log	Logarithm
ln	Natural logarithm
floor	Round down to the nearest integer
ceil	Round up to the nearest integer
sin	Sine
cos	Cosine
tan	Tangent
asin	Arcsin $(\sin^{-1})$

acos	Arccos (cos^{-1})
atan	Arctan (tan^{-1})
sinh	Hyperbolic sine
cosh	Hyperbolic cosine
tanh	Hyperbolic tangent
pi	Π
e	Base number for natural logarithm
exp(x)	e^{x}

2.8   Display Control

You may find that the parametric solids shown in the display seem to lack something. You would expect to see the silhouette of the model, which is not found. Instead, you see only some radial lines. These radial lines are called isolines. The density of the isolines is controlled by the AutoCAD system variable ISOLINES. Change the setting of this variable.

Command: **ISOLINES**
New values for ISOLINES <4>: **0**

When you set this variable, there should be no immediate change on the screen display. The new setting will take effect in the next regeneration. Issue the REGEN command.

Command: **REGEN**

As can be seen, all the isolines have gone. If you want to display the silhouette edges, you may set the AutoCAD system variable DISPSILH to 1.

Command: **DISPSILH**
New value for DISPSILH <0>: **1**

Again, you have to regenerate the screen display to see the change.

Command: **REGEN**

The silhouette edges now display. You should note that the silhouette edges depend on the viewing direction; there will be a slow regeneration each time you change the viewing angle.

To alter the viewing direction of an AutoCAD Designer object, you may use the AMVIEW command.

Command: **AMVIEW**
(Angle = 15)
Angle/Down/eXit/Left/Right/Sketch/Up/<Fit>: **L**
Regenerating drawing.
Angle/Down/eXit/Fit/Left/Right/Sketch/<Up>: **X**

As stated earlier in this chapter, there are short cut keys. The short cut keys for rotating the view are:

[Rotates the view to the left.
]   Rotates the view to the right.
=   Rotates the view upward.
-                Rotates the view downward.

To visualize the solid model that you have created, you may use the RENDER command. This command outputs a photo-realistic image to the screen or to a file.

Command: **RENDER**

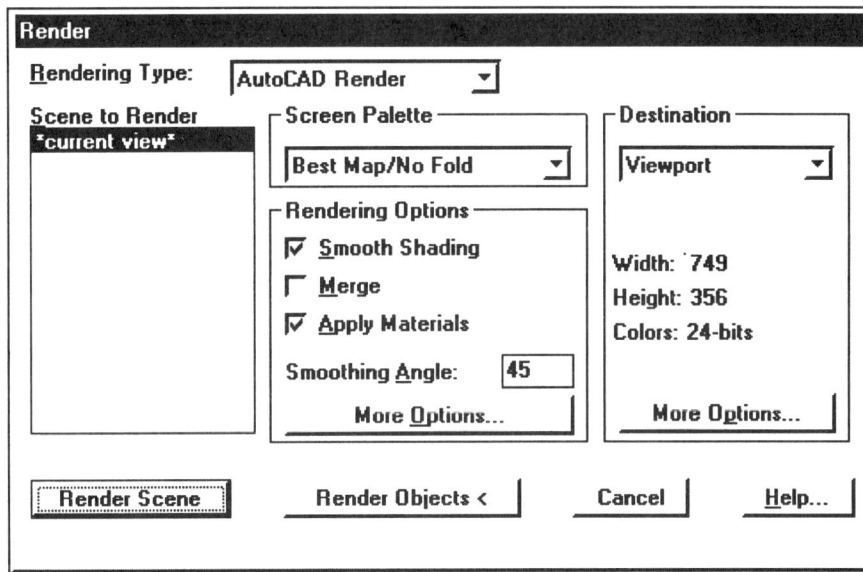

The RENDER command may take some time to produce an image. If you want to have a quick shading image, you may use the SHADE command.

Command: **SHADE**

If you want to have a line diagram with hidden lines removed, you may use the HIDE command.

Command: **HIDE**

End the drawing session.

Command: **END**

2.9 Summary

In this chapter, you have applied the following AutoCAD Designer commands and variables in parametric solid model creation.

Utility commands:

AMABOUT	AMPARTVARS

Profile commands:

AMPROFILE	AMFIXPT

Geometric constraint commands:

AMADDCON	AMDELCON	AMSHOWCON

Parametric dimension commands:

AMDIMDSP	AMPARDIM	AMMODDIM

Sketched solid feature command:

AMEXTRUDE

Placed solid feature commands:

AMCHAMFER	AMFILLET	AMHOLE

Construction feature commands:

AMSKPLN	AMWORKAXIS	AMAXISDSP
AMWORKPLN	AMPLNDSP	

Solid feature edit commands:

AMARRAY	AMDELFEAT	AMEDITFEAT
AMUPDATE	AMREPLAY	

Display commands:

AMVIEW	RENDER	SHADE
HIDE		

Variables:

CMDDIA	DISPSILH	ISOLINES
PICKBOX	AMRULEMODE	AMCOMPSV
AMCONDSPSZ	AMSKANGTOL	AMSKMODE
AMSKSTYLE		

For a brief explanation of these commands and variables, refer to the appendix of this book.

In making the two solid models, you have learned how to resolve a rough sketch to a profile; to display, add, and delete geometric constraints to a profile; to add parametric dimensions to a profile; to extrude the first profile to form a base feature; and to extrude subsequent profiles to form an additional sketched feature that joins, cuts, or intersects the existing feature. To maintain parametric relationships between the solid features, you have created construction features and set up sketch planes for sketching. In addition, you have learned how to use various display tools.

In the next chapter, you will further enhance your learning by working on two sets of solid parts. In addition to extruding a profile linearly, you will sweep a profile along a path and revolve a profile about an axis. You will also learn how to set up global parameters to maintain parametric relationship between the solid parts in a single file and across a number of files.

2.10 Exercises

Now that you have made two parametric solid models with guidance, you will make the following models on your own.

Figure 2.49 shows the completed solid model of the lever of a toggle clamp assembly. Make a rough sketch of the outlines. Resolve this sketch to a profile. Then apply geometric constraints and parametric dimensions to fully constrain the profile. All unspecified radii are R10. After that, extrude the profile to form a solid feature. Finally, cut two holes on it. Save the file named LEVER.DWG.

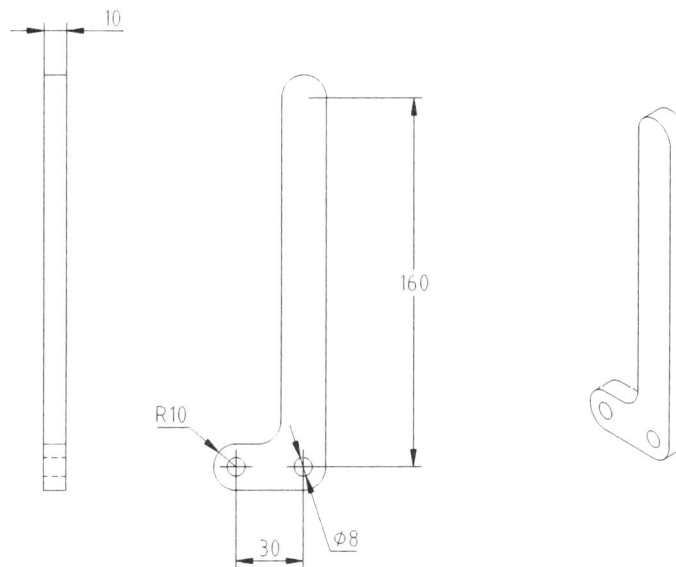

Figure 2.49 The toggle clamp lever

Figure 2.50 shows the completed solid model of the linkage bar of the toggle clamp assembly. To create this model, you would need two sketched features. First, create a rough sketch of the bar according to the top view. Then resolve it to a profile and fully constrain the profile. After that, extrude the profile to form a base solid feature. Next, you should set up a parametric work plane that is perpendicular to the sketch plane of the base solid feature. On this work plane, you then produce another rough sketch in accordance with the shape of the front view. Naturally, you also have to fully constrain the sketch. To produce the model, you should extrude the second sketch and intersect with the base solid. Finally, cut two holes on it. Save the file named LINK.DWG.

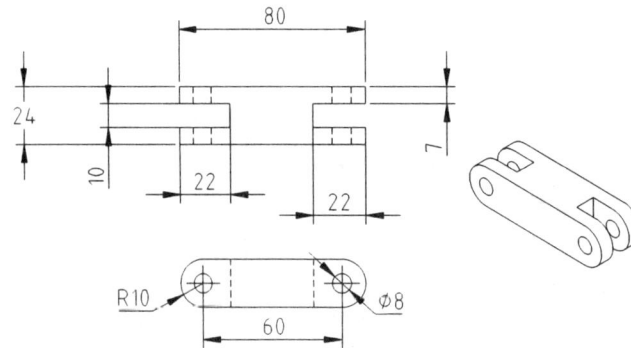

Figure 2.50 The toggle clamp linkage bar

Figure 2.51 shows the main body of the toggle clamp assembly. There are four sketched solid features, A, B, C, and D, and a number of placed holes.

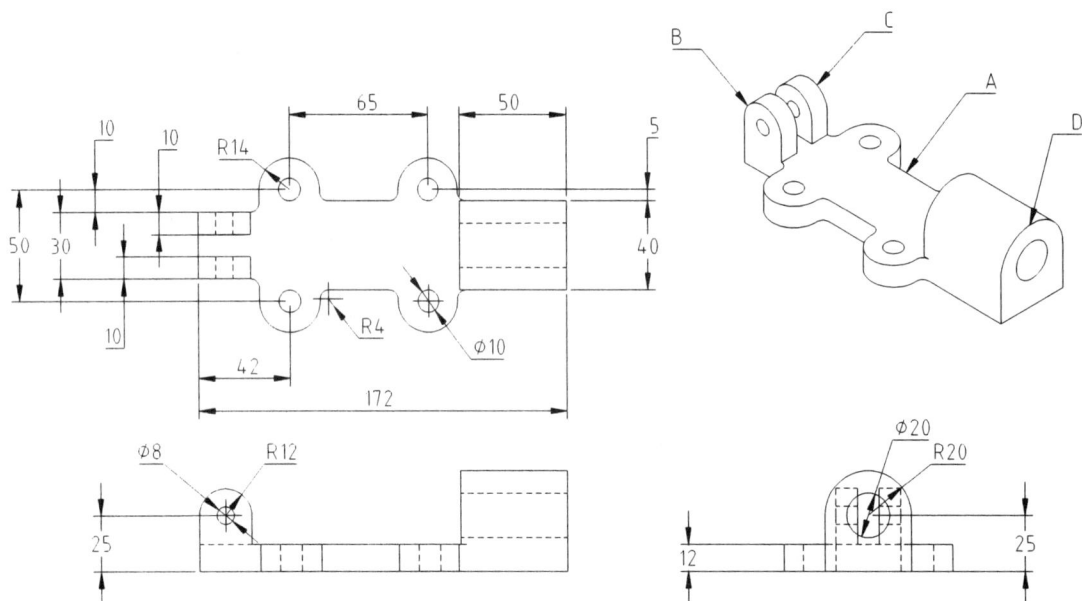

Figure 2.51 The toggle clamp main body

To begin with, you should produce a rough sketch A (Figure 2.52) for the feature A, resolve it, fully constrain it, and extrude it to form a solid. Sketched solid features B and C (Figure 2.51) are identical. To produce the sketched feature B, you have to set up a parametric work plane that is parallel to the ZX plane of the WCS. On this work plane, you may create the sketch B (Figure 2.52), fully constrain it, extrude it, and unite the extruded profile with the base solid. To make the sketched feature C (Figure 2.51), you should set the sketch plane to the upper face of the feature A (Figure 2.51) and then array the feature B. The last solid feature is the feature D (Figure 2.51). Again, you need a parametric work plane. This time, the plane should align with the ZY plane of the WCS.

Make the sketch C (Figure 2.52), resolve the sketch to a profile, fully constrain the profile, extrude the profile to form a solid, and unite the solid with the base solid.

To finish the model, you have to cut a number of holes. Save the file named BODY.DWG.

Figure 2.52 Three rough sketches

Chapter 3
Sweeping and Revolving

A complex solid part consists of a number of solid features. AutoCAD Designer classifies them as sketched solid features and placed solid features. A sketched solid feature originates from a sketch. A placed solid feature is simply added to the existing feature.

To make a sketched solid feature, you will begin from a rough sketch. The rough sketch need not be precise, because AutoCAD Designer will resolve it to form a profile, a path, or a cutting line. During resolution, AutoCAD Designer applies geometric constraints according to a set of rules and the settings of the system variables. Before you may use a resolved sketch for subsequent operation, you have to fully constrain it by applying geometric constraints and parametric dimensions. To remove a geometric constraint, you may use the AMDELCON command. To remove a parametric dimension, you may use the ERASE command. To create a sketched solid feature, you may extrude a profile linearly, revolve a profile about an axis, or sweep a profile along a path.

The first sketched solid feature of a solid model is the base feature. Subsequent sketched solid features may join, cut, or intersect the existing features. When you create the second sketch, you need to do it on a sketch plane. If a plane on the existing solid model is not available to place the sketch plane, then a work plane should be placed to position the sketch plane for the next sketch. To maintain a parametric relationship between the sketched solid features, you should create the sketched solid features on established parametric construction features. The construction features are work planes, work points, and work axes.

There are three kinds of placed solid features: the chamfer feature, fillet feature, and hole feature. These features are parametrically attached to the existing features.

In the previous chapter, you created two engineering components. You learned how to resolve a rough sketch to form a profile; how to fully constrain a profile; how to edit a profile; how to extrude a profile; how to join, cut, and intersect an extruded profile; how to add placed solid features; and how to edit a solid part.

In this chapter, you will build two sets of solid parts. They form two assemblies. You will assemble them together in the next chapter. In making the solid parts, you will learn how to resolve a sketch to a path, how to sweep a profile along a path to create a swept solid, how to revolve a profile about an axis to form a revolved solid, how to set up a set of global parameters to control the dimension values of a set of solid parts in a single file and across a set of files, how to set up a non-parametric work plane for subsequent preparation of a parametric work plane, and how to set up work points.

The first set of solid parts are the components of an universal joint assembly. See Figure 3.1. The second set of solid parts are the components of an electric motor casing. See Figure 3.2.

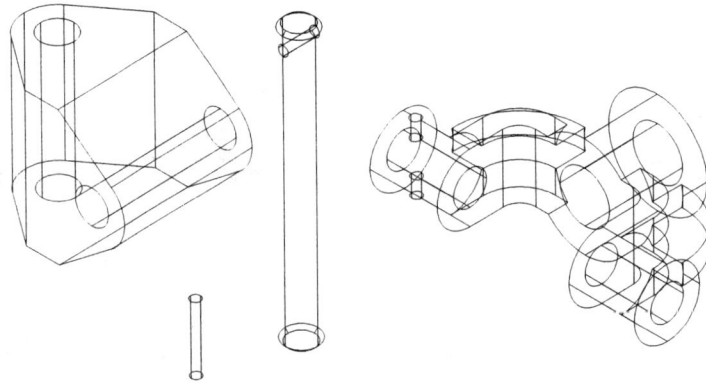

Figure 3.1 Components for an universal joint

Figure 3.2 Components for an electric motor casing

3.1   Universal Joint Main Body

The universal joint assembly consists of four solid parts: the main body, the yoke, the yoke pin, and the lock pin. You will create them one by one. The first solid part to create is the main body. Take some time to analyze this part. It consists of a number of sketched solid features and placed solid features.

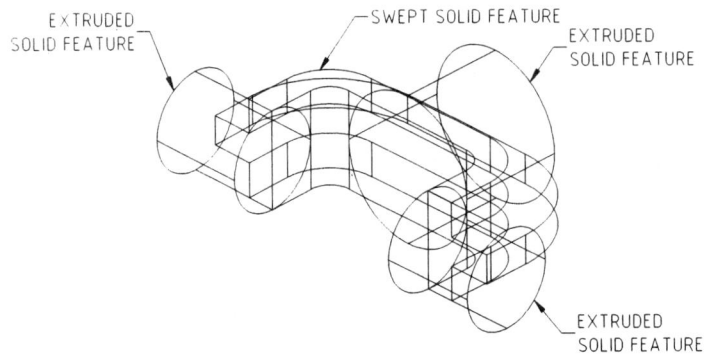

Figure 3.3 Breakdown of the sketched solid features of the main body

Refer to Figure 3.3. There are four sketched solid features. The base feature is a swept solid. The other three are extruded solids. After making the sketched solid features, you need to add four placed solid features to complete the model.

Start a new drawing with the NEW command.

<File>   **<New...>**

Command: **NEW**

To begin, run the DDLMODES command to create four additional layers, and set the current layer to SKETCH1.

<Data>   **<Layers...>**

Command: **DDLMODES**

Layer	Color
SKETCH1	**cyan**
SKETCH2	**green**
SOLID1	**yellow**
SOLID2	**magenta**

Current layer: **SKETCH1**

You need to sketch on a known screen size in order to have a better perception of the dimensional aspect of the sketch. Execute the LIMITS command to set the drawing limits. Then run the ZOOM command to zoom to the limits. Also, set the line type scale to 15 with the LTSCALE command.

<Data>   **<Drawing Limits>**

Command: **LIMITS**
ON/OFF/<Lower left corner>: **0,0**
Upper right corner: **297,210**

[Zoom]   **[Zoom All]**

Command: **ZOOM**
All/Center/Dynamic/Extents/Left/Previous/Vmax/Window/<Scale(X/XP)>: **ALL**

Command: **ZOOM**
All/Center/Dynamic/Extents/Left/Previous/Vmax/Window/<Scale(X/XP)>: **[Select a point near (70,70).]**
Other corner: **[Select a point near (180,120).]**

<Options>   **<Linetypes>**   **<Global Linetype Scale>**

Command: **LTSCALE**
New scale factor: **15**

Displaying the grid mesh and placing the UCS icon at the origin position also help you during sketching. Issue the GRID command and the UCS command.

Command: **GRID**
Grid spacing(X) or ON/OFF/Snap/Aspect: **10**

Command: **UCS**
ON/OFF/All/Noorigin/ORigin: **OR**

To create a swept solid, you need to prepare two sketches. First, you will create the sketch for the path. Next, you will create the sketch for the cross-section. To make the path, use the AMPATH command. To make the cross-section, use the AMPROFILE command. Each sketch needs a sketch plane. For the first sketch, you may sketch on the XY plane of the current UCS.

Apply the PLINE command to make a rough sketch. Remember, you do not need to be precise. The coordinates illustrated below serve only as a guide.

[Draw]   **[Polyline]**

Command: **PLINE**
From point: **100,90**
Arc/Close/Halfwidth/Length/Undo/Width/
<Endpoint of line>: **[Select a point near (100,100).]**
Arc/Close/Halfwidth/Length/Undo/Width/<Endpoint of line>: **A**
Angle/CEnter/CLose/Direction/Halfwidth/Line/Radius/Second pt/Undo/Width/
<Endpoint of arc>: **[Select a point near (105,105).]**
Angle/CEnter/CLose/Direction/Halfwidth/Line/Radius/Second pt/Undo/Width/
<Endpoint of arc>: **L**
Arc/Close/Halfwidth/Length/Undo/Width/
<Endpoint of line>: **[Select a point near (135,105).]**
Arc/Close/Halfwidth/Length/Undo/Width/<Endpoint of line>: **A**
Angle/CEnter/CLose/Direction/Halfwidth/Line/Radius/Second pt/Undo/Width/
<Endpoint of arc>: **[Select a point near (140,100).]**
Angle/CEnter/CLose/Direction/Halfwidth/Line/Radius/Second pt/Undo/Width/
<Endpoint of arc>: **L**
Arc/Close/Halfwidth/Length/Undo/Width/
<Endpoint of line>: **[Select a point near (140,90).]**
Arc/Close/Halfwidth/Length/Undo/Width/<Endpoint of line>: **[Enter]**

In addition to the polyline, execute the LINE command to create a line segment. Then change its line type to HIDDEN. See Figure 3.4.

[Draw]   **[Line]**

Command: **LINE**
From point: **[Select a point near (90,90).]**
To point: **[Select a point near (150,90).]**
To point: **[Enter]**

<Edit>   **<Properties...>**

Select objects: **LAST**

Select objects: **[Enter]**

[Properties
Linetype...   **HIDDEN**
OK   ]

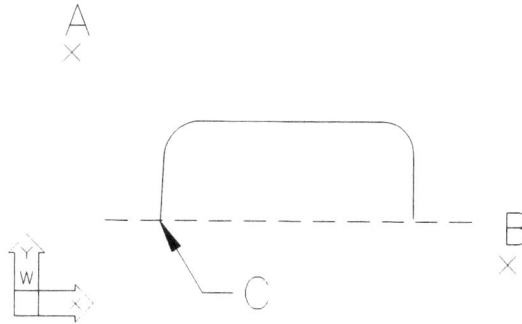

Figure 3.4 A rough sketch created

The rough sketch is completed. Before you resolve it, you may need to check the variables that affect the outcome of resolving. Apply the AMPARTVARS command.

   <Parts>   **<Preferences...>**

Command: **AMPARTVARS**

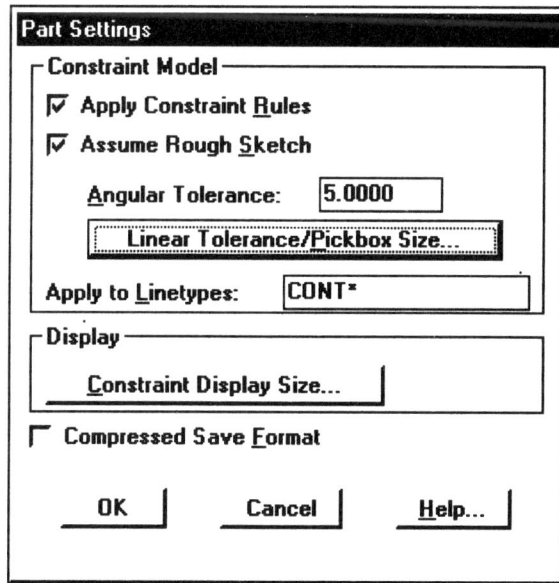

To resolve the polyline and the line segment to form a path, run the AMPATH command. See Figure 3.5.

\<Parts\>   \<Sketch\>   \<Path\>

Command: **AMPATH**
Select objects: **[Select A (Figure 3.4).]**
Other corner: **[Select B (Figure 3.4).]**
Select objects: **[Enter]**
Specify start point of path: **[Select C (Figure 3.4).]**

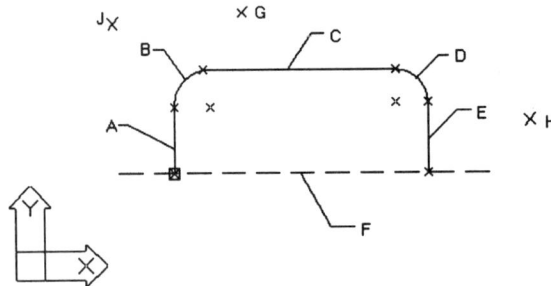

Figure 3.5 A resolved path with construction line

The line that has a different line type becomes a construction line. Although it is a part of the resolved sketch, the profile will not sweep along it. You may make use of it to place geometric constraints and parametric dimensions to constrain the sweeping path.

Apply the AMSHOWCON command to display the geometric constraints that AutoCAD Designer automatically applies to the path and the construction line.

\<Parts\>   \<Sketch\>   \<Constraints\>   \<Show\>

Command: **AMSHOWCON**
All/Select/Next/\<eXit\>: **ALL**
All/Select/Next/\<eXit\>: **[Enter]**

Knowing what geometric constraints AutoCAD Designer has already applied, execute the AMADDCON command to add geometric constraints and the AMDELCON command to delete redundant constraints where appropriate.

\<Parts\>   \<Sketch\>   \<Constraints\>   \<Add\>

Command: **AMADDCON**

[Vertical constraint: **Apply to A and E (Figure 3.5).**
 Horizontal constraint: **Apply to C and F (Figure 3.5).**
 Radius constraint: **Apply to B and D (Figure 3.5).**
 Tangent constraint: **Apply to A/B, B/C, C/D, and D/E (Figure 3.5).**
 Exit   ]

After constraining the path geometrically, you need to add parametric dimensions to complete the constraint. The part that you are going to create is one of the components of an assembly. In order to maintain a parametric relationship across their dimensions, you have to establish a set of global parameters. Execute the AMPARAM command to set up seven global parameters. While you are setting up the parameters, you may add comments to facilitate future reference.

<Parts>   **<Parameters...>**

Command: **AMPARAM**

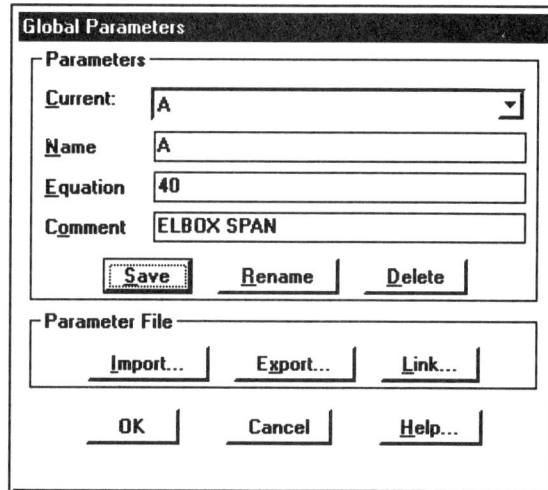

```
┌─────────────────────────────────────────┐
│ Global Parameters                        │
│  ┌─ Parameters ─────────────────────────┐│
│  │ Current:  [A                     ▼]  ││
│  │                                      ││
│  │ Name      [A                      ]  ││
│  │                                      ││
│  │ Equation  [40                     ]  ││
│  │                                      ││
│  │ Comment   [ELBOX SPAN             ]  ││
│  │                                      ││
│  │    [ Save ]   [ Rename ]  [ Delete ] ││
│  └──────────────────────────────────────┘│
│  ┌─ Parameter File ─────────────────────┐│
│  │   [Import...]  [Export...]  [Link...]││
│  └──────────────────────────────────────┘│
│       [ OK ]     [ Cancel ]   [ Help... ]│
│                                          │
└─────────────────────────────────────────┘
```

[Parameters:

Name	Equation	Comment	
A	40	**ELBOW SPAN**	**Save**
B	15	**ELBOW DEPTH**	**Save**
C	5	**BOSS**	**Save**
D	40	**YOKE THICKNESS**	**Save**
F	10	**YOKE PIN DIA**	**Save**
G	3	**LOCK PIN**	**Save**
H	15	**BOSS THICKNESS**	**Save**
J	10	**ELBOW HALF THICKNESS**	**Save**

OK   ]

Set the parametric dimension to equation display.

<Parts>   **<Display>**   **<Dim Display>**

Command: **AMDIMDSP**
Parameters/Equations/<Numeric>: **E**

Having created a set of global parameters, and having set the dimension display to equation, issue the AMPARDIM command to add parametric dimensions to the path to fully constrain it. When you add dimensions, use the global parameters. See Figure 3.6.

<Parts>   **<Sketch>**   **<Add Dimension>**

Command: **AMPARDIM**
Select first object: **[Select A (Figure 3.5).]**
Select second object or place dimension: **[Select E (Figure 3.5).]**
Specify dimension placement: **[Select G (Figure 3.5).]**

Undo/Hor/Ver/Align/Par/Enter Dimension value: **A**

The parameter name in the illustration is D0.

Select first object: **[Select C (Figure 3.5).]**
Select second object or place dimension: **[Select F (Figure 3.5).]**
Specify dimension placement: **[Select H (Figure 3.5).]**
Undo/Hor/Ver/Align/Par/Enter Dimension value: **B**

The parameter name in the illustration is D1.

Select first object: **[Select B (Figure 3.5).]**
Select second object or place dimension: **[Select J (Figure 3.5).]**
Undo/Enter Dimension value: **5**

The parameter name in the illustration is D2.

Solved fully constrained sketch.
Select first object: **[Enter]**

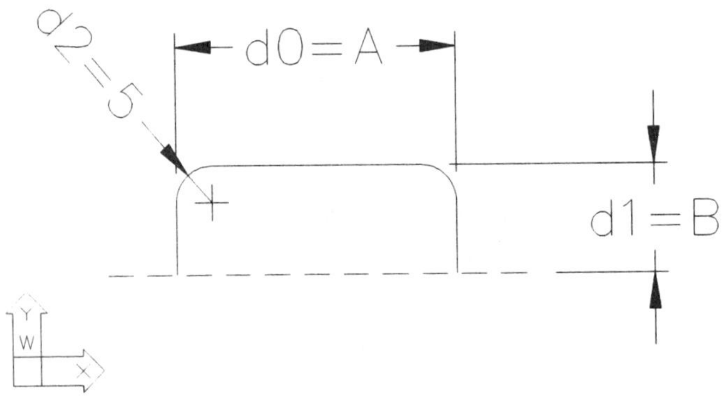

Figure 3.6 Fully constrained path

The path for sweeping is completed. Set the display to an isometric view.

Command: **8**

Use the AMWORKPLN command to create a work plane, and set the sketch plane to the new work plane. To make a work plane for a swept profile, you need to specify only one modifier, "Sweep Profile." See Figure 3.7.

<Parts>   **<Feature>**   **<Work Plane...>**

Command: **AMWORKPLN**

[1st Modifier: **Sweep Profile**
 Create Sketch Plane: **YES**
 OK   ]

Rotate/Z-flip/<Accept>: **[R, if the Y axis is not pointing upward.]**

Rotate/Z-flip/<Accept>: **[Z, if the X axis is not pointing to the right.]**
Rotate/Z-flip/<Accept>: **[Accept, if the Y axis is pointing upward, and the X axis is pointing to the right.]**

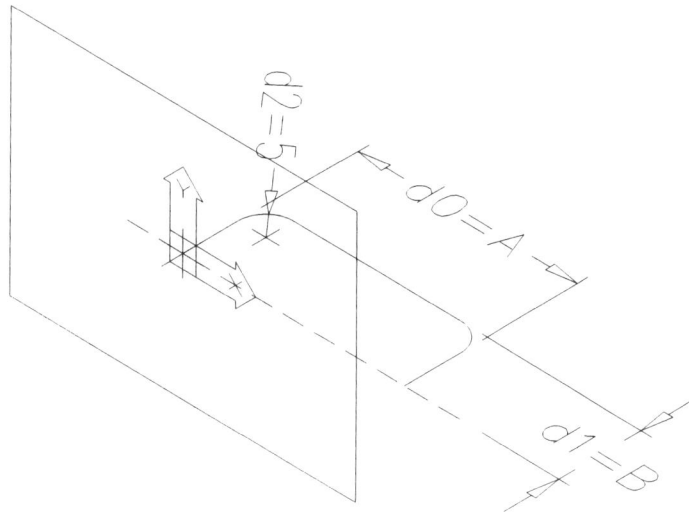

Figure 3.7 New sketch plane set on the work plane

Having prepared a work plane for sketching, you will work on the profile that represents the cross-section.

You have placed the path on the layer SKETCH1. To have better control of the entities, you will put the sketch for the profile on the layer SKETCH2. Turn off the layer SKETCH1, and set the current layer to SKETCH2.

    <Data>   **<Layers...>**

Command: **DDLMODES**

Layer	
SKETCH1	**Off**
Current layer:	**SKETCH2**

After turning off the layer SKETCH1, you may still find a point displayed on the sketch plane. This is the starting point of the path. You should constrain your profile sketch with reference to this point.

Set the display to the plan view of the current UCS. Then apply the PLINE command to create a rough sketch. See Figure 3.8.

    Command: **9**

    [Draw]   **[Polyline]**

    Command: **PLINE**
    From point: **[Select a point near (0,10).]**

Arc/Close/Halfwidth/Length/Undo/Width/
<Endpoint of line>: **[Select a point near (-6,10).]**
Arc/Close/Halfwidth/Length/Undo/Width/
<Endpoint of line>: **[Select a point near (-6,3).]**
Arc/Close/Halfwidth/Length/Undo/Width/
<Endpoint of line>: **[Select a point near (-15,3).]**
Arc/Close/Halfwidth/Length/Undo/Width/
<Endpoint of line>: **[Select a point near (-15,-3).]**
Arc/Close/Halfwidth/Length/Undo/Width/
<Endpoint of line>: **[Select a point near (-6,-3).]**
Arc/Close/Halfwidth/Length/Undo/Width/
<Endpoint of line>: **[Select a point near (-6,-10).]**
Arc/Close/Halfwidth/Length/Undo/Width/
<Endpoint of line>: **[Select a point near (0,-10).]**
Arc/Close/Halfwidth/Length/Undo/Width/<Endpoint of line>: **C**

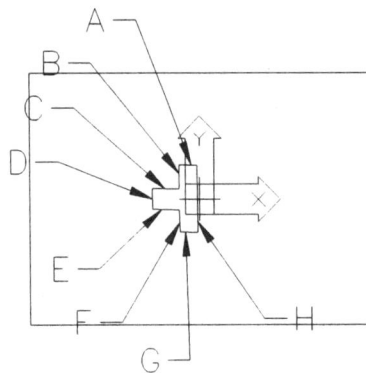

Figure 3.8 A sketch created on the new sketch plane

The sketch that you have produced is the cross-section of the swept solid. Run the AMPROFILE command to resolve it to a profile.

<Parts>   **<Sketch>**   **<Profile>**

Command: **AMPROFILE**
Select objects for sketch:
Select objects: **LAST**
Select objects: **[Enter]**

After resolving, run the AMSHOWCON command to display the geometric constraints that AutoCAD Designer has applied to the profile automatically. Because there are two resolved sketches, you have to choose which to display.

<Parts>   **<Sketch>**   **<Constraints>**   **<Show>**

Command: **AMSHOWCON**
Select sketch for which to display constraints: **[Select A (Figure 3.8).]**
All/Select/Next/<eXit>:**ALL**
All/Select/Next/<eXit>:**[Enter]**

In order properly to constrain the profile geometrically, apply the AMADDCON command. See Figure 3.9.

\<Parts\>   **\<Sketch\>**   **\<Constraints\>**   **\<Add\>**

Command: **AMADDCON**

[Vertical constraint: **Apply to B, D, F, and H (Figure 3.8).**
 Horizontal constraint: **Apply to A, C, E, and G (Figure 3.8).**
 Collinear constraint: **Apply to B and F (Figure 3.8).**
Exit   ]

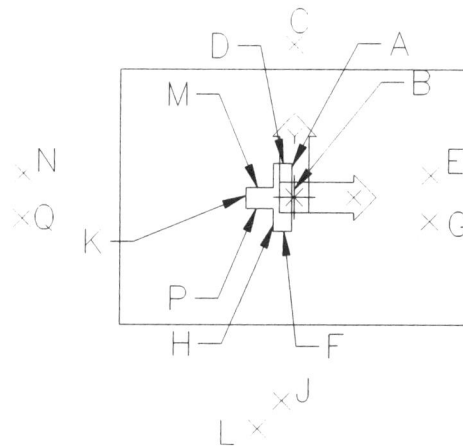

Figure 3.9 Geometrically constrained profile

Before making the swept solid, you have to fully constrain the cross-section. Run the AMPARDIM command to add parametric dimensions. When you add dimensions, use the global parameters that you have already set up. See Figure 3.10.

\<Parts\>   **\<Sketch\>**   **\<Add Dimension\>**

Command: **AMPARDIM**
Select first object: **[Select B (Figure 3.9).]**
Select second object: **[Select A (Figure 3.9).]**
Specify dimension placement: **[Select C (Figure 3.9).]**
Undo/Hor/Ver/Align/Par/Enter Dimension value: **0**

Select first object: **[Select B (Figure 3.9).]**
Select second object: **[Select D (Figure 3.9).]**
Specify dimension placement: **[Select E (Figure 3.9).]**
Undo/Hor/Ver/Align/Par/Enter Dimension value: **J**

Select first object: **[Select B (Figure 3.9).]**
Select second object: **[Select F (Figure 3.9).]**
Specify dimension placement: **[Select G (Figure 3.9).]**
Undo/Hor/Ver/Align/Par/Enter Dimension value: **J**

Select first object: **[Select B (Figure 3.9).]**

Select second object or place dimension: **[Select H (Figure 3.9).]**
Specify dimension placement: **[Select J (Figure 3.9).]**
Undo/Hor/Ver/Align/Par/Enter Dimension value: **6**

Select first object: **[Select B (Figure 3.9).]**
Select second object or place dimension: **[Select K (Figure 3.9).]**
Specify dimension placement: **[Select L (Figure 3.9).]**
Undo/Hor/Ver/Align/Par/Enter Dimension value: **H**

Select first object: **[Select D (Figure 3.9).]**
Select second object: **[Select M (Figure 3.9).]**
Specify dimension placement: **[Select N (Figure 3.9).]**
Undo/Hor/Ver/Align/Par/Enter Dimension value: **J-3**

Select first object: **[Select F (Figure 3.9).]**
Select second object: **[Select P (Figure 3.9).]**
Specify dimension placement: **[Select Q (Figure 3.9).]**
Undo/Hor/Ver/Align/Par/Enter Dimension value: **J-3**

Solved fully constrained sketch.
Select first object: **[Enter]**

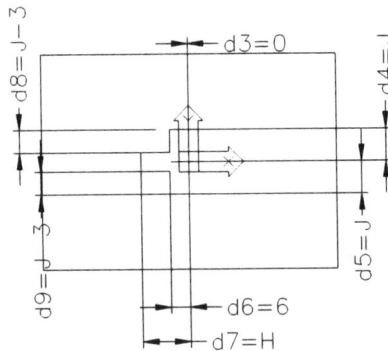

Figure 3.10 Fully constrained profile

Now you have two resolved sketches; one is a path and the other a profile. To create a swept solid feature, you will sweep the profile along the path.

Before doing that, set the current layer to SOLID. The solid feature will be placed on this layer.

<Data>   **<Layers...>**

Command: **DDLMODES**
Current layer: **SOLID1**

Set the display back to an isometric view. Then produce a swept solid feature with the AMSWEEP command. See Figure 3.11

Command: **8**

\<Parts\>   **\<Feature\>**   **\<Sweep...\>**

Command: **AMSWEEP**

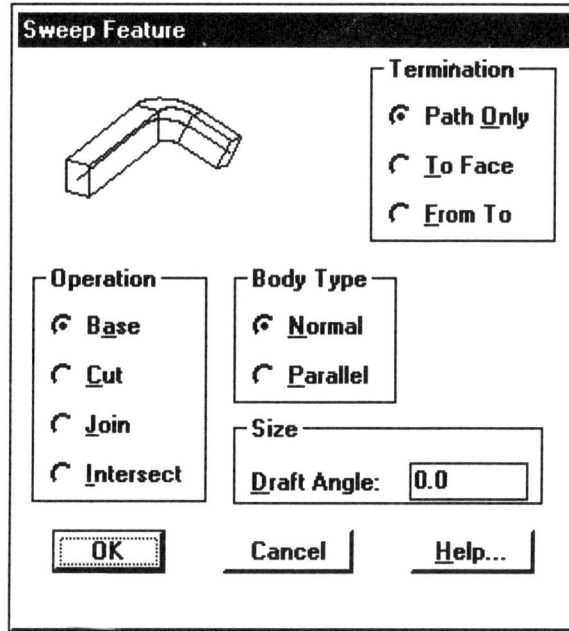

[Termination: **Path Only**
 Operation: **Base**
 Body Type: **Normal**
 Size:
     Draft Angle: **0**
OK   ]

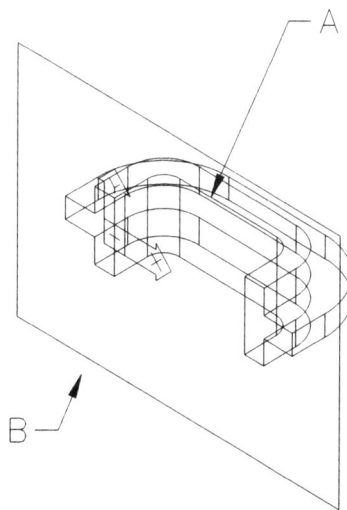

Figure 3.11 A swept solid created

You have created a swept solid feature. Because this is the first sketched solid feature, it is the base feature. You will produce more sketched solid features and placed solid features on this base feature. To put the next rough sketch on layer SKETCH1, set this layer current.

<Data>   <Layers...>

Command: **DDLMODES**
Current layer: **SKETCH1**

The second sketched solid feature is a boss that joins the base feature at the middle part. Create a work plane and set up the sketch plane with the AMWORKPLN command. To minimize confusion and to clean up the screen, run the AMPLNDSP command to turn off the display of the last work plane. See Figure 3.12.

<Parts>   <Feature>   <Work Plane...>

Command: **AMWORKPLN**

[1st Modifier: **Planar Parallel**
 2nd Modifier: **On Edge/Axis**
 Create Sketch Plane: **YES**
 OK   ]

worldX/worldY/worldZ/<Select work axis or straight edge>: **[Select A (Figure 3.11).]**
worldXy/worldYz/worldZx/Ucs/<Select work plane or planar face>: **[Select A (Figure 3.11).]**
Next/<Accept>: **[Accept, if the plane parallel to the current sketch plane is highlighted. Otherwise, Next.]**
worldX/worldY/worldZ/<Select work axis or straight edge>: **[Select A (Figure 3.11).]**
Rotate/Z-flip/<Accept>: **[R, if the Y axis is not pointing upward.]**
Rotate/Z-flip/<Accept>: **[Z, if the X axis is not pointing to the right.]**
Rotate/Z-flip/<Accept>: **[Accept, if the Y axis direction is pointing upward, and the X-axis direction is pointing to the right.]**

<Parts>   <Display>   <Work Plane>   <Off>

Command: **AMPLNDSP**
Display/ON/<OFf>: **OFF**
Select/<All>: **SELECT**
Select work planes to hide:
Select objects: **[Select B (Figure 3.11).]**
Select objects: **[Enter]**

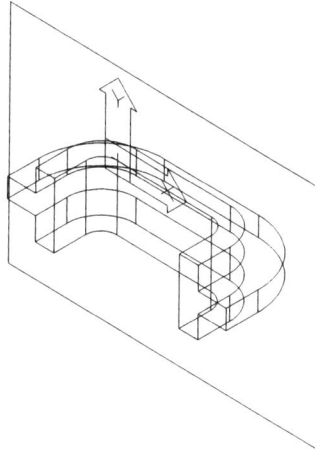

Figure 3.12 New work plane created, sketch plane set, and last work plane hidden

Having set the sketch plane to the new work plane, set the display to the plan view of the current UCS. Then run the CIRCLE command to make a circle. Next, resolve the circle to form a profile with the AMPROFILE command. See Figure 3.13.

Command: **9**

[Draw]   [Circle Center Radius]

Command: **CIRCLE**

<Parts>   <Sketch>   <Profile>

Command: **AMPROFILE**
Select objects for sketch:
Select objects: **LAST**
Select objects: **[Enter]**

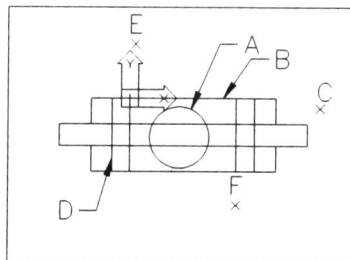

Figure 3.13 A circle drawn and resolved

You will extrude this circle to form an extruded solid feature. Before so doing, you should fully constrain the profile. Run the AMPARDIM command to add three parametric dimensions. See Figure 3.14.

<Parts>   **<Sketch>**   **<Add Dimension>**

Command: **AMPARDIM**
Select first object: **[Select A (Figure 3.13).]**
Select second object or place dimension: **[Select B (Figure 3.13).]**
Specify dimension placement: **[Select C (Figure 3.13).]**
Undo/Hor/Ver/Align/Par/Enter Dimension value: **J**

Select first object: **[Select A (Figure 3.13).]**
Select second object or place dimension: **[Select D (Figure 3.13).]**
Specify dimension placement: **[Select E (Figure 3.13).]**
Undo/Hor/Ver/Align/Par/Enter Dimension value: **A/2**

Select first object: **[Select A (Figure 3.13).]**
Select second object or place dimension: **[Select F (Figure 3.13).]**
Undo/Enter Dimension value: **3*J**

Solved fully constrained sketch.
Select first object: **[Enter]**

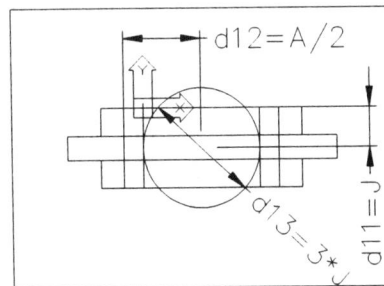

Figure 3.14 Fully constrained profile

Set the display to an isometric view.

Command: **8**

Execute the AMEXTRUDE command to extrude the profile, and join it to the base solid feature. See Figure 3.15. If you forget the parameter name of the dimensions, you may run the AMREPLAY command to replay the sequence of operation.

<Parts>   **<Utilities>**   **<Replay>**

Command: **AMREPLAY**

Note down the parameter names.

<Parts>   **<Feature>**   **<Extrude...>**

Command: **AMEXTRUDE**

[Termination: **Blind**

Operation: **Join**
Size:
    Distance: **H*1.5**
    Draft Angle: **0**
OK   ]

Direction Flip/<Accept>: **[Accept, if the arrow is pointing to the negative Z axis direction. Otherwise, Flip.]**

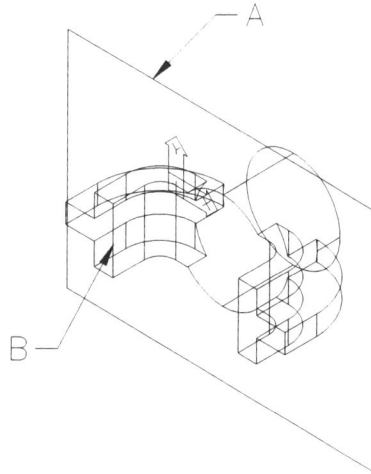

Figure 3.15 Profile extruded

You have created the second sketched solid feature, a boss, at the central part of the elbow-shaped main body. Create another work plane, and set the sketch plane to this new work plane by running the AMWORKPLN command. See Figure 3.16.

<Parts>   **<Feature>**   **<Work Plane...>**

Command: **AMWORKPLN**

[1st Modifier: **Planar Parallel**
 2nd Modifier: **On Edge/Axis**
 Create Sketch Plane: **YES**
OK   ]

worldX/worldY/worldZ/<Select work axis or straight edge>: **[Select B (Figure 3.15).]**
worldXy/worldYz/worldZx/Ucs/<Select work plane or planar face>: **[Select B (Figure 3.15).]**
Next/<Accept>: **[Accept, if the face in the current ZY plane is highlighted. Otherwise, Next.]**
worldX/worldY/worldZ/<Select work axis or straight edge>: **[Select B (Figure 3.15).]**
Rotate/Z-flip/<Accept>: **[R, if the Y axis is not pointing upward.]**
Rotate/Z-flip/<Accept>: **[Z, if the X axis is not pointing to the right.]**
Rotate/Z-flip/<Accept>: **[Accept, if the Y axis is pointing upward, and the X axis is pointing to the right.]**

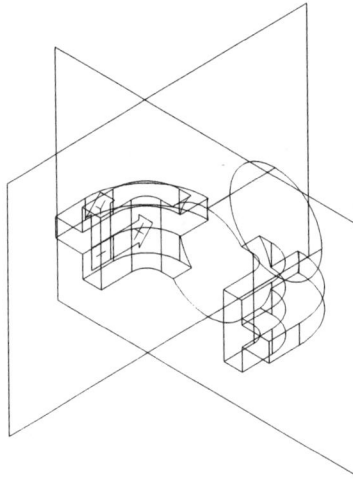

Figure 3.16 New work plane created and sketch plane set

The third sketched solid feature is also a boss. You will make it from a circle. Draw the circle with the CIRCLE command. Then resolve it to form a profile with the AMPROFILE command. See Figure 3.17.

[Draw]   **[Circle Center Radius]**

Command: **CIRCLE**

<Parts>   **<Sketch>**   **<Profile>**

Command: **AMPROFILE**
Select objects for sketch:
Select objects: **LAST**
Select objects: **[Enter]**

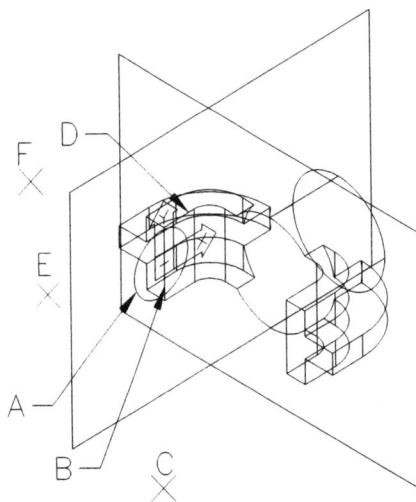

Figure 3.17 A circle drawn and resolved

Run the AMPARDIM command to add three parametric dimensions to fully constrain the profile. See Figure 3.18.

<Parts>   **<Sketch>**   **<Add Dimension>**

Command: **AMPARDIM**
Select first object: **[Select A (Figure 3.17).]**
Select second object or place dimension: **[Select B (Figure 3.17).]**
Specify dimension placement: **[Select C (Figure 3.17).]**
Undo/Hor/Ver/Align/Par/Enter Dimension value: **0**

Select first object: **[Select A (Figure 3.17).]**
Select second object or place dimension: **[Select D (Figure 3.17).]**
Specify dimension placement: **[Select E (Figure 3.17).]**
Undo/Hor/Ver/Align/Par/Enter Dimension value: **J**

Select first object: **[Select A (Figure 3.17).]**
Select second object or place dimension: **[Select F (Figure 3.17).]**
Undo/Enter Dimension value: **J*2**
Solved fully constrained sketch.
Select first object: **[Enter]**

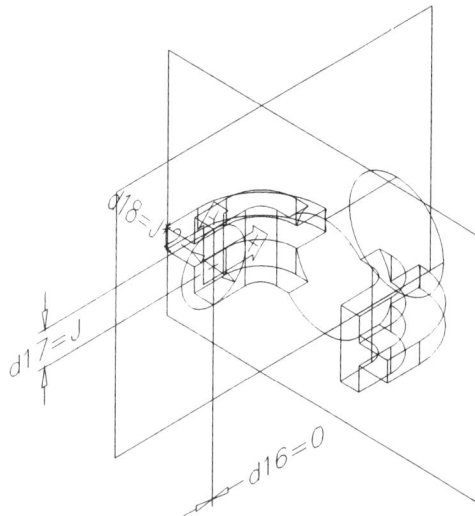

Figure 3.18 Fully constrained profile

Run the AMEXTRUDE command to extrude the profile and to join it to the base feature. See Figure 3.19.

<Parts>   **<Feature>**   **<Extrude...>**

Command: **AMEXTRUDE**

[Termination: **Blind**
Operation: **Join**
Size:

Distance:	**H+C**
Draft Angle:	**0**

OK   ]

Direction Flip/<Accept>: **[Accept, if the arrow is point to the negative Z axis direction. Otherwise, Flip.]**

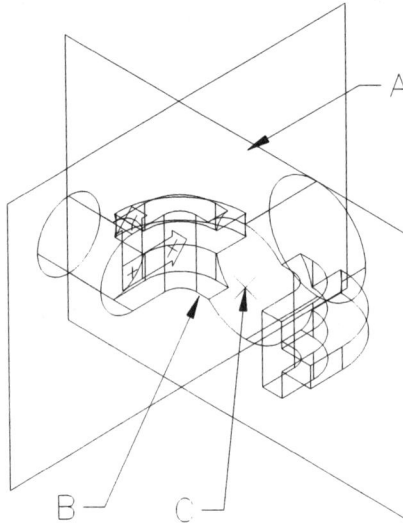

Figure 3.19 The second boss created

There should be three bosses on the elbow-shaped main body. You have produced two bosses and joined them to the main body. The third boss is similar to the second boss. Although you may create the third boss by following a procedure similar to that which you used to create the second boss, it is faster if you polar-array the second boss to form the third boss. To array polarly, you need a center for array. You may use a work point for this purpose. Execute the AMSKPLN command to select a sketch plane. Then run the AMWORKPT command to create a work point. See Figure 3.20.

<Parts>   <Sketch>   <Sketch Plane>

Command: **AMSKPLN**
worldXy/worldYz/worldZx/Ucs/<Select work plane or planar face>: **[Select A (Figure 3.19).]**
worldX/worldY/worldZ/<Select work axis or straight edge>: **[Select B (Figure 3.19).]**
Rotate/Z-flip/<Accept>: **[R, if the Y axis is not pointing upward.]**
Rotate/Z-flip/<Accept>: **[Z, if the X axis is not pointing to the right.]**
Rotate/Z-flip/<Accept>: **[Accept, if the Y axis is pointing upward, and the X axis is pointing to the right.]**

<Parts>   <Feature>   <Work Point>

Command: **AMWORKPT**
Location on sketch plane: **[Select C (Figure 3.19).]**

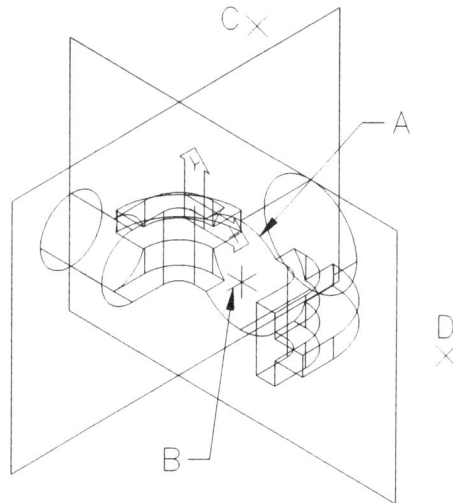

Figure 3.20 A work point created on a selected work plane

The work point you have just created does not have any dimensional relationship with the existing features. To constrain the work point parametrically, you need to add parametric dimensions. Run the AMPARDIM command. See Figure 3.21.

<Parts> **<Sketch>** **<Add Dimension>**

Command: **AMPARDIM**
Select first object: **[Select A (Figure 3.20).]**
Select second object or place dimension: **[Select B (Figure 3.20).]**
Specify dimension placement: **[Select C (Figure 3.20).]**
Undo/Hor/Ver/Align/Par/Enter Dimension value: **0**

Select first object: **[Select A (Figure 3.20).]**
Select second object or place dimension: **[Select B (Figure 3.20).]**
Specify dimension placement: **[Select D (Figure 3.20).]**
Undo/Hor/Ver/Align/Par/Enter Dimension value: **0**

Solved fully constrained sketch.
Select first object: **[Enter]**

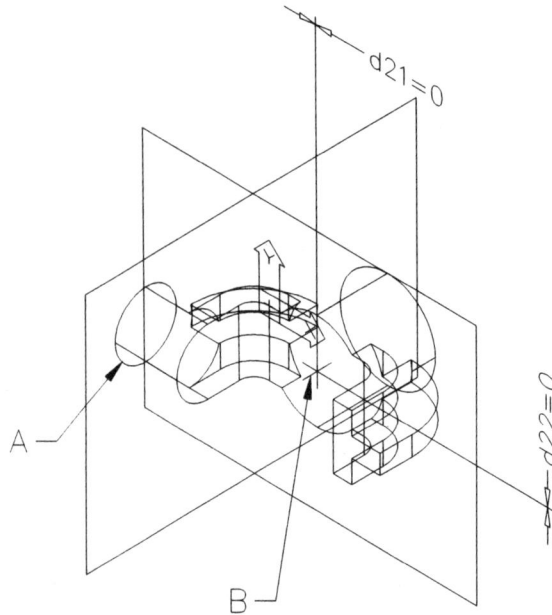

Figure 3.21 Fully constrained work point

Having fully constrained a work point, you may now array the second boss to form the third boss. Issue the AMARRAY command. See Figure 3.22.

<Parts>   **<Feature>**   **<Array...>**

Command: **AMARRAY**
Select feature: **[Select A (Figure 3.21).]**

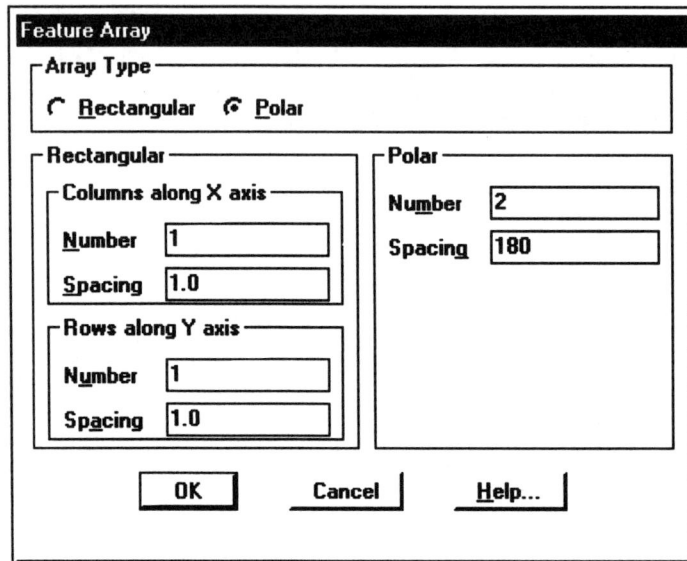

[Array Type: **Polar**
  Polar:
    Number: **2**

```
        Spacing:                180
OK                                          ]
```

Select work point: **[Select B (Figure 3.21).]**

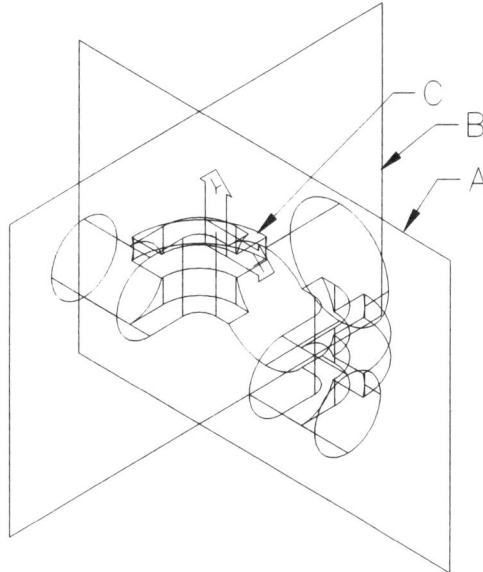

Figure 3.22 The third boss arrayed from the second boss

To clean up the screen, run the AMPLNDSP command to turn off the display of the work planes.

<Parts>   <Display>   <Work Plane>   <Off>

```
Command: AMPLNDSP
Display/ON/<OFf>: OFF
Select/<All>: SELECT
Select work planes to hide:
Select objects: [Select A, and B (Figure 3.22).]
Select objects: [Enter]
```

At this point, you have completed all the sketched solid features of the main body. To complete the model, you will add placed solid features to it. There are four holes on the model. Three of them are concentric with the three bosses. The fourth hole is perpendicular to the axis of the second boss. For the three concentric holes, you may simply place them directly by specifying the concentric features. For the perpendicular hole, you need to assign a work point. To assign a work point, you will create a work plane that is parallel to the top surface of the model. Then you will set the sketch plane to this work plane. Finally, you may set the work point on this sketch plane.

Run the AMWORKPLN command to create a work plane, and set the sketch plane to this work plane. See Figure 3.23.

<Parts>   <Feature>   <Work Plane...>

Command: **AMWORKPLN**

[1st Modifier: **Planar Parallel**
 2nd Modifier: **On Edge/Axis**
 Create Sketch Plane: **YES**
OK   ]

worldX/worldY/worldZ/<Select work axis or straight edge>: **[Select C (Figure 3.22).]**
worldXy/worldYz/worldZx/Ucs/<Select work plane or planar face>: **[Select C (Figure 3.22).]**
Next/<Accept>: **[Accept, if the upper face is highlighted. Otherwise, Next.]**
worldX/worldY/worldZ/<Select work axis or straight edge>: **[Select C (Figure 3.22).]**
Rotate/Z-flip/<Accept>: **[R, if the Y axis direction is not the same as Figure 3.23.]**
Rotate/Z-flip/<Accept>: **[Z, if the X axis direction is not the same as Figure 3.23).]**
Rotate/Z-flip/<Accept>: **[Accept, if the Y axis and the X axis direction are the same as Figure 3.23.]**

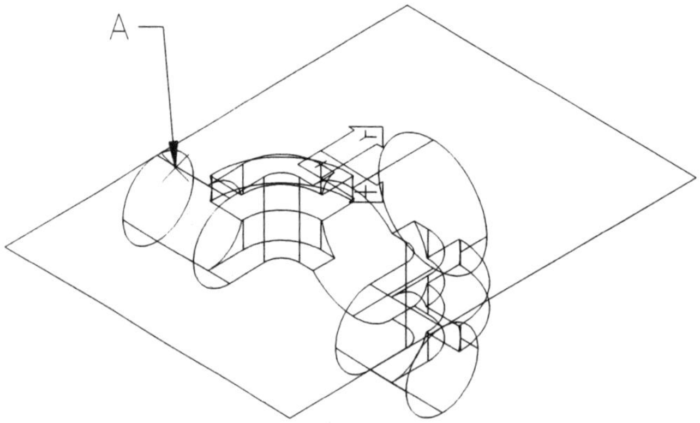

Figure 3.23 The sketch plane set to the newly created work plane

On this new sketch plane, run the AMWORKPT to create a work point. See Figure 3.24.

<Parts>   <Feature>   <Work Point>

Command: **AMWORKPT**
Location on sketch plane: **[Select A (Figure 3.23).]**

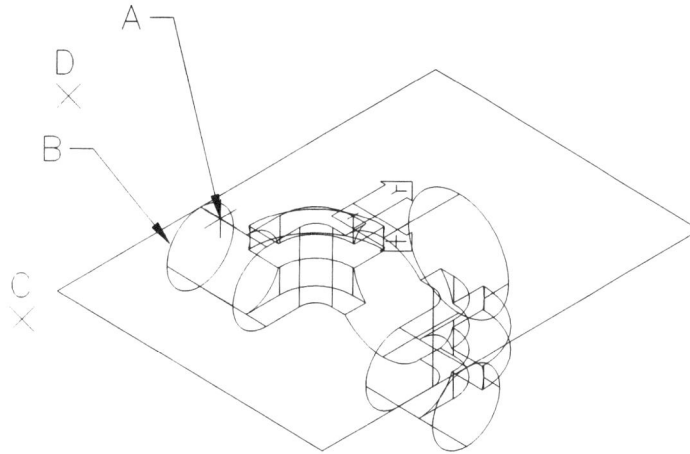

Figure 3.24 A work point created

You have to constrain the work point before you can use it. Apply the AMPARDIM command to create two parametric dimensions on the work point. See Figure 3.25.

<Parts>   <Sketch>   <Add Dimension>

Command: **AMPARDIM**
Select first object: **[Select A (Figure 3.24).]**
Select second object or place dimension: **[Select B (Figure 3.24).]**
Specify dimension placement: **[Select C (Figure 3.24).]**
Undo/Hor/Ver/Align/Par/Enter Dimension value: **H/4**

Select first object: **[Select A (Figure 3.24).]**
Select second object: **[Select B (Figure 3.24).]**
Specify dimension placement: **[Select D (Figure 3.24).]**
Undo/Hor/Ver/Align/Par/Enter Dimension value: **0**

Solved fully constrained sketch.
Select first object: **[Enter]**

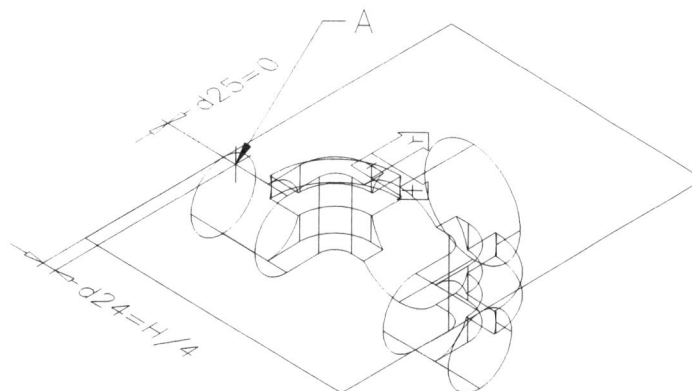

Figure 3.25 Fully constrained work point

You have fully constrained the work point. Apply the AMHOLE command to place a hole feature there. See Figure 3.26.

<Parts>   **<Feature>**   **<Hole...>**

Command: **AMHOLE**

[Operation: **Drilled**
 Termination: **Through**
 Placement: **On Point**
 Drill Size: **3**
OK   ]

Select work point: **[Select A (Figure 3.25).]**
Direction Flip/<Accept>: **[Accept, if the arrow is pointing downward. Otherwise, Flip.]**

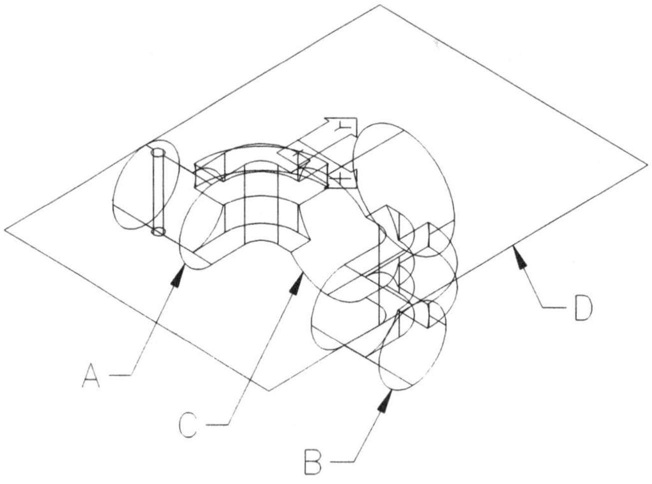

Figure 3.26 A hole created on the work point

The main body is near completion. Run the AMHOLE command to place three concentric holes. After that, turn off the display of the work plane. See Figure 3.27.

<Parts>   **<Feature>**   **<Hole...>**

Command: **AMHOLE**

[Operation: **Drilled**
 Termination: **Through**
 Placement: **Concentric**
 Drill Size: **F**
OK   ]

worldXy/worldYz/worldZx/Ucs/<Select work plane or planar face>: **[Select A (Figure 3.26).]**
Select concentric edge: **[Select A (Figure 3.26).]**

\<Parts>	**\<Feature>**	**\<Hole...>**

Command: **AMHOLE**

[Operation:	**Drilled**
Termination:	**Through**
Placement:	**Concentric**
Drill Size:	**F**
OK	]

worldXy/worldYz/worldZx/Ucs/\<Select work plane or planar face>: **[Select A (Figure 3.26).]**
Select concentric edge: **[Select B (Figure 3.26).]**

\<Parts>	**\<Feature>**	**\<Hole...>**

Command: **AMHOLE**

[Operation:	**Drilled**
Termination:	**Through**
Placement:	**On Point**
Drill Size:	**F*1.5**
OK	]

worldXy/worldYz/worldZx/Ucs/\<Select work plane or planar face>: **[Select A (Figure 3.26).]**
Select concentric edge: **[Select C(Figure 3.26).]**

\<Parts>	**\<Display>**	**\<Work Plane>**	**\<Off>**

Command: **AMPLNDSP**
Display/ON/\<OFf>: **OFF**
Select/\<All>: **S**
Select work planes to hide:
Select objects: **[Select D (Figure 3.26).]**
Select objects: **[Enter]**

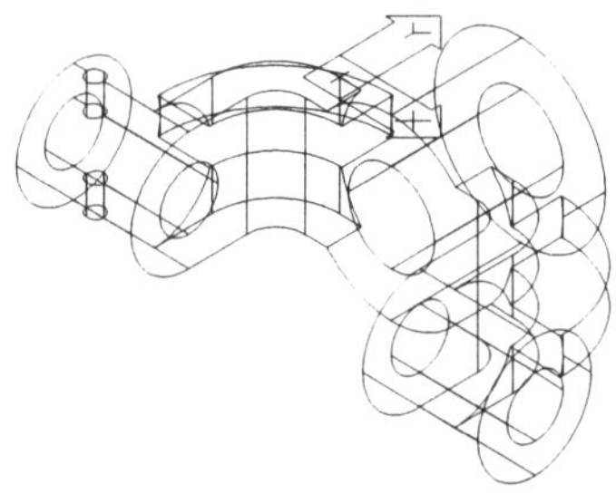

Figure 3.27 The completed main body

You have completed the main body of the universal joint assembly.

3.2 Second Solid Part in a File

Now you will work on the second component. It is the yoke of the universal joint. This is a symmetrical object. Because both its top view and its front view are the same, you may use two identical sketches to create the base feature and the second sketched solid feature. As usual, you will make a sketch, resolve it to form a profile, and extrude it to form a solid feature. To produce the second feature, you do not have to do sketching again. The profile of the second sketched feature is identical to the base feature, so you may simply copy the sketch from the base feature to form the sketch of the second feature. The final solid is an intersection of the second sketched feature with the base feature, plus two placed holes.

You will create this component in the same drawing file of the main body of the universal joint. To start another solid part in a drawing, run the AMNEWPART command.

<Parts>   **<Part>**   **<New>**

Command: **AMNEWPART**
Select native solid or (RETURN): **[Enter]**

The AMNEWPART command allows you to start a brand new solid part or to convert a native solid to form a static base feature. A native solid does not have a parts history or parametric information. Therefore, you cannot edit or change a native solid. If you convert a native solid to AutoCAD Designer solid, you can have only a static base feature with the form, shape, and size of the native solid. You may create additional sketched solid features and add placed solid features to it. The additional solid features are parametric and editable. However, the base feature that comes from a native solid is static and is not editable.

Run the DDLMODES command to set the current layer to SKETCH1. Use the UCS command to set the UCS back to WORLD.

<Data>   **<Layers...>**

Command: **DDLMODES**
Current layer: **SKETCH1**

Command: **UCS**
Origin/ZAxis/3point/OBject/View/X/Y/Z/Prev/Restore/Save/De/?/<World>: **[Enter]**

Apply the short cut key to set to a plan view. Then apply the PLINE command to create a rough sketch. See Figure 3.28.

Command: **5**

[Draw]   **[Polyline]**

Command: **PLINE**

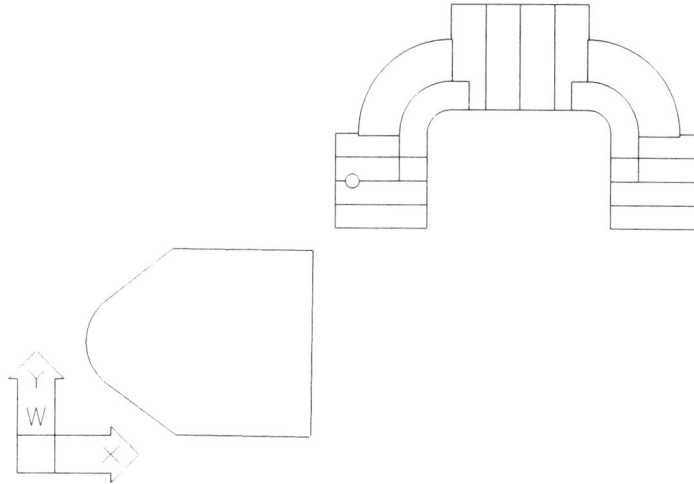

Figure 3.28 A sketch for the new part drawn on the WCS

Execute the AMPROFILE command to resolve the sketch to a profile for extrusion. See Figure 3.29.

\<Parts>   **\<Sketch>**   **\<Profile>**

Command: **AMPROFILE**
Select objects for sketch:
Select objects: **LAST**
Select objects: **[Enter]**

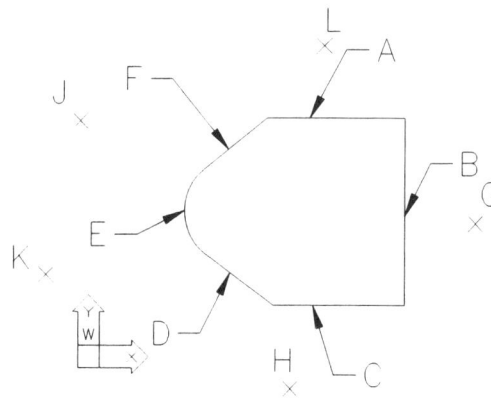

Figure 3.29 Resolved profile

Depending on how you make the sketch, the geometric constraints that AutoCAD Designer applies to the sketch may be different. In order properly to constrain the sketch geometrically, run the AMADDCON command.

<Parts>   **<Sketch>**   **<Constraints>**   **<Add>**

Command: **AMADDCON**

[Vertical constraint: **Apply to B (Figure 3.29).**
 Horizontal constraint: **Apply to A and C (Figure 3.29).**
 Tangent constraint: **Apply to D/E, and E/F (Figure 3.29).**
 Exit   ]

After setting the geometric constraints, apply the AMPARDIM command to add parametric dimensions to fully constrain the resolved sketch. See Figure 3.30.

<Parts>   **<Sketch>**   **<Add Dimension>**

Command: **AMPARDIM**
Select first object: **[Select A (Figure 3.29).]**
Select second object or place dimension: **[Select C (Figure 3.29).]**
Specify dimension placement: **[Select G (Figure 3.29).]**
Undo/Hor/Ver/Align/Par/Enter Dimension value: **D**

The parameter name in the illustration is D0. The first parameter name of a new part starts from D0 again.

Select first object: **[Select E (Figure 3.29).]**
Select second object or place dimension: **[Select B (Figure 3.29).]**
Specify dimension placement: **[Select H (Figure 3.29).]**
Undo/Hor/Ver/Align/Par/Enter Dimension value: **40**

Select first object: **[Select C (Figure 3.29).]**
Select second object or place dimension: **[Select H (Figure 3.29).]**
Undo/Hor/Ver/Align/Par/Enter Dimension value: **30**

Select first object: **[Select E (Figure 3.29).]**
Select second object or place dimension: **[Select J (Figure 3.29).]**
Undo/Enter Dimension value: **10**

Select first object: **[Select E (Figure 3.29).]**
Select second object or place dimension: **[Select C (Figure 3.29).]**
Specify dimension placement: **[Select K (Figure 3.29).]**
Undo/Hor/Ver/Align/Par/Enter Dimension value: **D/2**

Select first object: **[Select A (Figure 3.29).]**
Select second object or place dimension: **[Select L (Figure 3.29).]**
Undo/Hor/Ver/Align/Par/Enter Dimension value: **30**

Solved fully constrained sketch.
Select first object: **[Enter]**

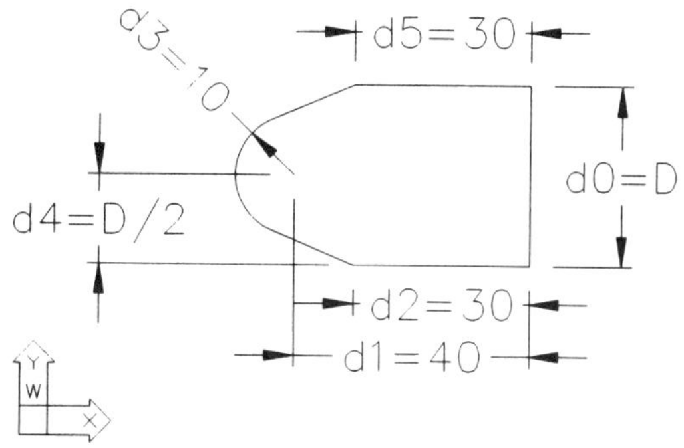

Figure 3.30 Fully constrained profile

You have fully constrained the profile. Change the display to an isometric view, and then set the current layer to SOLID2.

Command: **8**

<Data>   **<Layers...>**

Command: **DDLMODES**
Current layer: **SOLID2**

Execute the AMEXTRUDE command to extrude the profile to form the base solid feature of the second component. See Figure 3.31.

<Parts>   **<Feature>**   **<Extrude...>**

Command: **AMEXTRUDE**

[Termination: **Mid-Plane**
 Operation: **Base**
 Size:
    Distance: **D**
    Draft Angle: **0**
OK   ]

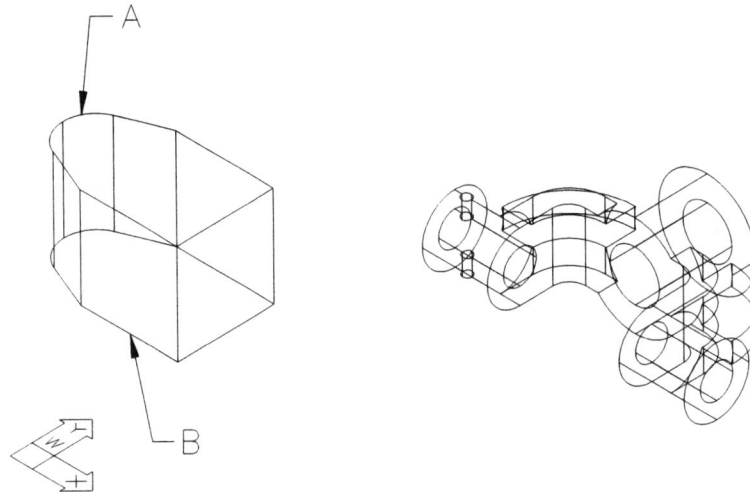

Figure 3.31 Base feature of the second component created

Now you have two solid parts residing on a single drawing file. Only one solid part can be active a time. If you want to add features or to edit the features of a part, then that part must be the active part.

To find out which part is the active part, you may run the AMSHOWACT command.

<Parts>   **<Utilities>**   **<Show Active>**

Command: **AMSHOWACT**

To select a part to be the active part, you may apply the AMACTPART command.

<Parts>   **<Part>**   **<Make Active>**

Command: **AMACTPART**
Select Part: **[Select A (Figure 3.31).]**

As mentioned earlier, this component has two sketched solid features. The second sketched solid feature is identical to the base feature and intersects it. Run the DDLMODES command to set the current layer to SKETCH1.

<Data>   **<Layers...>**

Command: **DDLMODES**
Current layer: **SKETCH1**

The second sketched solid feature needs a work plane for setting the sketch plane. Apply the AMWORKAXIS command to create a work axis. Then run the AMWORKPLN command to make a work plane and to set the location of the sketch plane. See Figure 3.32.

<Parts>   **<Feature>**   **<Work Axis>**

Command: **AMWORKAXIS**
Select cylinder/cone/torus: **[Select A (Figure 3.31).]**

<Parts>   **<Feature>**   **<Work Plane...>**

Command: **AMWORKPLN**

[1st Modifier: **On Edge/Axis**
 2nd Modifier: **Planar Parallel**
 Create Sketch Plane: **YES**
OK   ]

worldX/worldY/worldZ/<Select work axis or straight edge>: **[Select the newly created work axis, C (Figure 3.32).]**
worldXy/worldYz/worldZx/Ucs/<Select work plane or planar face>: **[Select B (Figure 3.31).]**
Next/<Accept>: **[Accept, if the vertical plane is highlighted. Otherwise, Next.]**
worldX/worldY/worldZ/<Select work axis or straight edge>: **[Select B (Figure 3.31).]**
Rotate/Z-flip/<Accept>: **[R, if the Y axis direction is not the same as Figure 3.32.]**
Rotate/Z-flip/<Accept>: **[Z, if the X axis direction is not the same as Figure 3.32.]**
Rotate/Z-flip/<Accept>: **[Accept, if the Y axis and X axis direction are the same as Figure 3.32.]**

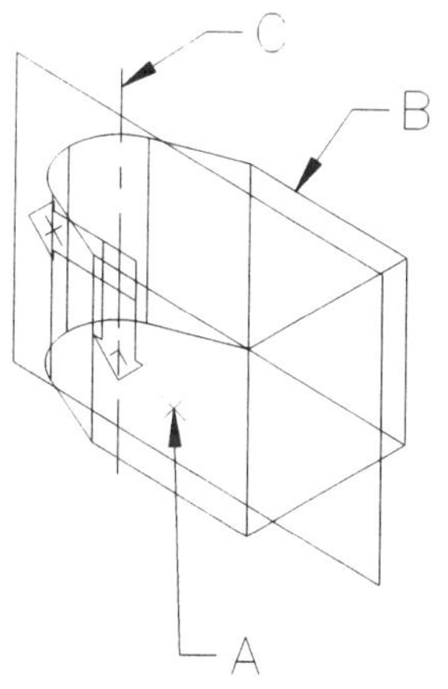

Figure 3.32 Work axis, and work plane created

To reiterate, this component is symmetrical. The cross-section of the second sketched solid feature is identical to that of the base feature. It is not necessary to create the second sketch. To save time, you may copy the sketch of the base feature to form the sketch for the second sketched solid feature. Run the AMCOPYSKETCH command. See Figure 3.33.

<Parts>   **<Sketch>**   **<Copy Sketch>**

Command: **AMCOPYSKETCH**
Feature/<Sketch>: **FEATURE**

Select feature: **[Select B (Figure 3.32).]**
Sketch center: **[Select A (Figure 3.32).]**
Sketch center: **[Enter]**

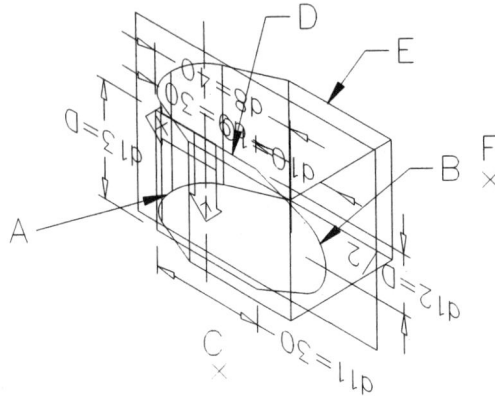

Figure 3.33 A sketch copied from the base feature

Basically, the copied sketch is the same as the original sketch. The constraints on the general form, shape, and size are already there. All you need to do is add two parametric dimensions to constrain the location of the second sketch in reference to the base feature. See Figure 3.34.

<Parts>   **<Sketch>**   **<Add Dimension>**

Command: AMPARDIM
Select first object: **[Select A (Figure 3.33).]**
Select second object or place dimension: **[Select B (Figure 3.33).]**
Specify dimension placement: **[Select C (Figure 3.33).]**
Undo/Hor/Ver/Align/Par/Enter Dimension value: **30**

Select first object: **[Select D (Figure 3.33).]**
Select second object or place dimension: **[Select E (Figure 3.33).]**
Specify dimension placement: **[Select F (Figure 3.33).]**
Undo/Hor/Ver/Align/Par/Enter Dimension value: **0**

Solved fully constrained sketch.
Select first object: **[Enter]**

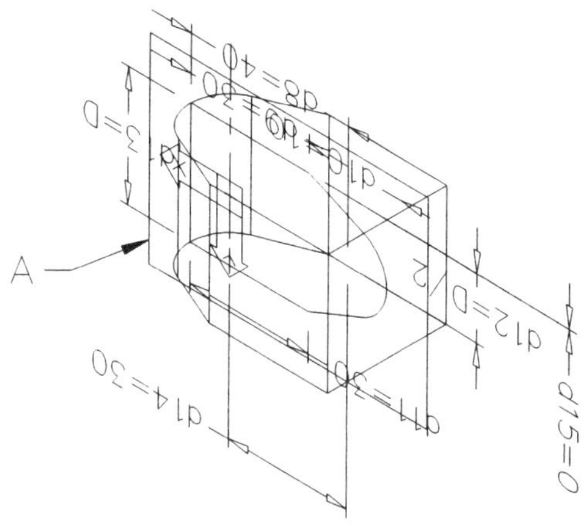

Figure 3.34 Fully constrained second sketch

To clean up the screen, run the AMPLNDSP command to turn off the display of the work plane. Then apply the AMEXTRUDE command to extrude the second sketch to form a sketched solid feature and to intersect with the base feature. See Figure 3.35.

\<Parts\>   **\<Display\>**   **\<Work Plane\>**   **\<Off\>**

Command: **AMPLNDSP**
Display/ON/\<OFF\>: OFF
Select/\<All\>: **SELECT**
Select objects: **[Select A (Figure 3.34).]**
Select objects: **[Enter]**

\<Parts\>   **\<Feature\>**   **\<Extrude...\>**

Command: **AMEXTRUDE**

[Termination: **Mid Plane**
 Operation: **Intersect**
 Size:
    Distance: **D**
    Draft Angle: **0**
OK   ]

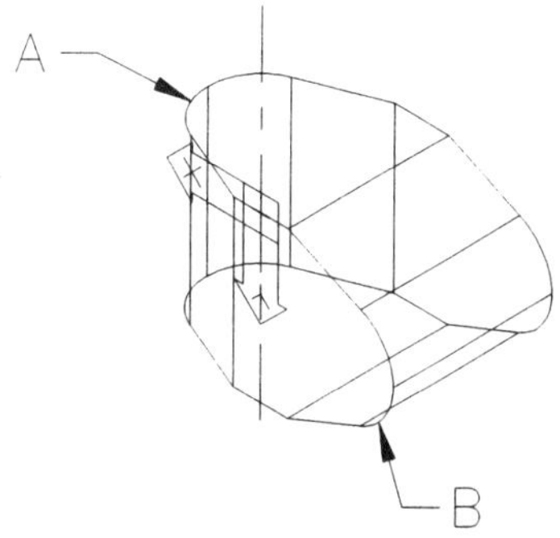

Figure 3.35 The second sketched solid feature intersected with the base feature

To complete the second solid part, issue the AMHOLE command to place two holes on it. See Figure 3.36.

<Parts>   <Feature>   <Hole...>

Command: **AMHOLE**

[Operation: **Drilled**
 Termination: **Through**
 Placement: **Concentric**
 Drill Size: **F**
OK   ]

worldXy/worldYz/worldZx/Ucs/<Select work plane or planar face>: **[Select A (Figure 3.35).]**
Select concentric edge: **[Select A (Figure 3.35).]**

<Parts>   <Feature>   <Hole...>

Command: **AMHOLE**

[Operation: **Drilled**
 Termination: **Through**
 Placement: **Concentric**
 Drill Size: **F**
OK   ]

worldXy/worldYz/worldZx/Ucs/<Select work plane or planar face>: **[Select B (Figure 3.35).]**
Select concentric edge: **[Select B (Figure 3.35).]**

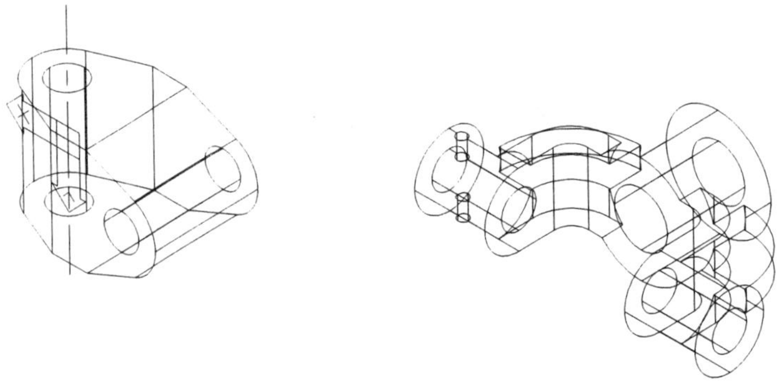

Figure 3.36 Second solid part created

You have completed the yoke of the universal joint assembly.

3.3 The Third Part of the Universal Joint

The third part of the universal joint is a chamfered circular rod with a through hole drilled perpendicular to the axis. You will put this part on the same drawing file with the last two solid parts. Therefore, run the AMNEWPART command to activate a new part.

    <Parts>   **<Part>**   **<New>**

Command: **AMNEWPART**
Select native solid or (RETURN) : **[Enter]**

    Run the UCS command to set the UCS to WORLD. Then use the CIRCLE command to create a circle to serve as a rough sketch. See Figure 3.37.

Command: **UCS**
Origin/ZAxis/3point/OBject/View/X/Y/Z/Prev/Restore/Save/Del/?/<World>: **[Enter]**

[Draw]   **[Circle Center Radius]**

Command: **CIRCLE**

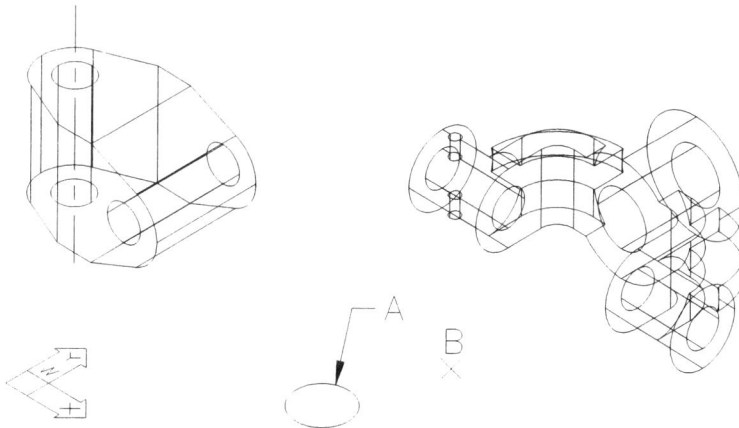

Figure 3.37 A circle drawn

    Run the AMPROFILE command to resolve the circle to form a profile. Next, use the AMPARDIM command to add a parametric dimension to fully constrain it. See Figure 3.38.

    <Parts>   **<Sketch>**   **<Profile>**

Command: **AMPROFILE**
Select objects for sketch:
Select objects: **LAST**
Select objects: **[Enter]**

<Parts>   **<Sketch>**   **<Add Dimension>**

Command: **AMPARDIM**
Select first object: **[Select A (Figure 3.37).]**
Select second object or place dimension: **[Select B (Figure 3.37).]**
Undo/Enter Dimension value: **F**

Solved fully constrained sketch.
Select first object: **[Enter]**

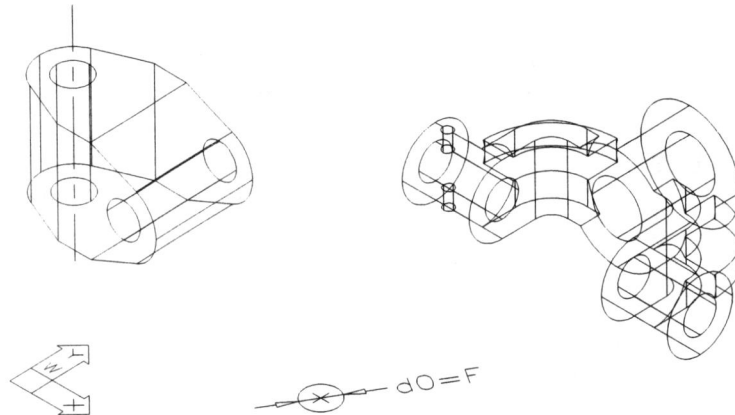

Figure 3.38 Profile fully constrained

To produce the base solid feature, issue the AMEXTRUDE command to extrude the resolved profile. To maintain a parametric relationship with the existing solid parts, the distance of extrusion is expressed as a function of four global variables. They add together to form the total length of extrusion.

<Parts>   **<Feature>**   **<Extrude...>**

Command: **AMEXTRUDE**

[Termination: **Blind**
 Operation: **Base**
 Size:
    Distance: **D+2*H+2*C+2*F/10**
    Draft angle: **0**
 OK   ]

Direction Flip/<Accept>: **[Accept, if the arrow is pointing upward. Otherwise, Flip.]**

Issue the AMWORKAXIS command to create a work axis at the axis location of the extruded circular base feature. See Figure 3.39.

<Parts>   **<Feature>**   **<Work Axis>**

Command: **AMWORKAXIS**
Select cylinder/cone/torus: **[Select A (Figure 3.39).]**

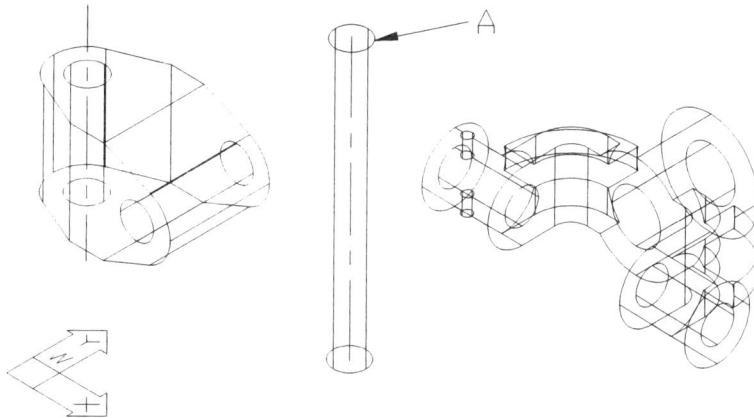

Figure 3.39 A base feature created

The third component consists of one sketched feature and three placed features. The placed features are two chamfered edges and a hole. To place the hole perpendicular to the axis, you need a work point. In turn, the work point needs a work plane. The work plane for the work point has to be parallel to the axis and tangential to the outer face of the base feature. In order to create this work plane, you have to create an intermediate work plane to define the orientation. The intermediate work plane does not have to be parametrically linked to the solid. Instead, it is simply a plane set to the XZ plane of the current UCS. Using the non-parametric work plane as a bridge, you may then create a parametric work plane that is parallel to the XZ plane and also tangential to the cylindrical feature.

Run the AMWORKPLN command to create the intermediate work plane. This work plane is set to the XZ plane of the current UCS. It has no reference to the active solid part. It is non-parametric. See Figure 3.40.

<Parts>   **<Feature>**   **<Work Plane...>**

Command: **AMWORKPLN**

[1st Modifier: **World XZ**
 Create Sketch Plane: **NO**
 OK   ]

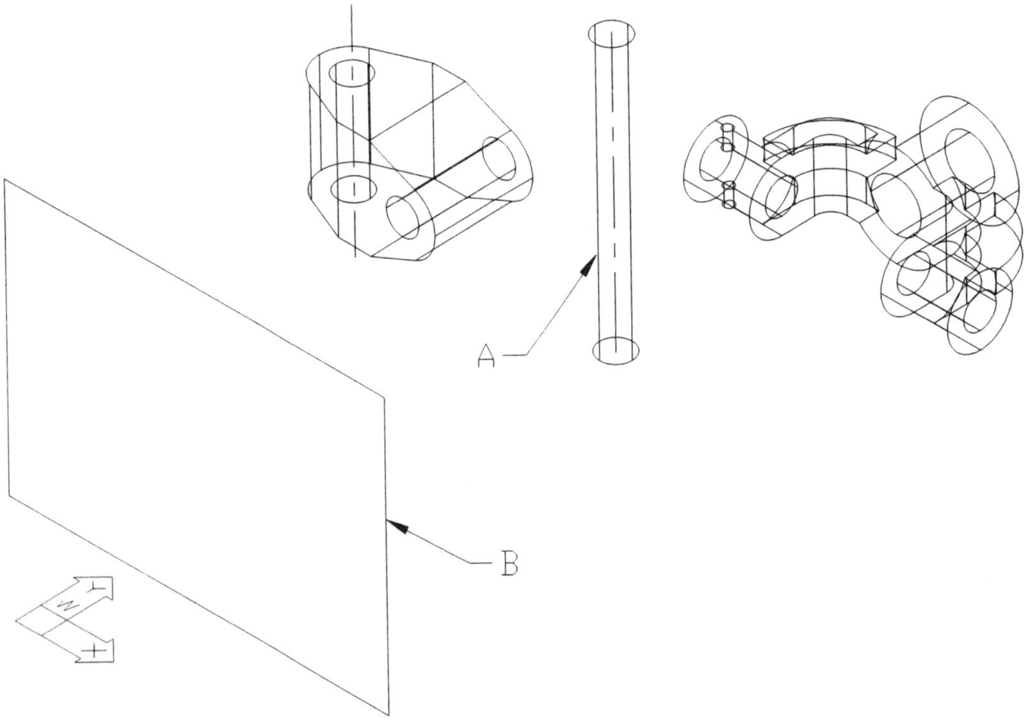

Figure 3.40 A non-parametric work plane created

Having created a non-parametric work plane that is parallel to the XZ plane of the current UCS, you may now run the AMWORKPLN command to create a parametric work plane that is parallel to the last work plane and tangential to the cylindrical feature. In creating this work plane, you should also set the sketch plane. See Figure 3.41.

\<Parts\>   **\<Feature\>**   **\<Work Plane...\>**

Command: **AMWORKPLN**

[1st Modifier: **Tangent**
 2nd Modifier: **Planar Parallel**
 Create Sketch Plane: **YES**
OK   ]

Select cylindrical face: **[Select A (Figure 3.40).]**
worldXy/worldYz/worldZx/Ucs/\<Select work plane or planar face\>: **[Select B (Figure 3.40).]**
Flip/\<Accept\>: **[Accept, if the arrow is pointing toward the last work plane. Otherwise, Flip.]**
worldX/worldY/worldZ/\<Select work axis or straight edge\>: **WORLDZ**
Rotate/Z-flip/\<Accept\>: **[R, if the Y axis is not pointing upward.]**
Rotate/Z-flip/\<Accept\>: **[Z, if the X axis is not pointing to the right.]**
Rotate/Z-flip/\<Accept\>: **[Accept, if the Y axis is pointing upward, and the X axis is pointing to the right.]**

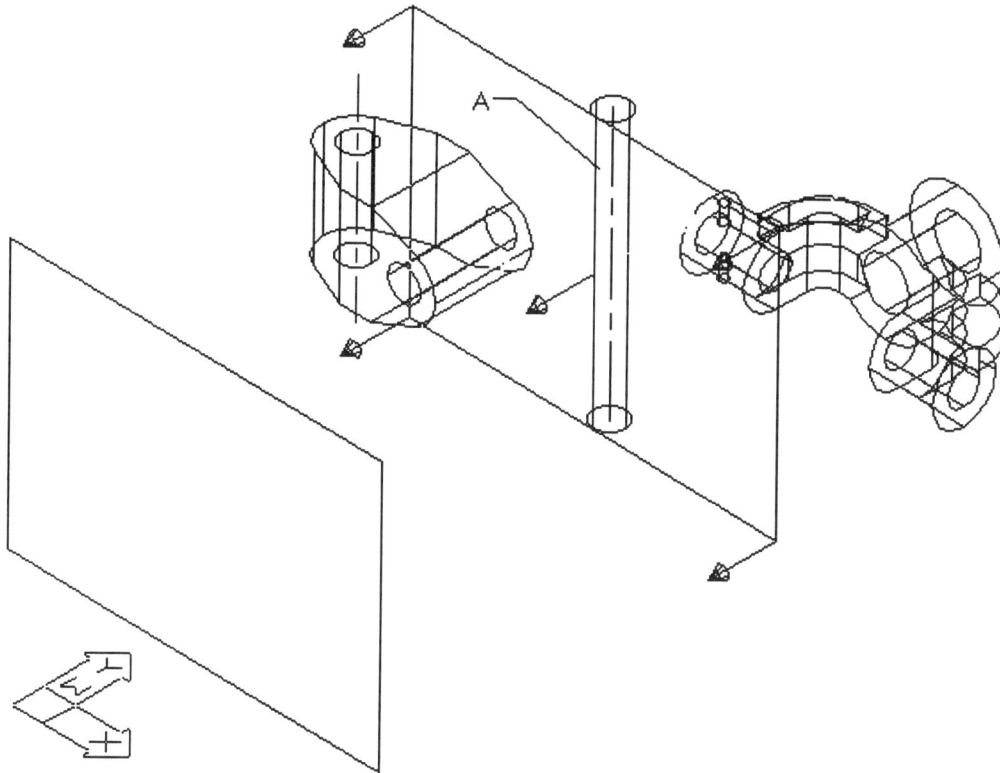

Figure 3.41 A parametric work plane created

On the current sketch plane, use the AMWORKPT command to make a work point. See Figure 3.42.

<Parts>   **<Feature>**   **<Work Point>**

Command: **AMWORKPT**
Location on sketch plane: **[Select A (Figure 3.41).]**

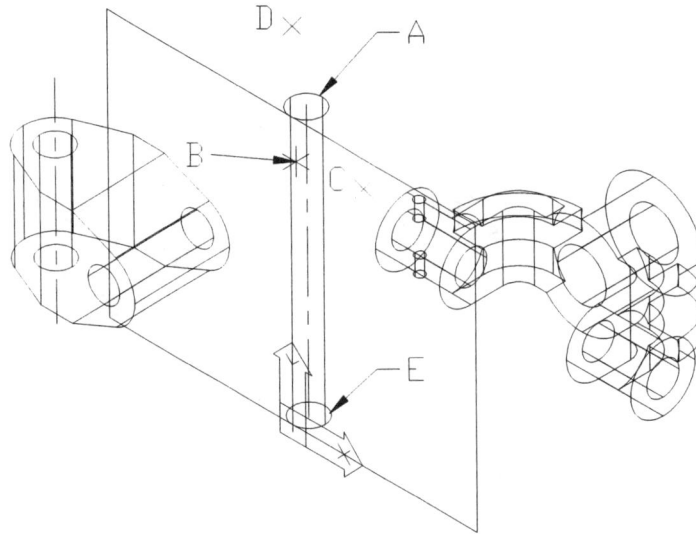

Figure 3.42 A work point created

Use the AMPARDIM command to add two parametric dimensions to fully constrain the work point. Then issue the AMHOLE command to place a through hole on this work point. See Figure 3.43.

<Parts>   **<Sketch>**   **<Add Dimension>**

Command: **AMPARDIM**
Select first object: **[Select A (Figure 3.42).]**
Select second object or place dimension: **[Select B (Figure 3.42).]**
Specify dimension placement: **[Select C (Figure 3.42).]**
Undo/Hor/Ver/Align/Par/Enter Dimension value: **H/4+F/10**

Select first object: **[Select A (Figure 3.42).]**
Select second object or place dimension: **[Select B (Figure 3.42).]**
Specify dimension placement: **[Select D (Figure 3.42).]**
Undo/Hor/Ver/Align/Par/Enter Dimension value: **0**

Solved fully constrained sketch.
Select first object: **[Enter]**

<Parts>   **<Feature>**   **<Hole...>**

Command: **AMHOLE**

[Operation: **Drilled**
 Termination: **Through**
 Placement: **On Point**
 Drill Size: **3**
 OK   ]

Select work point: **[Select B (Figure 3.42).]**
Direction Flip/<Accept>: **[Accept, if the arrow is pointing toward the center of the solid. Otherwise, Flip.]**

To complete the solid model, issue the AMCHAMFER command to place two chamfer features at the two ends of the base solid feature. See Figure 3.43.

<Parts>   **<Feature>**   **<Chamfer...>**

Command: **AMCHAMFER**

[Operation: **Equal Distance**
Parameters: Distance1: **F/10**
OK   ]

Pick the edge to chamfer: **[Select A (Figure 3.42).]**
Pick the edge to chamfer: **[Select E (Figure 3.42).]**
Pick the edge to chamfer: **[Enter]**

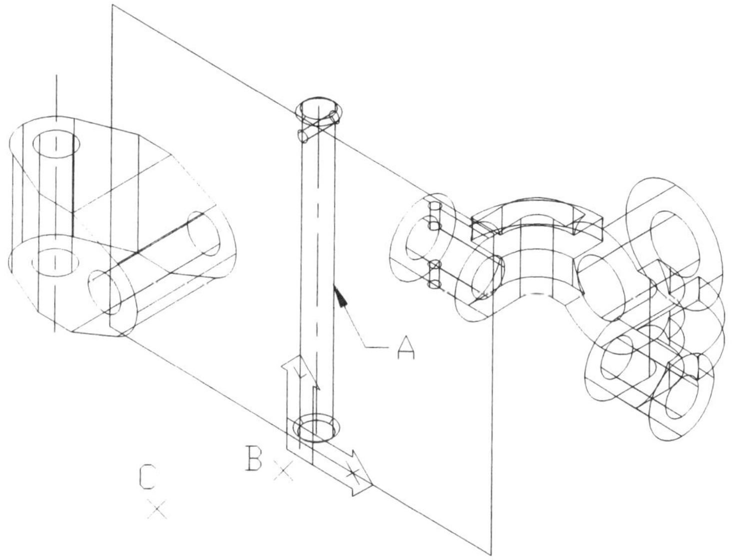

Figure 3.43 Third solid part created

You have completed the third part of the universal joint assembly. Apply the AMPLNDSP command to turn off the display of the work planes and the AMAXISDSP command to turn off the display of the work axis.

<Parts>   **<Display>**   **<Work Plane>**   **<Off>**

Command: **AMPLNDSP**
Display/ON/<OFf>: **OFF**
Select/<All>: **ALL**

<Parts>   **<Display>**   **<Work Axis>**   **<Off>**

Command: **AMAXISDSP**
ON/<OFf>: **OFF**

The AMPLNDSP command, the AMAXISDSP command, and the AMPTDSP command work on the active solid part. Check your drawing. If there are still any construction features on any solid parts that you would like to turn off, you have to run the AMACTPART command to select the relevant part to make it the active part. Then you may run the AMPLNDSP command, the AMAXISDSP command, and the AMPTDSP command again.

<Parts>   **<Part>**   **<Make Active>**

Command: **AMACTPART**
Select Part: **[Select the part that you want to be active.]**

<Parts>   **<Display>**   **<Work Plane>**   **<Off>**

Command: **AMPLNDSP**
Display/ON/<OFf>: **OFF**
Select/<All>: **ALL**

<Parts>   **<Display>**   **<Work Axis>**   **<Off>**

Command: **AMAXISDSP**
ON/<OFf>: **OFF**

<Parts>   **<Display>**   **<Work Point>**   **<Off>**

Command: **AMPTDSP**
ON/<OFf>: **OFF**

3.4   The Fourth Part of the Universal Joint

The fourth part of the universal joint is a circular lock pin. Simply speaking, it is an extruded solid feature created from a circular sketch. In order to illustrate how to create similar parts, you will use the COPY command to copy the third solid part, and then you will do editing.

Apply the UCS command to set the UCS to WORLD. Then issue the COPY command to copy the third solid to form the fourth solid part. See Figure 3.44.

Command: **UCS**
Origin/ZAxis/3point/OBject/View/X/Y/Z/Prev/Restore/Save/Del/?/<World>: **[Enter]**

[Modify]   **[Copy Object]**
Command: **COPY**
Select objects: **[Select A (Figure 3.43).]**
Select objects: **[Enter]**
<Base point or displacement>/Multiple: **[Select B (Figure 3.43).]**
Second point of displacement: **[Select C (Figure 3.43).]**

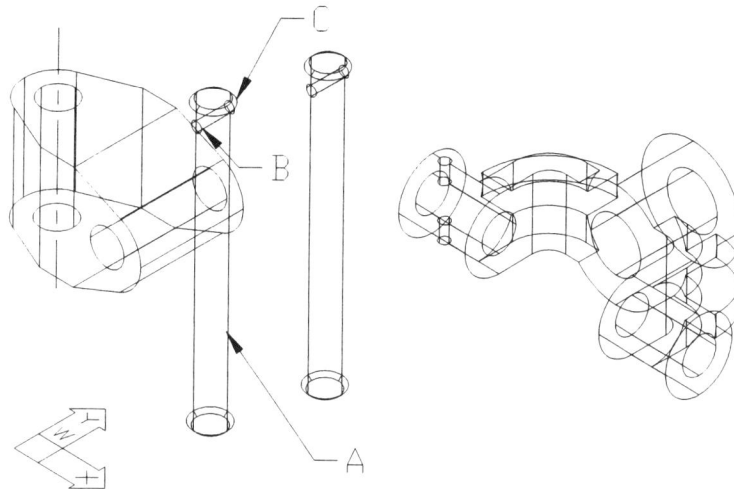

Figure 3.44 A solid part copied from the third solid part

There are four solid parts in this drawing file. To edit the fourth solid part, you have to run the AMACTPART command to select it as active.

<Parts>   **<Part>**   **<Make Active>**

Command: **AMACTPART**
Select Part: **[Select A (Figure 3.44).]**

Next, use the AMDELFEAT command to delete the placed hole feature and the chamfer features. Then issue the AMEDITFEAT command to change the parametric dimensions. After that, apply the AMUPDATE command to update the change. See Figure 3.45.

<Parts>   **<Feature>**   **<Delete>**

Command: **AMDELFEAT**
Select feature: **[Select B (Figure 3.44).]**
Next/<Accept>: **[Accept, if the hole is highlighted. Otherwise, Next.]**
Highlighted features will be deleted. Continue ? No/<Yes>: **YES**

<Parts>   **<Feature>**   **<Delete>**

Command: **AMDELFEAT**
Select feature: **[Select C (Figure 3.44).]**
Next/<Accept>: **[Accept, if the chamfer is highlighted. Otherwise, Next.]**
Highlighted features will be deleted. Continue ? No/<Yes>: **YES**

<Parts>   **<Feature>**   **<Delete>**

Command: **AMDELFEAT**
Select feature: **[Select the other chamfered edge (Figure 3.44).]**
Next/<Accept>: **[Accept, if the chamfer is highlighted. Otherwise, Next.]**
Highlighted features will be deleted. Continue ? No/<Yes>: **YES**

<Parts>   <Edit Feature>

Command: **AMEDITFEAT**
Sketch/surfCut/<select Feature>: **[Select A (Figure 3.44).]**
Select object: **[Select the dimension that governs the height of extrusion.]**
Enter new value for dimension: **J*2**
Select object: **[Select the dimension that governs the diameter of the cylinder.]**
Enter new value for dimension: **G**
Solved fully constrained sketch.
Select object: **[Enter]**

<Parts>   <Update>

Command: **AMUPDATE**

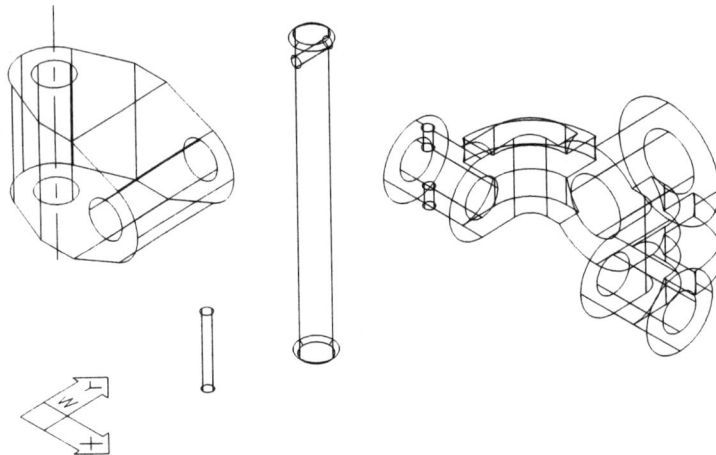

Figure 3.45 The fourth solid part completed

You have completed the fourth part of the universal joint assembly. Now you should have four solid parts created in a single drawing file.

Save your work. Before saving, you may set the AMCOMPSV variable to 1 to save the file to a compressed format. A compressed file is smaller. It takes you less time to open it again. However, it will take you some time to rebuild the parts history if you are going to update the solid parts.

Command: **AMCOMPSV**
New value for AMCOMPSV: **1**

<Parts>   <Preferences...>

Command: **AMPARTVARS**

```
┌─────────────────────────────────────────┐
│ Part Settings                            │
│ ┌─Constraint Model──────────────────┐   │
│ │  ☑ Apply Constraint Rules          │   │
│ │  ☑ Assume Rough Sketch             │   │
│ │                                     │   │
│ │   Angular Tolerance:   ┌────────┐  │   │
│ │                        │4.0000  │  │   │
│ │                        └────────┘  │   │
│ │      Linear Tolerance/Pickbox Size...│ │
│ │                                     │   │
│ │  Apply to Linetypes:  ┌──────────┐ │   │
│ │                       │CONT*     │ │   │
│ │                       └──────────┘ │   │
│ │ ┌─Display─────────────────────────┐│   │
│ │ │  Constraint Display Size...      ││   │
│ │ └─────────────────────────────────┘│   │
│ └─────────────────────────────────────┘  │
│  ☑ Compressed Save Format                │
│                                           │
│  ┌────────┐   ┌────────┐   ┌────────┐    │
│  │   OK   │   │ Cancel │   │ Help...│    │
│  └────────┘   └────────┘   └────────┘    │
└─────────────────────────────────────────┘
```

<File>   <Save...>

Command: **QSAVE**

[File name: **U_JOINT.DWG**
OK   ]

To demonstrate how the global parameters affect the dimensions of a set of solid parts collectively, run the AMPARAM command to change the value of a global parameter, and then update the change with the AMUPDATE command.

<Parts>   <Parameters...>

Command: **AMPARAM**

[Parameters:
Name	Equation	Comment	
A	**50**	**ELBOX SPAN**	**Save**
OK			]

<Parts>   <Update>

Command: **AMUPDATE**

Because you have saved the file before, quit the drawing with the QUIT command.

<File>   <Exit>

Command: **QUIT**

[**Discard changes**
OK   ]

In the next chapter, you will assemble the solid parts together. To continue the drawing session, proceed to prepare the parts for the second assembly.

3.5   The Electric Motor Casing

The second assembly is a set of electric motor casings. It has three solid parts. Unlike the universal joint assembly, in which you created all the solid parts in a single file, you will put each solid part in an individual file. In order to establish a dimensional relationship between the solid parts, you will, as in the last assembly, maintain a set of global parameters. Because the solid parts reside on separate files, you need a global parameter file. You may create a global parameter file in two ways. You may use a text editor to make one, or you may build up a set of parameters in a drawing file and then export them to an external file. All other drawing files that use the global parameters may import the global parameters from the parameter file or link to the parameter file.

Each time you have to create a drawing, you need to do several things, such as setting up limits and layers. If you need the same settings in a number of files, as in this assembly, you should create a prototype drawing.

Start a new drawing with the NEW command.

<File>   <New...>

Command: **NEW**

To prepare a prototype drawing, run a series of commands to make appropriate settings. Then apply the SAVE command.

Run the LIMITS command to set the drawing limits and the ZOOM command to zoom to those limits. This provides a known area of working space.

<Data>   <Drawing Limits>

Command: **LIMITS**
Reset Model space limits:
ON/OFF/<Lower left corner>: **0,0**
Upper right corner: **40,30**

[Standard Toolbar]   [Zoom All]

Command: **ZOOM**
All/Center/Dynamic/Extents/Left/Previous/Vmax/Window/<Scale(X/XP)>: **A**

In addition to zooming to a known display window size, it will be helpful to display the grid mesh on the screen. Issue the GRID command to display a grid mesh of 1 unit times 1 unit.

Command: **GRID**
Grid spacing(X) or ON/OFF/Snap/Aspect: **1**

To make rough sketches and to create solids, you should create two layers. Run the DDLMODES command.

<Data>   <Layers...>

Command: **DDLMODES**

Layer	Color
SKETCH	**cyan**
SOLID	**magenta**

Current layer: **SKETCH**

To be prepared for creating parametric solid models, run the UCSICON command to set the UCS icon to display at the origin position, and issue the AMPARTVARS command to set the preferences.

Command: **UCSICON**
ON/OFF/All/Noorigin/ORigin: **OR**

<Parts>   <Preferences...>

Command: **AMPARTVARS**

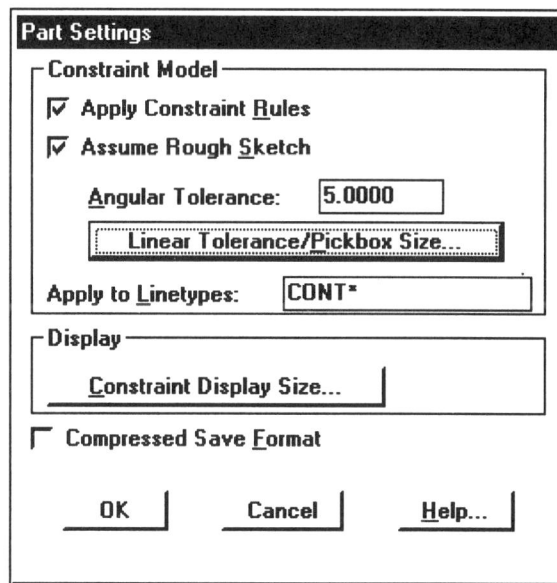

Part Settings
- **Constraint Model**
  - ☑ Apply Constraint **R**ules
  - ☑ Assume Rough **S**ketch

    Angular Tolerance: 5.0000

    Linear Tolerance/Pickbox Size...

  Apply to **L**inetypes: CONT*
- **Display**
  - **C**onstraint Display Size...

☐ Compressed Save **F**ormat

OK   Cancel   Help...

To have a better line type proportion to display the construction lines, run the LTSCALE command to set the line type scale to 5.

<Options>   <Linetypes>   <Global Linetype Scale>

Command: **LTSCALE**
New scale factor: **5**

Because you will use global parameters, you should set the dimension display to show an equation. Execute the AMDIMDSP command.

<Parts>   <Display>   <Dim Display>

Command: **AMDIMDSP**
Parameter/Equations/<Numeric>: **E**

You will need the above settings in each of the three drawings of the electric motor casing assembly. Save the drawing as a prototype for the three solid parts that you are going to create.

<File>   **<Save...>**

Command: **QSAVE**
[File name: **PROTO_32.DWG**
OK   ]

3.6   Front Cap of the Motor Casing Assembly

Basically, the three solid parts are solids of revolution. You will make rough sketches, resolve them to form profiles, and revolve them to form solid features.

To begin, you will create the front cap of the motor casing. This solid part is a solid of revolution with four tapped holes. The completed solid model is shown in Figure 3.53.

Run the NEW command to start a new drawing. Use the prototype that you have saved.

<File>   **<New...>**

Command: **NEW**

[Prototype...: **PROTO_32**
OK   ]

As shown in Figure 3.46, use the PLINE command to make a rough sketch.

[Draw]   **[Polyline]**

Command: **PLINE**

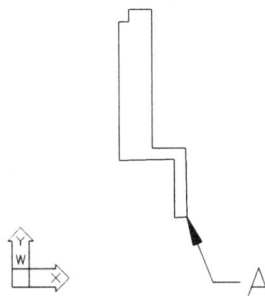

Figure 3.46 A rough sketch created

Execute the AMPROFILE command to resolve the rough sketch to form a profile. Set the fix point of the profile at A with the AMFIXPT command, and set the insertion base point at A with the BASE command. See Figure 3.47.

<Parts>   **<Sketch>**   **<Profile>**

Command: **AMPROFILE**
Select objects for sketch:
Select objects: **[Select A (Figure 3.46).]**
Select objects: **[Enter]**

<Parts>   **<Sketch>**   **<Fix Point>**

Command: **AMFIXPT**
Specify new fixed point for sketch: **END** of **[Select A (Figure 3.46).]**

Command: **BASE**
Base point: **END** of **[Select A (Figure 3.46).]**

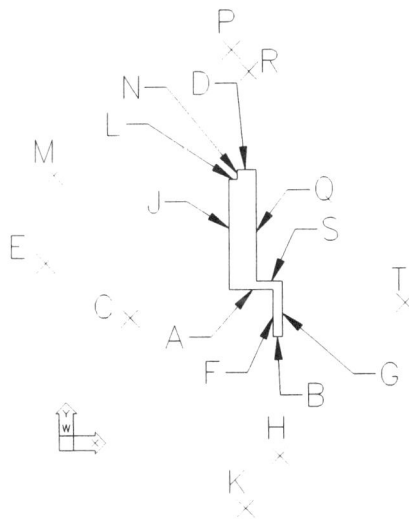

Figure 3.47 Resolved sketch

In order to find out what type of geometric constraints AutoCAD Designer has applied to the profile, run the AMSHOWCON command.

<Parts>   **<Sketch>**   **<Constraints>**   **<Show>**

Command: **AMSHOWCON**
All/Select/Next/<eXit>: **ALL**
All/Select/Next/<eXit>: **[Enter]**

Check your screen display. Then run the AMADDCON command to add the necessary geometric constraints. Also, apply the AMDELCON command to delete any geometric constraints that are inappropriate.

<**Parts**>   <**Sketch**>   <**Constraints**>   <**Add**>

Command: **AMADDCON**

[Vertical constraint: **Apply to J, F, G, Q, and N (Figure 3.47).**
 Horizontal constraint: **Apply to A, B, S, D, and L (Figure 3.47).**
Exit   ]

<**Parts**>   <**Sketch**>   <**Constraints**>   <**Delete**>

Command: **AMDELCON**
Size/All/<Select>: **[Select the Collinear constraint, if any.]**

Establish a set of global parameters by running the AMPARAM command. To make the parameters accessible by other drawing files, use the "Export" option to write the parameters to an external file. After exporting, use the "Link" option to maintain a linkage with the external parameter file.

<**Parts**>   <**Parameters...**>

Command: **AMPARAM**

[Parameter:
Name	Equation	Comment	
OR	**18**	**CASING OUTSIDE RADIUS**	**SAVE**
BR	**5**	**BEARING OUTSIDE RADIUS**	**SAVE**
BT	**5**	**BEARING THICKNESS**	**SAVE**
CT	**1**	**CASING STEP**	**SAVE**
PR	**14.5**	**PITCH CIRCLE RADIUS**	**SAVE**
SH	**3**	**SHAFT DIAMETER**	**SAVE**

Export...
    [Specify a valid file name.   ]
Link...
    [Select the file that you have exported.   ]
OK   ]

Now you have created an external parameter file and linked the parameters in this drawing file to that file. If you wish to create a parameter file with a text editor, you may consult the following, which is the content of the parameter file that you have created:

```
/* Exported Global Parameters */
OR = 18 /* CASING OUTSIDE RADIUS */
BR = 5 /* BEARING OUTSIDE RADIUS */
BT = 5 /* BEARING THICKNESS */
CT = 1 /* CASING STEP */
PR = 14.5 /* PITCH CIRCLE RADIUS */
SH = 3 /* SHAFT DIAMETER */
```

In order to fully constrain the resolved sketch, run the AMPARDIM command to add parametric dimensions. See Figure 3.48.

<Parts>   **<Sketch>**   **<Add Dimension>**

Command: **AMPARDIM**
Select first object: **[Select A (Figure 3.47).]**
Select second object or place dimension: **[Select B (Figure 3.47).]**
Specify dimension placement: **[Select C (Figure 3.47).]**
Undo/Hor/Ver/Align/Par/Enter Dimension value: **BR**

Select first object: **[Select D (Figure 3.47).]**
Select second object or place dimension: **[Select B (Figure 3.47).]**
Specify dimension placement: **[Select E (Figure 3.47).]**
Undo/Hor/Ver/Align/Par/Enter Dimension value: **OR**

Select first object: **[Select F (Figure 3.47).]**
Select second object or place dimension: **[Select G (Figure 3.47).]**
Specify dimension placement: **[Select H (Figure 3.47).]**
Undo/Hor/Ver/Align/Par/Enter Dimension value: **CT**

Select first object: **[Select F (Figure 3.47).]**
Select second object or place dimension: **[Select J (Figure 3.47).]**
Specify dimension placement: **[Select K (Figure 3.47).]**
Undo/Hor/Ver/Align/Par/Enter Dimension value: **BT**

Select first object: **[Select L (Figure 3.47).]**
Select second object or place dimension: **[Select D (Figure 3.47).]**
Specify dimension placement: **[Select M (Figure 3.47).]**
Undo/Hor/Ver/Align/Par/Enter Dimension value: **CT**

Select first object: **[Select N (Figure 3.47).]**
Select second object or place dimension: **[Select J (Figure 3.47).]**
Specify dimension placement: **[Select P (Figure 3.47).]**
Undo/Hor/Ver/Align/Par/Enter Dimension value: **CT**

Select first object: **[Select J (Figure 3.47).]**
Select second object or place dimension: **[Select Q (Figure 3.47).]**
Specify dimension placement: **[Select R (Figure 3.47).]**
Undo/Hor/Ver/Align/Par/Enter Dimension value: **3**

Select first object: **[Select B (Figure 3.47).]**
Select second object or place dimension: **[Select S (Figure 3.47).]**
Specify dimension placement: **[Select T (Figure 3.47).]**
Undo/Hor/Ver/Align/Par/Enter Dimension value: **6**

Solved fully constrained sketch.
Select first object: **[Enter]**

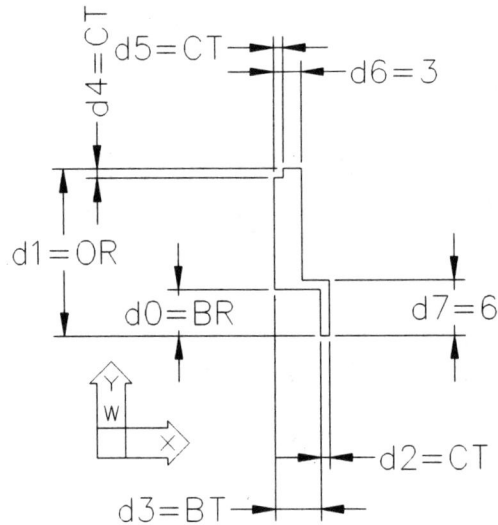

Figure 3.48 Fully constrained profile

You have fully constrained the profile. Set the current layer to SOLID. Apply the short cut key [8] to set to an isometric view. Then run the AMREVOLVE command to revolve the profile to form a solid feature. See Figure 3.49.

<Data>   **<Layers...>**

Command: **DDLMODES**
Current layer: **SOLID**

Command: **8**

<Parts>   **<Feature>**   **<Revolve...>**

Command: **AMREVOLVE**

[Termination: **Full**
 Operation: **Base**
OK   ]

Select revolution axis: **[Select B (Figure 3.47).]**

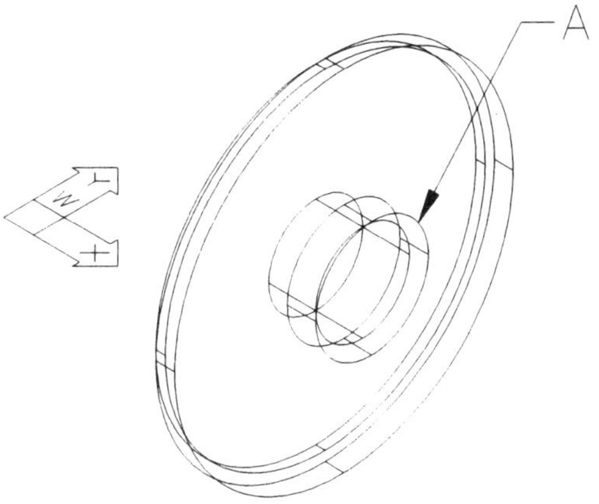

Figure 3.49 A solid of revolution created

There is a central hole in the solid feature. Apply the AMHOLE command to place a hole feature concentric with the model. See Figure 3.50.

\<Parts\>   **\<Feature\>**   **\<Hole...\>**

Command: **AMHOLE**

[Operation: **Drilled**
 Termination: **Through**
 Placement: **Concentric**
 Drill Size: **SH**
OK   ]

worldXy/worldYz/worldZx/Ucs/\<Select work plane or planar face\>: **[Select A (Figure 3.49).]**
Select concentric edge: **[Select A (Figure 3.49).]**

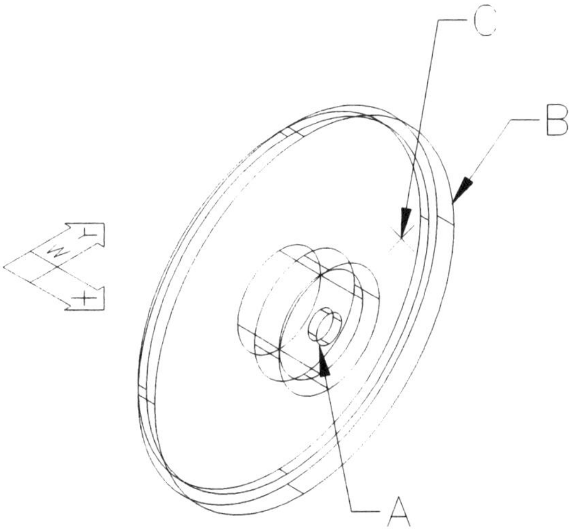

Figure 3.50 A hole placed centrally

Using the last hole as reference, apply the AMHOLE command to place a tapped hole on the face of the solid. Note once again that the threaded convention of the tapped hole will not show up in the model. See Figure 3.51.

<Parts>   **<Feature>**   **<Hole...>**

Command: **AMHOLE**

```
[Operation:              Drilled
Termination:             Through
Tapped...
    [Tapped Thread Options:   YES
        Major DIA:            2
        Thread Depth:
            Full Depth:       YES
    OK                                    ]
Placement:               From Hole
Drill Size:
    DIA:                 1.6
OK                                                  ]
```

worldXy/worldYz/worldZx/Ucs/<Select work plane or planar face>:**[Select A (Figure 3.50).]**
worldX/worldY/worldZ/<Select work axis or straight edge>: **WORLDY**
Rotate/Z-flip/<Accept>: **[Enter]**
Select x direction reference hole: **[Select B (Figure 3.50).]**
Select y direction reference hole/<Previous>: **P**
Select hole location: **[Select C (Figure 3.50).]**
Enter x distance: **PR**
Enter y distance: **0**

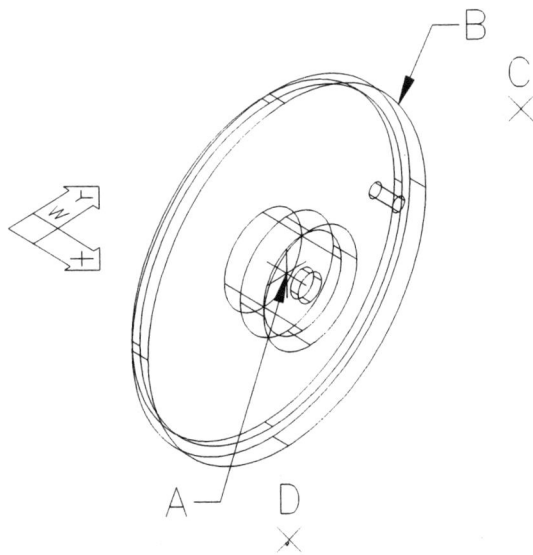

Figure 3.51 A tapped hole placed

There are four tapped holes in all; make a work point with the AMWORKPT command. Then use the AMPARDIM command to add two parametric dimensions to fully constrain the work point. See Figure 3.52.

<Parts>   **<Feature>**   **<Work Point>**

Command: **AMWORKPT**
Location on sketch plane: **[Select A (Figure 3.51).]**

<Parts>   **<Sketch>**   **<Add Dimension>**

Command: **AMPARDIM**
Select first object: **[Select A (Figure 3.51).]**
Select second object or place dimension: **[Select B (Figure 3.51).]**
Specify dimension placement: **[Select C (Figure 3.51).]**
Undo/Hor/Ver/Align/Par/Enter Dimension value: **0**

Select first object: **[Select A (Figure 3.51).]**
Select second object or place dimension: **[Select B (Figure 3.51).]**
Specify dimension placement: **[Select D (Figure 3.51).]**
Undo/Hor/Ver/Align/Par/Enter Dimension value: **0**

Solved fully constrained sketch.
Select first object: **[Enter]**

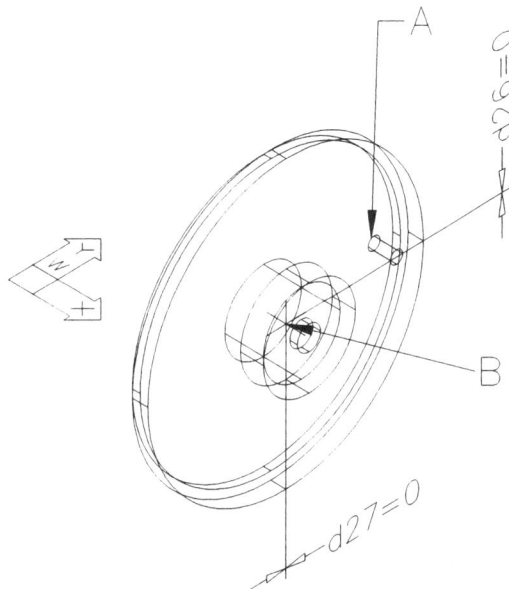

Figure 3.52 Work point fully constrained

Having fully constrained the work point, run the AMARRAY command to polar-array the tapped hole. See Figure 3.53.

<Parts>   **<Feature>**   **<Array...>**

Command: **AMARRAY**
Select feature: **[Select A (Figure 3.52).]**
Next/<Accept>: **[Accept, if the tapped hole is highlighted. Otherwise, Next.]**

[Array Type: **Polar**
 Polar:
     Number: **4**
     Spacing: **90**
OK   ]

Select work point: **[Select B (Figure 3.52).]**

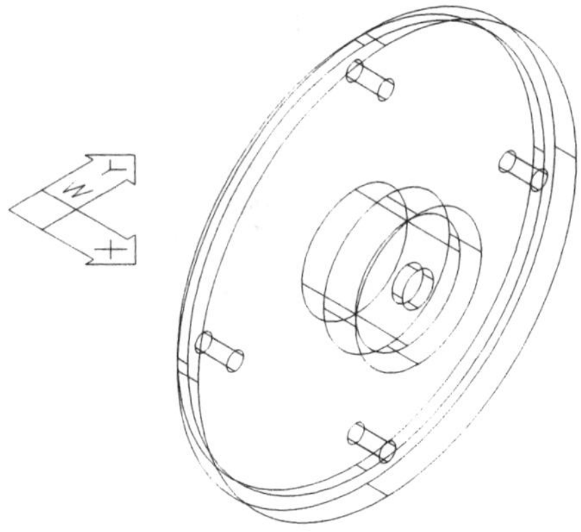

Figure 3.53 Front cap of the motor casing completed

You have completed the front cap of the electric motor casing. Use the QSAVE command to save your work.

<File>   **<Save...>**

Command: **QSAVE**

[File name: **MOTOR_1.DWG**
OK   ]

3.7   Rear Cap of the Motor Casing

See Figure 3.66. The rear cap of the electric motor casing consists of two sketched solid features and three placed hole features. The base solid feature is a solid of revolution. The second sketched solid feature is a solid of extrusion that intersects with the base solid feature. Run the NEW command to begin a new drawing. Use the same prototype drawing that you used for the front cap.

<File>   **<New...>**

Command: **NEW**

[Prototype...:   **PROTO_32**
OK   ]

Using the prototype drawing saves you a lot of preparation time. You may run the PLINE command to make a rough sketch. See Figure 3.54.

[**Draw**]   [**Polyline**]

Command: **PLINE**

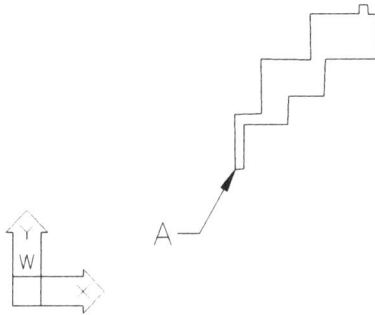

Figure 3.54 A rough sketch created

Apply the AMPROFILE command to resolve the rough sketch to form a profile for subsequently making a solid of revolution. Set the fix point at A with the AMFIXPT command, and the insertion base point at A with the BASE command. See Figure 3.55.

<**Parts**>   <**Sketch**>   <**Profile**>

Command: **AMPROFILE**
Select objects for sketch:
Select objects: **LAST**
Select objects: **[Enter]**

<**Parts**>   <**Sketch**>   <**Fix Point**>

Command: **AMFIXPT**
Specify new fixed point for sketch: **END** of **[Select A (Figure 3.54).]**

Command: **BASE**
Base point: **END** of **[Select A (Figure 3.54).]**

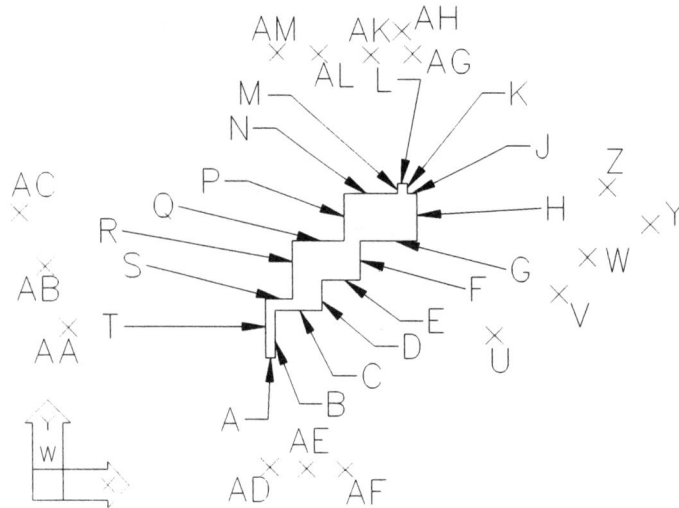

Figure 3.55 Resolved sketch

Apply the AMSHOWCON command to check the geometric constraints that AutoCAD Designer has applied for you automatically. Then run the AMADDCON command to add the necessary geometric constraints, and use the AMDELCON command to delete the irrelevant constraints.

<Parts>   **<Sketch>**   **<Constraints>**   **<Show>**

Command: **AMSHOWCON**
All/Select/Next/<eXit>: **ALL**
All/Select/Next/<eXit>: **[Enter]**

<Parts>   **<Sketch>**   **<Constraints>**   **<Add>**

Command: **AMADDCON**

[Horizontal constraint: **Apply to A, C, E, G, J, N, Q, and S (Figure 3.55).**
 Vertical constraint: **Apply to B, D, F, H, K, M, P, R, and T (Figure 3.55).**
Exit   ]

<Parts>   **<Sketch>**   **<Constraints>**   **<Delete>**

Command: **AMDELCON**
Size/All/<Select>: **[Select all the Collinear constraints.]**

After adding the necessary geometric constraints, import the set of global parameters from the external parameter file. Remember to link the parameters to the external file to keep their values up to date all the time.

<Parts>   **<Parameters...>**

Command: **AMPARAM**

[Parameter File:
    Import...
    [Select the file that you have output from the last component.]
OK   ]

Creating new global parameter : OR
    initial value : 18
Creating new global parameter : BR
    initial value : 5
Creating new global parameter : BT
    initial value : 5
Creating new global parameter : CT
    initial value : 1
Creating new global parameter : PR
    initial value : 14.5
Creating new global parameter : SH
    initial value : 3

Making use of the global parameters, run the AMPARDIM command to fully constrain the profile. See Figure 3.56.

    <Parts>   **<Sketch>**   **<Add Dimension>**

Command: **AMPARDIM**
Select first object: **[Select A (Figure 3.55).]**
Select second object or place dimension: **[Select C (Figure 3.55).]**
Specify dimension placement: **[Select U (Figure 3.55).]**
Undo/Hor/Ver/Align/Par/Enter Dimension value: **BR**

Select first object: **[Select A (Figure 3.55).]**
Select second object or place dimension: **[Select L (Figure 3.55).]**
Specify dimension placement: **[Select Y (Figure 3.55).]**
Undo/Hor/Ver/Align/Par/Enter Dimension value: **OR**

Select first object: **[Select A (Figure 3.55).]**
Select second object or place dimension: **[Select S (Figure 3.55).]**
Specify dimension placement: **[Select AA (Figure 3.55).]**
Undo/Hor/Ver/Align/Par/Enter Dimension value: **6**

Select first object: **[Select A (Figure 3.55).]**
Select second object or place dimension: **[Select Q (Figure 3.55).]**
Specify dimension placement: **[Select AB (Figure 3.55).]**
Undo/Hor/Ver/Align/Par/Enter Dimension value: **12**

Select first object: **[Select A (Figure 3.55).]**
Select second object or place dimension: **[Select N (Figure 3.55).]**
Specify dimension placement: **[Select AC (Figure 3.55).]**
Undo/Hor/Ver/Align/Par/Enter Dimension value: **17**

Select first object: **[Select A (Figure 3.55).]**
Select second object or place dimension: **[Select E (Figure 3.55).]**
Specify dimension placement: **[Select V (Figure 3.55).]**
Undo/Hor/Ver/Align/Par/Enter Dimension value: **8**
Select first object: **[Select A (Figure 3.55).]**
Select second object or place dimension: **[Select G (Figure 3.55).]**

Specify dimension placement: **[Select W (Figure 3.55).]**
Undo/Hor/Ver/Align/Par/Enter Dimension value: **12**

Select first object: **[Select J (Figure 3.55).]**
Select second object or place dimension: **[Select L (Figure 3.55).]**
Specify dimension placement: **[Select Z (Figure 3.55).]**
Undo/Hor/Ver/Align/Par/Enter Dimension value: **CT**

Select first object: **[Select H (Figure 3.55).]**
Select second object or place dimension: **[Select K (Figure 3.55).]**
Specify dimension placement: **[Select AG (Figure 3.55).]**
Undo/Hor/Ver/Align/Par/Enter Dimension value: **CT**

Select first object: **[Select K (Figure 3.55).]**
Select second object or place dimension: **[Select M (Figure 3.55).]**
Specify dimension placement: **[Select AH (Figure 3.55).]**
Undo/Hor/Ver/Align/Par/Enter Dimension value: **CT**

Select first object: **[Select M (Figure 3.55).]**
Select second object or place dimension: **[Select P (Figure 3.55).]**
Specify dimension placement: **[Select AK (Figure 3.55).]**
Undo/Hor/Ver/Align/Par/Enter Dimension value: **5.5**

Select first object: **[Select P (Figure 3.55).]**
Select second object or place dimension: **[Select R (Figure 3.55).]**
Specify dimension placement: **[Select AL (Figure 3.55).]**
Undo/Hor/Ver/Align/Par/Enter Dimension value: **5.5**

Select first object: **[Select R (Figure 3.55).]**
Select second object or place dimension: **[Select T (Figure 3.55).]**
Specify dimension placement: **[Select AM (Figure 3.55).]**
Undo/Hor/Ver/Align/Par/Enter Dimension value: **3**

Select first object: **[Select T (Figure 3.55).]**
Select second object or place dimension: **[Select B (Figure 3.55).]**
Specify dimension placement: **[Select AD (Figure 3.55).]**
Undo/Hor/Ver/Align/Par/Enter Dimension value: **CT**

Select first object: **[Select B (Figure 3.55).]**
Select second object or place dimension: **[Select D (Figure 3.55).]**
Specify dimension placement: **[Select AE (Figure 3.55).]**
Undo/Hor/Ver/Align/Par/Enter Dimension value: **BT**

Select first object: **[Select D (Figure 3.55).]**
Select second object or place dimension: **[Select F (Figure 3.55).]**
Specify dimension placement: **[Select AF (Figure 3.55).]**
Undo/Hor/Ver/Align/Par/Enter Dimension value: **4**

Solved fully constrained sketch
Select first object: **[Enter]**

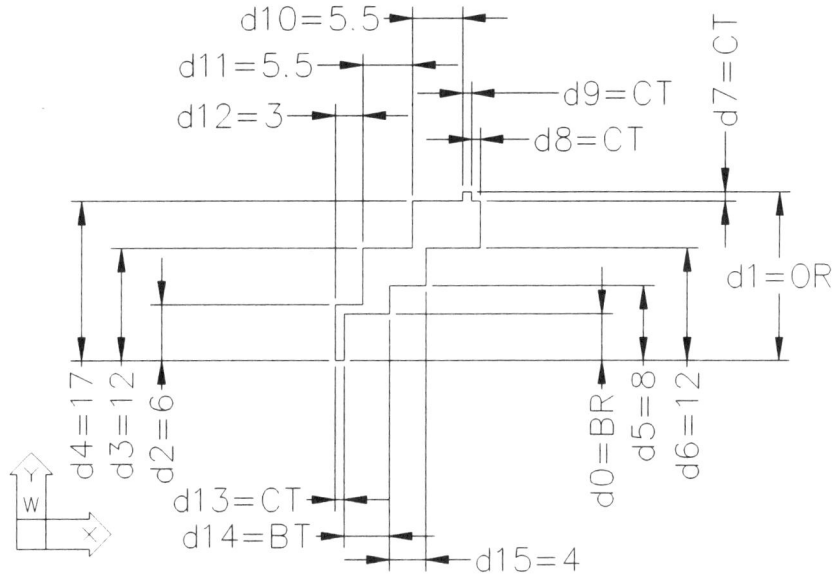

Figure 3.56 Fully constrained profile

You have fully constrained the profile with geometric constraints and parametric dimensions. Set the current layer to SOLID. Apply the VPOINT command to set the display to an isometric view. Then run the AMREVOLVE command to make a solid of revolution from the fully constrained profile. See Figure 3.57.

<Data> **<Layers...>**

Command: **DDLMODES**
Current layer: **SOLID**

<View> **<3D Viewpoint>** **<Vector>**

Command: **VPOINT**
Rotate/<View point> <1.0000,-1.0000,1.0000>: **R**
Enter angle in XY plane from X axis: **225**
Enter angle from XY plane: **25**

<Parts> **<Feature>** **<Revolve...>**

Command: **AMREVOLVE**
Select revolution axis: **[Select A (Figure 3.56).]**

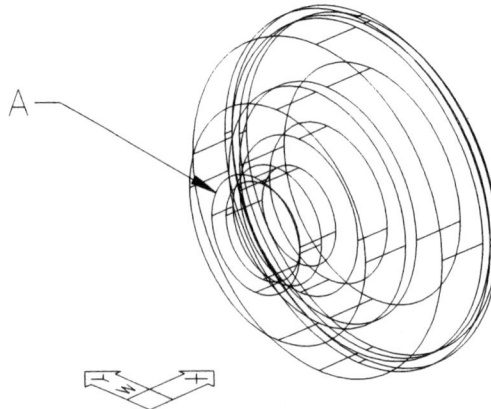

Figure 3.57 A solid of revolution created

You have created a solid of revolution from a fully constrained profile. It is the base solid feature of this component. Before making the second sketched solid feature, use the AMHOLE command to place a hole. See Figure 3.58.

\<Parts\>   **\<Feature\>**   **\<Hole...\>**

Command: **AMHOLE**

[Operation: **Drilled**
 Termination: **Through**
 Placement: **Concentric**
 Drill Size: **SH**
OK   ]

worldXy/worldYz/worldZx/Ucs/\<Select work plane or planar face\>: **[Select A (Figure 3.57).]**
Select concentric edge: **[Select A (Figure 3.57).]**

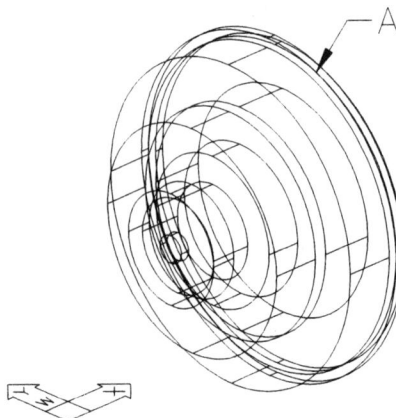

Figure 3.58 A hole placed concentrically

Having added a hole feature, you will build the second sketched solid feature. To create the second sketched solid feature, you need two construction features: a work axis and a work plane.

Run the AMWORKAXIS command to create a work axis. Then use the AMWORKPLN command to create a work plane. Set the sketch plane to the new work plane. See Figure 3.59.

<Parts>   **<Feature>**   **<Work Axis>**

Command: **AMWORKAXIS**
Select cylinder/cone/torus: **[Select A (Figure 3.58).]**

<Parts>   **<Feature>**   **<Work Plane...>**

Command: **AMWORKPLN**

[1st Modifier: **On Edge/Axis**
 2nd Modifier: **Planar Parallel**
 Create Sketch Plane: **YES**
 OK   ]

worldX/worldY/worldZ/<Select work axis or straight edge>: **[Select the newly created work axis.]**
worldXy/worldYz/worldZx/Ucs/<Select work plane or planar face>: **UCS**
worldX/worldY/worldZ/<Select work axis or straight edge>: **[Select the newly created work axis.]**
Rotate/Z-flip/<Accept>: **[Enter]**

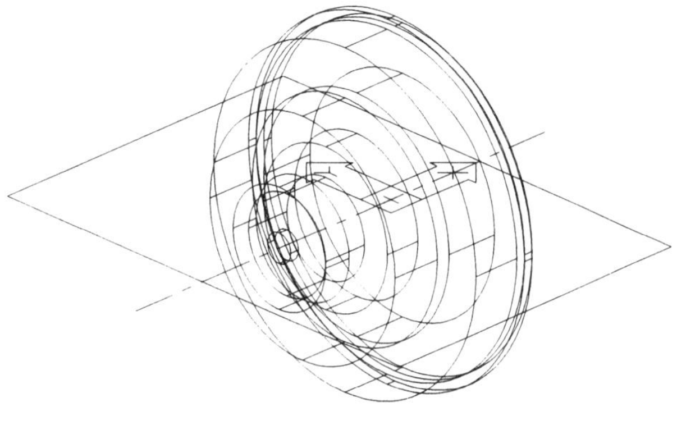

Figure 3.59 A work axis and a work plane created

Return to a plan view. Set the current layer to SKETCH with the DDLMODES command. Then make a sketch with the PLINE command. See Figure 3.60. You will use this sketch to create a solid of extrusion. This solid will intersect with the base feature.

Command: **5**

<Data>   **<Layers...>**

Command: **DDLMODES**
Current Layer: **SKETCH**

[Draw]   [Polyline]

Command: **PLINE**

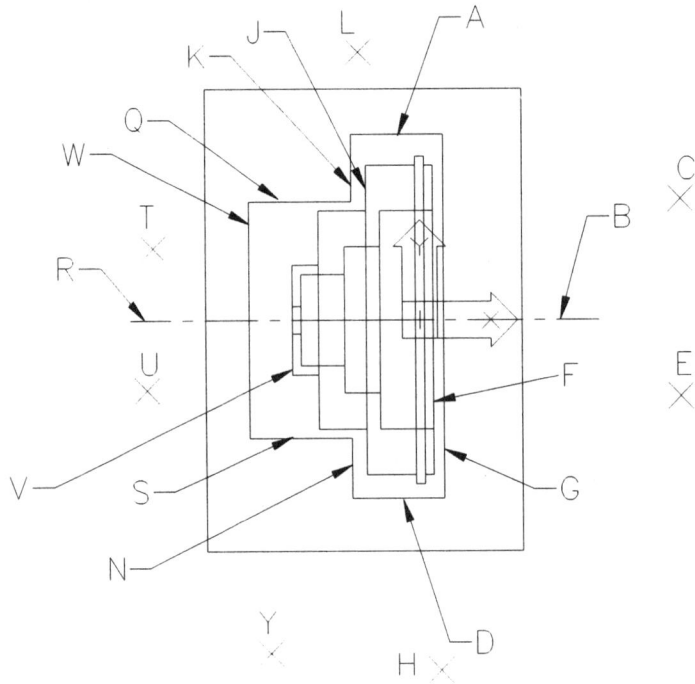

Figure 3.60 A sketch created

Resolve the rough sketch to form a profile with the AMPROFILE command. After resolution, run the AMADDCON command to finish the geometric constraints, and use the AMPARDIM command to add parametric dimensions. See Figure 3.61.

<Parts>   <Sketch>   <Profile>

Command: **AMPROFILE**
Select objects for sketch:
Select objects: **LAST**
Select objects: **[Enter]**

<Parts>   <Sketch>   <Constraints>   <Add>

Command: **AMADDCON**

[Horizontal constraint: **Apply to B, K, N, and W (Figure 3.60).**
 Vertical constraint: **Apply to A, Q, S, and D (Figure 3.60).**
 Collinear constraint: **Apply to K and N (Figure 3.60).**
 Exit   ]

<Parts>   **<Sketch>**   **<Add Dimension>**

Command: **AMPARDIM**
Select first object: **[Select A (Figure 3.60).]**
Select second object or place dimension: **[Select B (Figure 3.60).]**
Specify dimension placement: **[Select C (Figure 3.60).]**
Undo/Hor/Ver/Align/Par/Enter Dimension value: **OR**

Select first object: **[Select B (Figure 3.60).]**
Select second object or place dimension: **[Select D (Figure 3.60).]**
Specify dimension placement: **[Select E (Figure 3.60).]**
Undo/Hor/Ver/Align/Par/Enter Dimension value: **OR**

Select first object: **[Select F (Figure 3.60).]**
Select second object: **[Select G (Figure 3.60).]**
Specify dimension placement: **[Select H (Figure 3.60).]**
Undo/Hor/Ver/Align/Par/Enter Dimension value: **0**

Select first object: **[Select J (Figure 3.60).]**
Select second object: **[Select K (Figure 3.60).]**
Specify dimension placement: **[Select L (Figure 3.60).]**
Undo/Hor/Ver/Align/Par/Enter Dimension value: **0**

Select first object: **[Select Q (Figure 3.60).]**
Select second object: **[Select R (Figure 3.60).]**
Specify dimension placement: **[Select T (Figure 3.60).]**
Undo/Hor/Ver/Align/Par/Enter Dimension value: **6**

Select first object: **[Select R (Figure 3.60).]**
Select second object or place dimension: **[Select S (Figure 3.60).]**
Specify dimension placement: **[Select U (Figure 3.60).]**
Undo/Hor/Ver/Align/Par/Enter Dimension value: **6**

Select first object: **[Select V (Figure 3.60).]**
Select second object or place dimension: **[Select W (Figure 3.60).]**
Specify dimension placement: **[Select Y (Figure 3.60).]**
Undo/Hor/Ver/Align/Par/Enter Dimension value: **0**

Solved fully constrained sketch.
Select first object: **[Enter]**

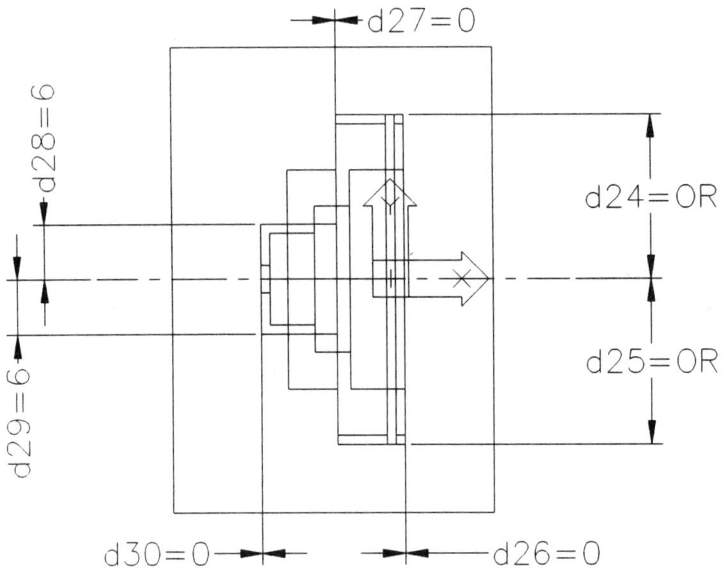

Figure 3.61 Fully constrained profile

You have fully constrained the second sketch. Set back to an isometric view with the VPOINT command. Then issue the AMEXTRUDE command to extrude the resolved sketch and to intersect with the base solid feature. See Figure 3.62.

<View>   **<3D Viewpoint>**   **<Vector>**

Command: **VPOINT**
Rotate/<View point> <1.0000,-1.0000,1.0000>: **R**
Enter angle in XY plane from X axis: **225**
Enter angle from XY plane: **25**

<Parts>   **<Feature>**   **<Extrude...>**

Command: **AMEXTRUDE**

[Termination: **Mid Plane**
 Operation: **Intersect**
 Size:
    Distance: **2*OR**
    Draft Angle: **0**
OK   ]

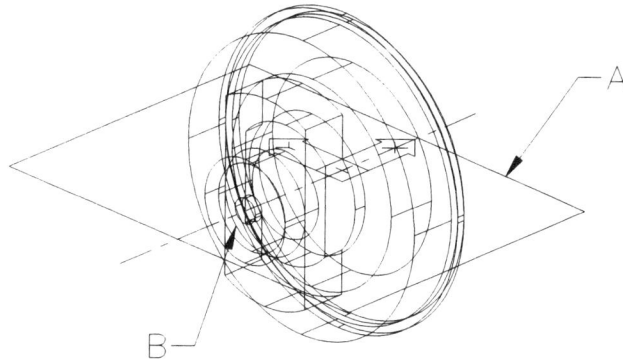

Figure 3.62 Second sketched solid feature intersected with the base solid feature

You have completed two sketched solid features of the rear cap of the electric motor casing. To complete the model, you need to add two more placed solid features.

Before making these features, turn off the display of the current work plane by using the AMPLNDSP command, and make a work point with the AMWORKPT command. See Figure 3.63.

```
<Parts>            <Display>          <Work Plane>        <Off>

Command: AMPLNDSP
Display/ON/<OFf>: OFF
Select/<All>: SELECT
Select work planes to hide:
Select objects: [Select A (Figure 3.62).]
Select objects: [Enter]


<Parts>           <Feature>         <Work Point>

Command: AMWORKPT
Location on sketch plane: [Select B (Figure 3.62).]
```

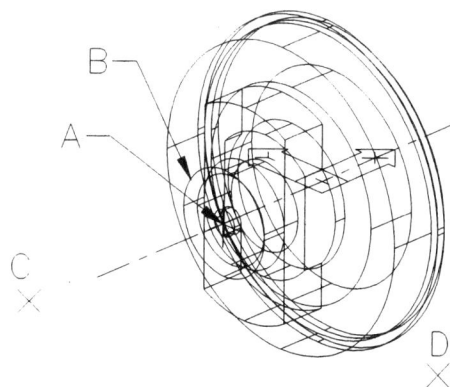

Figure 3.63 A work point created

Before you can use the work point as the center of polar array, you have to fully constrain it. Run the AMPARDIM command. See Figure 3.64.

<Parts>   **<Sketch>**   **<Add Dimension>**

Command: **AMPARDIM**
Select first object: **[Select A (Figure 3.63).]**
Select second object or place dimension: **[Select B (Figure 3.63).]**
Specify dimension placement: **[Select C (Figure 3.63).]**
Undo/Hor/Ver/Align/Par/Enter Dimension value: **0**

Select first object: **[Select A (Figure 3.63).]**
Select second object or place dimension: **[Select B (Figure 3.63).]**
Specify dimension placement: **[Select D (Figure 3.63).]**
Undo/Hor/Ver/Align/Par/Enter Dimension value: **0**

Solved fully constrained sketch.
Select first object: **[Enter]**

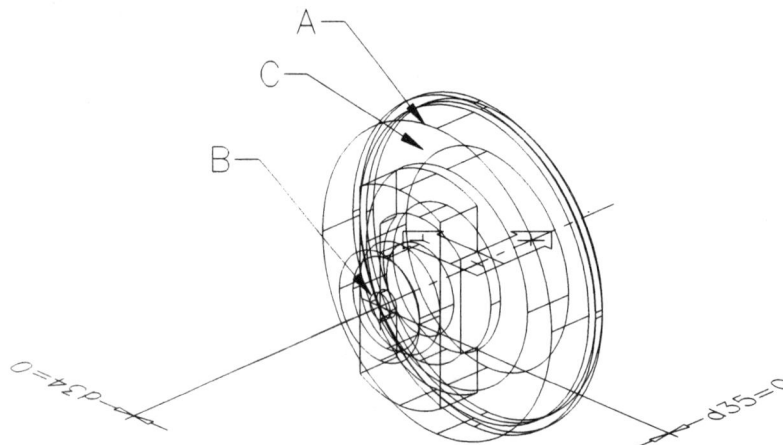

Figure 3.64 Work point fully constrained

Using the central hole as reference, run the AMHOLE command to add a hole. See Figure 3.65.

<Parts>   **<Feature>**   **<Hole...>**

Command: **AMHOLE**

[Operation: **Drilled**
 Termination: **Through**
 Placement: **From Hole**
 Drill Size:
   Dia: **SH**
OK   ]

worldXy/worldYz/worldZx/Ucs/<Select work plane or planar face>: **[Select A (Figure 3.64).]**
worldX/worldY/worldZ/<Select work axis or straight edge>: **WORLDY**
Rotate/Z-flip/<Accept>: **[R, if the Y axis direction is not pointing upward.]**
Rotate/Z-flip/<Accept>: **[Z, if the X axis direction is not pointing to the right.]**
Rotate/Z-flip/<Accept>: **[Accept, if the Y axis direction is pointing upward, and the X axis direction is pointing to the right.]**
Select x direction reference hole: **[Select B (Figure 3.64).]**
Select y direction reference hole/<Previous>: **[Enter]**
Select hole location: **[Select C (Figure 3.64).]**
Enter x distance: **0**
Enter y distance: **PR**

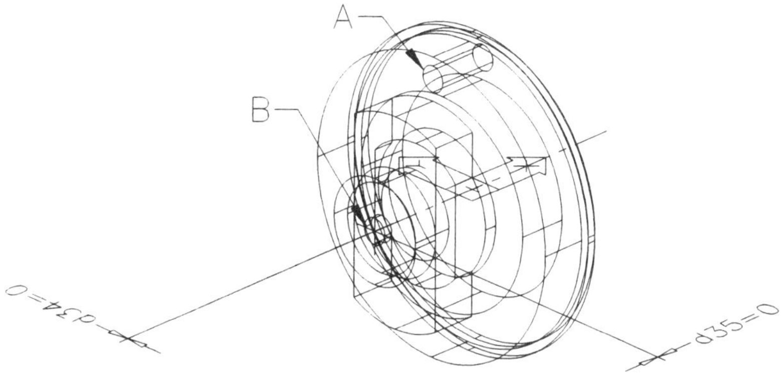

Figure 3.65 A hole placed

You have placed a hole feature on one of the faces of the solid part. To complete the model, run the AMARRAY command and use the work point as the center of the polar array to create one more hole. See Figure 3.66.

<Parts>   **<Feature>**   **<Array...>**

Command: **AMARRAY**
Select feature: **[Select A (Figure 3.65).]**
Next/<Accept>: **[Accept, if the last hole is highlighted. Otherwise, Next.]**

[Array Type: **Polar**
 Polar:
     Number: **2**
     Spacing: **180**
OK   ]

Select work point: **[Select B (Figure 3.65).]**

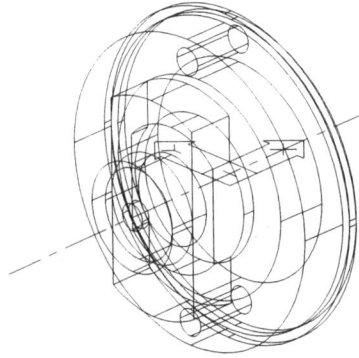

Figure 3.66 Placed hole arrayed

You have completed the rear cap of the electric motor casing. Run the QSAVE command to save it to a file.

<File>   **<Save...>**

Command: **QSAVE**

[File name: **MOTOR_2.DWG**
OK   ]

3.8   Motor Casing Main Body

The main body consists of a base solid feature only. You will make a rough sketch on the XY plane of the current UCS. Then you will resolve it and fully constrain it. Finally, you will revolve it about an axis.

Apply the NEW command to start a new drawing. Use the last prototype drawing.

<File>   **<New...>**

Command: **NEW**

[Prototype...:   **PROTO_32**
OK   ]

Make a rough sketch using the PLINE command and the LINE command. Then change the line type property of the line so that AutoCAD Designer will recognize it as a construction line. See Figure 3.67.

[Draw]   **[Polyline]**

Command: **PLINE**

[Draw]   **[Line]**

Command: **LINE**

<Edit>   <Properties...>

Select objects: **LAST**
Select objects: **[Enter]**

[Properties
Linetype...   **HIDDEN**
OK   ]

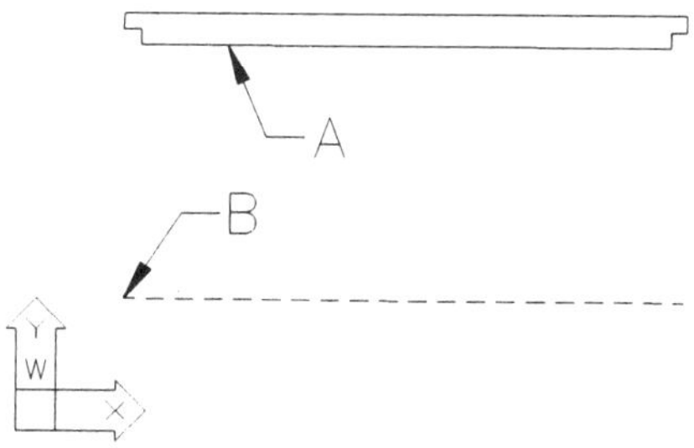

Figure 3.67 A rough sketch created

Resolve the rough sketch, including the hidden line, by applying the AMPROFILE command. The continuous line will become the profile for subsequently making a solid feature. The hidden line will become a construction line. You will use this line as the axis when making the solid of revolution.

<Parts>   <Sketch>   <Profile>

Command: **AMPROFILE**
Select objects for sketch:
Select objects: **[Select A and B (Figure 3.67).]**
Select objects: **[Enter]**

Set the fix point and the insertion base point at B with the AMFIXPT command and the BASE command, respectively. See Figure 3.68.

<Parts>   <Sketch>   <Fix Point>

Command: **AMFIXPT**
Specify new fixed point for sketch: **END** of **[Select B (Figure 3.67).]**

Command: **BASE**
Base point: **END** of **[Select B (Figure 3.67).]**

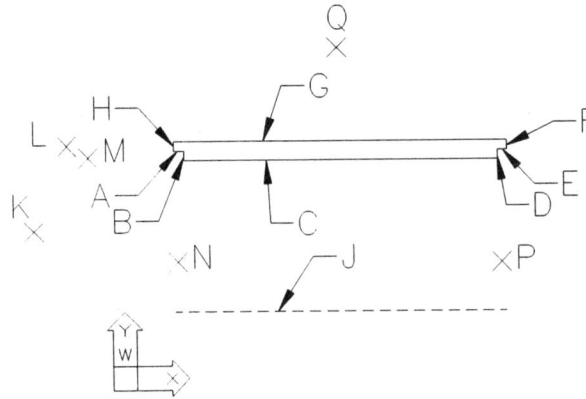

Figure 3.68 Rough sketch resolved

Execute the AMADDCON command to add the necessary geometric constraints to the profile.

<Parts>   <Sketch>   <Constraints>   <Add>

Command: **AMADDCON**

[Horizontal constraint: **Apply to G, A, C, E, and J (Figure 3.68).**
 Vertical constraint: **Apply to H, B, D, and F (Figure 3.68).**
 Collinear constraint: **Apply to A and E (Figure 3.68).**
 Exit   ]

After adding the geometric constraints, execute the AMPARAM command to import the set of global parameters from the external parameter file.

Then fully constrain the profile by adding parametric dimensions with the AMPARDIM command. See Figure 3.69.

<Parts>   <Parameters...>

Command: **AMPARAM**
Creating new global parameter : OR
        initial value : 18
Creating new global parameter : BR
        initial value : 5
Creating new global parameter : BT
        initial value : 5
Creating new global parameter : CT
        initial value : 1
Creating new global parameter : PR
        initial value : 14.5
Creating new global parameter : MR
        initial value : 13
Creating new global parameter : SH
        initial value : 3

<Parts>   <Sketch>   <Add Dimension>

Command: **AMPARDIM**
Select first object: **[Select G (Figure 3.68).]**
Select second object or place dimension: **[Select J (Figure 3.68).]**
Specify dimension placement: **[Select K (Figure 3.68).]**
Undo/Hor/Ver/Align/Par/Enter Dimension value: **OR**

Select first object: **[Select G (Figure 3.68).]**
Select second object or place dimension: **[Select A (Figure 3.68).]**
Specify dimension placement: **[Select L (Figure 3.68).]**
Undo/Hor/Ver/Align/Par/Enter Dimension value: **CT**

Select first object: **[Select A (Figure 3.68).]**
Select second object or place dimension: **[Select C (Figure 3.68).]**
Specify dimension placement: **[Select M (Figure 3.68).]**
Undo/Hor/Ver/Align/Par/Enter Dimension value: **CT**

Select first object: **[Select H (Figure 3.68).]**
Select second object or place dimension: **[Select B (Figure 3.68).]**
Specify dimension placement: **[Select N (Figure 3.68).]**
Undo/Hor/Ver/Align/Par/Enter Dimension value: **CT**

Select first object: **[Select D (Figure 3.68).]**
Select second object or place dimension: **[Select F (Figure 3.68).]**
Specify dimension placement: **[Select P (Figure 3.68).]**
Undo/Hor/Ver/Align/Par/Enter Dimension value: **CT**

Select first object: **[Select H (Figure 3.68).]**
Select second object or place dimension: **[Select F (Figure 3.68).]**
Specify dimension placement: **[Select Q (Figure 3.68).]**
Undo/Hor/Ver/Align/Par/Enter Dimension value: **36**

Solved fully constrained sketch.
Select first object: **[Enter]**

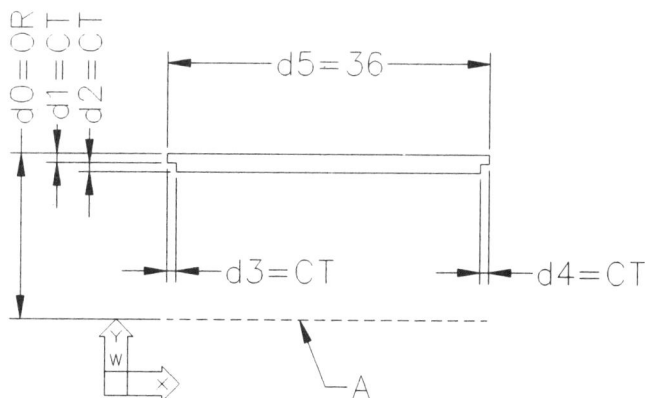

Figure 3.69 Profile fully constrained

After fully constraining the profile, set the current layer to SOLID by running the DDLMODES command.

<Data>   <Layers...>

Command: **DDLMODES**
Current Layer: **SOLID**

Set to an isometric view with the short cut key [8]. Then execute the AMREVOLVE command to create the solid feature. See Figure 3.70.

Command: **8**

<Parts>   <Feature>   <Revolve...>

Command: **AMREVOLVE**

[Termination: **Full**
 Operation: **Base**
OK   ]

Select revolution axis: **[Select A (Figure 3.69).]**

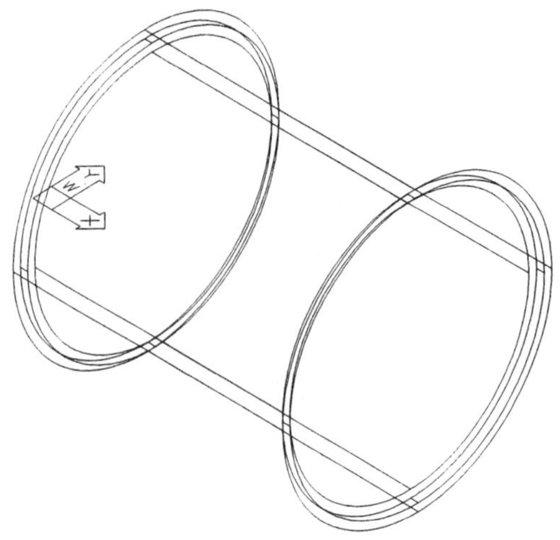

Figure 3.70 Main body completed

You have completed the third solid part of the electric motor casing. Run the QSAVE command to save your drawing.

<File>   <Save...>

Command: **QSAVE**

[File name: **MOTOR_3.DWG**
OK   ]

Like the first set of solid parts that you created earlier in this chapter, you will assemble the solid parts of the electric motor casing in the next chapter.

3.9   Solid Parts Utilities

Before proceeding to the next chapter to assemble the solid parts created in this chapter, run the AMLISTPART command to gain information about the active solid part.

   <Parts>   **<Utilities>**   **<List>**

Command: AMLISTPART
Part/<Feature>: PART
ALI/Select/<ACtive>: ACTIVE
Handle = 45
   Bounding Box: Lower Bound X = 0.0000 , Y = -18.0000 , Z = -18.0000
       Upper Bound X = 36.0000 , Y = 18.0000 , Z = 18.0000
Features :
Closed profile
Revolution Full
Work axis Centerline
Part is active.

   <Parts>   **<Utilities>**   **<List>**

Command: **AMLISTPART**
Part/<Feature>: **FEATURE**
Select feature:
Children/Parents/<List>: **CHILDREN**
Revolution Full
Operation: Base
Work axis Centerline
Press <ENTER> to continue: **[Enter]**

   <Parts>   **<Utilities>**   **<List>**

Command: **AMLISTPART**
Part/<Feature>: **FEATURE**
Select feature:
Children/Parents/<List>: **PARENTS**
Revolution Full
Operation: Base
Closed profile
Press <ENTER> to continue: **[Enter]**

A solid part contains edge data, surface data, and volume data. You may make use of a solid part to determine the mass properties of a part. Apply the AMPARTPROP command. See Figure 3.71.

   <Parts>   **<Utilities>**   **<Mass Properties>**

Command: **AMPARTPROP**

```
┌─────────────────────────────────────────────────────────────────────┐
│                          Part Properties                             │
├─────────────────────────────────────────────────────────────────────┤
│ Density:  1            Moments of Inertia      Mass * Moments of Inertia
│                                                                      
│ Mass:          7483.27   Ix: 2.36352e+006      MIx:1.76869e+010     
│ Volume:        7483.27   Iy: 4.85402e+006      MIy:3.6324e+010      
│ Surface Area: 8130.44    Iz: 5.04376e+006      MIz:3.77439e+010     
│ Centroid                 Products of Inertia    Radii of Gyration    
│  x:  20.0225             Ixy:754484             kx: 17.7719          
│  y:  5.03546             Ixz:-1.20749e-010      ky: 25.4686          
│  z:  -1.93893e-015       Iyz:-1.18536e-011      kz: 25.9616          
│ Principal Axes                                  Principal Moments    
│  i:  1          0         0                      Ii: 2.17378e+006    
│  j:  0          1         0                      Ij: 1.85396e+006    
│  k:  0          0         1                      Ik: 1.85396e+006    
│                                                                      
│ Write to File...                                                     
│                       [ OK ]   [ Cancel ]   [ Help... ]             
└─────────────────────────────────────────────────────────────────────┘
```

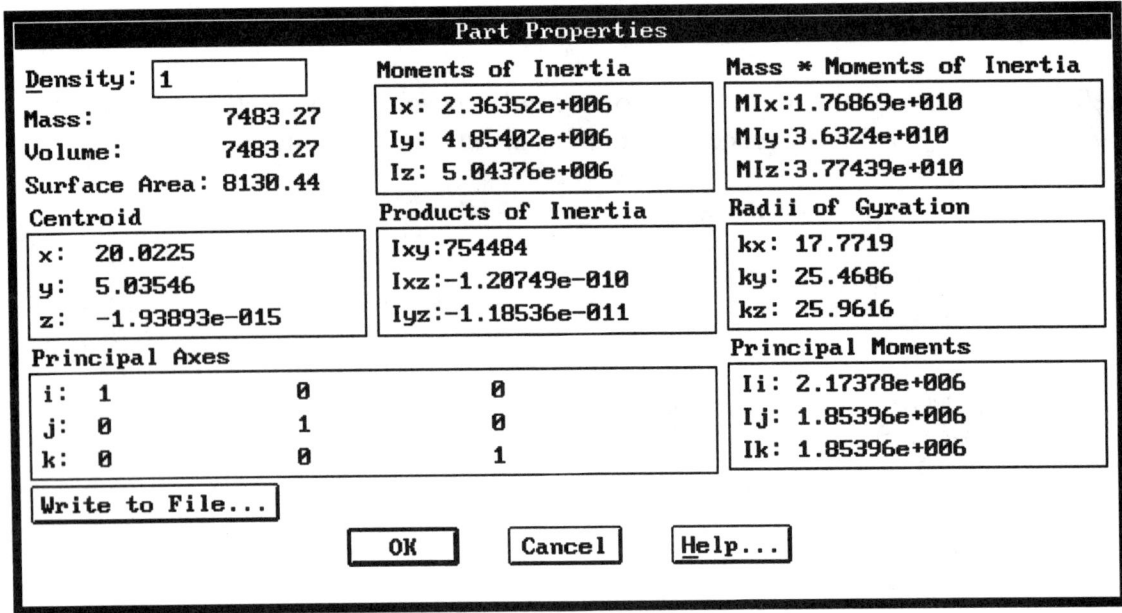

Figure 3.71 Dialog box of the AMPARTPROP command

The solid parts that you have created are parametric and are dimension-driven. You may edit their features as well as their dimensions. If for any reason you want to freeze the solid part such that it cannot be edited, you may convert it to a static base feature by running the AMMAKEBASE command.

<Parts>   **<Utilities>**   **<Make Base>**

Command: **AMMAKEBASE**
Drawing view information and ability to edit existing features will be lost.
Create base from highlighted part ? No/<Yes>: **N**

If you respond YES to the above command prompt, the parametric data of the solid will be lost. Although you cannot edit it any more, you may still add additional features to it. The resulting solid is similar to a solid converted from a native solid by running the AMNEWPART command.

Do not save your drawing. Instead, apply the QUIT command.

<File>   **<Exit>**

Command: **QUIT**

3.10 Summary

In addition to the commands that you learned in Chapter 2, you have applied the following AutoCAD Designer commands to create parametric solid models in this chapter.

Solid part management commands:

AMACTPART   AMMAKEBASE   AMNEWPART

Global parameter command:

AMPARAM

Solid features creation commands:

AMPATH   AMSWEEP   AMREVOLVE

Utility commands:

AMLISTPART   AMPARTPROP

For a brief explanation of these commands, refer to the appendix of this book.

By now, you should be able to make extruded, revolved, and swept solid features from rough sketches; to compose complex solid parts by joining, cutting, and intersecting sketched solid features; to add placed solid features; to make use of construction features in model building; and to set up global parameters.

To reiterate, you begin from rough sketches. AutoCAD Designer resolves the rough sketch to form a profile, a path, or a cutting line. You will learn how to apply a cutting line to produce an offset section in Chapter 5. You should fully constrain the resolved sketch by adding geometric constraints and parametric dimensions.

There are two types of features — solid features and construction features. Solid features include sketched solid features and placed solid features. You may create sketched solid features by extruding, revolving, and sweeping. Placed solid features are fillets, chamfers and holes. You may simply place them on the solid parts. To set up a parametric relationship between solid features, you may use construction features. Work planes, work axes, and work points are construction features.

In this chapter, you created two sets of solid parts. The first set consists of the parts for a universal joint. You have saved them in a single drawing file. The second set consists of the parts for an electric motor casing. You saved them in separate files. Besides modeling, you also worked on solid part utilities.

In the next chapter, you will learn how to create assembly and sub-assembly. You will assemble parts from a single file and parts from separate files.

3.11 Exercises

To further enhance your knowledge on parametric solid modeling, you will make the following models on your own.

Figure 3.72 shows the solid model of the clamp bar of the toggle clamp assembly. It consists of two sketched solid features and one placed solid feature.

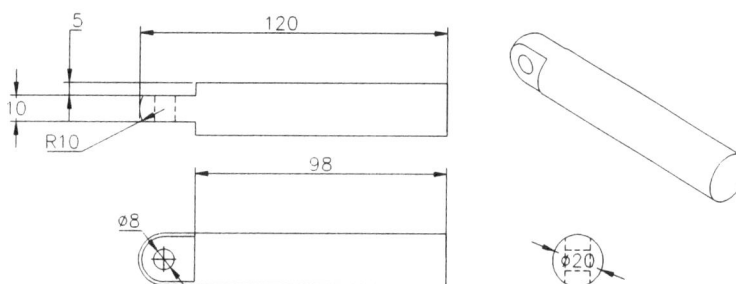

Figure 3.72 The clamp bar

To build the model, you should make a rough sketch A (Figure 3.73). Convert it to a profile, fully constrain it, and extrude it to form the base solid feature. Then you should place a hole feature on it. To complete the model, you should create the second sketch B (Figure 3.73), fully constrain it, revolve it, and intersect the revolved solid with the base solid. Save the file named CLAMP.DWG.

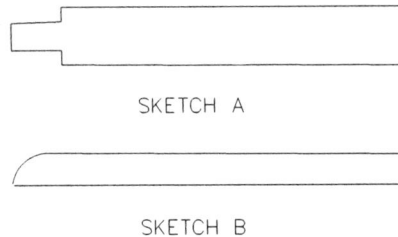

SKETCH A

SKETCH B

Figure 3.73 The two rough sketches required

Figure 3.74 shows two swivel pins of the toggle clamp assembly. The two pins are similar in shape but differ in length.

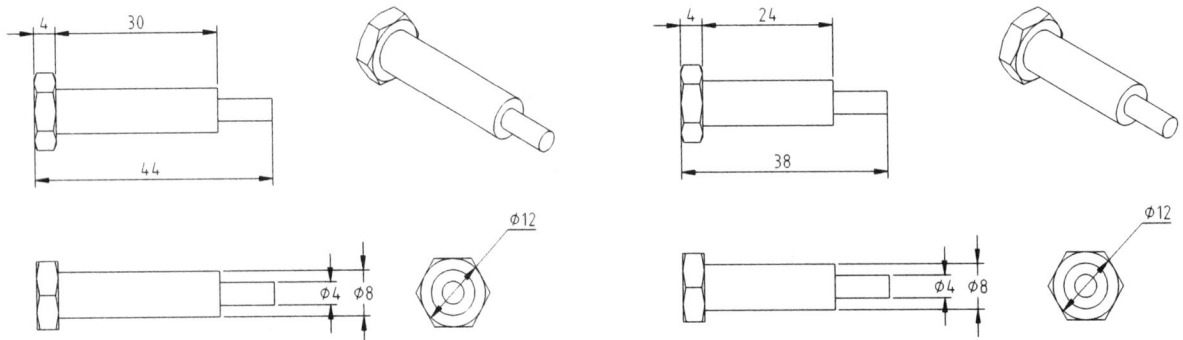

Figure 3.74 The swivel pins

Refer to the dimensions of the pin (left of Figure 3.74). Make a rough sketch A (Figure 3.75), fully constrain it, and revolve it to form a base solid feature.

Set up a parametric work plane on the left end face of the base solid that is perpendicular to the axis of rotation. Then produce a rough sketch corresponding to sketch B (Figure 3.75). Fully constrain it, extrude it to form a solid, and intersect the extruded solid with the base solid. The first pin is completed. Save the file named PIN1.DWG.

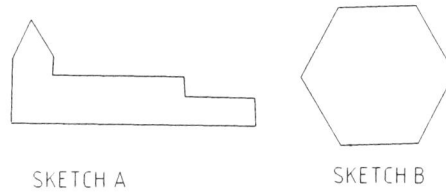

SKETCH A   SKETCH B

Figure 3.75 The rough sketches

Save to another file named PIN2.DWG. Edit the length dimension (See Figure 3.74), and update the drawing. Save the file again.

Chapter 4
Assembly Modeling

In the last two chapters, you learned how to create dimension-driven parametric solid models from rough sketches. In Chapter 2, you created two solid parts. In Chapter 3, you created two sets of solid parts. To maintain a dimensional relationship between the solid parts in a file, and across a number of files, you established global parameters and a global parameter file. By now, you should be able to recognize and create two types of features: solid features and construction features. The solid features are sketched solid features and placed solid features. The construction features are work planes, work axes, and work points.

With the two sets of solid parts prepared in Chapter 3, you will learn how to form assemblies and sub-assemblies in this chapter and how to prepare an exploded view in the next chapter.

The first assembly is a universal joint. It consists of four distinctive solid parts, which you created in a single drawing file. Figure 4.1 shows the assembly.

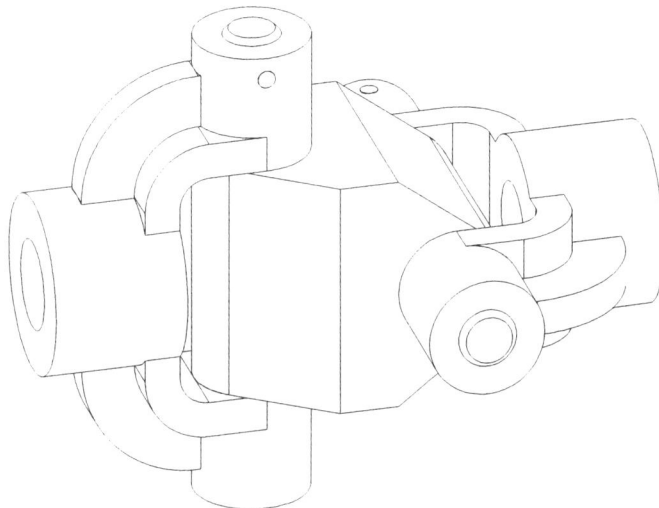

Figure 4.1 The universal joint assembly

The second assembly is an electric motor casing. It has three solid parts; you put them in separate files. Figure 4.2 is the assembly.

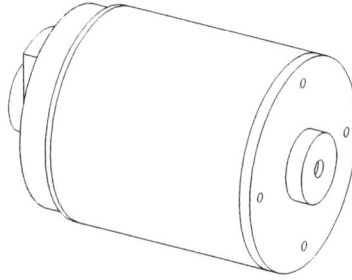

Figure 4.2 The electric motor casing assembly

4.1   Creating Component Definitions from Solid Parts

You should have completed Chapter 3 before you start working on this chapter. If you have not done so, you should go back to Chapter 3.

Run the OPEN command to retrieve the drawing of the universal joint, "U_JOINT". If you have saved your file under a different file name, you should replace "U_JOINT" with your file name in the following delineation.

    \<File\>   **\<Open...\>**

    Command: **OPEN**

    [File name: **U_JOINT.DWG**
    OK   ]

Alternatively, you may run the NEW command and use the saved file of the universal joint as the prototype drawing.

    \<File\>   **\<New...\>**

    Command: **NEW**

    [Prototype... : **U_JOINT.DWG**
    OK   ]

In a solid part, there are construction features as well as solid features. The construction features are work planes, work axes, and work points. These construction features are useful not only in the course of making the solid part but also during the process of assembly. You may use them as reference objects.

Run the AMAXISDSP command to turn on the display of the work axes. Then use the AMWORKAXIS command to create work axes on all the circular features. You should use the AMACTPART command to select a part to make it active before you create work axes on it.

    \<Parts\>   **\<Display\>**   **\<Work Axis\>**   **\<On\>**

    Command: **AMAXISDSP**
    ON/\<OFf\>: **ON**

<Parts>   **<Part>**   **<Make Active>**

Command: **AMACTPART**
Select Part: **[Select a solid part.]**

<Parts>   **<Display>**   **<Work Axis>**   **<On>**

Command: **AMWORKAXIS**
Select cylinder/cone/torus: **[Select a circular feature.]**
Next/<Accept>: **[Enter]**

Check your drawing against Figure 4.3. Create and display all the work axes.

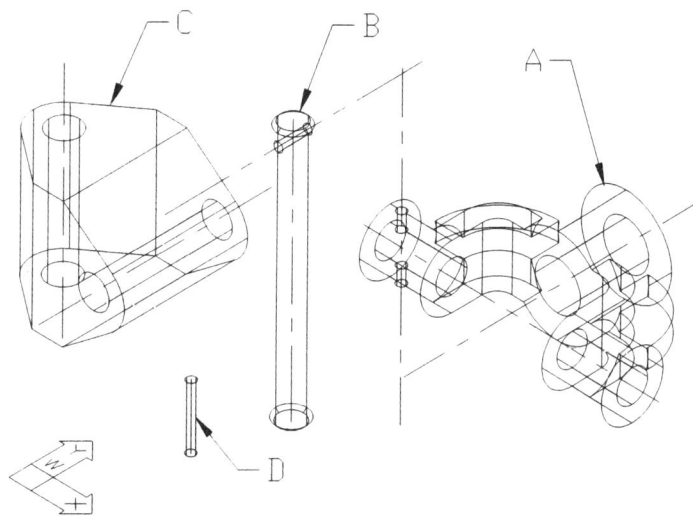

Figure 4.3 Work axes created and displayed

To start the assembly process, you have to put the solid parts into memory as component definitions. Run the AMNEW command on the main body of the universal joint.

<Assemblies>   **<Component Definition>**   **<Create...>**

Command: **AMNEW**

```
┌─────────────────────────────────────────────┐
│ Create Component                             │
│   ┌─ Components ─────────────────────┐       │
│   │ ⊙ Parts                          │       │
│   │                                  │       │
│   │ ○ SubAssembly                    │       │
│   └──────────────────────────────────┘       │
│                  □ Externalize               │
│                  ☑ Auto-Insert               │
│    ┌─────────┐   ┌─────────┐   ┌─────────┐   │
│    │   OK    │   │ Cancel  │   │ Help... │   │
│    └─────────┘   └─────────┘   └─────────┘   │
└─────────────────────────────────────────────┘
```

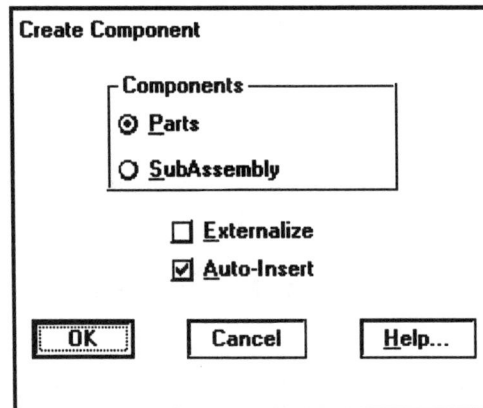

[Component: **Parts**
 Externalize: **NO**
 Auto-Insert: **YES**
OK   ]

Select base part: **[Select A (Figure 4.3).]**
Name for new component: **MAIN**
Select next part: **[Enter]**

The AMNEW command enables you to create component definitions from solid parts or to initialize sub-assemblies. You will work on both in this assembly.

Using the AMNEW command to create a component definition from a solid part is similar to making a block with the BLOCK command. You will select a solid part to put it into memory as a component definition. You have to assign a name to the component definition in much the same way as you would assign a block name. Much like the BLOCK command, the AMNEW command deletes the original solid part after putting it into memory as a component definition.

Refer to the dialog box of this command. You will find two more options. The "Externalize" option writes the component definition to an external drawing file, in much the same way as the WBLOCK command would do. The "Auto-Insert" option automatically inserts the component back to the drawing file from the memory. Thus it saves you time.

Repeat the AMNEW command on the pivot pin of the universal joint. This time, do not auto-insert the component definition.

<Assemblies>   <Component Definition> <Create...>

Command: **AMNEW**

[Component: **Parts**
 Externalize: **NO**
 Auto-Insert: **NO**
OK   ]

Select parts to convert to components: **[Select B (Figure 4.3).]**
Select parts to convert to components: **[Enter]**
Name for new component: **PIN**

Run the AMNEW command two more times on the yoke and the lock pin of the assembly. See Figure 4.4.

<Assemblies>   <Component Definition>   <Create...>

Command: **AMNEW**

[Component: **Parts**
 Externalize: **NO**
 Auto-Insert: **NO**
OK   ]

Select parts to convert to components: **[Select C (Figure 4.3).]**
Select parts to convert to components: **[Enter]**
Name for new component: **YOKE**

<Assemblies>   <Component Definition>   <Create...>

Command: **AMNEW**

[Component: **Parts**
 Externalize: **NO**
 Auto-Insert: **NO**
OK   ]

Select parts to convert to components: **[Select D (Figure 4.3).]**
Select parts to convert to components: **[Enter]**
Name for new component: **LOCK**

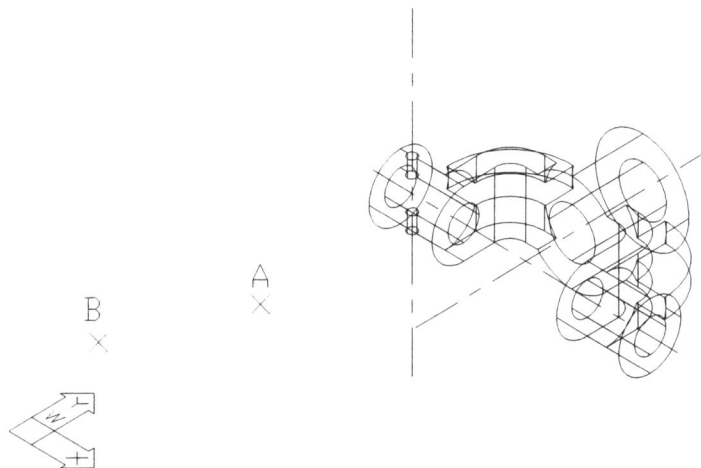

Figure 4.4 Solid parts put away as component definitions and the main body auto-inserted

You have put the four solid parts of the universal joint into memory as component definitions. While you did that, you also instanced the first component back to the drawing by using the "Auto-Insert" option of the AMNEW command. The main body shown in Figure 4.4 is an instance of the component shown in Figure 4.3.

4.2   Instancing Component Definitions to the Assembly

To instance a component definition to a drawing file, you may auto-insert a component while you put a solid part into memory as a component definition, or you may use the AMINSERT command to do instancing. Run this command to instance two component definitions, the pin and the lock, to the drawing. See Figure 4.5.

<Assemblies>   <Instances>   <Insert...>

Command: **AMINSERT**

[Component definition: **PIN**
Insert <   ]

Select insertion point: **[Select A (Figure 4.4).]**
Select insertion point: **[Enter]**

[Component definition: **LOCK**
Insert <   ]

Select insertion point: **[Select B (Figure 4.4).]**
Select insertion point: **[Enter]**

[**Done**   ]

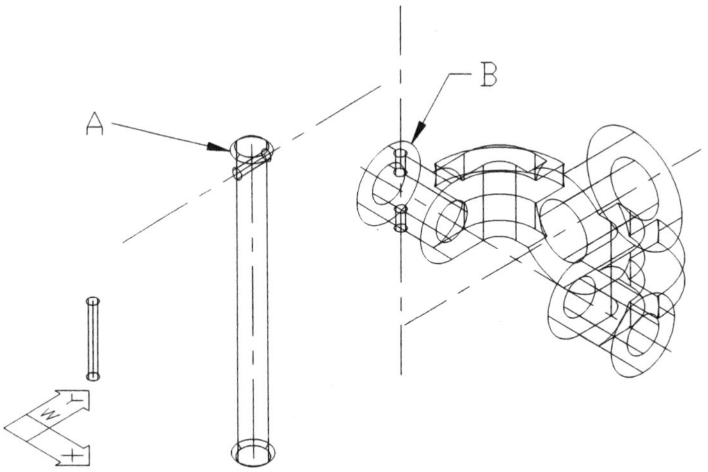

Figure 4.5 Two more component definitions instanced

Now you have four component definitions stored in the memory, and you have three instances.

4.3   Constraining the Instances

In an assembly drawing, each instance except the first one has six degrees of freedom — three degrees of freedom in linear translation and three degrees of freedom in rotational translation. The first instance of an assembly is said to be grounded, because it has no degrees of freedom. You will constrain all other instances with reference to this grounded instance.

Because you have applied the "Auto-Insert" option on the main body, this becomes the first instance of the assembly. It is grounded.

To find out the number of degrees of freedom, and the type of freedom, of the instances, you may run the AMASSMVIS command.

<Assemblies>   **<Instances>**   **<Set Visibility...>**

Command: **AMASSMVIS**

[Component:
**Select All
CG On
DOF On
Done**   ]

In your screen display, you should see the center of gravity (CG) symbols, and the degree of freedom (DOF) symbols. You may find that, except for the main body, there are three mutually perpendicular lines with arrow heads, and three circular arcs with arrow heads. The three lines signify the three degrees of freedom of linear translation. The three circular arcs signify the three degrees of freedom of angular rotation.

For the main body, you should find three mutually perpendicular lines without any arrow heads and also the CG symbol. An instance like this one is fully constrained in terms of assembly.

The two system variables that involve assembly are AMAUTOASSEMBLE and AMVIEWRESTORE. You may enter the variable name at the command prompt and then change its value. Alternatively, you may use the AMASSMVARS command to set the values. When the AMAUTOASSEMBLE variable equals one, the instances translate toward the grounded instance as you add assembly constraints. Otherwise, the instances do not move. The AMVIEWRESTORE variable concerns sub-assemblies. If its value is one, AutoCAD Designer restores the last sub-assembly view each time you change the edit target. You will work on "Target" later.

<Assemblies>   **<Preferences>**

Command: **AMASSMVARS**

[AutoAssemble: **YES**
 ViewRestore: **YES**
OK   ]

Run the AMCONSTRAIN command to constrain the pin instance.

<Assemblies>   **<Constraints>**   **<Create...>**

Command: **AMCONSTRAIN**

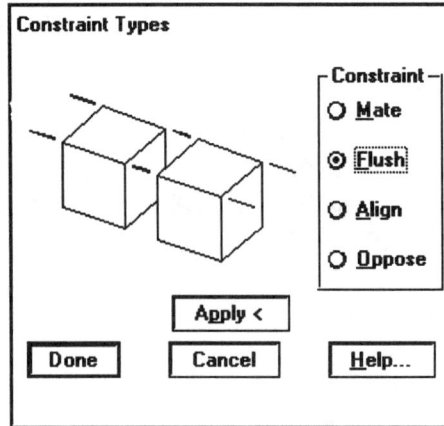

[Constraint: **Flush**
Apply <   ]

Select first plane edge: **[Select A (Figure 4.5).]**
Select second plane edge: **[Select B (Figure 4.5).]**
Distance to offset planes: **0**

[**Done**   ]

There are four types of assembly constraints. You may use the options provided by the AMCONSTRAIN command. They are "Align," "Flush," "Mate," and "Oppose." To apply such constraints directly, you may use the AMALIGN command, the AMFLUSH command, the AMMATE command, and the AMOPPOSE command.

Because you have set the AMAUTOASSEMBLE variable to one, the pin instance translates accordingly. See Figure 4.6.

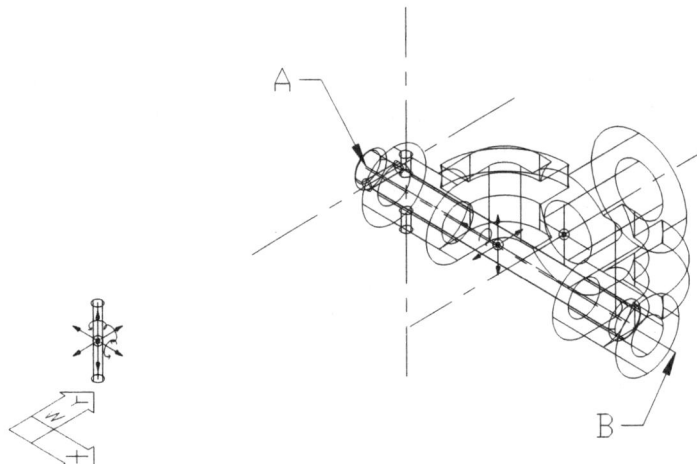

Figure 4.6 The end of the pin instance flushed with the main body instance

You have applied an assembly constraint to the pin instance. You may find that the symbol representing the six degrees of freedom has changed. Some of the freedoms are removed.

Run the AMMATE command to apply the mate constraint. See Figure 4.7.

[Assemblies]   **[Mate]**

Command: **AMMATE**
Reference geometry for mate constraint Line/Point/<Select plane>: **LINE**
Select reference line to constrain: **[Select A (Figure 4.6).]**
Reference geometry for mate constraint PLane/POint/<Select line>: **[Select B (Figure 4.6).]**

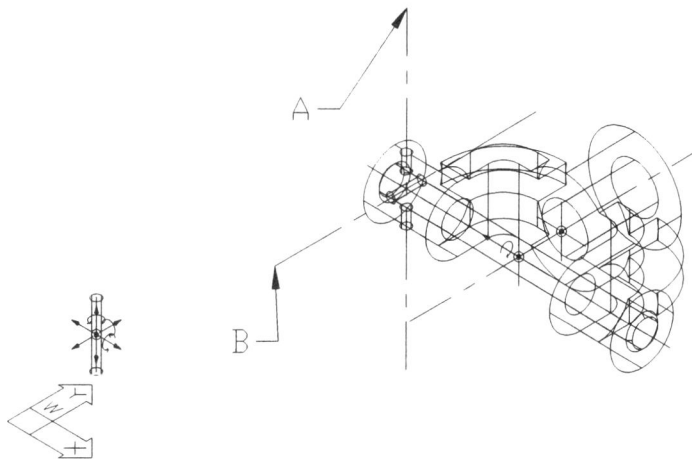

Figure 4.7 Two axes mated

The AMMATE command that you have applied is equivalent to the "Mate" option of the AMCONSTRAIN command. After mating, more freedom is removed.

Change the AMAUTOASSEMBLE setting to 0. Then run the AMMATE command to add one more mating constraint to the assembly.

Command: **AMAUTOASSEMBLE**
New value for AMAUTOASSEMBLE: **0**

[Assemblies]   **[Mate]**

Command: **AMMATE**
Reference geometry for mate constraint Line/Point/<Select plane>: **LINE**
Select reference line to constrain: **[Select A (Figure 4.7).]**
Reference geometry for mate constraint PLane/POint/<Select line>: **[Select B (Figure 4.7).]**

This time, only the degree-of-freedom symbol changes. The pin instance does not translate at all. To assemble the instances together after applying the assembly constraint, run the AMASSEMBLE command. See Figure 4.8.

<Assemblies>   **<Constraints>**   **<Assemble>**

Command: **AMASSEMBLE**

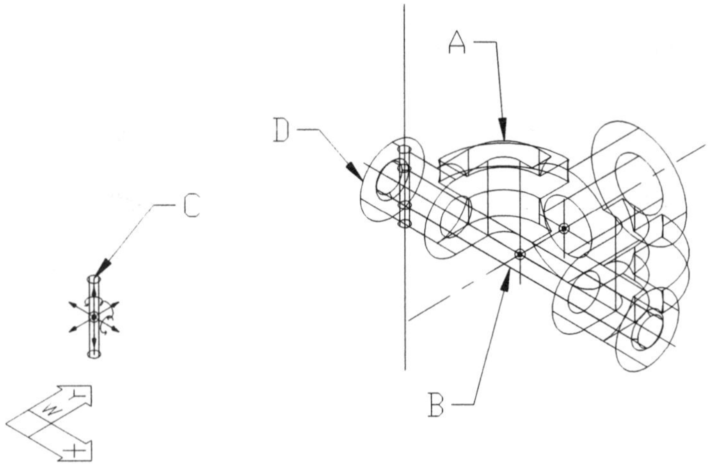

Figure 4.8 The pin instance fully constrained to the grounded main body instance

To do the assembly automatically as you apply the assembly constraint, set AMASSEMBLE to 1 again.

Command: **AMAUTOASSEMBLE**
New value for AMAUTOASSEMBLE: **1**

Whereas the AMCONSTRAIN, AMALIGN, AMFLUSH, AMMATE, and AMOPPOSE commands apply assembly constraints to the instances, the AMEDITCONST command edits and removes assembly constraints. Run the AMEDITCONST command on the pin instance.

<Assemblies>   **<Constraints>**   **<Edit...>**

Command: **AMEDITCONST**

[Select Component: **PIN_1**
OK   ]

Flush plane/plane constraint with 0.000000 offset...
All/Delete/Edit/eXit/Previous/<Next>: **[Enter]**
Line/line constraint...
All/Delete/Edit/eXit/Previous/<Next>: **[Enter]**
Line/line constraint...
All/Delete/Edit/eXit/Next/<Previous>: **[Enter]**
Line/line constraint...
All/Delete/Edit/eXit/Next/<Previous>: **[Enter]**
Flush plane/plane constraint with 0.000000 offset...
All/Delete/Edit/eXit/Previous/<Next>: **X**

You have properly assembled the pin instance to the grounded instance, the main body. To find out whether there is any interference between the two instances, apply the AMINTERFERE command.

<Assemblies> **<Analysis>** **<Interference>**

Command: **AMINTERFERE**
Nested component selection? Yes/<No>: **YES**
Select the first set of components.
Select component: **[Select A (Figure 4.8).]**
Select component: **[Enter]**
Select the second set of components.
Select component: **[Select B (Figure 4.8).]**
Select component: **[Enter]**
Components do not interfere.

To continue, you will assemble the lock pin instance to the grounded instance. Run the AMOPPOSE command. See Figure 4.9.

[Assemblies] **[Oppose]**

Command: **AMOPPOSE**
Reference geometry for oppose constraint Line/<Select plane>: **LINE**
Select reference line to constrain: **[Select C (Figure 4.8).]**
Reference geometry for oppose constraint PLane/<Select line>: **[Select D (Figure 4.8).]**
Flip the line direction? Yes/<No>: **[Enter]**
Oppose angle: **0**

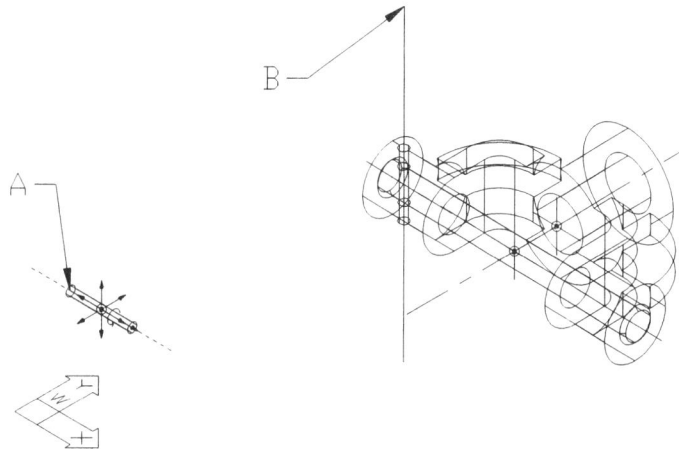

Figure 4.9 The lock pin instance translated angularly for 90 degrees

It would seem that the last assembly constraint was applied wrongly. Execute the AMDELCONST command to delete the assembly constraints that you have applied to the lock pin instance.

<Assemblies> **<Constraints>** **<Delete...>**

Command: **AMDELCONST**

[Select Component: **LOCK_1**
 All Constraints: **YES**
OK   ]

All constraints removed

Upon removal of the assembly constraints, you may find that all degrees of freedom come back again.

To apply constraint to the lock pin instance again, run the AMMATE command. See Figure 4.10.

[Assemblies]   **[Mate]**

Command: **AMMATE**
Reference geometry for mate constraint Line/Point/<Select plane>: **LINE**
Select reference line to constrain: **[Select A (Figure 4.9).]**
Reference geometry for mate constraint PLane/POint/<Select line>: **[Select B (Figure 4.9).]**

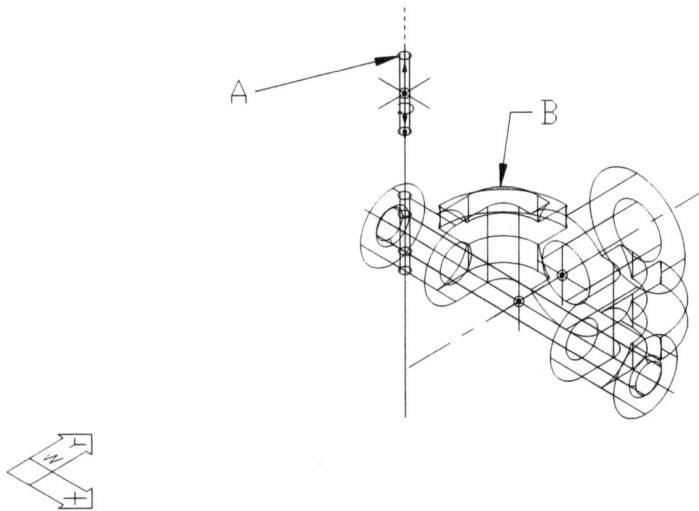

Figure 4.10 Two axes mated

To constrain the lock pin instance further, apply the AMFLUSH command. See Figure 4.11.

[Assemblies]   **[Flush]**

Command: **AMFLUSH**
Select first plane edge: **[Select A (Figure 4.10).]**
Select second plane edge: **[Select B (Figure 4.10).]**
Next/<Accept>: **[Accept, if the top face is highlighted. Otherwise, Next.]**
Distance to offset planes: **0**

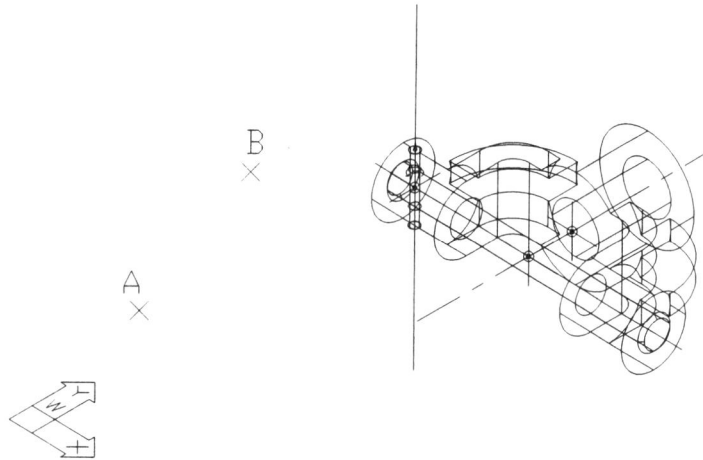

Figure 4.11 The lock pin instance assembled

Take a closer look at the DOF (degree of freedom) symbol of the lock pin instance; you may find that there is still one degree of freedom left. It is a freedom of rotation about the lock pin's own axis. Since this freedom does not affect the functionality of the assembly, you should leave it as it is. You may consider that you have properly assembled the pin instance, and the lock instance to the grounded instance, the main body.

Now you will instance the yoke to the assembly. Run the AMINSERT command.

\<Assemblies\>   **\<Instances\>**   **\<Insert...\>**

Command: **AMINSERT**

[Component definition: **YOKE**
Insert \<   ]

Select insertion point: **[Select A (Figure 4.11).]**
Select insertion point: **[Select B (Figure 4.11).]**
Select insertion point: **[Enter]**

[Done   ]

You have made two instances of this component definition. Because you need only one instance instead of two, run the AMDELCOMP command to delete the extra instance. See Figure 4.12. The name given to the first instance of the yoke is YOKE_1, the second is YOKE_2. Therefore, to delete the second instance of the yoke, you should select the instance YOKE_2.

Command: **AMDELCOMP**

[Select Component: **YOKE_2**
OK   ]

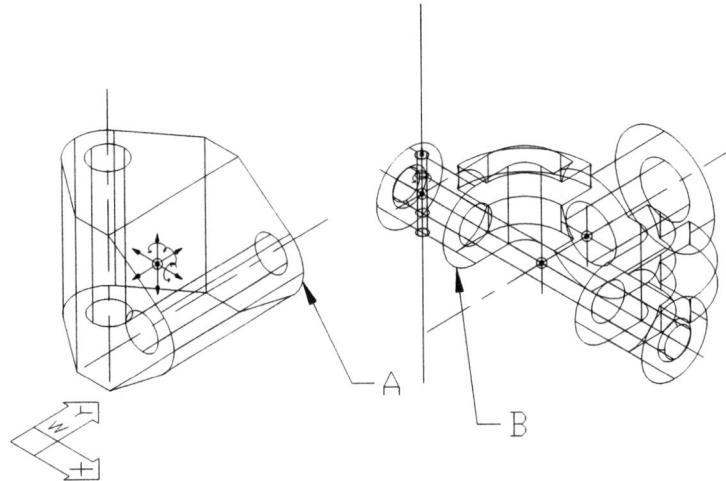

Figure 4.12 The yoke instanced

The new instance is free in all respects. Run the AMOPPOSE command to add the assembly constraints to it. See Figure 4.13

[Assemblies]   **[Oppose]**

Command: **AMOPPOSE**
Reference geometry for oppose constraint Line/<Select plane>: **[Select A (Figure 4.12).]**
Reference geometry for oppose constraint Line/<Select plane>>: **[Select B (Figure 4.12).]**
Oppose angle <0>: **[Enter]**

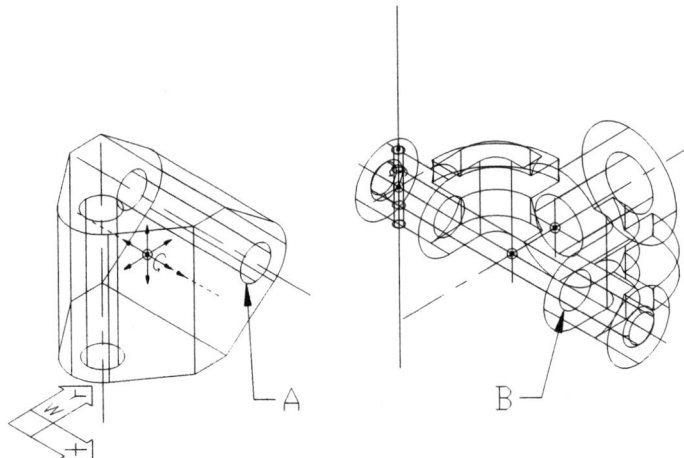

Figure 4.13 Two faces opposed

Issue the AMMATE command to constrain the yoke instance against the main instance. See Figure 4.14.

[Assemblies]   **[Mate]**

Command: **AMMATE**
Reference geometry for mate constraint Line/Point/<Select plane>: **LINE**
Select reference line to constrain: **[Select A (Figure 4.13).]**
Reference geometry for mate constraint PLane/POint/<Select line>: **[Select B (Figure 4.13).]**

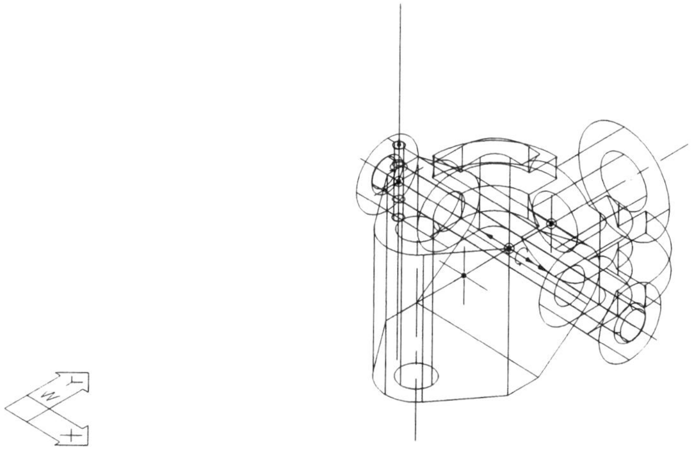

Figure 4.14 The yoke instance properly assembled

You have successfully assembled four instances together.

4.4   Sub-Assembly and Target

In engineering design, it is not uncommon to break down a very complicate design that has a lot of parts into a number of sub-assemblies of fewer parts. This is useful for practical reasons, because it is easier to handle small assemblies. In AutoCAD Designer, you may create sub-assemblies as well as assemblies.

Refer to the assembly drawing in Figure 4.1. Although there are not too many parts in this project, for the sake of demonstrating how to create and work on sub-assemblies, you will produce a sub-assembly and then assemble the sub-assembly to the main assembly.

To start a sub-assembly, you will use the AMNEW command.

      <Assemblies>   **<Component Definition>**   **<Create...>**

Command: **AMNEW**

[Component: **SubAssembly**
 Auto-Insert: **NO**
OK   ]
Name for new subassembly: **SUB1**

Besides allowing you to select a solid part to become a component definition, the AMNEW command lets you to begin a new sub-assembly.

By now, you have a main assembly and a sub-assembly in your drawing. In AutoCAD Designer terms, you have two targets. The first target is the main assembly -- the current target. There are four instances in it. They are the main body instance, the pin instance, the lock instance, and the yoke instance. The second target is the sub-assembly. For the time being, it is empty.

At any one time, you may work on only one target. Currently, you are working on the main assembly target. The name of the target is the file name of this drawing, if you have already specified one. The name can be "unnamed" if you have not specified a file name for the current drawing. To choose a target to work on, you may use the AMTARGET command. Run this command to set the working target to the sub-assembly, SUB1. Click the "DOF" button to display the degree-of-freedom symbol.

<Assemblies>   **<Instances>**   **<Edit Target...>**

Command: **AMTARGET**

[Select Edit Target: **SUB1**
 DOF: **YES**
 OK   ]

After you have changed the edit target, your screen display switches to the sub-assembly. The sub-assembly is empty for the time being, so your screen shows nothing.

When you have more than one target in your drawing, you may switch between the targets from time to time. To restore the model space views for each sub-assembly target, set the AMVIEWRESTORE variable to 1.

Command: **AMVIEWRESTORE**
New value for AMVIEWRESTORE: **1**

The sub-assembly needs three instances. They are instances for the main body, the pin, and the lock pin. Run the AMINSERT command. See Figure 4.15.

<Assemblies>   **<Instances>**   **<Insert...>**

Command: **AMINSERT**

[Component definition: **MAIN**
 Insert <   ]

Select insertion point: **[Select A (Figure 4.15).]**
Select insertion point: **[Enter]**

[Component definition: **PIN**
 Insert <   ]

Select insertion point: **[Select B (Figure 4.15).]**
Select insertion point: **[Enter]**

[Component definition: **LOCK**
 Insert <   ]

Select insertion point: **[Select C (Figure 4.15).]**
Select insertion point: **[Enter]**

[Done   ]

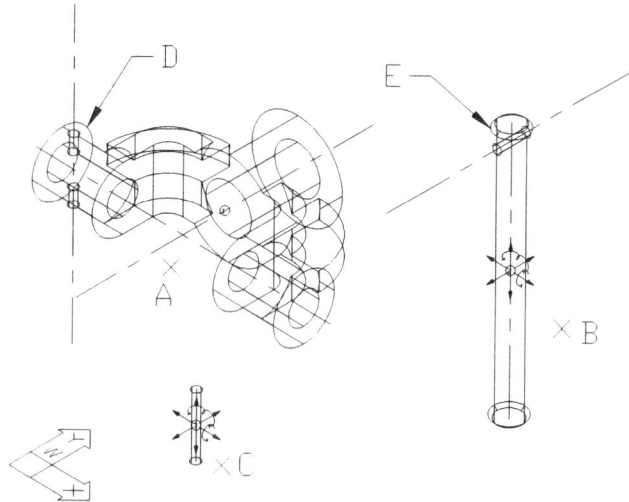

Figure 4.15 Sub-assembly having three instances

Refer to your screen display. You may find that the DOF (degree of freedom) symbol of the first instance, the main, is different from those of other instances. This instance is the grounded instance of the sub-assembly. It has no freedom of translation at all in the sub-assembly. Other instances translate relative to it. The procedure of applying assembly constraints to the instances of a sub-assembly is the same as that for an assembly. You need to use the AMCONSTRAINT command to apply "Align," "Flush," "Mate," and "Oppose" constraints. Alternatively, you may use the AMALIGN command, the AMFLUSH command, the AMMATE command, and the AMOPPOSE command. To edit assembly constraints, you may use the AMEDITCONST command. To delete assembly constraints, you should apply the AMDELCONST command.

To constrain the pin instance to the main body instance, run the AMFLUSH command. See Figure 4.16.

[Assemblies]   **[Flush]**

Command: **AMFLUSH**
Select first plane edge: **[Select D (Figure 4.16).]**
Select second plane edge: **[Select E (Figure 4.16).]**
Distance to offset planes: **0**

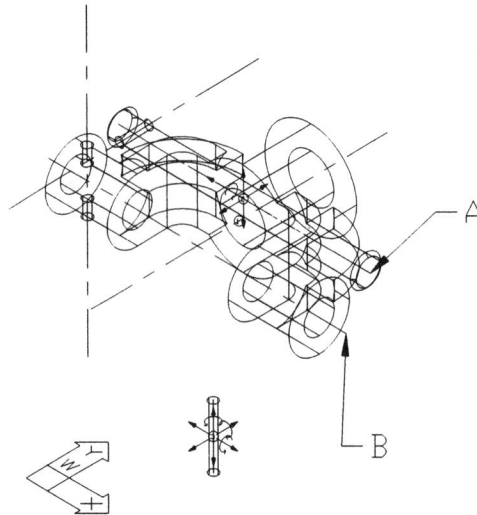

Figure 4.16 End face of the pin instance flushed with that of the main body instance

After flushing the two faces, use the AMMATE command to mate two axes. See Figure 4.17.

[**Assemblies**]   [**Mate**]

Command: **AMMATE**
Reference geometry for mate constraint Line/Point/<Select plane>: **LINE**
Select reference line to constrain: **[Select A (Figure 4.16).]**
Reference geometry for mate constraint PLane/POint/<Select line>: **[Select B (Figure 4.16).]**

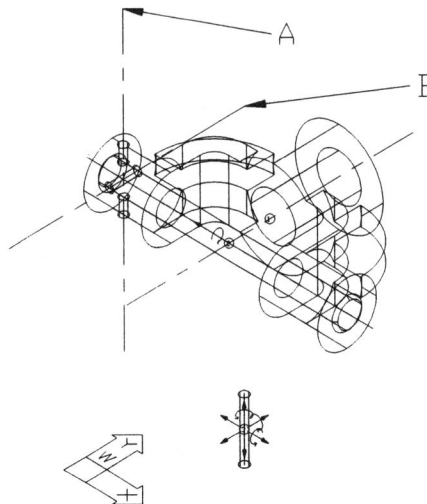

Figure 4.17 Two axes mated

Repeat the AMMATE command to mate two more axes to fully constrain the pin instance to the main body instance. See Figure 4.18.

[Assemblies]   **[Mate]**

Command: **AMMATE**
Reference geometry for mate constraint Line/Point/<Select plane>: **LINE**
Select reference line to constrain: **[Select A (Figure 4.18).]**
Reference geometry for mate constraint PLane/POint/<Select line>: **[Select B (Figure 4.18).]**

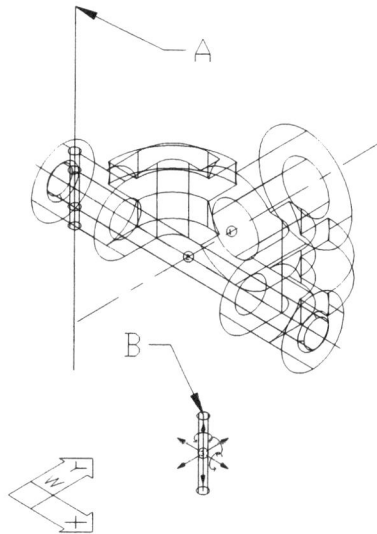

Figure 4.18 The pin instance fully constrained

You have fully constrained the pin instance relative to the main body instance. To continue, run the AMMATE command to mate the work axis of the lock pin instance to that of the main body. See Figure 4.19.

[Assemblies]   **[Mate]**

Command: **AMMATE**
Reference geometry for mate constraint Line/Point/<Select plane>: **LINE**
Select reference line to constrain: **[Select A (Figure 4.18).]**
Reference geometry for mate constraint PLane/POint/<Select line>: **[Select B (Figure 4.18).]**

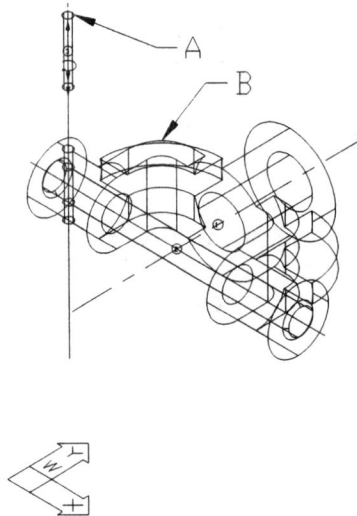

Figure 4.19 The lock instance mated with the pin instance

Execute the AMFLUSH command to apply a flush constraint on the lock pin instance. See Figure 4.20.

[**Assemblies**]   [**Flush**]

Command: **AMFLUSH**
Select first plane edge: **[Select A (Figure 4.19).]**
Select second plane edge: **[Select B (Figure 4.19).]**
Distance to offset planes: **0**

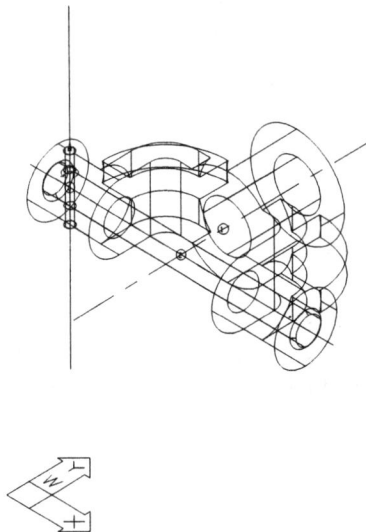

Figure 4.20 The lock instance flushed to the main instance

Refer to your screen. You may find that, as in the main assembly, there is one degree-of-freedom left in the lock pin instance. It is a freedom of rotation about the lock pin's own work axis. This freedom does not affect the final functionality of the assembly or the sub-assembly, so you may leave it as it is. You have completed the sub-assembly.

4.5   Final Assembly of the Universal Joint

To complete the entire assembly, you have to switch your edit target. Currently, there are two targets, the main assembly and the sub-assembly. Run the AMTARGET command.

Note that the target name of the main assembly is the name of your drawing file. Change the "U_JOINT" in the following delineation to your file name.

\<Assemblies\>   **\<Instances\>**   **\<Edit Target...\>**

Command: **AMTARGET**

[Select Edit Target: **U_JOINT**
 DOF: **YES**
 OK   ]

After you change the target, your sub-assembly disappears. The screen shows the main assembly again. It should resemble Figure 4.14, which is where you left off before starting the sub-assembly.

To complete the overall assembly, you need to instance the sub-assembly and apply assembly constraints accordingly. Issue the AMINSERT command. See Figure 4.21.

\<Assemblies\>   **\<Instances\>**   **\<Insert...\>**

Command: **AMINSERT**

[Component definition: **SUB1**
 Insert \<   ]

Select insertion point: **[Select A (Figure 4.21).]**
Select insertion point: **[Enter]**

[Done   ]

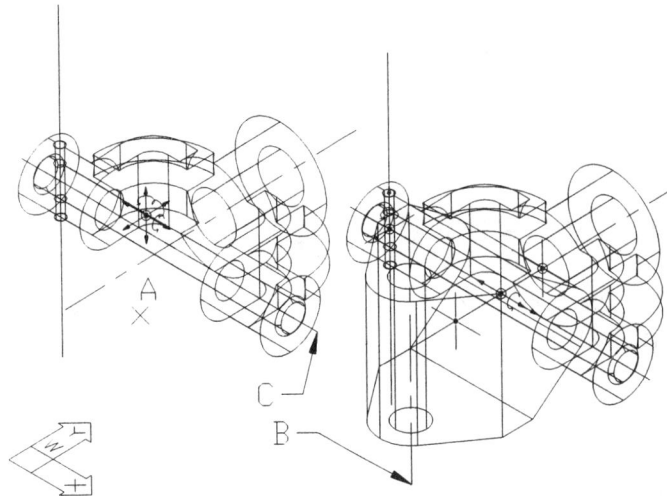

Figure 4.21 The sub-assembly instanced to the main assembly

At this point, you may ask, "Could we not make the sub-assembly from the outset?" Yes, we could. If you have made a sub-assembly, you do not have to assemble the pin instance, the lock instance, and the main instance twice. Instead, you may instance the sub-assembly twice to the drawing. However, the aim of this project is to demonstrate the different ways of handling an assembly.

In this assembly project, you have made an assembly from the component instances, as well as the sub-assembly instance.

Apply the AMALIGN command to align an axis of the sub-assembly instance with that of the yoke instance. See Figure 4.22.

[Assemblies]   **[Align]**

Command: **AMALIGN**
Reference geometry for alignment constraint Line/<Select plane>: **LINE**
Select reference line to constrain: **[Select B (Figure 4.21).]**
Flip the line direction? Yes/<No>: **[Enter]**
Reference geometry for alignment constraint PLane/<Select line>: **[Select C (Figure 4.21).]**
Flip the line direction? Yes/<No>: **[Enter]**
Alignment angle: **0**

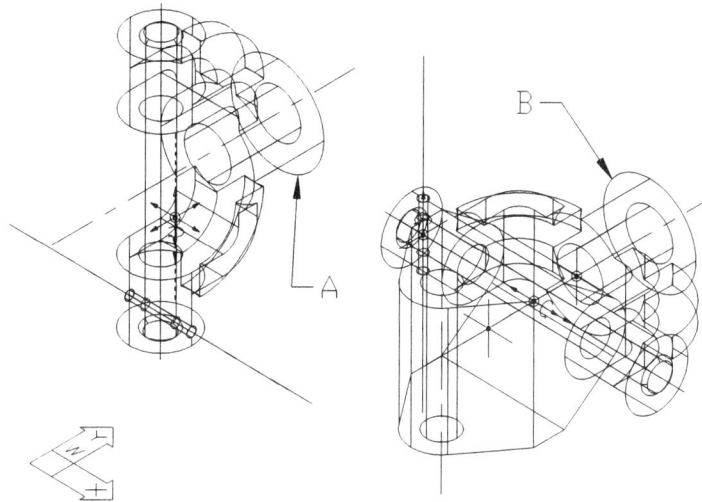

Figure 4.22 The axis of the sub-assembly instance aligned with the yoke instance

To constrain the sub-assembly instance further, apply the AMOPPOSE command. See Figure 4.23.

[**Assemblies**]   [**Oppose**]

Command: **AMOPPOSE**
Reference geometry for oppose constraint Line/<Select plane>: **[Select A (Figure 4.22).]**
Reference geometry for oppose constraint Line/<Select plane>: **[Select B (Figure 4.22).]**
Oppose angle: **0**

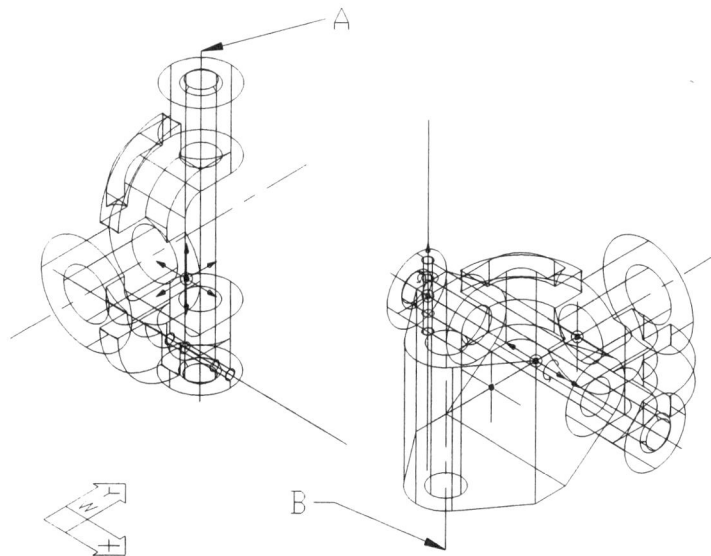

Figure 4.23 The sub-assembly instance opposed to the main instance

   Issue the AMMATE command to mate the axis of the sub-assembly instance to that of the yoke instance. See Figure 4.24.

   [Assemblies]   **[Mate]**

   Command: **AMMATE**
   Reference geometry for mate constraint Line/Point/<Select plane>: **LINE**
   Select reference line to constrain: **[Select A (Figure 4.23).]**
   Reference geometry for mate constraint PLane/POint/<Select line>: **[Select B (Figure 4.23).]**

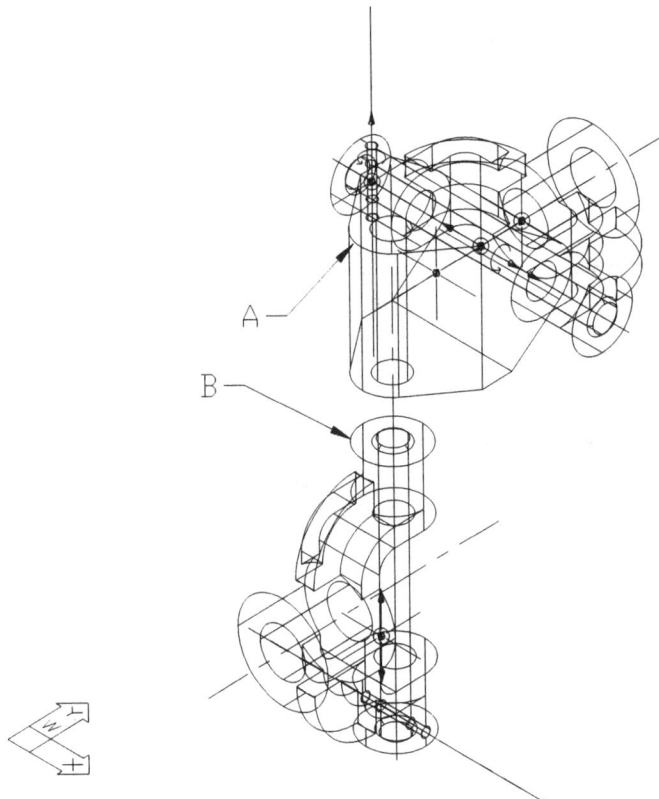

Figure 4.24 The axis of the sub-assembly instance aligned with the yoke instance

   To complete the assembly, repeat the AMMATE command to mate two planes together. See Figure 4.25.

   [Assemblies]   **[Mate]**

   Command: **AMMATE**
   Reference geometry for mate constraint Line/Point/<Select plane>: **[Select A (Figure 4.24).]**
   Reference geometry for mate constraint Line/Point/<Select plane>: **[Select B (Figure 4.24).]**
   Distance to offset planes: **0**

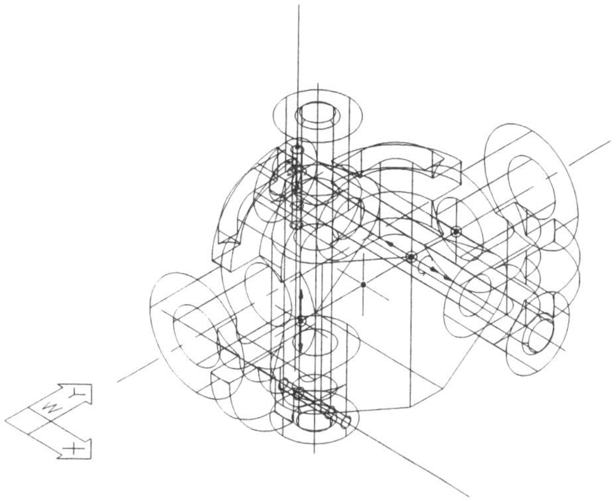

Figure 4.25 The completed assembly of the universal joint

You have assembled the instances of the universal joint properly. In your file, there are four component definitions. They are the main, yoke, pin, and lock component definitions. You have instanced them to the assembly and have assembled them properly. You have also created a sub-assembly. Doing so set up the second target in the drawing. Working on the sub-assembly is similar to working on the main assembly. After making a sub-assembly, you have instanced it to the main assembly and assembled it properly.

Before you save the file, you should check for interference between the instances. Run the AMINTERFERE command. You should maintain the good habit of checking interference from time to time.

Save your drawing.

<File>   **<Save As...>**

Command: **SAVEAS**

[File name: **U_JOINT.DWG**
OK   ]

4.6   Assembling Solid Parts in a Single Drawing File

Let us review how to make an assembly from a set of solid parts in a drawing. The starting point is to create all the necessary solid parts. Then you may use the AMNEW command to put the solid parts into memory as local component definitions. When you run the AMNEW command, you may choose to externalize the component definition. To externalize a component definition creates an external file having the solid part that the component definition represents. The external file then links to the current file. It becomes an external component definition and is accessible from the current drawing file. You need to assign a name to each component definition, whether external or local.

You should repeat this command on all the solid parts on a local drawing. After creating the component definitions, you may use the AMINSERT command to insert them to the assembly. The inserted component definition is an instance. It is not a solid part. See Figure 4.26.

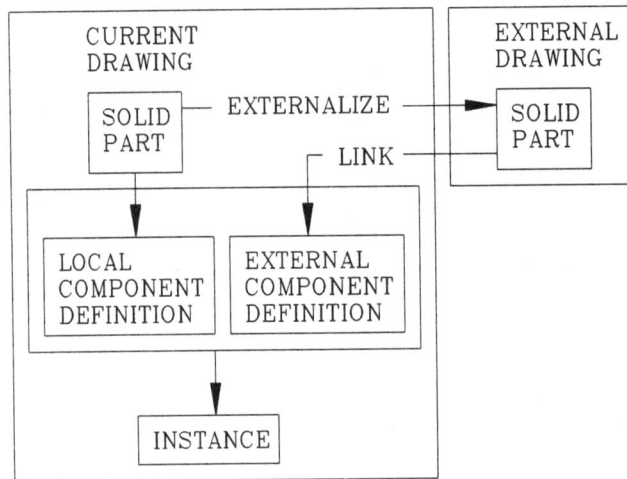

Figure 4.26 Creating local and external component definitions with the AMNEW command

To assemble the instances together, you may use the AMCONSTRAIN command. Alternatively, you may apply the AMALIGN, the AMFLUSH, the AMMATE, or the AMOPPOSE command.

You may edit the assembly constraints with the AMEDITCONST command or delete assembly constraints with the AMDELCONST command. To find out the number of degrees of freedom, you may display the CG and DOF symbol with the AMASSMVIS command.

After assembling the instances together, you may check interference with the AMINTERFERE command. When you apply assembly constraints to the instances, they translate. If you do not want them to translate, you may use the AMASSMVARS command to operate the AMAUTOASSEMBLE variable. After that, you may apply the AMASSEMBLE command to assemble the instances together.

For practical reasons, you may need to establish sub-assemblies in a drawing. You may use the AMNEW command to start a sub-assembly. After you have started a sub-assembly, there are more than one target in a drawing. The main assembly and the sub-assemblies are targets. To select which target to work on, you need to use the AMTARGET command. You may apply the AMINSERT command to insert a sub-assembly as an instance in exactly the same way as ordinary component definitions. When you switch between edit targets, you may choose to restore the last sub-assembly view by manipulating the AMVIEWRESTORE variable. The AMASSMVARS command also operates this variable.

4.7   Solid Parts, Component Definitions, and Instances

In your assembly drawing, there may be a lot of instances of component definitions. To find out where an instance is used, you may apply the AMWHEREUSE command.

<Assemblies>   **<Component Definition>**   **<Where Used...>**

Command: **AMWHEREUSE**
Cataloged component to inquire (? for list) <?>: **?**
 LOCAL COMPONENTS:
MAIN
PIN
YOKE
LOCK
SUB1
 EXTERNAL COMPONENTS:
Cataloged component to inquire (? for list) <?>: **MAIN**
List the components? No/<Yes>: **YES**
Highlight the components? No/<Yes>: **YES**
Output to a file? Yes/<No>: **NO**
    MAIN is used in:
        MAIN_1|
Press RETURN to continue. **[Enter]**
        SUB1_1|MAIN_2|
Press RETURN to continue. **[Enter]**

There are two types of component definitions, local and external. The above inquiry shows that there are five local components but no external components. You did not take the "Externalize" option when you defined the component definitions, so all component definitions are stored locally.

You have to distinguish three types of objects. They are solid parts, component definitions, and instances. Solid parts are parametric solid models that you may edit. Component definitions derive from the solid parts. Local component definitions exist in the memory of an assembly drawing. They behave like blocks. External component definitions are solid parts that are saved in attached external drawing files.

Instances refer to the component definitions. They are similar to the inserted block objects or externally referenced objects.

To manage the component definitions in a project, you may use the AMCOMPMAN command. See Figure 4.27.

<Assemblies>   **<Component Definition>**   **<Manage...>**

Command: **AMCOMPMAN**

```
┌────────────────────────────────────────────────────────────────┐
│ Component Manager                                                │
│      Current Edit Target:           U_JOINT                      │
│                                                                  │
│ Local Components                      External Components        │
│ ┌──────────────────┐  ┌──────────────────┐  ┌─────────────────┐ │
│ │ MAIN             │  │   Localize <-    │  │                 │ │
│ │ PIN              │  └──────────────────┘  │                 │ │
│ │ YOKE             │  ┌──────────────────┐  │                 │ │
│ │ LOCK             │  │  Externalize ->  │  │                 │ │
│ │ SUB1             │  └──────────────────┘  │                 │ │
│ │                  │  ┌──────────────────┐  │                 │ │
│ │                  │  │     Delete       │  │                 │ │
│ │                  │  └──────────────────┘  │                 │ │
│ │                  │  ┌──────────────────┐  │                 │ │
│ │                  │  │    Rename...     │  │                 │ │
│ │                  │  └──────────────────┘  │                 │ │
│ │                  │  ┌──────────────────┐  │                 │ │
│ │                  │  │    Attach...     │  │                 │ │
│ │                  │  └──────────────────┘  │                 │ │
│ │                  │  ┌──────────────────┐  │                 │ │
│ │                  │  │    Insert <      │  │                 │ │
│ └──────────────────┘  └──────────────────┘  └─────────────────┘ │
│                                                                  │
│        ┌────────┐   ┌────────┐   ┌────────┐                      │
│        │  Done  │   │ Cancel │   │ Help...│                      │
│        └────────┘   └────────┘   └────────┘                      │
└────────────────────────────────────────────────────────────────┘
```

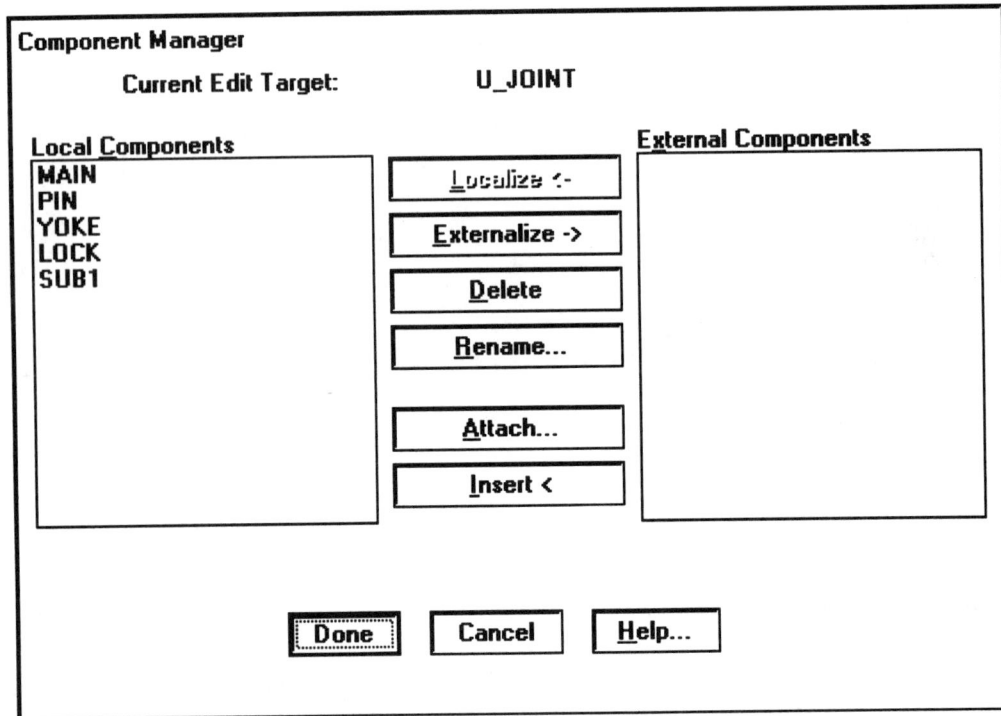

Figure 4.27 Dialog box of the AMCOMPMAN command

This command provides six options. They are "Localize," "Externalize," "Delete," "Rename," "Attach," and "Insert."

As explained above, component definitions can exist locally or externally. You may decide whether a component definition is local or external when you create one, or you may use the AMCOMPMAN command to externalize a local one and localize an external one.

To externalize a local component definition removes the component definition locally, writes the component definition to an external file as a solid part, attaches to that external file, and uses the solid part in that external file as an external component definition.

Command: **AMCOMPMAN**
Attach/Delete/Externalize/Localize/Rename/<Insert>: **E**
Catalogued component to externalize (? for list) <?>:

To localize an external component definition copies the solid part to the local file as a component definition and removes the attachment. See Figure 4.28.

Command: **AMCOMPMAN**
Attach/Delete/Externalize/Localize/Rename/<Insert>: **L**
Catalogued component to localize (? for list) <?>:

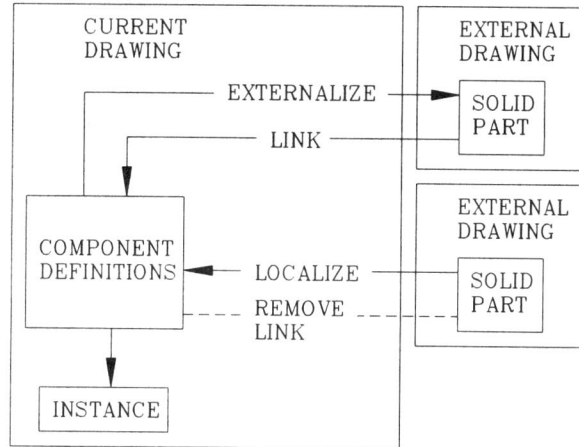

Figure 4.28 Managing component definitions with the AMCOMPMAN command —
externalizing and localizing

If you want to remove a component definition, local or external, you may use the "Delete" option. Operating this option removes the local component definition, or detaches the external link, and deletes all the instances of the component definition.

[Assemblies]   **[Delete Component]**

Command: **AMCOMPMAN**
Attach/Delete/Externalize/Localize/Rename/<Insert>: **D**
Catalogued component to delete (? for list) <?>:

The "Rename" option of this command is different from the AMRENAME command. This option renames a component definition. The AMRENAME command renames an instance.

Command: **AMCOMPMAN**
Attach/Delete/Externalize/Localize/Rename/<Insert>: **R**
Catalogued component to rename (? for list) <?>: **[Specify a component definition.]**

[Assemblies]   **[Rename Component]**

Command: **AMRENAME**
Component to rename Name/<Select>: **[Select an instance.]**

Returning to the options of the AMCOMPMAN command, the "Attach" option establishes a link to an external drawing file. See Figure 4.29. The solid part that is contained in the external file becomes the external component definition. You may use the AMINSERT command or the "Insert" option of the AMCOMPMAN command to instance it to the current drawing.

Command: **AMCOMPMAN**
Attach/Delete/Externalize/Localize/Rename/<Insert>: **A**
External file to attach:

Command: **AMCOMPMAN**
Attach/Delete/Externalize/Localize/Rename/<Insert>: **I**
Catalogued component to insert (? for list) <?>:

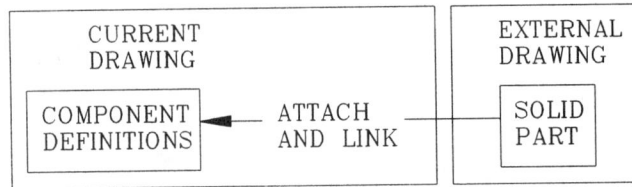

Figure 4.29 Managing component definitions with the AMCOMPMAN command –– attach and link up

External drawings can have solid parts and component definitions. To import the solid part of an external drawing to make it a local component definition, you may use the "Attach" and then the "Localize" options of the AMCOMPMAN command.

To import a component definition of an external drawing to make it a local component definition, you may use the AMCOMPIN command. This command copies the component definitions, not the solid parts. If there is no component definition in the external file, it will copy nothing. See Figure 4.30.

[Assemblies]   **[Input Component Definition]**

Command: **AMCOMPIN**
No components in specified file.

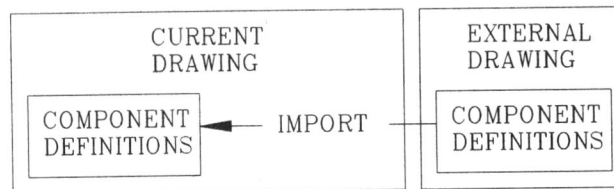

Figure 4.30 Importing component definitions from an external drawing file

The counterpart of the AMCOMPIN command is the AMCOMPOUT command. The AMCOMPOUT command outputs a local component definition to an external drawing file as a component definition. See Figure 4.31.

[Assemblies]   **[Output Component Definition]**

Command: **AMCOMPOUT**
Name of component to output (? for list) <?>:

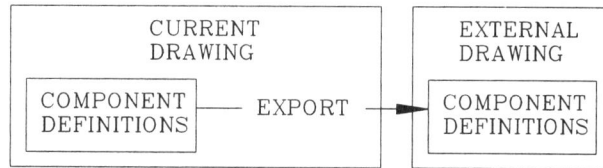

Figure 4.31 Exporting component definitions to an external drawing file

An instance points to a local or external component definition. You may change the component definition that an instance points to. For example, the "YOKE_1" instance refers to the component definition "YOKE." You may change its component definition to "MAIN" by using the AMREPLACE command

<Assemblies>   <Instances>   <Replace...>

Command: **AMREPLACE**
Select components to replace Name/<Select>: **[Enter]**
Select component: **[Select an instance on the screen.]**
Select component: **[Enter]**
Definition to replace components (? to list) <?>: **MAIN**
Replace all instances No/<Yes>: **YES**
Warning: All constraints will be removed from components(s).
 Continue? No/<Yes>: **YES**

To manage the instances within a drawing, you may use the AMBROWSE command. This command allows you to do five tasks. They are "Insert," "Rename," "Reorder," "Delete," and "Hide." See Figure 4.32.

The "Insert" option is similar to the AMINSERT command and to the "Insert" option of the AMCOMPMAN command.

The "Rename" option is similar to the AMRENAME command. It renames an instance, not a component definition as the "Rename" option of the AMCOMPMAN command does.

The "Reorder" option changes the order of instancing and constraining, including the grounded instance.

The "Delete" option is similar to the AMDELCOMP command. It deletes the instance, not the component definition as the "Delete" option of the AMCOMPMAN command does.

The "Hide" option is similar to the "Hide" option of the AMASSMVIS command. It controls the visibility of individual instances.

<Assemblies>   <Instances>   <Browse...>

Command: **AMBROWSE**

```
╔═══════════════════════════════════════════════════════════════════════╗
║              Assembly Browser Tool - [U_JOINT]                          ║
╠═══════════════════════════════════════════════════════════════════════╣
║                                                                         ║
║  Current Edit Target:      U_JOINT                   ┌─────────────┐    ║
║  Component Definition:                               │ Edit Target │    ║
║                                                      └─────────────┘    ║
║  Select Component:                                                      ║
║  ┌────────────────────────────────────────────────┐  Component         ║
║  │ +U_JOINT                                       │  ┌──────────────┐   ║
║  │                                                │  │ Insert...    │   ║
║  │                                                │  └──────────────┘   ║
║  │                                                │  ┌──────────────┐   ║
║  │                                                │  │ Rename...    │   ║
║  │                                                │  └──────────────┘   ║
║  │                                                │  ┌──────────────┐   ║
║  │                                                │  │ Reorder...   │   ║
║  │                                                │  └──────────────┘   ║
║  │                                                │  ┌──────────────┐   ║
║  │                                                │  │ Delete       │   ║
║  │                                                │  └──────────────┘   ║
║  │                                                │  ┌──────────────┐   ║
║  │                                                │  │ Pick <       │   ║
║  │                                                │  └──────────────┘   ║
║  │                                                │  ┌──────────────┐   ║
║  │                                                │  │ Show         │   ║
║  │                                                │  └──────────────┘   ║
║  └────────────────────────────────────────────────┘  □ Hide           ║
║                                                                         ║
║  * indicates component is external                                      ║
║                                                                         ║
║            ┌──────┐  ┌────────┐  ┌─────────┐                            ║
║            │ Done │  │ Cancel │  │ Help... │                            ║
║            └──────┘  └────────┘  └─────────┘                            ║
╚═══════════════════════════════════════════════════════════════════════╝
```

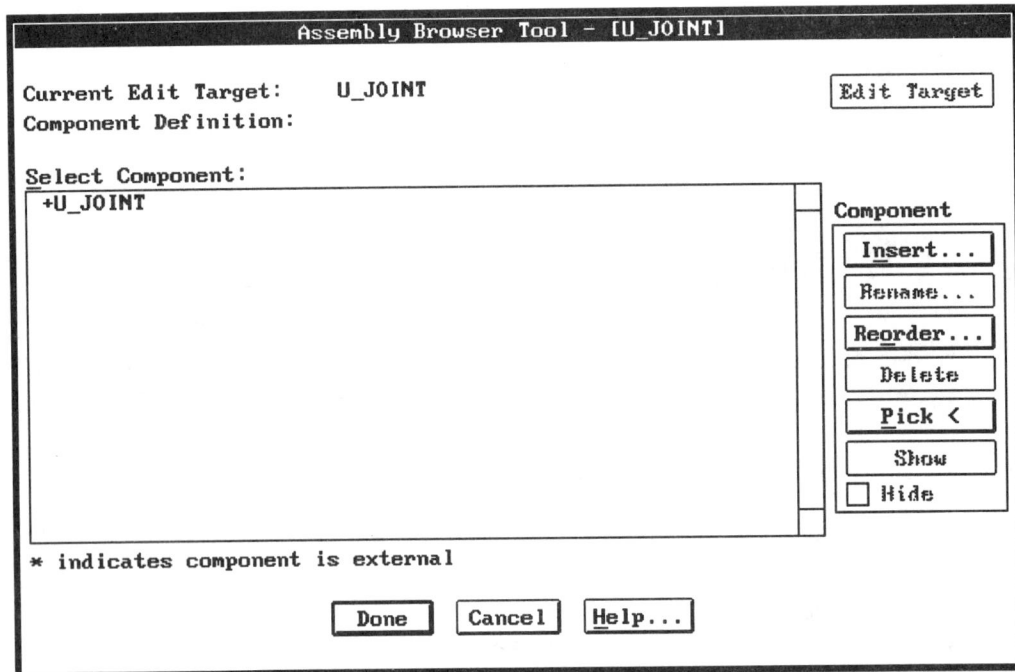

Figure 4.32 Dialog box of the AMBROWSE command

An assembly may consist of a number of external component definitions, and there are cases where you have to change the external solid part after constraining the instances in the assembly. Any change to the external solid part may affect the validity of an assembly. To detect any change that might have been made to the external drawings, you may use the AMAUDIT command. This command compares the time and date stamp of the external drawing with the assembly drawing. The command makes a report on whether the assembly needs any updating. Run this command.

    <Assemblies>   **<Component Definition>**   **<External References>**   **<Audit...>**

Command: **AMAUDIT**
All files up to date

If the AMAUDIT command reports an out-of-date external component definition, you should apply the AMUPDATE command and the AMASSEMBLE command. Then you may have to re-apply the assembly constraints to the instances again.

While you are working on an assembly drawing that links to external component definitions, you may use the AMREFRESH command to reload all external definitions from time to time to keep the assembly drawing up to date. This is necessary when you are working on the assembly drawing and someone else is working on the external component definitions in a network environment.

4.8   Instancing from External Component Definitions

Assembly drawings consist of component definitions and instances. The component definitions can be local or external. In the universal joint assembly, you created all the solid parts in a single drawing and put them away in memory as local component definitions. Then you instanced them back to the drawing and applied assembly constraints accordingly.

If you wish to produce four separate part drawings from the last assembly drawing, you may use the "Externalize" option of the AMNEW command from the outset or use the "Externalize" option of the AMCOMPMAN command later on. In the course of externalizing, four drawings will be created. Each will attach to the current assembly drawing as an external component definition. After externalizing the components, you may edit the solid parts. To check whether the external component definitions of an assembly are up to date, you may use the AMAUDIT command. To reload an external component definition, you may use the AMREFRESH command.

In the last chapter, you created two sets of solid parts. You have finished the first assembly. Now you will work on the second one. It is a set of three drawings. Each drawing contains a solid part.

Start a new drawing with the NEW command.

> **<File>**   **<New...>**
>
> Command: **NEW**
>
> [File name: **MOTOR.DWG**   ]

Because you have created all the solid parts in separate drawing files, you need to use the AMCOMPMAN command to attach them to the current drawing to become external component definitions.

> **<Assemblies>**   **<Component Definition>**   **<External References>**   **<Attach...>**
>
> Command: **AMCOMPMAN**
> Attach/Delete/Externalize/Localize/Rename/<Insert>: **ATTACH**
> External file to attach: **MOTOR_1**
>
> **<Assemblies>**   **<Component Definition>**   **<External References>**   **<Attach...>**
>
> Command: **AMCOMPMAN**
> Attach/Delete/Externalize/Localize/Rename/<Insert>: **ATTACH**
> External file to attach: **MOTOR_2**
>
> **<Assemblies>**   **<Component Definition>**   **<External References>**   **<Attach...>**
>
> Command: **AMCOMPMAN**
> Attach/Delete/Externalize/Localize/Rename/<Insert>: **ATTACH**
> External file to attach: **MOTOR_3**

After attachment, the solid parts in the external drawing files become external component definitions of the current drawing. If you prefer, you may use the

AMCOMPMAN command to localize the component definitions. If you do that, the solid parts from the external drawing will be copied to the current drawing to form local component definitions. As a result, the attachment link will be lost. Any change to the external drawings will have no effect on the current assembly drawing. For the time being, leave them as external component definitions.

Set to an isometric view.

Command: **8**

Use the "Insert" option of the AMCOMPMAN command to instance three component definitions. See Figure 4.33.

<Assemblies>   **<Component Definition>**   **<Manage...>**

Command: **AMCOMPMAN**

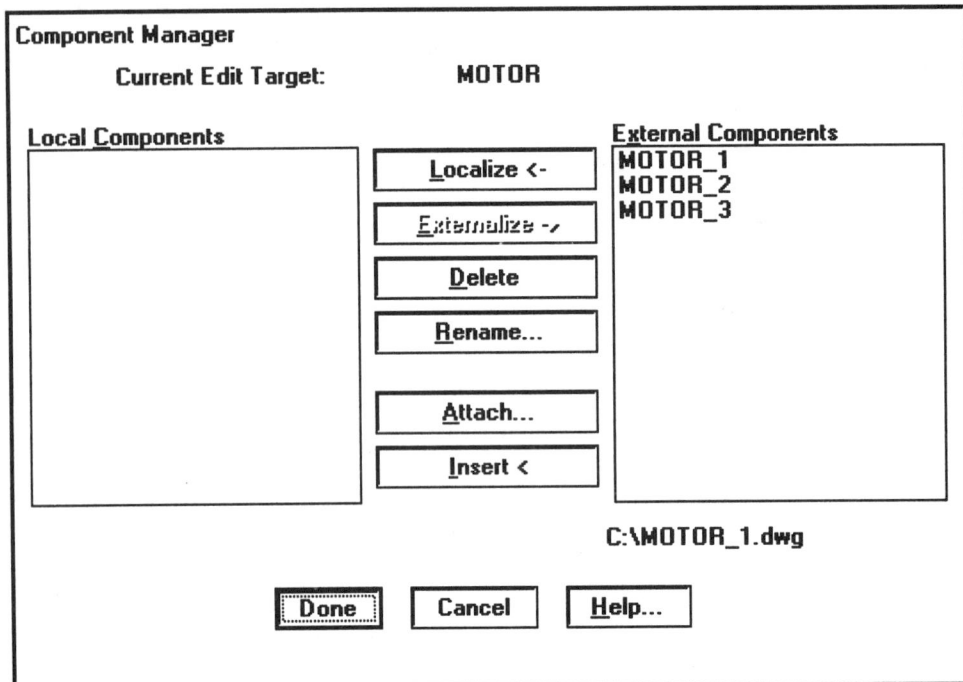

```
Component Manager
       Current Edit Target:              MOTOR

Local Components                                    External Components
                          ┌──────────────┐         ┌──────────────────┐
                          │  Localize <- │         │ MOTOR_1          │
                          └──────────────┘         │ MOTOR_2          │
                          ┌──────────────┐         │ MOTOR_3          │
                          │ Externalize -/│        │                  │
                          └──────────────┘         │                  │
                          ┌──────────────┐         │                  │
                          │   Delete     │         │                  │
                          └──────────────┘         │                  │
                          ┌──────────────┐         │                  │
                          │  Rename...   │         │                  │
                          └──────────────┘         │                  │
                                                   │                  │
                          ┌──────────────┐         │                  │
                          │  Attach...   │         │                  │
                          └──────────────┘         │                  │
                          ┌──────────────┐         │                  │
                          │  Insert <    │         │                  │
                          └──────────────┘         └──────────────────┘

                                               C:\MOTOR_1.dwg

                 ┌────────┐   ┌────────┐   ┌────────┐
                 │  Done  │   │ Cancel │   │ Help...│
                 └────────┘   └────────┘   └────────┘
```

[INSERT   **MOTOR_3**
Select insertion point: **[Select B (Figure 4.33).]**
Select insertion point: **[Enter]**

INSERT   **MOTOR_1**
Select insertion point: **[Select A (Figure 4.33).]**
Select insertion point: **[Enter]**

INSERT   **MOTOR_2**
Select insertion point: **[Select C (Figure 4.33).]**
Select insertion point: **[Enter]**

Done   ]

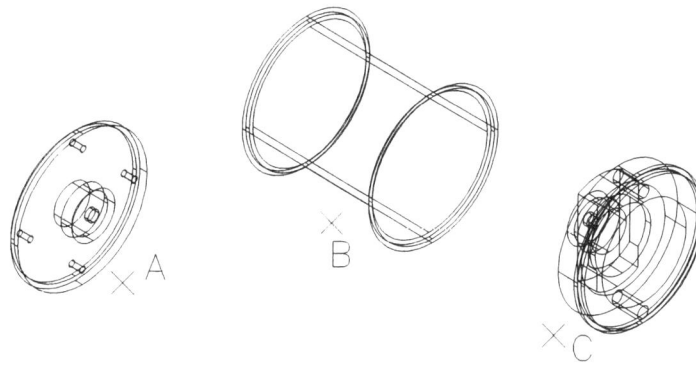

Figure 4.33 External component definitions instanced

Now your drawing has three instances from three external component definitions. To find out which is the MOTOR_1 instance, apply the AMWHEREUSE command.

\<Assemblies\>   **\<Component Definition\>**   **\<Where Used...\>**

Command: **AMWHEREUSE**
Cataloged component to inquire (? for list) \<?\>: **?**
 LOCAL COMPONENTS:

 EXTERNAL COMPONENTS:
MOTOR_1
MOTOR_2
MOTOR_3
Cataloged component to inquire (? for list) \<?\>: **MOTOR_1**
List the components? No/\<Yes\>: **NO**
Highlight the components? No/\<Yes\>: **YES**
Output to a file? Yes/\<No\>: **NO**
Press RETURN to continue. **[Enter]**

As can be seen in the foregoing list, there are three external component definitions but no local component definitions. The highlighted object is the instance of the MOTOR_1 component definition.

Run the QSAVE command to save your drawing.

\<File\>   **\<Save...\>**

Command: **QSAVE**

[File name: **MOTOR.DWG**
OK   ]

Construction features are very useful in providing references in assembly. Open the part drawings, MOTOR_1, and use the AMWORKAXIS command to create work axes.

\<File\>   **\<Open...\>**

Command: **OPEN**

[File name: **MOTOR_1.DWG**
OK   ]

As shown in Figure 4.34, run the AMWORKAXIS command to create work axes.

<Parts>   **<Feature>**   **<Work Axis>**

Command: **AMWORKAXIS**
Select cylinder/cone/torus: **[Select the cylindrical feature.]**

Execute the SAVE command.

<File>   **<Save...>**

Command: **QSAVE**

[File name: **MOTOR_1.DWG**
OK   ]

Repeat the OPEN command, AMWORKAXIS command, and SAVE command on the other two part drawings, MOTOR_2 and MOTOR_3.

Now issue the OPEN command to open the assembly drawing MOTOR.DWG again. See Figure 4.34.

<File>   **<Open...>**

Command: **OPEN**

[File name: **MOTOR.DWG**
OK   ]

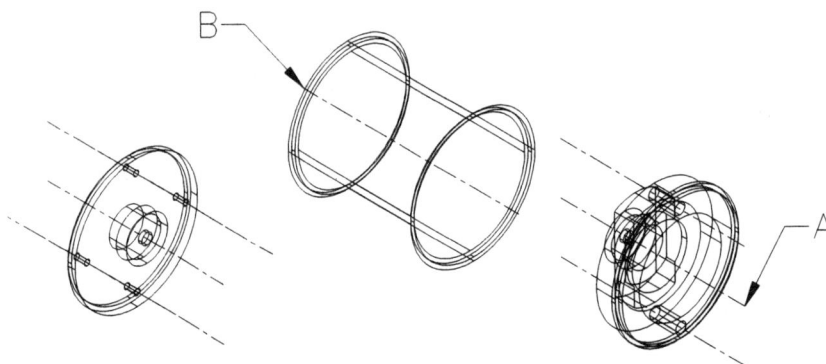

Figure 4.34 Work axes created on external components

Apply the AMMATE command to mate two axes of the instances together. See Figure 4.35.

[Assemblies]   **[Mate]**

Command: **AMMATE**
Reference geometry for mate constraint Line/Point/<Select plane>: **LINE**
Select reference line to constrain: **[Select A (Figure 4.34).]**
Reference geometry for mate constraint PLane/POint/<Select line>: **[Select B (Figure 4.34).]**

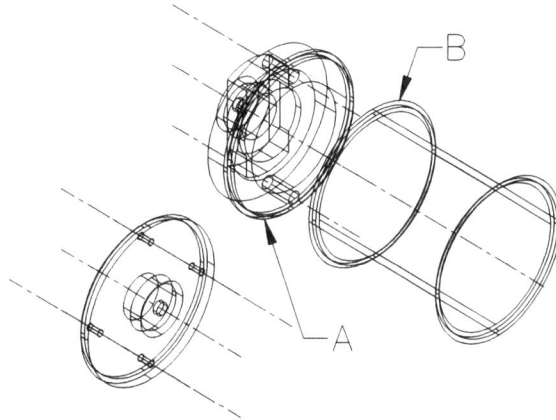

Figure 4.35 Axes mated

Repeat the AMMATE command on two planes. See Figure 4.36.

[Assemblies]   **[Mate]**

Command: **AMMATE**
Reference geometry for mate constraint Line/Point/<Select plane>: **[Select A (Figure 4.35).]**
Reference geometry for mate constraint Line/Point/<Select plane>: **[Select B (Figure 4.35).]**
Distance to offset planes: **0**

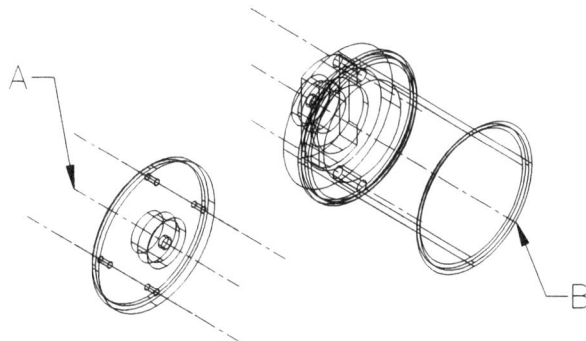

Figure 4.36 Two planes mated

Execute the AMMATE command again. See Figure 4.37.

[Assemblies]   **[Mate]**

Command: **AMMATE**
Reference geometry for mate constraint Line/Point/<Select plane>: **LINE**
Select reference line to constrain: **[Select A (Figure 4.36).]**
Reference geometry for mate constraint PLane/POint/<Select line>: **[Select B (Figure 4.36).]**

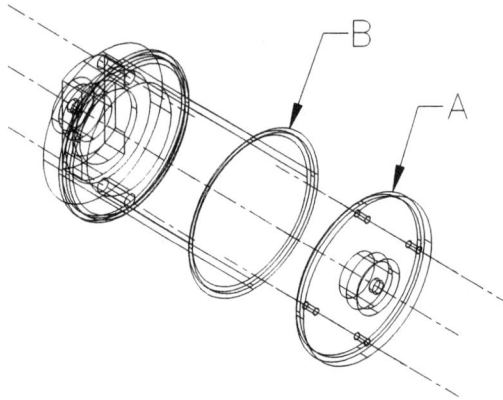

Figure 4.37 Axes mated

Repeat the AMMATE command on two planes. See Figure 4.38.

[Assemblies]   **[Mate]**

Command: **AMMATE**
Reference geometry for mate constraint Line/Point/<Select plane>: **[Select A (Figure 4.37).]**
Reference geometry for mate constraint Line/Point/<Select plane>: **[Select B (Figure 4.37).]**
Distance to offset planes: **0**

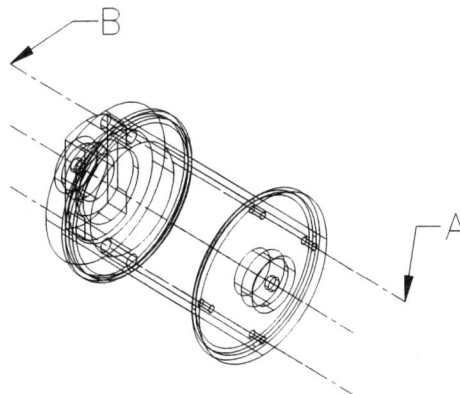

Figure 4.38 Two planes mated

Finally, apply the AMMATE command to complete the assembly. See Figure 4.39.

[Assemblies]   **[Mate]**

Command: **AMMATE**
Reference geometry for mate constraint Line/Point/<Select plane>: **LINE**
Select reference line to constrain: **[Select A (Figure 4.38).]**
Reference geometry for mate constraint PLane/POint/<Select line>: **[Select B (Figure 4.38).]**

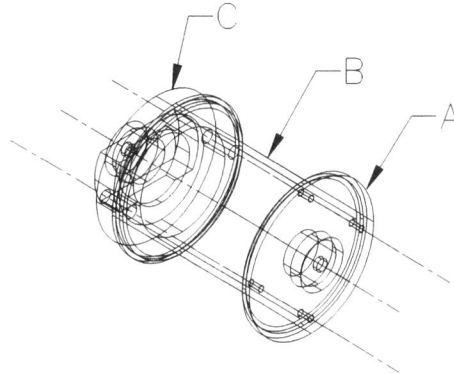

Figure 4.39 Instances properly assembled

You have completed the assembly drawing of the electric motor casing. Run the QSAVE command.

<File>   **<Save...>**

Command: **QSAVE**

[File name: **MOTOR.DWG**
OK   ]

In this assembly, all the instances refer to the external component definitions. The external component definitions are solid parts in three separate drawing files. If you make any changes to the external solid parts, the content of the assembly drawing changes as well. You may apply the AMAUDIT command on the assembly drawing to check the time and date stamp of the external files in order to determine whether you need to re-assemble the instances with the AMASSEMBLE command. In so doing, you might have to re-apply the assembly constraint by using the AMCONSTRAINT command. Someone can edit the external component definitions while you are working on this assembly drawing. To reload the external definitions, you may use the AMREFRESH command.

4.9 Assembly Utilities

Having properly assembled the instances together, you may now assign material to each component definition. Run the AMASSMPROP command. See Figure 4.40.

<Assemblies> **<Analysis>** **<Mass Properties>**

Command: **AMASSMPROP**
Select component Name/<Select>: **[Enter]**
Select component: **[Select A, B, and C (Figure 4.39).]**
Select component: **[Enter]**

[% Error: **1**
 Coordinate System: **WCS**
 Assembly units: **mm**
 Mass units: **g**
 Material...
   [Component definition: **MOTOR_1**
   Aluminum
   Assign
   Component definition: **MOTOR_2**
   Aluminum
   Assign
   Component definition: **MOTOR_3**
   Stain_Steel, Austenic
   Assign
   OK   ]
OK   ]

```
┌──────────────────────────────────────────────────────┐
│           Assembly Mass Property Results               │
│ Component: Multiple                                    │
│ Mass:    41095.5422 g                                 │
│ Volume:  15164.4067 cm^3                              │
│                                                        │
│ Center of Gravity          Principal moments:         │
│ ┌──────────────┐           ┌──────────────────────┐   │
│ │ X:    94.362 │           │ X:    420342032.8773 │   │
│ │ Y:    100    │           │ Y:    381759738.7918 │   │
│ │ Z:    0      │           │ Z:    792632143.9328 │   │
│ └──────────────┘           └──────────────────────┘   │
│ Radii of Gyration          Products:                  │
│ ┌──────────────┐           ┌──────────────────────┐   │
│ │ X:  101.1356 │           │ XY:   387785765.793  │   │
│ │ Y:  96.3824  │           │ YZ:   0              │   │
│ │ Z:  138.8796 │           │ ZX:   0              │   │
│ └──────────────┘           └──────────────────────┘   │
│ Principal Axes                                         │
│ ┌────────────────────────────────────────────────┐   │
│ │ I: 9386611.0281 alon [1,0,0]                    │   │
│ │ J: 15837324.4459 alo [0,1,0]                    │   │
│ │ K: 15754307.7377 alo [0,0,1]                    │   │
│ └────────────────────────────────────────────────┘   │
│                            ┌──────┐   ┌────────┐       │
│                            │ Done │   │ File...│       │
│                            └──────┘   └────────┘       │
└──────────────────────────────────────────────────────┘
```

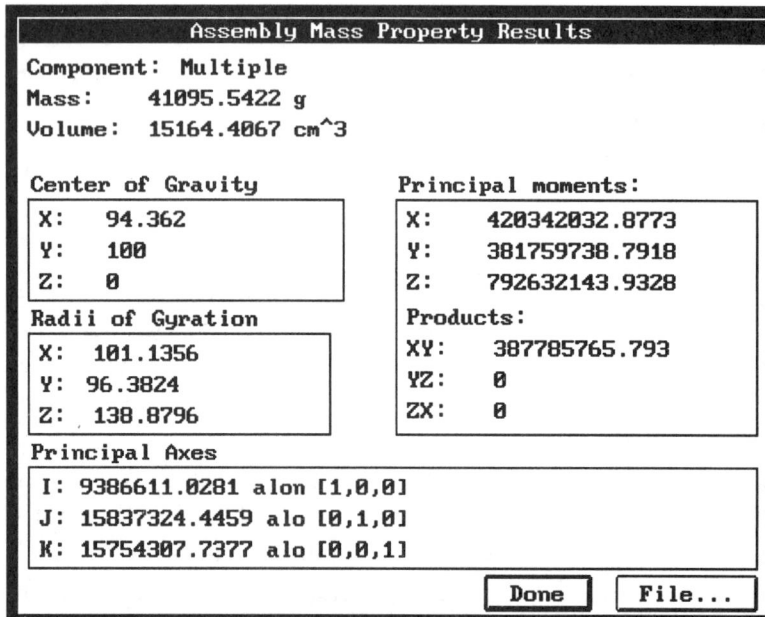

Figure 4.40 Assembly Mass Property Results dialog box

You may view the material assignment and the assembly constraint assignment of an instance by running the AMLISTASSM command.

<Assemblies>   **<Instances>**   **<Query>**

Command: **AMLISTASSM**
Select components Name/<Select>:
Select component: **[Select A, B, and C (Figure 4.39).]**
Select component: **[Enter]**

Component name: MOTOR_1_1
Definition name: MOTOR_1
Degrees of freedom
----
 1 Rotational degrees of freedom
 0 Translational degrees of freedom
Attributes on definition

MATERIAL: Aluminum
DENSITY: 2.710000

Component name: MOTOR_3_1   Base Part
Definition name: MOTOR_3
Degrees of freedom
----
 3 Rotational degrees of freedom
 3 Translational degrees of freedom
Attributes on definition

MATERIAL: Stainless_Steel, Austenic
DENSITY: 2.710000

Component name: MOTOR_2_1
Definition name: MOTOR_2
Degrees of freedom
----
 0 Rotational degrees of freedom
 0 Translational degrees of freedom
Attributes on definition

MATERIAL: Aluminum
DENSITY: 2.710000

Besides the material assignment, you may assign textural information to a component definition; each attribute has a name and a value. The value can be a string, an integer, or a real. For example, you may assign part number, manufacturing requirement, and so on.

Apply the AMASSIGN command to assign a string attribute, "PART NUMBER," to each component definition of the electric motor casing. In Chapter 5, you will include this attribute in the bill of material.

<Assemblies>   **<Component Definition>**   **<Assign Attributes...>**

Command: **AMASSIGN**

```
[Component definitions: MOTOR_1
 Add...
    [Attribute Name:      PART NUMBER
     Attribute Value: 01
     Column Data type: String
     OK                                    ]
 Component definitions:  MOTOR_2
 Add...
    [Attribute Name:      PART NUMBER
     Attribute Value: 02
     Column Data type: String
     OK                                    ]
 Component definitions:  MOTOR_3
 Add...
    [Attribute Name:      PART NUMBER
     Attribute Value: 03
     Column Data type: String
     OK                                    ]
 Done                                          ]
```

You have assigned materials and attributes to the assembly drawing. You will make use of them in the next chapter.

4.10 Summary

In this chapter, you applied the following AutoCAD Designer commands and variables to create two sets of assemblies.

Assembly constraint commands:

AMALIGN	AMCONSTRAINT	AMDELCONST
AMEDITCONST	AMFLUSH	AMMATE
AMOPPOSE		

Component definitions and instances management commands:

AMAUDIT	AMBROWSE	AMCOMPIN
AMCOMPMAN	AMCOMPOUT	AMDELCOMP
AMINSERT	AMNEW	AMREFRESH
AMRENAME	AMREPLACE	AMTARGET
AMWHEREUSE		

Assembly commands:

AMASSEMBLE	AMASSMVARS	AMASSMVIS
AMINTERFERE		

Assembly utility commands:

AMASSIGN	AMASSMPROP	AMLISTASSM

Assembly variables:

AMAUTOASSEMBLE
AMVIEWRESTORE

For a brief explanation of these commands and variables, refer to the appendix of this book.

By now, you should be able to put away a solid part in a drawing to make it become a local component definition or become an external component definition that resides in an attached external drawing. You should be able to manage solid parts, instances, and component definitions, both locally and externally. Most important, you should be able to apply assembly constraints to the instances to produce sub-assemblies and assemblies. Besides assembling the parts together, you also worked on assembly utilities.

In the next chapter, you will produce two-dimensional engineering drawings from the solid parts that you created in Chapter 2, and will produce exploded assembly drawings of the assemblies that you created in this chapter.

4.11 Exercises

Now that you have produced two sets of assemblies under guidance, you will assemble the parts of the toggle clamp assembly on your own.

Start a new drawing, and attach the components that you created in Chapter 2 and Chapter 3. Refer to Figures 2.49, 2.50, and 2.51 of Chapter 2, and to Figures 3.72 and 3.74 of Chapter 3. There are six component definitions.

Insert the component definitions as instances. See Figure 4.41.

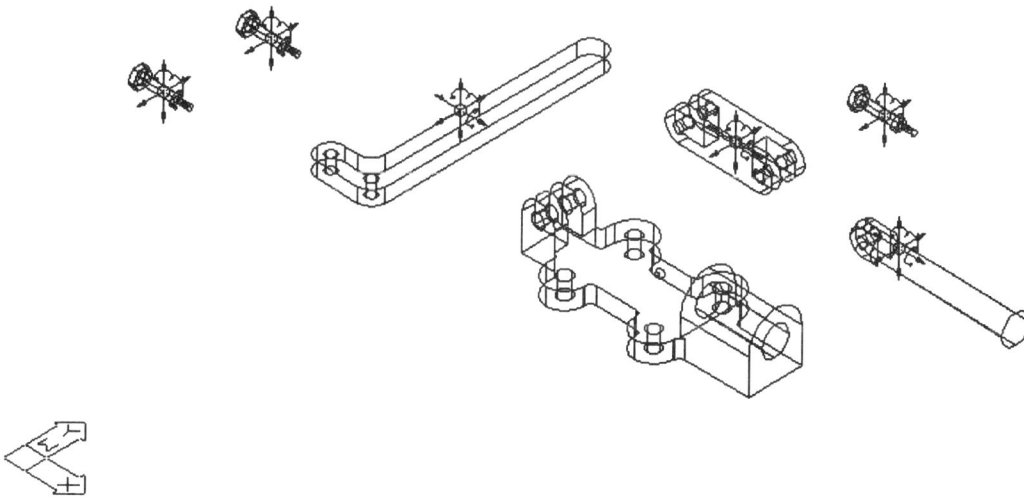

Figure 4.41 The parts for the toggle clamp assembly

As shown in Figure 4.42, apply assembly constraints to the instances to assemble them together properly.

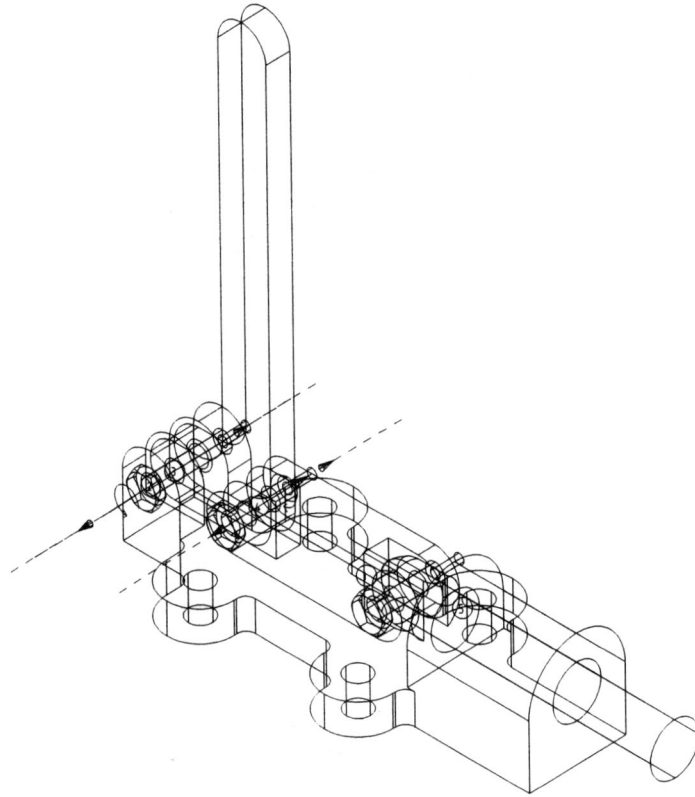

Figure 4.42 The toggle clamp assembly

After completing the assembly, save the drawing named TOGGLE.DWG.

Chapter 5

Documentation

AutoCAD Designer solid parts are three-dimensional feature-based parametric solid models. A solid model consists of edge data, surface data, and volume data. You may use a solid model for many purposes in manufacturing, such as computer-aided manufacturing, rapid prototyping, etc. However, there are occasions when you have to communicate a three-dimensional design in a conventional way by outputting a two-dimensional engineering drawing.

With an AutoCAD Designer solid part, you may output a two-dimensional engineering drawing. From a set of instances in an assembly, you may generate a bill of materials and an exploded view, in addition to an engineering drawing. The drawings and the solid parts associate to each other bidirectionally. If you update a solid part, the drawing changes. If you alter a parametric dimension in a drawing, the solid part is also modified.

Having created two solid parts in Chapter 2, and two sets of assembly in Chapters 3 and 4, you will produce engineering drawings and exploded assembly drawings in this chapter.

You will create the engineering drawings of the "LEVER" solid part and the "PLATE" solid part and exploded assembly drawings of the "U_JOINT" assembly set and the "MOTOR" assembly set.

5.1 Standard Practice

To produce a two-dimensional engineering document, you need to follow standard practice, such as ANSI, DIN, ISO, etc. Whatever the standard is, you need to place the engineering content of the drawing within a proper title block.

A title block is a rectangle, or four border lines, with margins around the edge of the paper. Within the title block, in addition to the engineering drawing itself, you need to include general engineering information. Typically, it should have the name of the company, possibly with the company logo, and textural data. You need to state who creates the drawing, who checks the drawing, who approves the drawing, the date, the plotting scale, the material, the surface finish requirement, and the tolerances, etc. Figure 5.1 shows a typical title block.

You should have a similar title block ready before you start creating engineering drawings in this chapter. If you have not got one, you should create one now. Then you should save it in the computer storage device for later insertion into the engineering drawing.

205

In making the title block, you may ask what the width of the margin between the four borders and the edges of the paper should be. The answer is that it depends on how much space your plotting device needs to clamp the paper while it prints. You may check it out by drawing a rectangle. Then plot the rectangle with your plotting device, using the "Fit to size" option. After plotting, measure the lengths of the lines printed. These lengths are the width and height of the rectangle that you should use to create a formal title block.

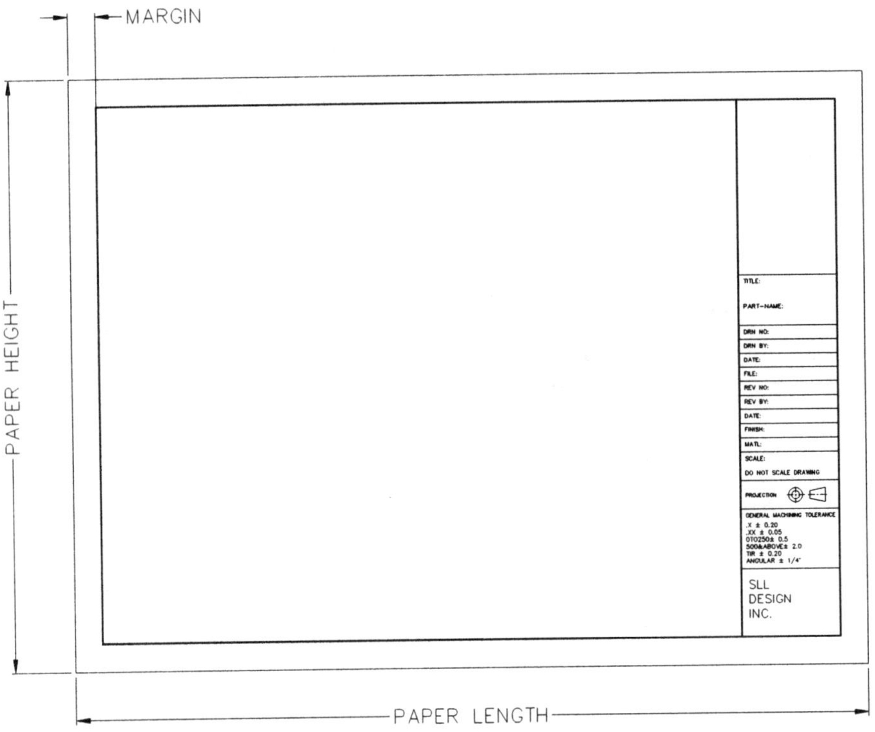

Figure 5.1 A typical title block for producing an engineering document

5.2 Engineering Drawing

With a proper title block ready, you may start to create a two-dimensional engineering drawing from a solid part.

Use the OPEN command to retrieve the second solid part that you created in Chapter 2. If you saved the file under a different name, replace "LEVER" in the following delineation with the name of your saved file. See Figure 5.2.

<File>   **<Open...>**

Command: **OPEN**

[File name: **LEVER.DWG**
OK   ]

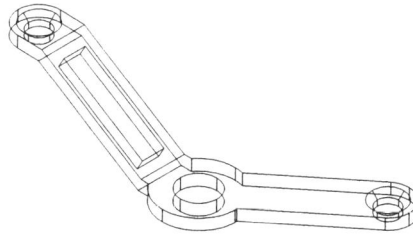

Figure 5.2 The second solid part created in Chapter 2

You will create a two-dimensional engineering drawing from this solid part. In an AutoCAD drawing, there are two working environments: model space environment and paper space environment. In AutoCAD Designer terms, they are model mode and drawing mode. To switch from one mode to another, you may issue the AMMODE command. Run this command to set to drawing mode.

<Drawings>   <Drawing Mode>

Command: **AMMODE**
Model/<Drawing>: **[Enter]**

After you switch to drawing mode, the solid part that you created in model mode disappears. The screen is blank because you have not done anything in this mode.

Before you may start to create a two-dimensional engineering drawing from the solid part, you need to place a title block. The title block gives you a better sense of the size of the working area of the paper. Make a layer called TITLE. Then run the INSERT command. See Figure 5.3. When you insert the title block, set the insertion scale to 1.

<Data>   <Layers...>

Command: **DDLMODES**

Layer
TITLE

Current layer: **TITLE**

Command: **INSERT**

[File name: **YOUR_TITLE_BLOCK**
OK   ]

Figure 5.3 A title block inserted

Now you have a title block inserted in drawing mode and a solid part created in model mode.

To create two-dimensional engineering drawings, you need to follow standard practice. You have to state whether you want to use first angle projection or third angle projection, to state the standard of screw thread representation, to state the line types, etc. Run the AMDWGVARS command.

<Drawings>   <Preferences...>

Command: **AMDWGVARS**

[Projection type of unfolded views: **Third Angle**
  Display parametric dimensions: **YES**
  Hide drawing viewport borders: **YES**
      [Drafting Standards
        Tapped Holes: **Ansi**
        Detail Views: **Ansi**
        Section Views: **Ansi**
        Display Vanish: **NO**
      OK   ]
      [Centerlines
        Parametric Sizing of Extension Lines: **YES**
        Centermark: **2**
        Gap: **2**
        Overshoot: **12**
        Centerline linetype: **CENTER**
      OK   ]
    Section symbol linetype: **PHANTOMS**

Hidden line linetype: **HIDDEN**
  OK   ]

The AMDWGVARS command sets the following variables:

* AMPROJTYPE   Projection type of unfolded views
* AMREUSEDIM   Display parametric dimensions
* AMVPBORDER   Hide drawing viewport borders
* AMSTDTAP   Tapped holes
* AMSTDDTL   Detail views
* AMSTDSCT   Section views
* AMLINETHICK   Thread thickness
* AMVANISH   Sets vanishes if tapped hole uses ANSI standard
* AMCLPAR   Parametric sizing of extension lines
* AMCLCM   Centermark
* AMCLGAP   Gap
* AMCLOSHT   Overshoot
* AMCLTYPE   Centerline line type
* AMSECLTYPE   Section symbol line type
* AMHIDLTYPE   Hidden line line type

Apply the LTSCALE command to set linetype scale to 8.

<Options>   <Linetypes>   <Global Linetype Scale>

Command: **LTSCALE**
New scale factor: **8**

After setting the drawing standard and the line type scale, you may apply the AMDWGVIEW command to create a series of engineering drawing views. This command allows you to create six types of views. They are base view, orthographic view, auxiliary view, isometric view, sectional view, and detail view.

Run the AMDWGVIEW command to create a top view. See Figure 5.4.

<Drawings>   <Create View>

Command: **AMDWGVIEW**

```
┌─────────────────────────────────────────────────┐
│ Create Drawing View                               │
│ ┌─Type────────┐  ┌─Hidden Lines──────────────┐   │
│ │              │  │ ☑ Calculate hidden lines  │   │
│ │  ◉ Base      │  │                           │   │
│ │  ○ Ortho     │  │ ☐ Hide hidden lines       │   │
│ │  ○ Aux       │  │ Linetype of hidden lines: │   │
│ │  ○ Iso       │  │ ┌──────────────────┬───┐  │   │
│ │  ○ Detail    │  │ │ HIDDEN           │ ▼ │  │   │
│ │              │  │ └──────────────────┴───┘  │   │
│ └──────────────┘  │ ☐ Display tangencies      │   │
│ ┌─Data Set─────┐  └───────────────────────────┘   │
│ │  ◉ Active Part│ ┌─Scale─────────────────────┐   │
│ │  ○ Assembly  │  │ ┌───────────────────────┐ │   │
│ │  ○ Select    │  │ │ 0.5                   │ │   │
│ │  ○ Group     │  │ └───────────────────────┘ │   │
│ │              │  │ ☐ Relative to Parent      │   │
│ └──────────────┘  └───────────────────────────┘   │
│                   ┌───────────────────────────┐   │
│                   │      Section View...       │   │
│                   └───────────────────────────┘   │
│                   Detail View Symbol  ┌─────────┐ │
│                                       └─────────┘ │
│   ┌────────┐    ┌────────┐    ┌────────┐          │
│   │   OK   │    │ Cancel │    │ Help...│          │
│   └────────┘    └────────┘    └────────┘          │
└─────────────────────────────────────────────────┘
```

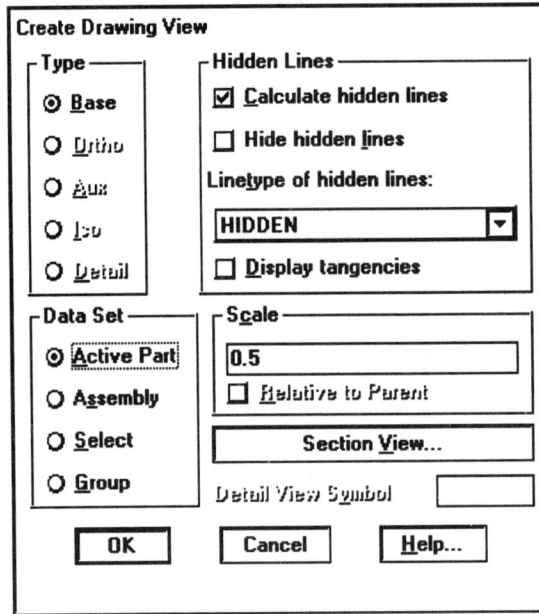

The first drawing view in a drawing is the base view. Therefore, you have to choose this option.

[Type:	**Base**
Hidden Lines	
Calculate hidden lines:	**YES**
Hide hidden lines:	**NO**
Linetype of hidden lines:	**HIDDEN**
Display tangencies:	**NO**
Data Set:	**Active Part**
Scale:	**0.5**
OK	]

After you click the "OK" button, the solid part in model mode appears again. You need to specify the orientation of the XY plane of the view. In this case, use the XY plane of the world coordinate system (WCS), and set the orientation of the X axis direction of the drawing view to align with that of the WCS.

```
worldXy/worldYz/worldZx/Ucs/<Select work plane or edge>: WORLDXY
worldX/worldY/worldZ/<Select work axis or straight edge>: WORLDX
Rotate/Z-flip/<Accept>: [Enter]
Location for base view: [Select A (Figure 5.3).]
Location for base view: [Enter]
```

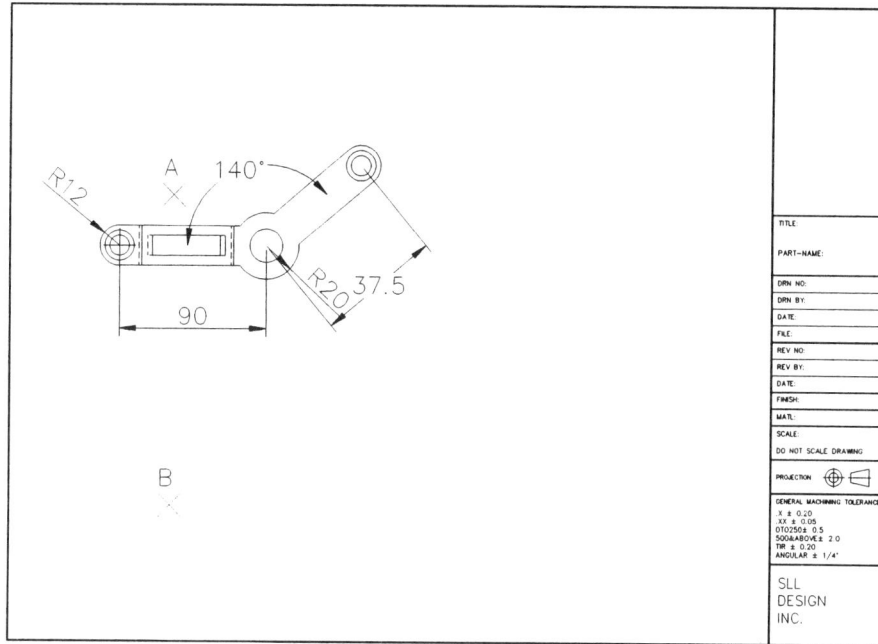

Figure 5.4 A top view created

You have a top view created. In the drawing view, there are some parametric dimensions that you have used to make the sketch elicit. Their positions may not be correct. Leave them as they are now. You will come back to dimensioning later. Continue the AMDWGVIEW command to make a front view. A front view is an orthographic view relative to a parent view. Choose the top view that you have created as the parent view. See Figure 5.5.

<Drawings>   <Create View>

Command: **AMDWGVIEW**

[Type: **Ortho**
  Hidden Lines
      Calculate hidden lines: **YES**
      Hide hidden lines: **NO**
      Linetype of hidden lines: **HIDDEN**
      Display tangencies: **NO**
OK   ]

Select parent view: **[Select A (Figure 5.4).]**
Location for orthographic view: **[Select B (Figure 5.4).]**
Location for orthographic view: **[Enter]**

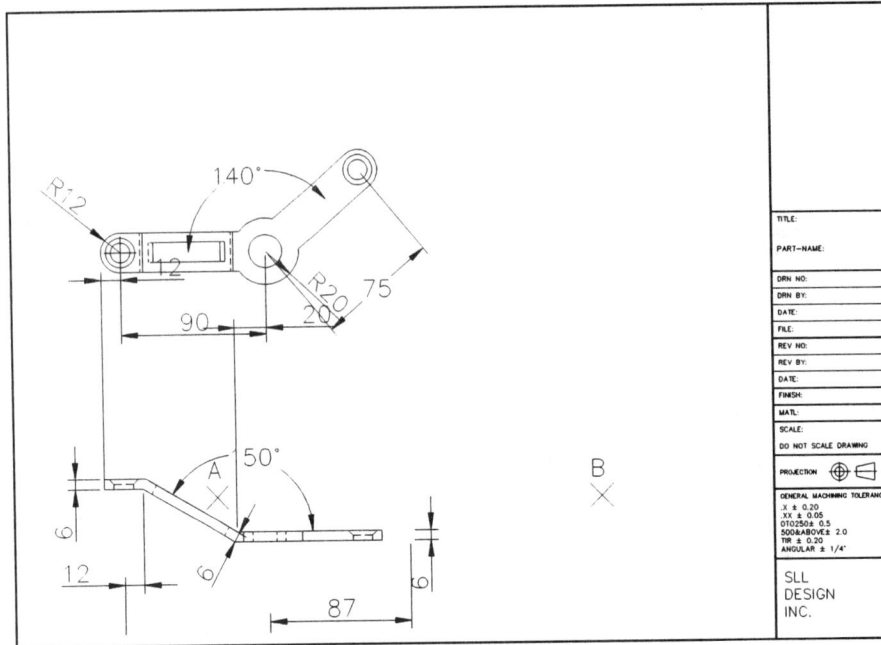

Figure 5.5 Front view created

After making the top view and the front view, you will produce a sectional side view. This is a full section. A section needs a section plane. You may use a construction feature for this purpose. Switch back to model mode with the AMMODE command. Then turn on the display of the work planes and work axes with the AMPLNDSP command and the AMAXISDSP command, respectively. See Figure 5.6.

<Drawings>	**<Drawing Mode>**		

Command: **AMMODE**
Drawing/<Model>: **MODEL**

<Parts>	**<Display>**	**<Work Plane>**	**<On>**

Command: **AMPLNDSP**
Display/ON/<OFf>: **ON**

<Parts>	**<Display>**	**<Work Axis>**	**<On>**

Command: **AMAXISDSP**
OFf/<ON>: **ON**

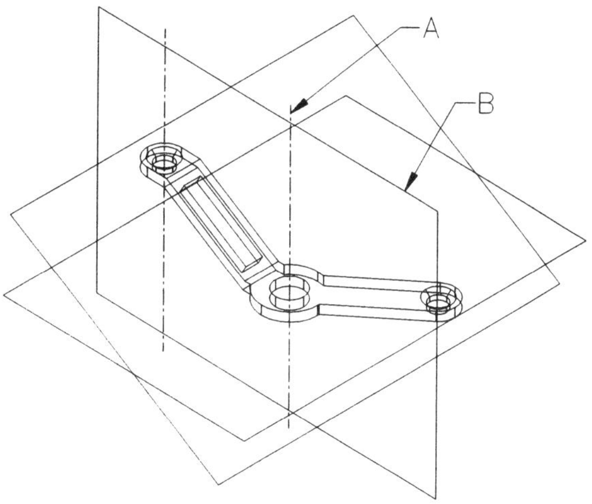

Figure 5.6 Work planes and work axes displayed in model mode

Run the AMWORKPLN command to create a work plane for use as a cutting plane. See Figure 5.7.

\<Parts\>   **\<Feature\>**   **\<Work Plane...\>**

Command: **AMWORKPLN**

[1st Modifier: **Planar Normal**
 2nd Modifier: **On Edge/Axis**
 Create Sketch Plane: **NO**
 OK   ]

worldX/worldY/worldZ/\<Select work axis or straight edge\>: **[Select A (Figure 5.6).]**
worldXy/worldYz/worldZx/Ucs/\<Select work plane or planar face\>: **[Select B (Figure 5.6).]**

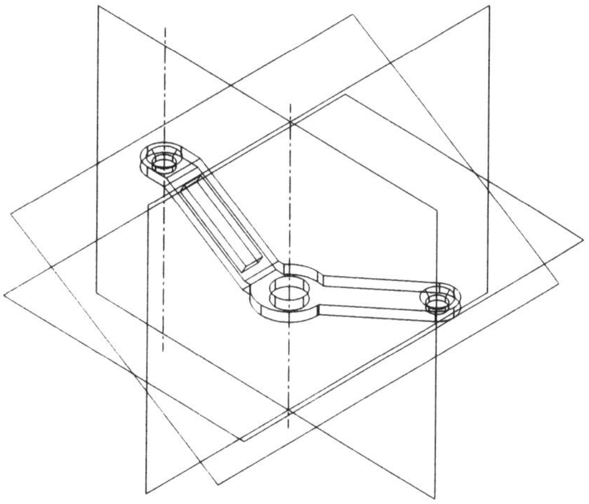

Figure 5.7 A work plane created

After creating a new work plane, run the AMMODE command to switch back to drawing mode. Then issue the AMDWGVIEW command to create a sectional side view. Use the new work plane that you have created as the cutting plane. See Figure 5.8.

<Drawings>   **<Drawing Mode>**

Command: **AMMODE**
Model/<Drawing>: **[Enter]**

<Drawings>   **<Create View>**

Command: **AMDWGVIEW**

[Type: **Ortho**
  Hidden Lines
     Calculate hidden lines: **YES**
     Hide hidden lines: **NO**
  Linetype of hidden lines: **HIDDEN**
  Display tangencies: **NO**
  Section View...
     [Type: **Full**
     Hatch: **YES**
        Pattern...
        [Pattern Properties:
        Pattern: **ANSI31**
        Scale: **50**
        Angle: **0**
        OK   ]
     Section Symbol: **A**
    OK   ]
OK   ]

Select parent view: **[Select A (Figure 5.5).]**
Location for orthographic view: **[Select B (Figure 5.5).]**
Location for orthographic view: **[Enter]**
Section through Point/Ucs/<Work plane>: **[Enter]**
Select work plane in parent view for the section: **[Select the work plane shown in the front view.]**

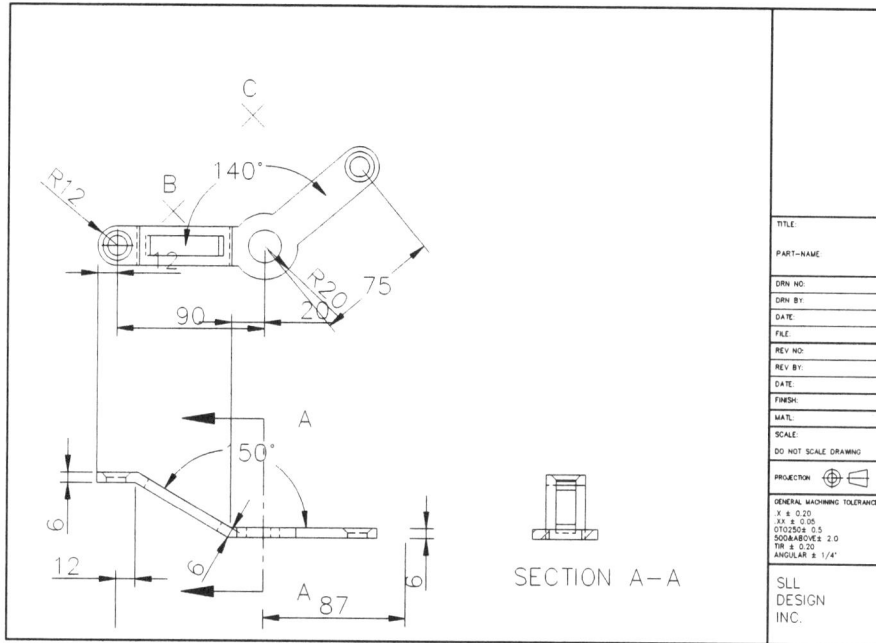

Figure 5.8 A sectional side view created

Each orthographic drawing view is related to its parent view. For the front view, the top view is its parent view. For the sectional side view, the front view is its parent view. If you move a parent view, all its descendant views will move accordingly. Issue the AMMOVEVIEW command to move the top view. See Figure 5.9.

<Drawings>   **<Edit View>**   **<Move>**

Command: **AMMOVEVIEW**
Select view to move: **[Select B (Figure 5.8).]**
2 descendant views will also be moved.
View location: **[Select C (Figure 5.8).]**
View location: **[Enter]**

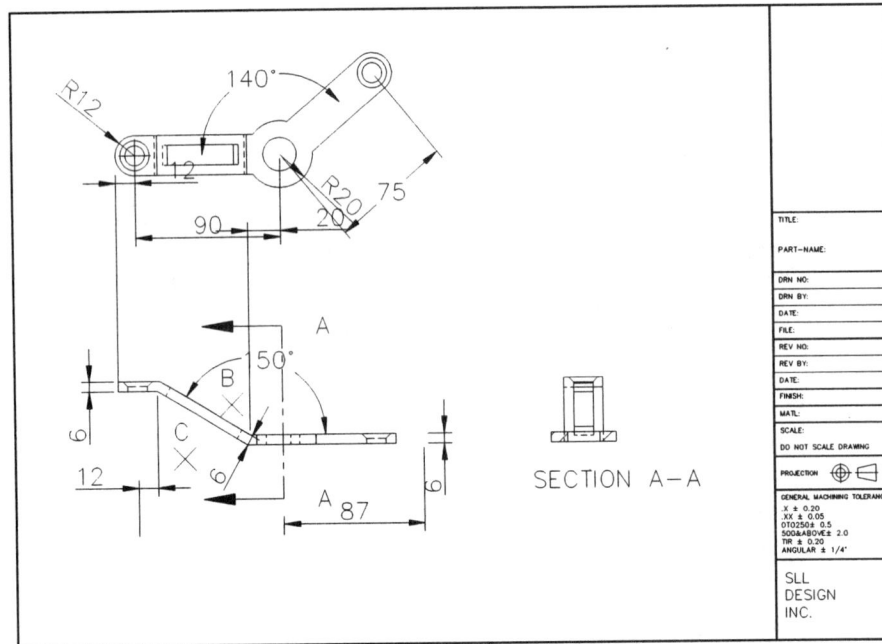

Figure 5.9 The top view and its descendant views moved

As you can see, the front view and the sectional side view move together with the top view. Repeat the AMMOVEVIEW command to move the front view. See Figure 5.10.

<Drawings>   **<Edit View>**   **<Move>**

Command: **AMMOVEVIEW**
Select view to move: **[Select B (Figure 5.9).]**
1 descendant view will also be moved.
View location: **[Select C (Figure 5.9).]**
View location: **[Enter]**

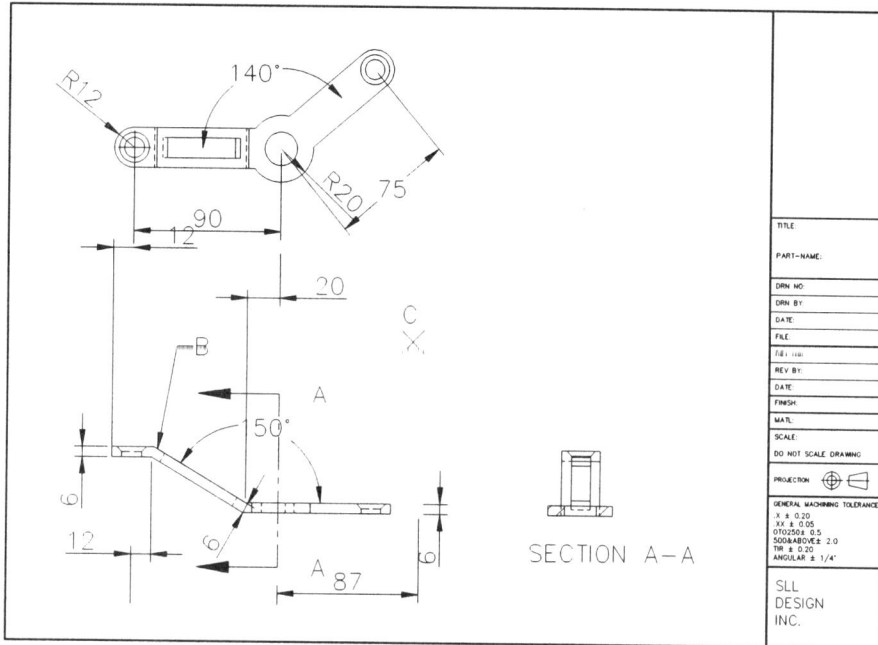

Figure 5.10 The front view and the sectional side view moved

This time, only the side view moves together with the front view. The top view does not move, because it is not a descendant view of the front view.

Create an auxiliary view with the AMDWGVIEW command. See Figure 5.11.

<Drawings>   **<Create View>**

Command: **AMDWGVIEW**

[Type:	**Aux**
Hidden Lines	
Calculate hidden lines:	**YES**
Hide hidden lines:	**NO**
Linetype of hidden lines:	**HIDDEN**
Display tangencies:	**NO**
OK	]

Select a straight edge in the parent view: **[Select B (Figure 5.10).]**
Select second point or <RETURN> to use the selected edge: **[Enter]**
Location for auxiliary view: **[Select C (Figure 5.10).]**
Location for auxiliary view: **[Enter]**

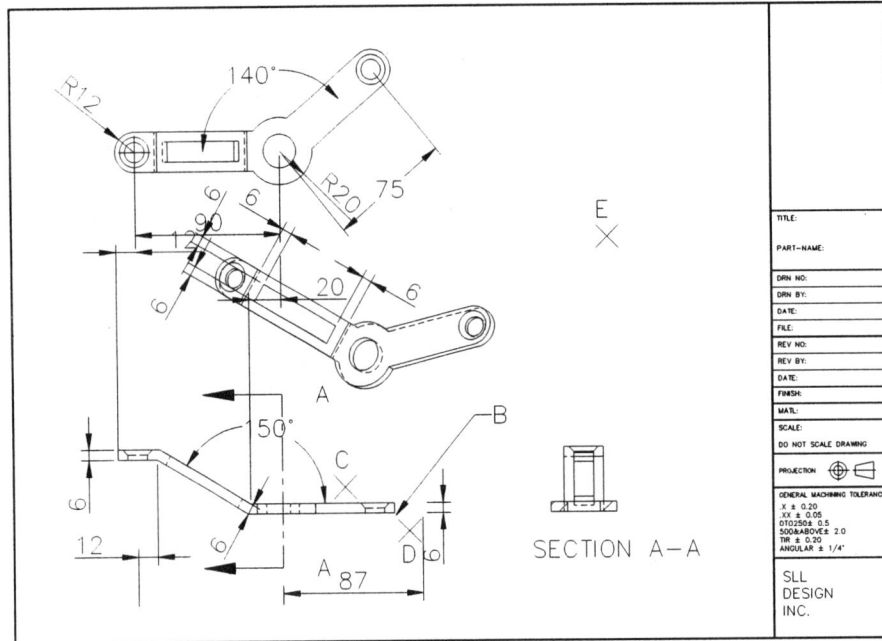

Figure 5.11 An auxiliary view created

As mentioned earlier, there are six types of view. You have created a base view, an orthographic view, a sectional view, and an auxiliary view. Now execute the AMDWGVIEW command to create a detail view. A detail view is an enlargement of a small portion of an existing drawing view. Select the right end of the front view to produce an enlarged portion. See Figure 5.12.

<Drawings>   **<Create View>**

Command: **AMDWGVIEW**

[Type: **Detail**
 Scale: **2**
 Relative to Parent: **NO**
 Detail View Symbol: **B**
OK   ]

Select vertex in parent view for detail center: **[Select B (Figure 5.11).]**
Drag rectangle around detail: **[Select C (Figure 5.11).]**
Other corner: **[Select D (Figure 5.11).]**
Location for detail view: **[Select E (Figure 5.11).]**
Location for detail view: **[Enter]**

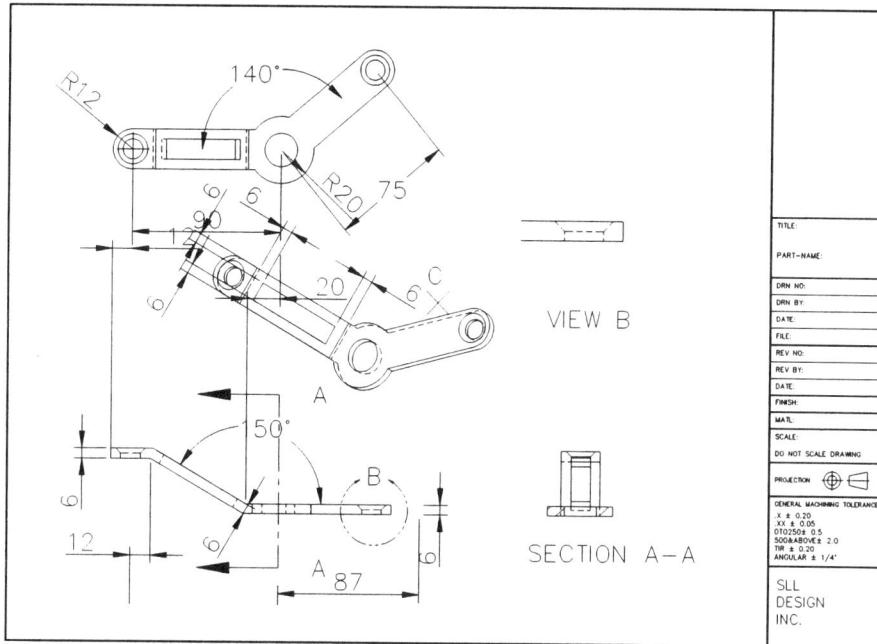

Figure 5.12 A detail view created

You may delete a drawing view that you do not want. Issue the AMDELVIEW command to delete the auxiliary view. See Figure 5.13.

<Drawings>   **<Edit View>**   **<Delete>**

Command: **AMDELVIEW**
Select view to delete: **[Select C (Figure 5.12).]**

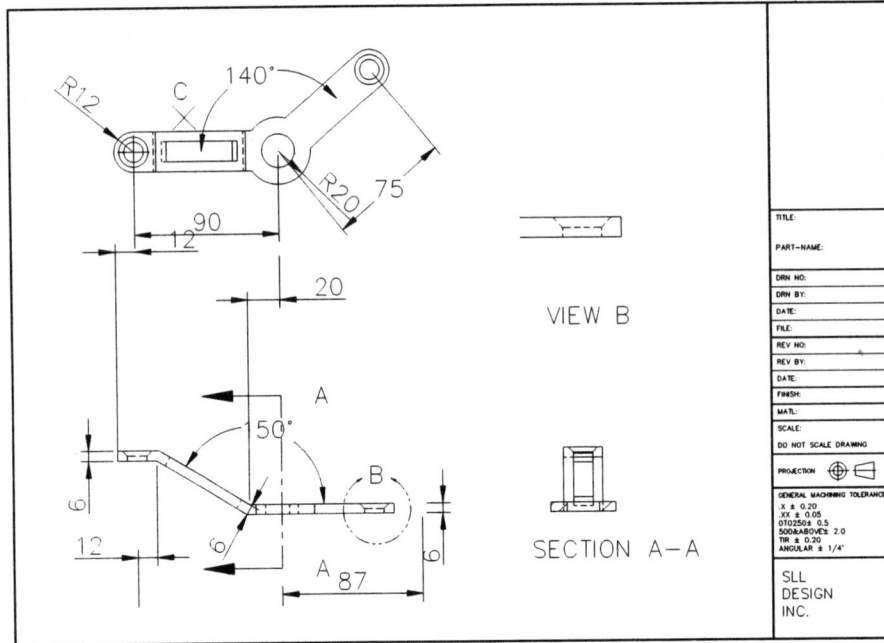

Figure 5.13 The auxiliary view deleted

After deleting the auxiliary view, edit the top view with the AMEDITVIEW command. Use this command to hide the hidden lines. See Figure 5.14.

<Drawings>   **<Edit View>**   **<Attributes>**

Command: **AMEDITVIEW**
Select view to edit: **[Select C (Figure 5.13).]**

[Hidden Lines
 Hide hidden lines: **YES**
OK   ]

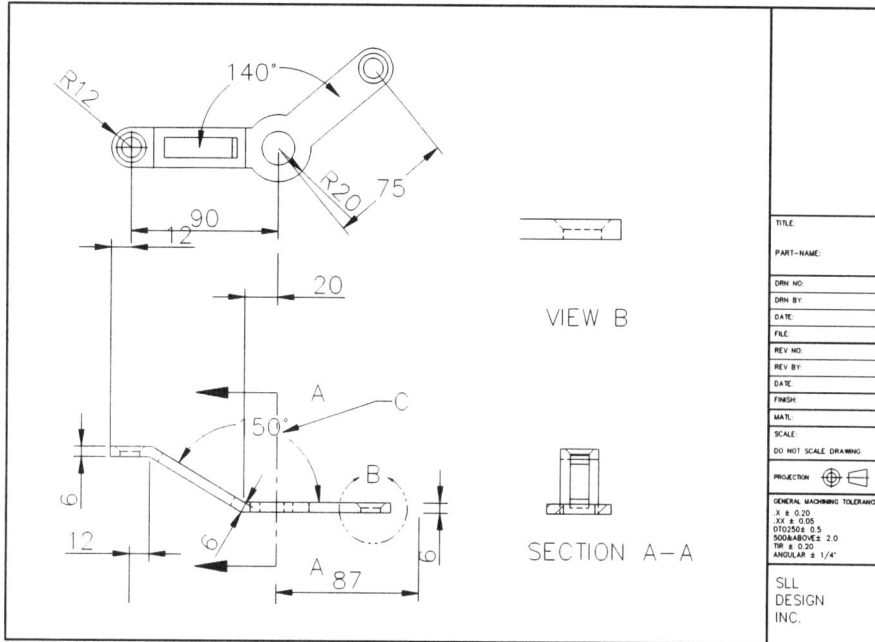

Figure 5.14 Hidden lines hidden in the top view

Now you have completed a two-dimensional engineering drawing of a solid part. This drawing consists of a top view, a front view, a sectional side view, and a detail view.

To sum up, drawing views are objects in drawing mode. You can create a view with the AMDWGVIEW command. You may move a view with the AMMOVEVIEW command. You may delete a view with the AMDELVIEW command. You may edit a view with the AMEDITVIEW command.

5.3   Bidirectional Associativity

The two-dimensional engineering drawing and the three-dimensional solid part associate to each other bidirectionally. Changes to either object cause corresponding changes to the other.

Run the AMMODDIM command on an angular dimension in the front view. Change its value from 150° to 160°. After that, run the AMUPDATE command. Both the drawing and the model change. See Figure 5.15.

    <Parts>   **<Change Dimension>**

Command: **AMMODDIM**
Select dimension to change: **[Select C (Figure 5.14).]**
New value for dimension: **160**
Select dimension to change: **[Enter]**

    <Parts>   **<Update>**

Command: **AMUPDATE**

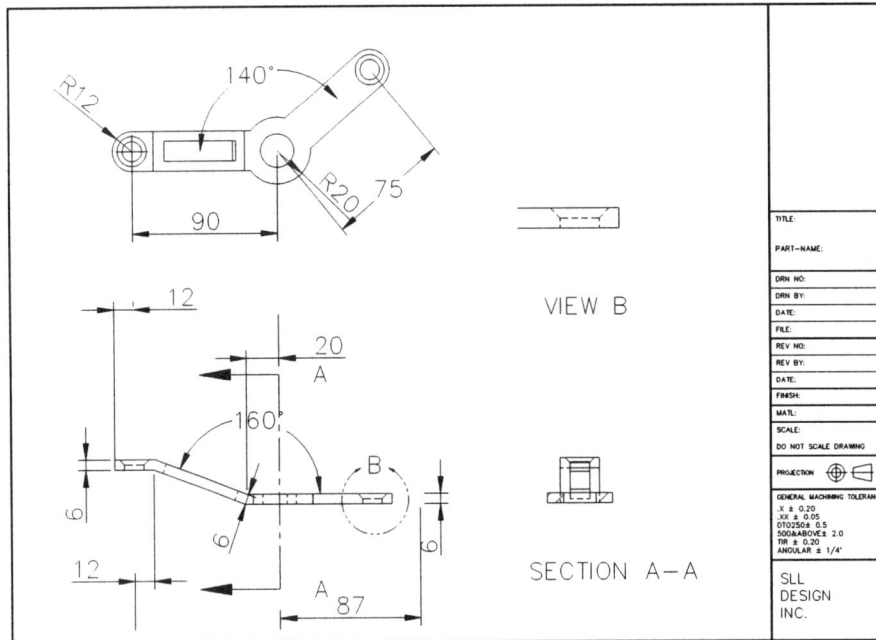

Figure 5.15 Bidirectional change

Apply the AMMODE command to switch to model mode. Then use the AMEDITFEAT command to edit the angular dimension of the base feature.

<Drawings>   **<Drawing Mode>**

Command: **AMMODE**
Drawing/<Model>: **[Enter]**

<Parts>   **<Edit Feature>**

Command: **AMEDITFEAT**
Sketch/surfCut/<select Feature>: **[Select the base feature.]**
Next/<Accept>: **[Enter]**
Select object: **[Select the 140 degree dimension.]**
Enter new value for dimension: **150**
Solved fully constrained sketch.
Select object: **[Enter]**

Issue the AMUPDATE command. Change back to drawing mode with the AMMODE command. Again, both the model and the drawing are updated. See Figure 5.16.

<Parts>   **<Update>**

Command: **AMUPDATE**

<Drawings>   **<Drawing Mode>**

Command: **AMMODE**
Model/<Drawing>: **[Enter]**
3 drawing views being updated.

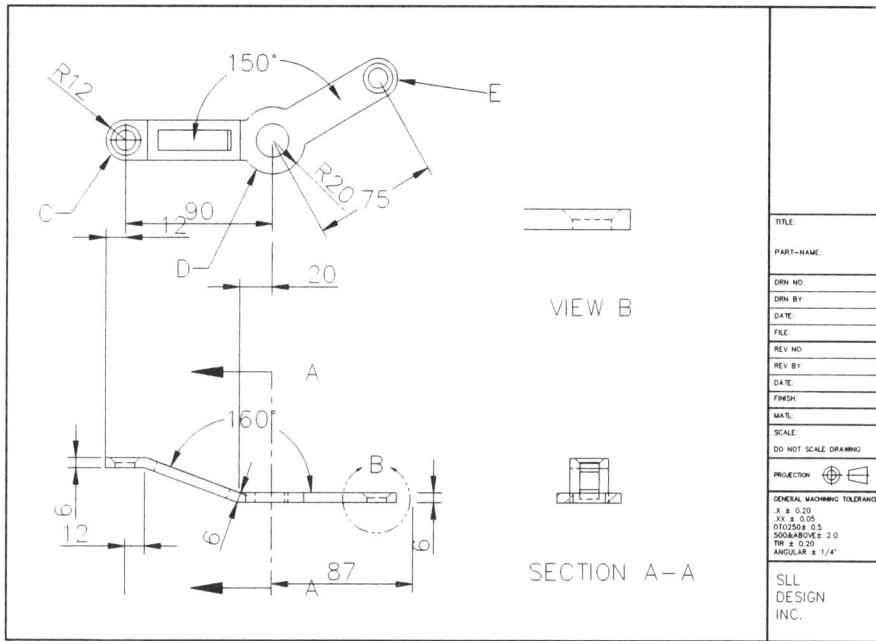

Figure 5.16 Drawing and model updated simultaneously

Remember, the drawing and the model associate to each other bidirectionally. Change to either party causes an automatic modification to the other.

To change a parametric dimension in drawing mode, you may use the AMMODDIM command. To modify a solid in model mode, you should use the AMEDITFEAT command. After changing a dimension or editing a feature, you should run the AMUPDATE command.

5.4 Center Lines

To complete the document, you will add parametric center lines to the drawing by using the AMCENLINE command. This command allows you to add a center line midway between two parallel lines or to add a pair of mutually perpendicular center lines to a circular object.

Apply the AMCENLINE command on the three circular objects of the top view. See Figure 5.17.

<Drawings>   <Annotation>   <Centerline>

Command: **AMCENLINE**
Select Edge: **[Select C (Figure 5.16).]**
Select mirrored edge or <RETURN>: **[Enter]**

<Drawings>   <Annotation>   <Centerline>

Command: **AMCENLINE**
Select Edge: **[Select D (Figure 5.16).]**
Select mirrored edge or <RETURN>: **[Enter]**

<Drawings>   **<Annotation>**   **<Centerline>**

Command: **AMCENLINE**
Select Edge: **[Select E (Figure 5.16).]**
Select mirrored edge or <RETURN>: **[Enter]**

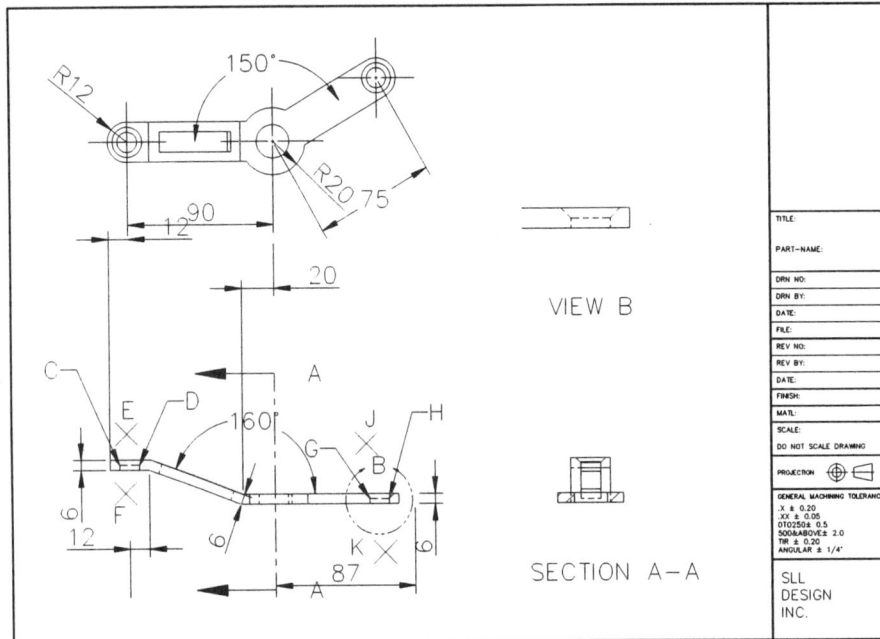

Figure 5.17 Three pairs of center lines created on the top view

    Repeat the AMCENLINE command on the front view to add two vertical center lines. See Figure 5.18.

<Drawings>   **<Annotation>**   **<Centerline>**

Command: **AMCENLINE**
Select Edge: **[Select C (Figure 5.17).]**
Select mirrored edge or <RETURN>: **[Select D (Figure 5.17).]**
Select first trim point: **[Select E (Figure 5.17).]**
Select second trim point: **[Select F (Figure 5.17).]**

<Drawings>   **<Annotation>**   **<Centerline>**

Command: **AMCENLINE**
Select Edge: **[Select G (Figure 5.17).]**
Select mirrored edge or <RETURN>: **[Select H (Figure 5.17).]**
Select first trim point: **[Select J (Figure 5.17).]**
Select second trim point: **[Select K (Figure 5.17).]**

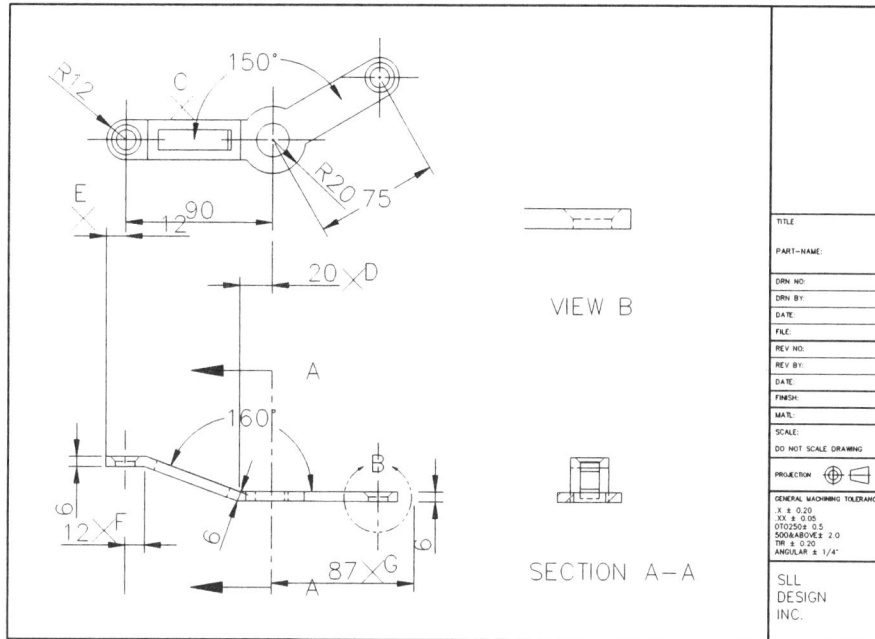

Figure 5.18 Two vertical center lines created on the front view

The engineering drawing with four projection views is completed. To get information about a particular drawing view, you may use the AMLISTDWG command.

```
<Drawings>          <List>

Command: AMLISTDWG
Select view: [Select C (Figure 5.18).]
     Base Drawing View
id = 1       view is ACTIVE and up to date
view scale   : 0.5000
view direction   : 0.0000,0.0000,1.0000
center point : 74.8066,157.0038  target point : 148.8961,127.0235,13.3626
visible layer : AM_VIS
hidden layer: AM_HID   hidden layer linetype    : HIDDEN
Hidden lines are blanked.
Tangent edges are not displayed.
View has 3 descendants, 5 dimensions, 3 notes.
One part represented
```

Because of differences between your drawing and the drawing illustrated here, the information delineated may not be the same as yours.

5.5   Dimensioning and Annotation

In an engineering document, you need to add dimensions and annotations in addition to graphical diagrams. This information is very important for onward manufacturing of the engineering part.

From what you have done, you should have noted that the parametric dimensions that you have used to create the sketched solid feature elicit in the drawing views. These dimensions, though valid in terms of constraining the sketch and the solid part, are sometimes wrongly placed or are irrelevant to manufacture. Before you may issue the drawing to the workshop, you have to make appropriate changes to the dimensions and add annotations.

Obviously, some dimensions that are used in building a solid part for intersection will not be needed in the drawing view. Therefore, you should use the AMHIDEDIM command to hide them. See Figure 5.19.

<Drawings>   <Dimension>   <Hide>

Command: **AMHIDEDIM**
Hide dimensions All/View/<Select>: **[Enter]**
Select dimension: **[Select D, E, F, and G (Figure 5.18).]**
Select dimension: **[Enter]**

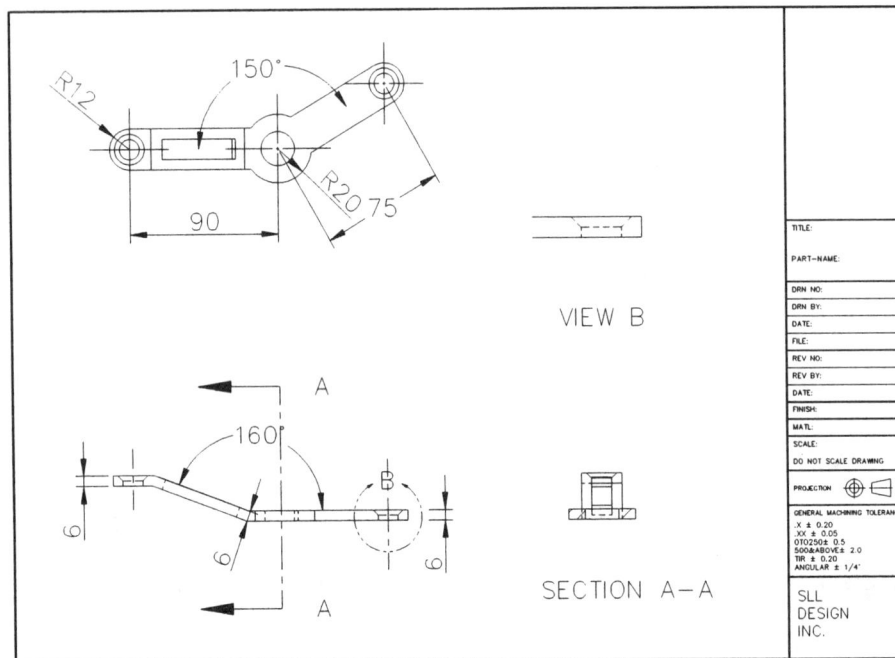

Figure 5.19 Four parametric dimensions hidden

If you want to display a hidden dimension, you may use the AMSHOWDIM command.

<Drawings>   <Dimension>   <Show>

Command: **AMSHOWDIM**
Show dimensions View/<All>: **VIEW**
Select view: **[Select a drawing view. Or, Enter to exit.]**

After hiding some dimensions, you may have to add some reference dimensions to your drawing. Before you do that, turn gripmode on by setting the GRIPS variable to 1. Then tidy up the positioning of the remaining parametric dimensions by manipulating the grip points.

Command: **GRIPS**
New value for GRIPS: **1**

To manipulate the grip points of a dimension, pick the dimension to highlight it. Then click the square grip box and drag it to a new position. Move the dimensions properly as shown in Figure 5.20.

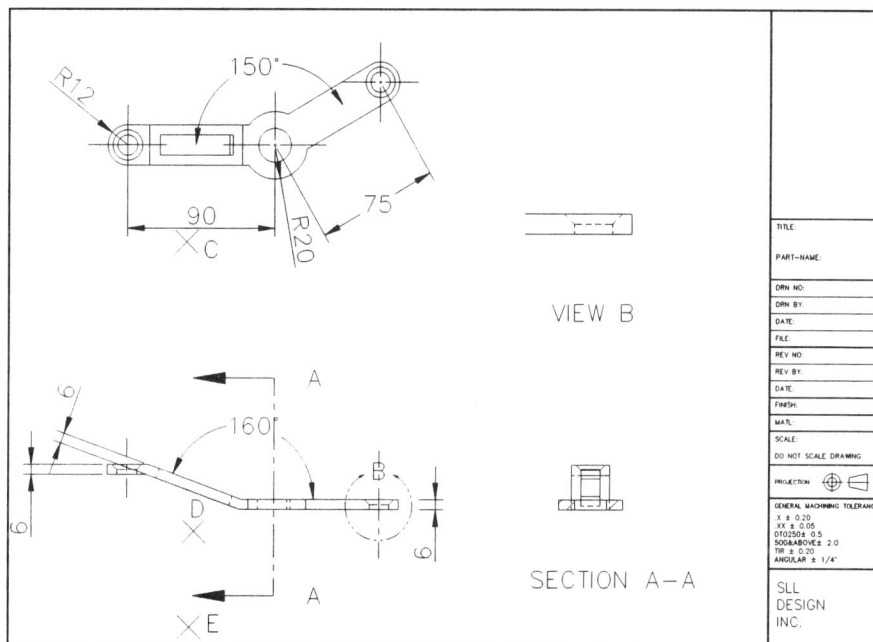

Figure 5.20 Dimensions moved by manipulating their grip points

You have moved the dimensions of a drawing view by manipulating their grips. To move the dimensions from one drawing view to another, you may use the AMMOVEDIM command. See Figure 5.21.

<Drawings>   **<Dimension>**   **<Move>**

Command: **AMMOVEDIM**
Flip/Reattach/<Move>: **MOVE**
Select dimension: **[Select C (Figure 5.20).]**
Select view to place dimension: **[Select D (Figure 5.20).]**
Location for dimension: **[Select E (Figure 5.20).]**
Location for dimension: **[Enter]**
Select dimension: **[Enter]**

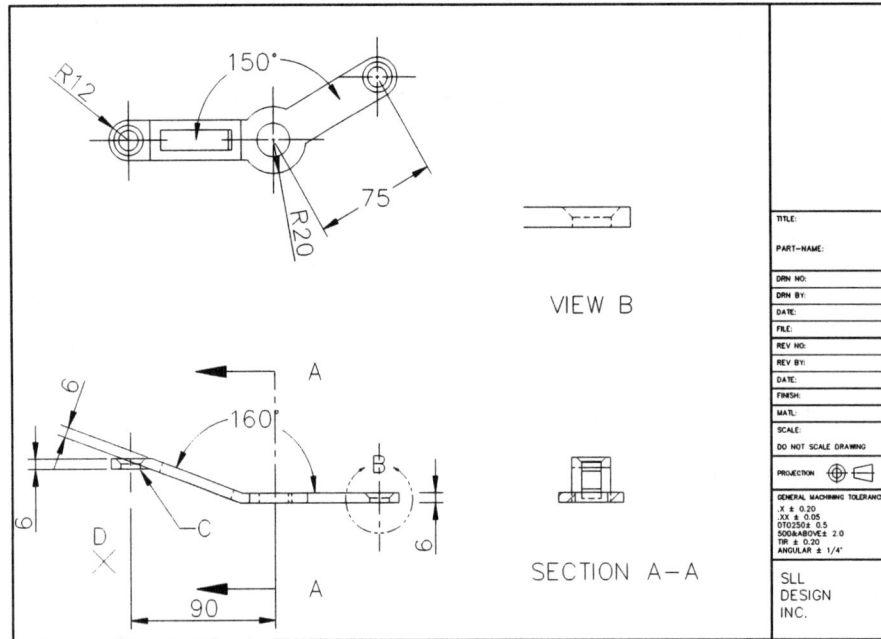

Figure 5.21 A dimension moved from one drawing view to another

It may be necessary to add some reference dimensions to the drawing. To add reference dimensions, use the AMREFDIM command. See Figure 5.22.

<Drawings>   <Dimension>   <Ref Dim>

Command: **AMREFDIM**
Select first object: **[Select C (Figure 5.21).]**
Select second object or place dimension: **[Select D (Figure 5.21).]**
Undo/Ref/Basic/Placement point: **[Enter]**
Select first object: **[Enter]**

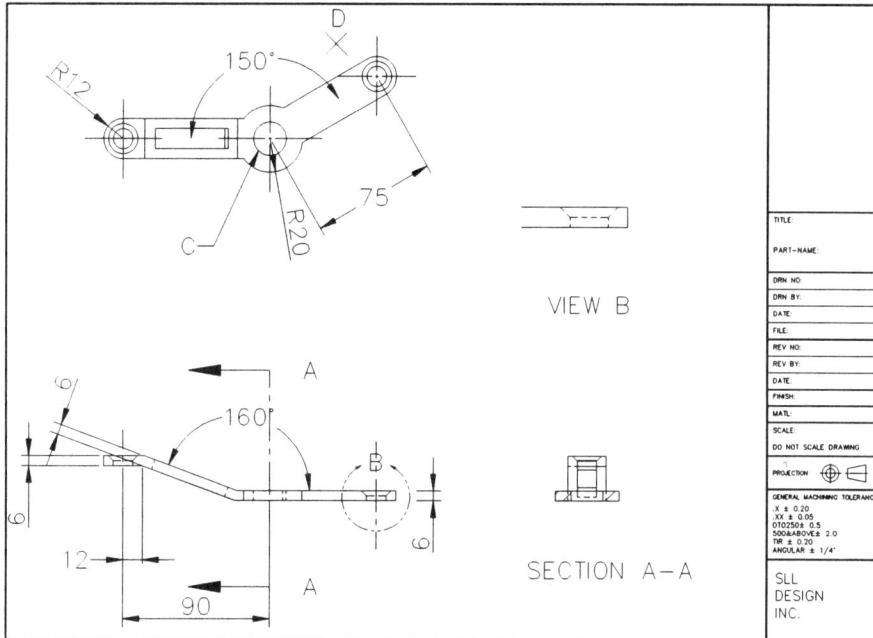

Figure 5.22 A reference dimension added

To sum up, there are two types of dimensions, parametric dimensions and reference dimensions. The parametric dimensions are dimensions that you used to create the parametric solid part. The reference dimensions are dimensions associated with the parametric solid part. You may modify the parametric dimensions to change the solid part. The reference dimensions only follow the change; they cannot drive the change. To create a reference dimension, you may use the AMREFDIM command. To move a dimension within a drawing view, you may manipulate its grip points. To move a dimension from one view to another, you may use the AMMOVEDIM command. To hide a dimension, you may use the AMHIDEDIM command. To display hidden dimensions, you may use the AMSHOWDIM command.

Apart from adding dimensions, you may want to include annotations to a drawing. Apply the AMHOLENOTE command to add a hole note to the central through hole. See Figure 5.23.

<Drawings>   <Annotation>   <Hole Note...>

Command: **AMHOLENOTE**
Edit/<New>: **NEW**
Select hole feature: **[Select C (Figure 5.22).]**

[Template: **THRU_DRILL**
OK   ]

Location for hole note: **[Select D (Figure 5.22).]**
Location for hole note: **[Enter]**
Select hole feature: **[Enter]**

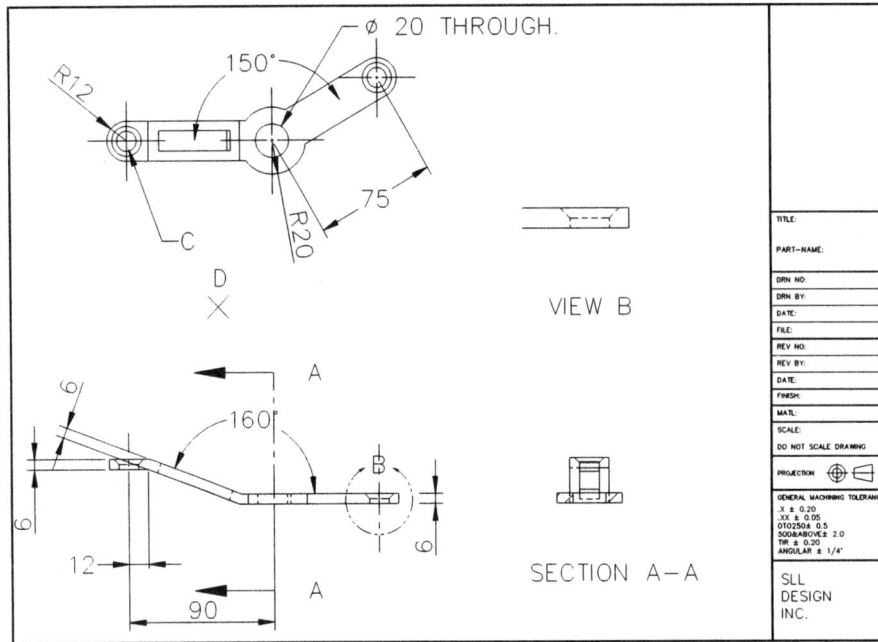

Figure 5.23 A hole note created

Hole notes use templates. Issue the AMTEMPLATE command to edit a template. Prefix the text "2 HOLES" to the default text string.

\<Drawings\>   \<Annotation\>   \<Template...\>

Command: **AMTEMPLATE**

[Template: **THRU_CSINK**
Edit Template
    [*Prefix the following line to the default text string:*
        2 HOLES   ]
SAVE
Template: ***EDITED***
OK   ]

After editing the template, apply the AMHOLENOTE command to one of the two counterbored holes. See Figure 5.24.

\<Drawings\>   \<Annotation\>   \<Hole Note...\>

Command: **AMHOLENOTE**
Edit/\<New\>: **NEW**
Select hole feature: **[Select C (Figure 5.23).]**

[Template: ***EDITED***
OK   ]

Location for hole note: **[Select D (Figure 5.23).]**
Location for hole note: **[Enter]**
Select hole feature: **[Enter]**

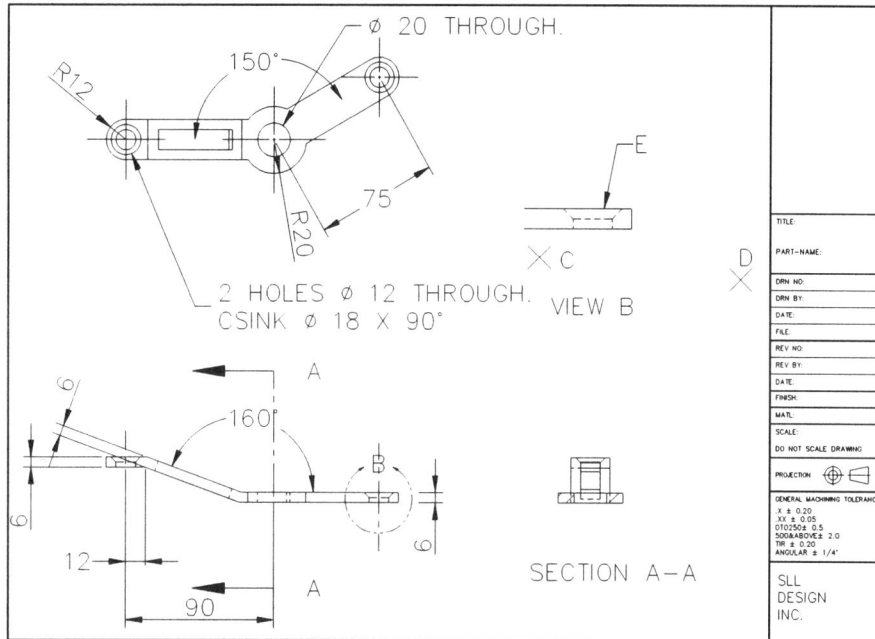

Figure 5.24 Another hole note created

You may attach geometric objects or text to a drawing view. Create a piece of text "SCALE: 2 TO 1" with the MTEXT command.

[Draw]   **[Text]**

Command: **MTEXT**
Attach/Rotation/Style/Height/Direction/<Insertion point>: **[Select C (Figure 5.24).]**
Attach/Rotation/Style/Height/Direction/Width/2Points/<Other corner>: **[Select D (Figure 5.24).]**

To associate the text to the top view, you may use the AMANNOTE command. See Figure 5.25.

<Drawings>   **<Annotation>**   **<Create>**

Command: **AMANNOTE**
Add/Delete/Move/<Create>: **CREATE**
Select objects to associate to view.
Select objects: **[Select the newly created text string.]**
Select objects: **[Enter]**
Select point in view to attach annotation: **[Select E (Figure 5.24).]**

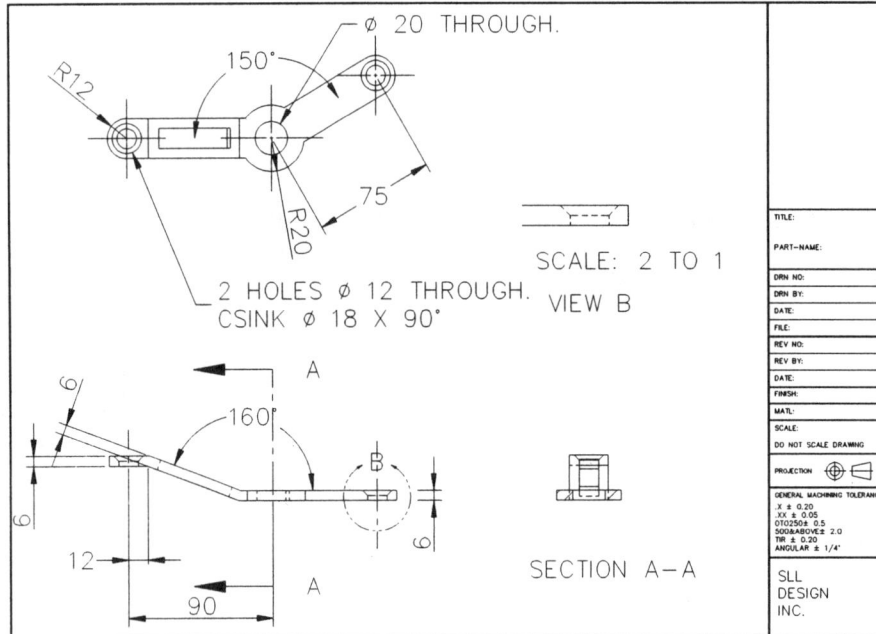

Figure 5.25 A text string attached to the top view

The engineering drawing is now completed. Use the QSAVE command to save your drawing.

<File>   <Save...>

Command: **QSAVE**

[File name: **LEVER.DWG**
OK   ]

5.6   Drawing Mode Output

Your drawing has two modes -- drawing mode and model mode. If you wish to output a purely two-dimensional drawing from the drawing mode of an AutoCAD Designer drawing, you may issue the AMDWGOUT command.

<Drawings>   <Drawing Out...>

Command: **AMDWGOUT**

[File name: **LEVER_2D.DWG**
OK   ]

Four drawing views found
Select objects, or <ret> for all:
Select objects: **[Enter]**

Now you have a two-dimensional drawing in addition to the drawing that consists of the engineering drawing and solid model.

The output drawing is an independent drawing. It has no associativity with the solid part, nor has it any solid part data.

5.7   Offset Section and Isometric View

In drawing mode, you may create six types of drawing views. They are base view, orthographic view, sectional view, auxiliary view, isometric view, and detail view. You learned how to create five types of views in the engineering drawing for the second solid part that you created in Chapter 2. Now you will produce the engineering drawing for the first solid part in the same chapter. In making the drawing, you will create an offset sectional view and an isometric view. Making an isometric view is similar to making other types of drawing views. Creating an offset section requires a parametric cutting plane.

In Chapters 1 and 2, you learned that a rough sketch can be resolved to form a profile, a path, or a cutting line. You worked on profiles in Chapters 2 and 3 and on paths in Chapter 3. Now you will create a rough sketch, resolve it to form a cutting line, and use this line as a cutting plane to create an offset section.

Run the OPEN command to open the first solid part that you saved in Chapter 2. See Figure 5.26.

<File>   **<Open...>**

Command: **OPEN**

[File name: **PLATE3.DWG**
OK   ]

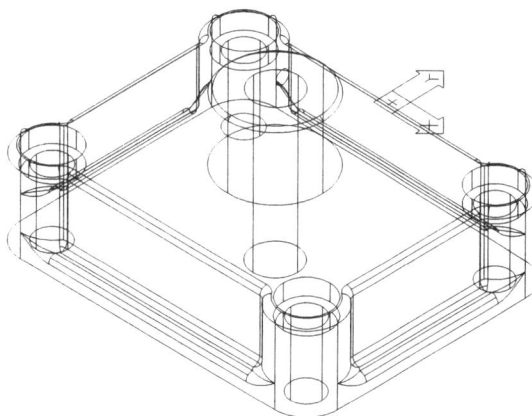

Figure 5.26 The first solid part saved in Chapter 2

Set the display to a plan view by using the short cut key [5]. See Figure 5.27.

Command: **5**

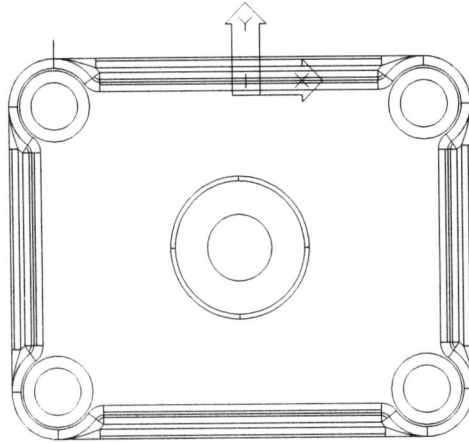

Figure 5.27 Plan view of WCS

An offset section needs an offset cutting plane. Issue the PLINE command to create a rough sketch. Then apply the AMCUTLINE command to resolve it to form a parametric cutting plane. See Figure 5.28.

[Draw]   **[Polyline]**

Command: **PLINE**

<Parts>   **<Sketch>**   **<Cutting Line>**

Command: **AMCUTLINE**
Select objects for section cutting line:
Select objects: **LAST**
Select objects: **[Enter]**

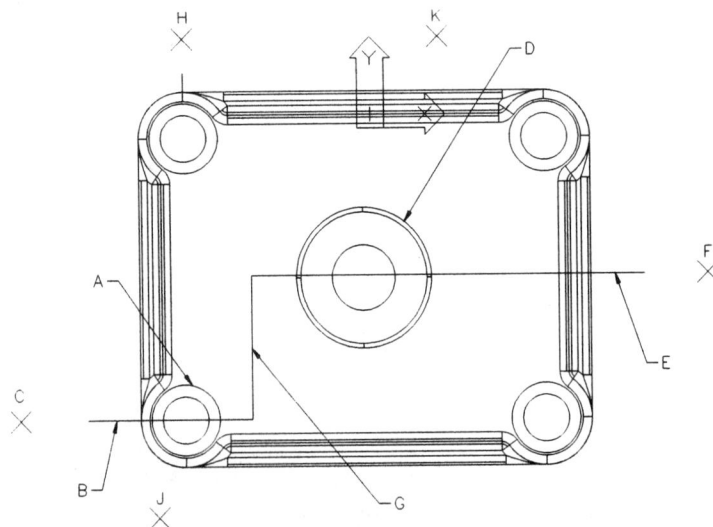

Figure 5.28 Resolved cutting line

Check the geometric constraints that AutoCAD Designer has applied to the cutting line by running the AMSHOWCON command. There should be two horizontal constraints and one vertical constraint. If not, use the AMADDCON command to add the necessary constraints.

Execute the AMPARDIM command to add five parametric dimensions to fully constrain the cutting line. See Figure 5.29.

\<Parts\>   \<Sketch\>   \<Add Dimension\>

Command: **AMPARDIM**
Select first object: **[Select A (Figure 5.28).]**
Select second object: **[Select B (Figure 5.28).]**
Specify dimension placement: **[Select C (Figure 5.28).]**
Undo/Hor/Ver/Align/Par/Enter Dimension value: **0**
Select first object: **[Select D (Figure 5.28).]**
Select second object: **[Select E (Figure 5.28).]**
Specify dimension placement: **[Select F (Figure 5.28).]**
Undo/Hor/Ver/Align/Par/Enter Dimension value: **0**
Select first object: **[Select A (Figure 5.28).]**
Select second object or place dimension: **[Select G (Figure 5.28).]**
Specify dimension placement: **[Select H (Figure 5.28).]**
Undo/Hor/Ver/Align/Par/Enter Dimension value: **30**
Select first object: **[Select B (Figure 5.28).]**
Select second object or place dimension: **[Select J (Figure 5.28).]**
Undo/Hor/Ver/Align/Par/Enter Dimension value: **70**
Select first object: **[Select E (Figure 5.28).]**
Select second object or place dimension: **[Select K (Figure 5.28).]**
Undo/Hor/Ver/Align/Par/Enter Dimension value: **170**
Solved fully constrained sketch.
Select first object: **[Enter]**

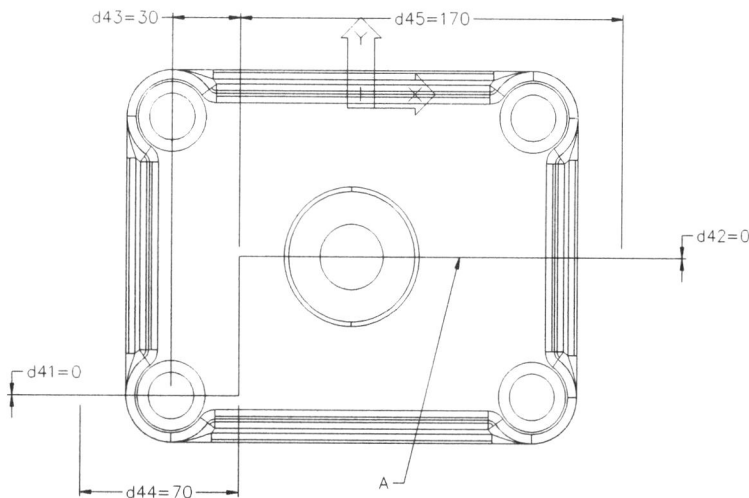

Figure 5.29 The cutting line fully constrained

Having fully constrained the cutting line, you may switch to drawing mode to produce the engineering drawing for this solid part. Apply the AMMODE command to set to drawing mode.

<Drawings>   <Drawing Mode>

Command: **AMMODE**
Model/<Drawing>: **[Enter]**

The solid part disappears temporarily. Use the LAYER command to make a new layer. Then run the INSERT command to insert a drawing title block. See Figure 5.30.

Command: **LAYER**
?/Make/Set/New/ON/OFF/Color/Ltype/Freeze/Thaw/LOck/Unlock: **MAKE**
New current layer: **TITLE**
?/Make/Set/New/ON/OFF/Color/Ltype/Freeze/Thaw/LOck/Unlock: **[Enter]**

Command: **INSERT**

[File name: **YOUR_TITLE_BLOCK**
OK   ]

Figure 5.30 The title block inserted to a new layer

Set the drawing standards by running the **AMDWGVARS** command. Then apply the **AMDWGVIEW** command to create a base view. See Figure 5.31.

<Drawings>   <Preferences...>

Command: **AMDWGVARS**

<Drawings>   **<Create View>**

Command: **AMDWGVIEW**

[Type: **Base**
  Hidden Lines
    Calculate hidden lines: **YES**
    Hide hidden lines: **NO**
    Linetype of hidden lines: **HIDDEN**
    Display tangencies: **NO**
  Data Set: **Active Part**
  Scale: **0.5**
OK   ]

worldXy/worldYz/worldZx/Ucs/<Select work plane or edge>: **WORLDXY**
worldX/worldY/worldZ/<Select work axis or straight edge>: **WORLDX**
Rotate/Z-flip/<Accept>: **[Enter]**
Location for base view: **[Select A (Figure 5.30).]**
Location for base view: **[Enter]**

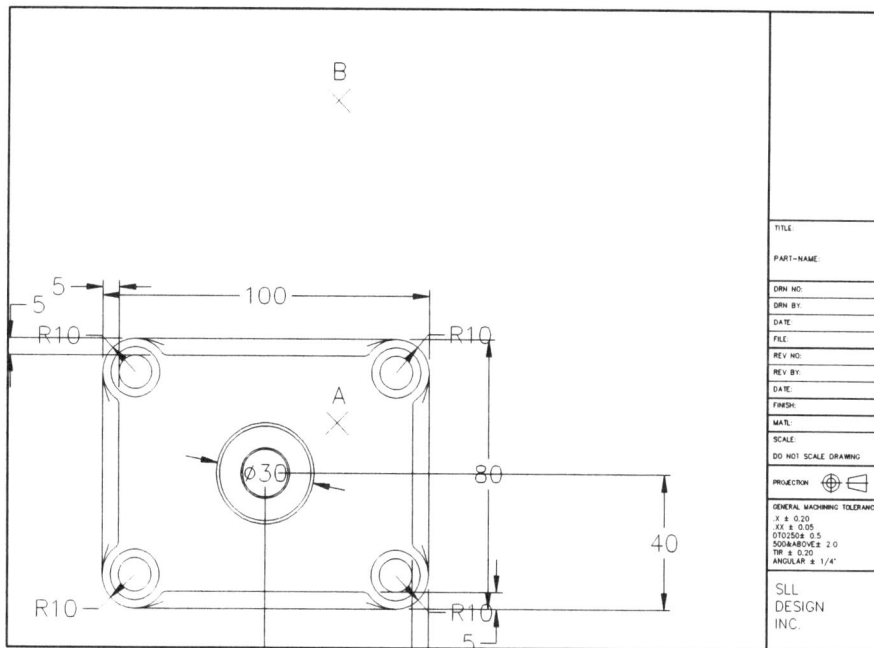

Figure 5.31 Top view created

Repeat the AMDWGVIEW command to create an offset section. Use the resolved cutting line as the cutting plane. See Figure 5.32.

<Drawings>   **<Create View>**

Command: **AMDWGVIEW**

[Type: **Ortho**
  Hidden Lines

Calculate hidden lines:	**YES**
Hide hidden lines:	**YES**
Display tangencies:	**NO**
Section View...	
[Type:	**Offset**
Hatch:	**YES**
Pattern...	
[Pattern Properties:	
Pattern:	**ANSI31**
Scale:	**50**
Angle:	**0**
OK	]
Section Symbol:	**A**]
OK	]

Select parent view: **[Select A (Figure 5.31).]**
Location for orthographic view: **[Select B (Figure 5.31).]**
Location for orthographic view: **[Enter]**

At this moment, the display switches to model mode. You may select the cutting line.

Select cutting line sketch: **[Select A (Figure 5.29).]**

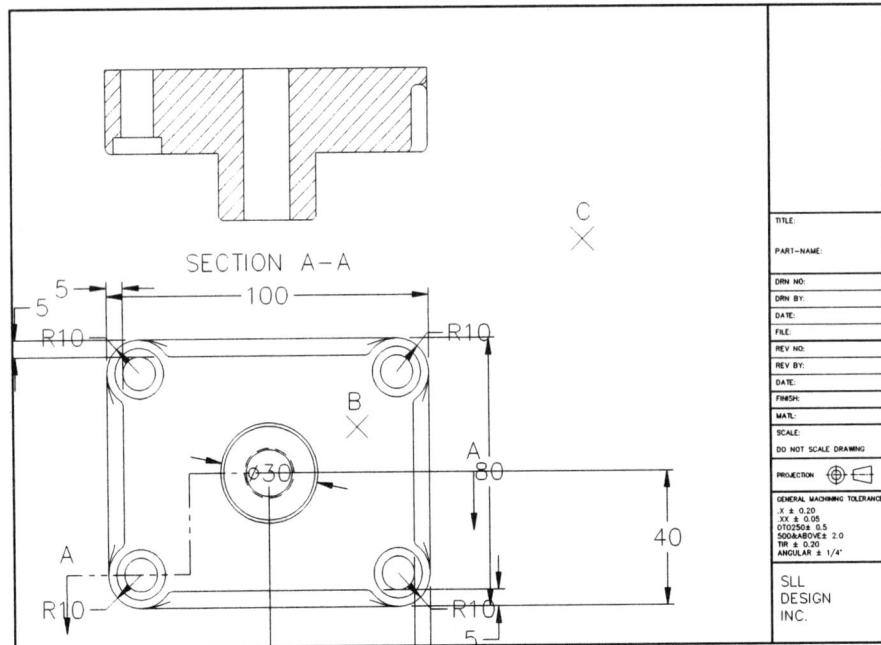

Figure 5.32 An offset sectional view created

After you have used the parametric cutting line to define an offset cutting plane, the cutting plane hides. Switch to model mode with the AMMODE command.

<Drawings>   **<Drawing Mode>**

Command: **AMMODE**
Drawing/<Model>: **[Enter]**

If you want to display the cutting line again, you may run the AMCLDSP command.

<Parts>   **<Display>**   **<Cutting Line>**   **<On>**

Command: **AMCLDSP**
Off/<ON>: **ON**

Switch back to drawing mode with the AMMODE command.

<Drawings>   **<Drawing Mode>**

Command: **AMMODE**
Model/<Drawing>: **[Enter]**

Run the AMDWGVIEW command again. This time, create an isometric view. See Figure 5.33.

<Drawings>   **<Create View>**

Command: **AMDWGVIEW**

[Type: **Iso**
  Hidden Lines
    Calculate hidden lines: **YES**
    Hide hidden lines: **YES**
    Display tangencies: **YES**
  Scale
    Scale: **1**
    Relative to Parent: **YES**
OK   ]

Select parent view: **[Select B (Figure 5.32).]**

You can have any one of the four different isometric views of any parent view by placing the location point, when asked for the position of the isometric view, to the left and up, right and up, left and down, and right and down. Once the isometric view is placed, you may use the AMMOVEVIEW command to move the given isometric view into its final position. You should also note that isometric views can be taken from any sectioned view.

Location for isometric view: **[Select C (Figure 5.32).]**
Location for isometric view: **[Enter]**

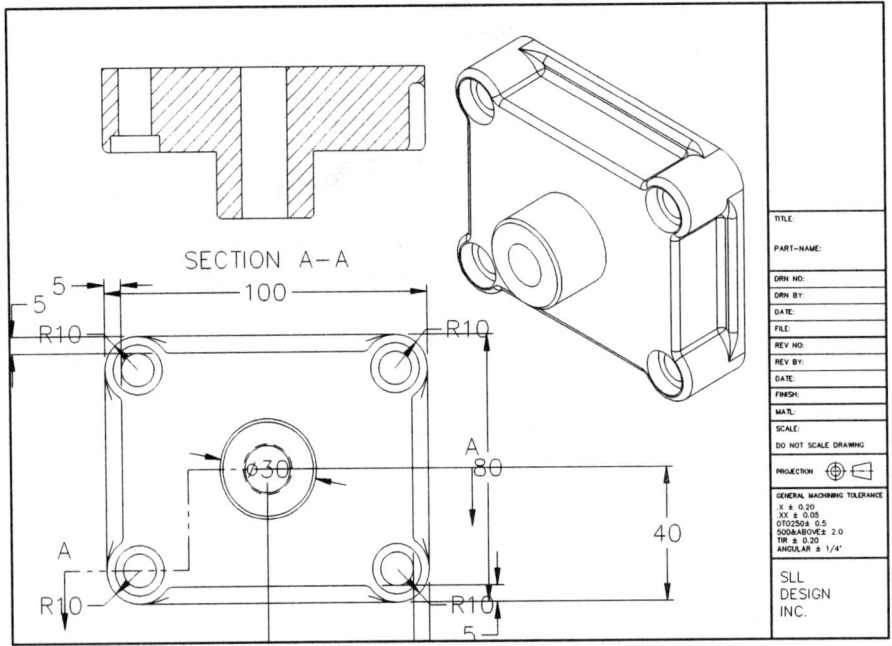

Figure 5.33 An isometric view created

Now you have created an engineering drawing. It has a base view and two projection views. One projection view is an offset section. The other one is an isometric view.

To complete the engineering drawing, you should make any necessary modification to the dimensions. You may have to use the AMHIDEDIM command to hide some parametric dimensions that you used to create the sketched solid feature but no longer need, to use the AMMOVEDIM command to move some dimensions from one view to another, and to use the AMREFDIM command to add some reference dimensions. See Figure 5.34.

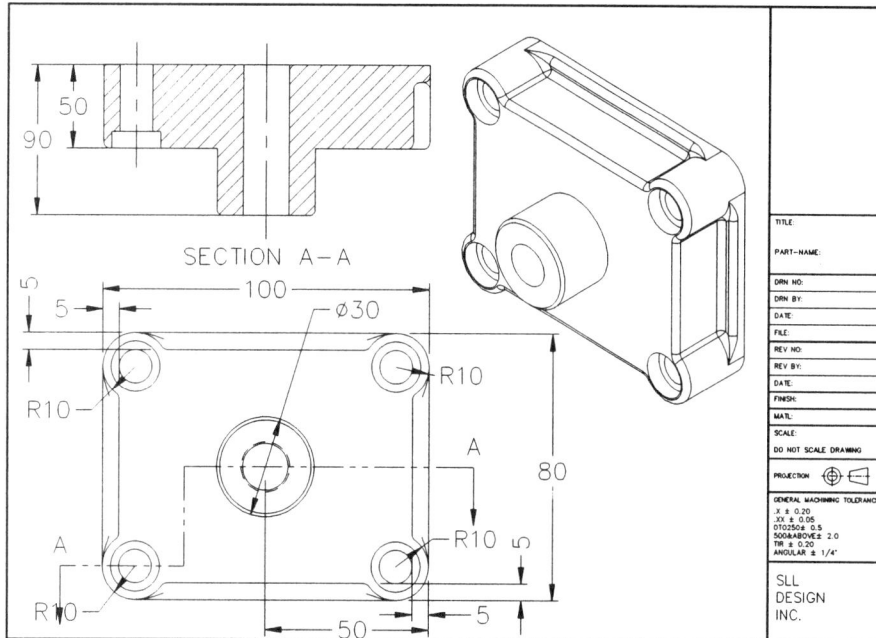

Figure 5.34 Dimensions properly placed

By now, you should be able to create six types of engineering views from a solid part. These are the base view, orthographic view, auxiliary view, isometric view, sectional view, and detail view. If you wish to output a two-dimensional drawing from the drawing mode entities, you may apply the AMDWGOUT command. Remember, the output drawing will be an independent two-dimensional drawing. Use the SAVE command to save your drawing.

> **<File>**   **<Save...>**
>
> Command: **QSAVE**
>
> [File name: **PLATE3.DWG**
> **OK**   ]

5.8   **Explode Assembly Drawing**

The basic procedure for preparing an engineering drawing from an assembly of instances is similar to that for a solid part. With an assembly, you may go one step further. You may create an exploded view of the instances and yet retain the assembly constraints that you have applied.

Run the OPEN command to retrieve the drawing "U_JOINT" from your storage memory. See Figure 5.35.

> **<File>**   **<Open...>**
>
> Command: **OPEN**

[File name: **U_JOINT.DWG**
OK   ]

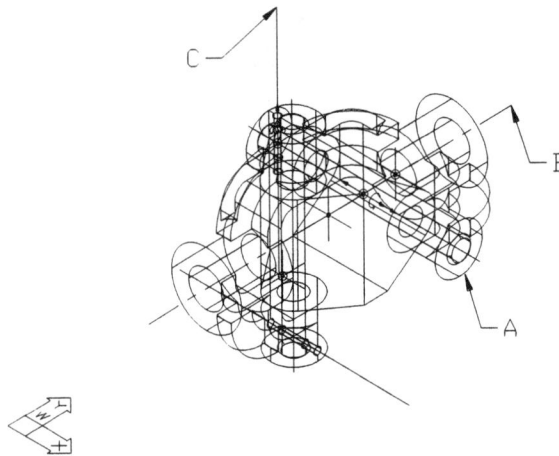

Figure 5.35 The assembled universal joint

In model mode, the instances assemble together properly according to the assembly constraints that you have applied. To explode the instances apart and yet keep the assembly constraints, you may set up scenes. In an assembly drawing, you may set up a number of scenes. You may have a scene with no explosion, together with an exploded view in memory. To create and manipulate scenes, run the AMSCENE command. Run this command to create two scenes. Set the explosion factor to zero for both scenes. You will work on the explosion factor later.

<Assemblies>   **<Scene>**   **<Create...>**

Command: **AMSCENE**

[Explosion Factor: **0**
 Automatic Update: **YES**
 Name: **U_JOINT1**
Save
 Explosion Factor: **0**
 Automatic Update: **YES**
 Name: **U_JOINT2**
Save
 Select Scene To Activate: **U_JOINT1**
OK   ]

You may suppress the visibility of instances in a scene. Run the AMSUPPRESS command to suppress the display of an instance. See Figure 5.36.

<Assemblies>   **<Scene>**   **<Set Visibility...>**

Command: **AMSUPPRESS**
Unsuppress all/<Select>: **[Select A (Figure 5.35).]**

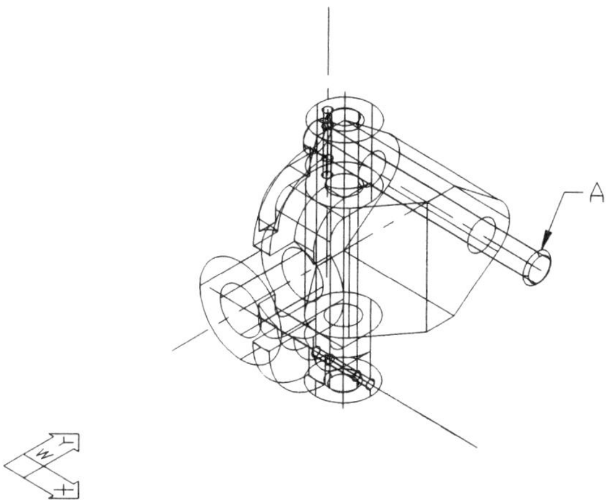

Figure 5.36 Display of an instance suppressed

There are two ways to create an exploded drawing: tweaking and exploding. To tweak the instances in a scene is to separate the instances. Use the AMTWEAK command on an instance. See Figure 5.37.

<Assemblies>   **<Scene>**   **<Exploded Views>**   **<Add Tweaks...>**

Command: **AMTWEAK**
Select component to tweak: **[Select A (Figure 5.36).]**

[Type: **Move**
OK   ]

Select reference geometry: **[Select A (Figure 5.35).]**
Distance: **-90**

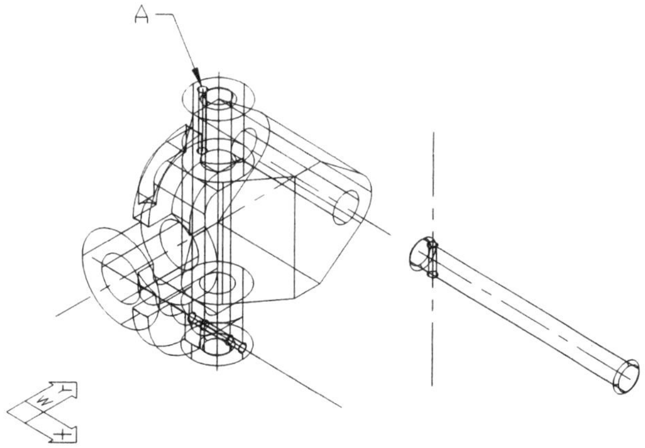

Figure 5.37 The PIN instance tweaked

Run the AMTWEAK command to tweak the LOCK instance. See Figure 5.38.

<Assemblies>   <Scene>   <Exploded Views>   <Add Tweaks...>

Command: **AMTWEAK**
Select component to tweak: **[Select A (Figure 5.37).]**

[Type: **Move**
OK   ]

Select reference geometry: **[Select B (Figure 5.35).]**
Distance: **-30**

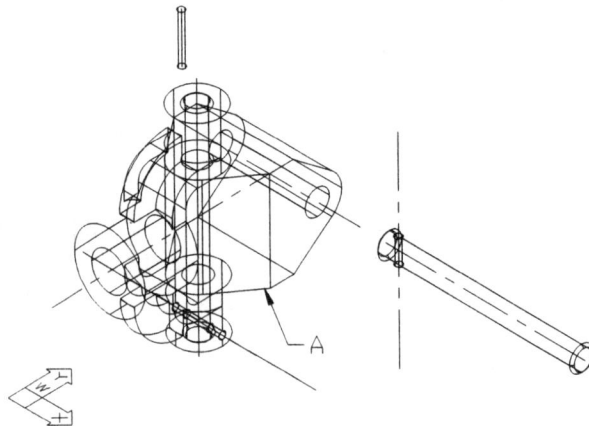

Figure 5.38 The LOCK instance tweaked

Apply the AMTWEAK command to tweak the YOKE instance. Then use the AMSUPPRESS command to unsuppress the display of all the instances. See Figure 5.39.

<Assemblies>   <Scene>   <Exploded Views>   <Add Tweaks...>

Command: **AMTWEAK**
Select component to tweak: **[Select A (Figure 5.38).]**

[Type: **Move**
OK   ]

Select reference geometry: **[Select C (Figure 5.35).]**
Distance: **-30**

<Assemblies>   <Scene>   <Set Visibility...>

Command: **AMSUPPRESS**
Unsuppress all/<Select>: **U**

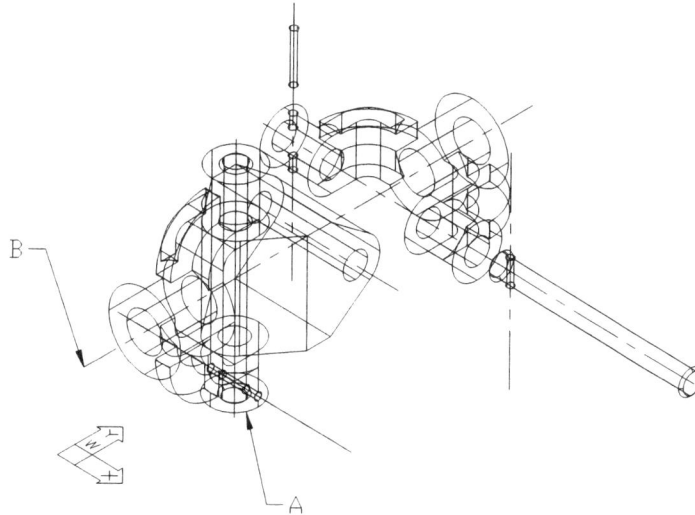

Figure 5.39 The YOKE instance tweaked and the main instance re-displayed

You have tweaked all the instances of the main assembly. To continue, you will tweak the instances of the sub-assembly. Run the AMTWEAK command. See Figure 5.40.

<Assemblies>   <Scene>   <Exploded Views>   <Add Tweaks...>

Command: **AMTWEAK**
Select component to tweak: **[Select A (Figure 5.39).]**
Component MAIN_2 Down/Up/<Continue>: **U**
Component SUB1_1 Down/Up/<Continue>: **[Enter]**

[Type: **Move**
OK   ]

Select reference geometry: **[Select B (Figure 5.39).]**
Distance: **40**

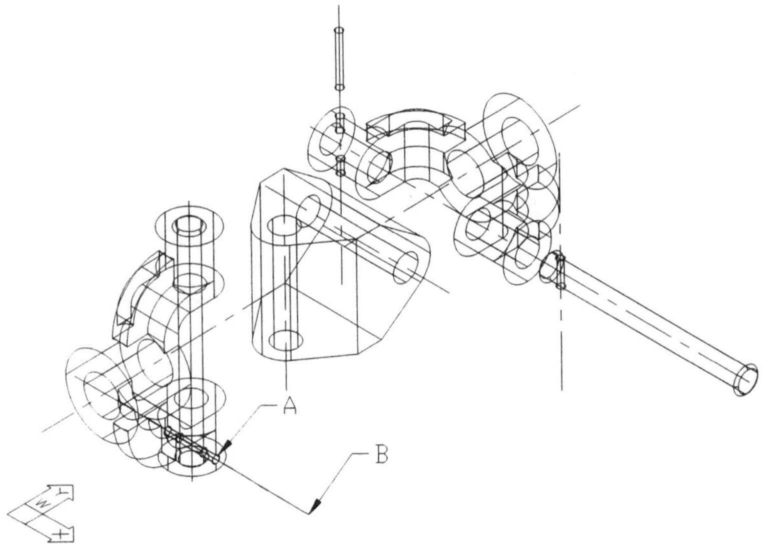

Figure 5.40 The MAIN instance of the sub-assembly tweaked

Issue the AMTWEAK command to tweak the LOCK instance of the sub-assembly. See Figure 5.41.

<Assemblies>   <Scene>   <Exploded Views>   <Add Tweaks...>

Command: **AMTWEAK**
Select component to tweak: **[Select A (Figure 5.40).]**
Component LOCK_2 Down/Up/<Continue>: **[Enter]**

[Type: **Move**
OK   ]

Select reference geometry: **[Select B (Figure 5.40).]**
Distance: **-30**

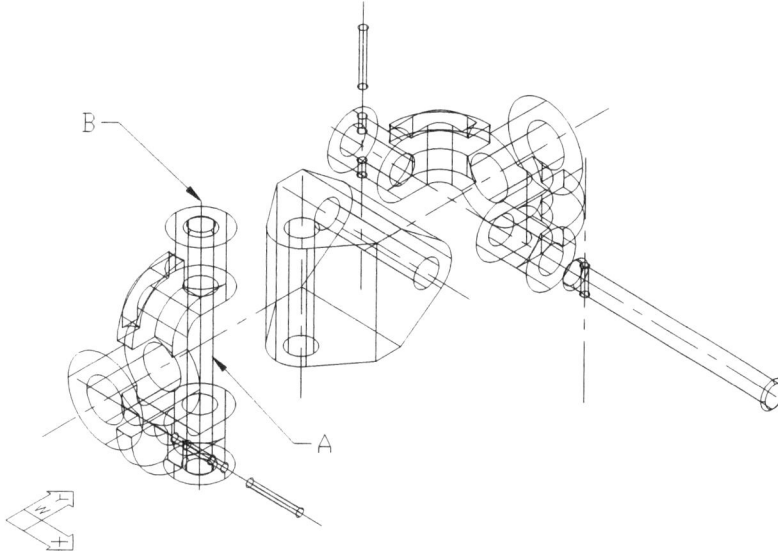

Figure 5.41 The LOCK instance of the sub-assembly tweaked

As you carried out the foregoing command, the instances tweaked accordingly, because you have set the current scene to update automatically. Issue the AMSCENE command to turn off automatic update. Then run the AMTWEAK command on the PIN instance of the sub-assembly.

<Assemblies>   **<Scene>**   **<Manage...>**

Command: **AMSCENE**

[Select Scene to Activate: **U_JOINT1**
 Explosion Factor: **0**
 Automatic Update: **NO**
 Name: **U_JOINT1**
 Save
 OK   ]

<Assemblies>   **<Scene>**   **<Exploded Views>**   **<Add Tweaks...>**

Command: **AMTWEAK**
Select component to tweak: **[Select A (Figure 5.41).]**
Component PIN_2 Down/Up/<Continue>: **[Enter]**

[Type: **Move**
 OK   ]

Select reference geometry: **[Select B (Figure 5.41).]**
Distance: **-100**

Because the scene does not update automatically, the instance does not tweak. To update the scene, issue the AMUPDATESCENE command. See Figure 5.42.

<Assemblies>   <Scene>   <Update>

Command: **AMUPDATESCENE**

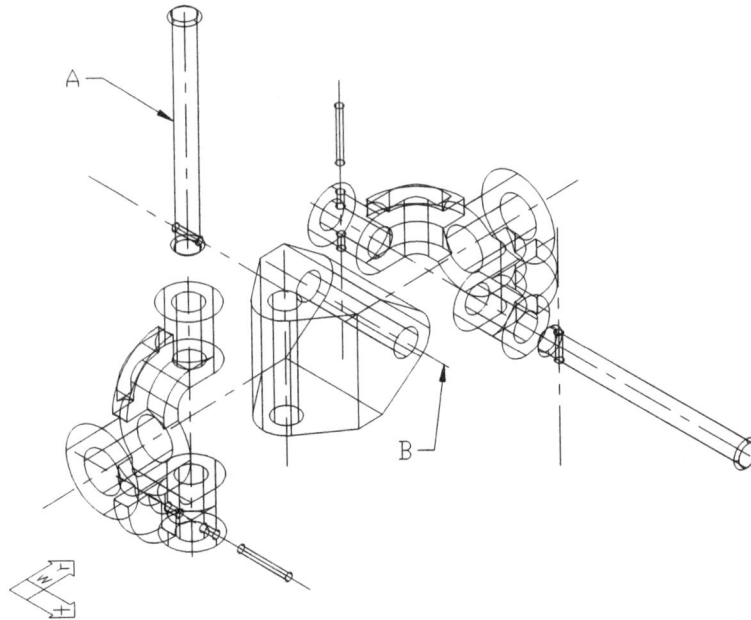

Figure 5.42 The scene updated

Set the scene to update automatically with the AMSCENE command.

<Assemblies>   <Scene>   <Manage...>

Command: **AMSCENE**

[Select Scene to Activate: **U_JOINT1**
 Explosion Factor: **0**
 Automatic Update: **YES**
 Name: **U_JOINT1**
 Save
 OK   ]

You may delete the tweak of an instance. Try the AMDELTWEAKS command on the PIN instance. Watch what happens to the drawing. Because the tweak is not to be deleted, run the U command to undo the deleting.

<Assemblies>   <Scene>   <Exploded Views>   <Remove Tweaks>

Command: **AMDELTWEAKS**
Select component to delete tweaks from: **[Select A (Figure 5.42).]**
Component PIN_2 Down/Up/<Continue>: **[Enter]**

Command: **U**

There are two scenes in this assembly. You have applied the AMTWEAK command to tweak the instances to create an explode view. You may want to know what has happened to the other scene. Apply the AMSCENE command to activate the other scene.

<**Assemblies**>   <**Scene**>   <**Manage...**>

Command: **AMSCENE**

[Select Scene To Activate: **U_JOINT2**
OK   ]

All the instances remain together properly. There is no tweaking in the other scene. By now, you should appreciate how you may maintain more than one scene in a drawing. You may keep a scene un-tweaked, a scene tweaked, and maybe a scene tweaked in another fashion. Run the AMSCENE command to select the U_JOINT1 scene.

<**Assemblies**>   <**Scene**>   <**Manage...**>

Command: **AMSCENE**

[Select Scene To Activate: **U_JOINT1**
OK   ]

In order to illustrate the relationship between the tweaked instances, you may add a trailing line to link up the tweaked instances. Run the AMTRAIL command to create a trail. See Figure 5.43.

<**Assemblies**>   <**Scene**>   <**Exploded Views**>   <**Create Trail...**>

Command: **AMTRAIL**
Select reference point on component: **[Select B (Figure 5.42).]**

[Offset at Current Position
     Distance: **0**
 Offset at Assembled Position
     Distance: **0**
OK   ]

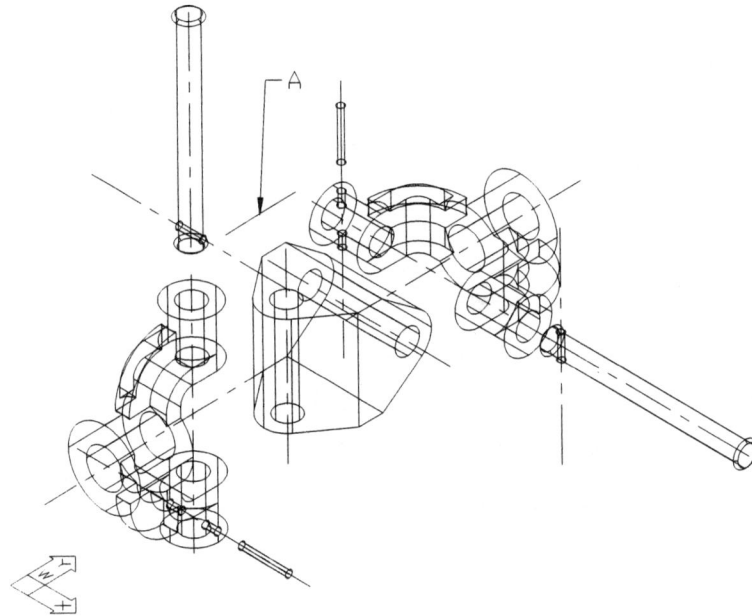

Figure 5.43 A trail added

To edit the length of a trail, run the AMEDITTRAIL command. See Figure 5.44.

<Assemblies>   <Scene>   <Exploded Views>   <Edit Trail...>

Command: **AMEDITTRAIL**
Select trail to edit: **[Select A (Figure 5.43).]**

[Offset at Current Position
     Distance: **20**
 Offset at Assembled Position
     Distance: **20**
OK   ]

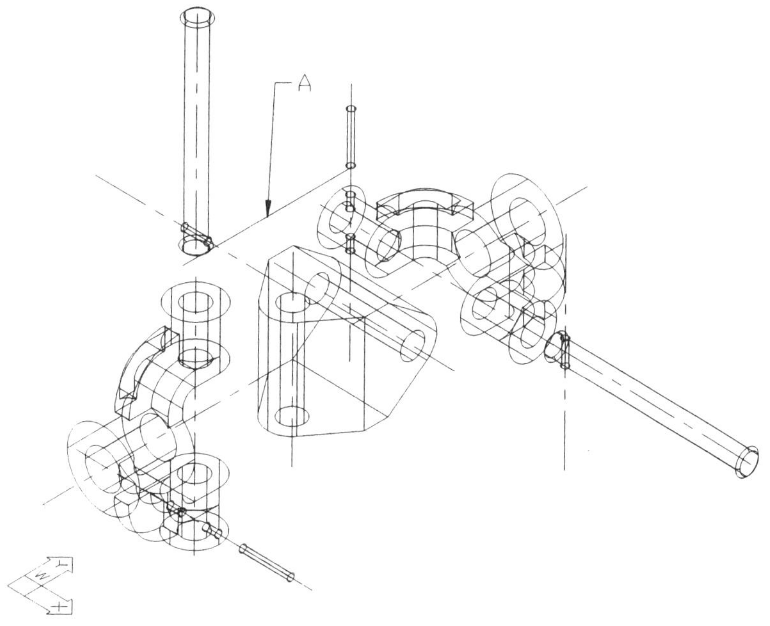

Figure 5.44 The trail edited

If you do not want the trail, you may delete it. Try the AMDELTRAIL command.

<Assemblies>   **<Scene>**   **<Exploded Views>**   **<Delete Trail...>**

Command: **AMDELTRAIL**
Select trail to delete: **[Select A (Figure 5.44).]**

Switch to drawing mode. You will prepare an engineering drawing from the scenes.

<Drawings>   **<Drawing Mode>**

Command: **AMMODE**
Model/<Drawing>: **[Enter]**

Before making drawing views, run the LAYER command to create a new layer. Then use the INSERT command to insert your title block. See Figure 5.45.

Command: **LAYER**
?/Make/Set/New/ON/OFF/Color/Ltype/Freeze/Thaw/LOck/Unlock: **MAKE**
New current layer: **TITLE**
?/Make/Set/New/ON/OFF/Color/Ltype/Freeze/Thaw/LOck/Unlock: **[Enter]**

Command: **INSERT**

[File name: **YOUR_TITLE_BLOCK**
OK   ]

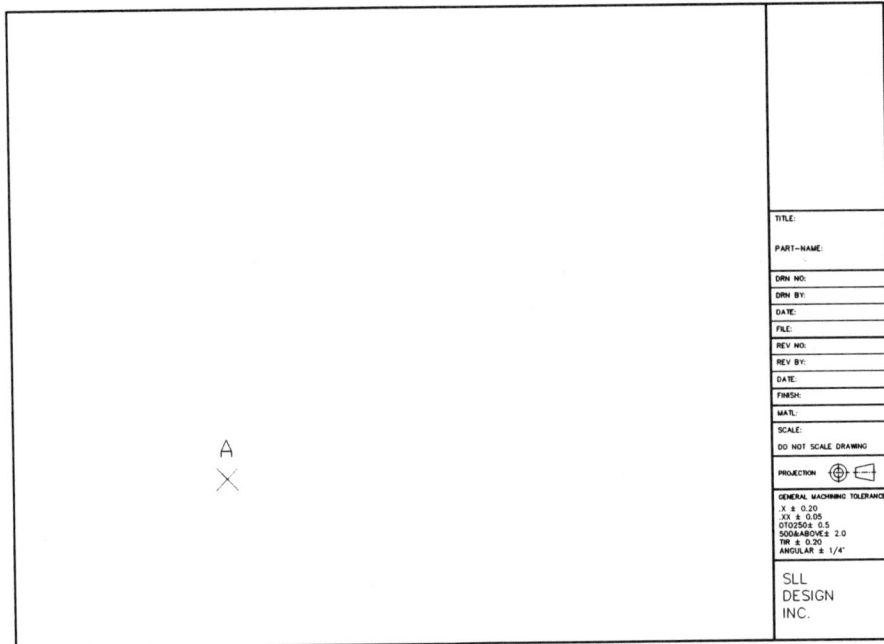

Figure 5.45 A title block inserted

With a title block inserted in position, issue the AMDWGVIEW command to create a base view. There are two scenes in this assembly. Select the scene with tweaked instances. See Figure 5.46.

<Drawings>   **<Create View>**

Command: **AMDWGVIEW**

[Type:	**Base**
Hidden Lines	
Calculate hidden lines:	**YES**
Hide hidden lines:	**YES**
Display tangencies:	**NO**
Data Set:	**Assembly**
Scale:	**0.5**
OK	]

[Select Scene:	**U_JOINT1**
OK	]

worldXy/worldYz/worldZx/Ucs/<Select work plane or edge>: **WORLDZX**
worldX/worldY/worldZ/<Select work axis or straight edge>: **WORLDX**
Rotate/Z-flip/<Accept>: **[Enter]**
Location for base view: **[Select A (Figure 5.45).]**
Location for base view: **[Enter]**

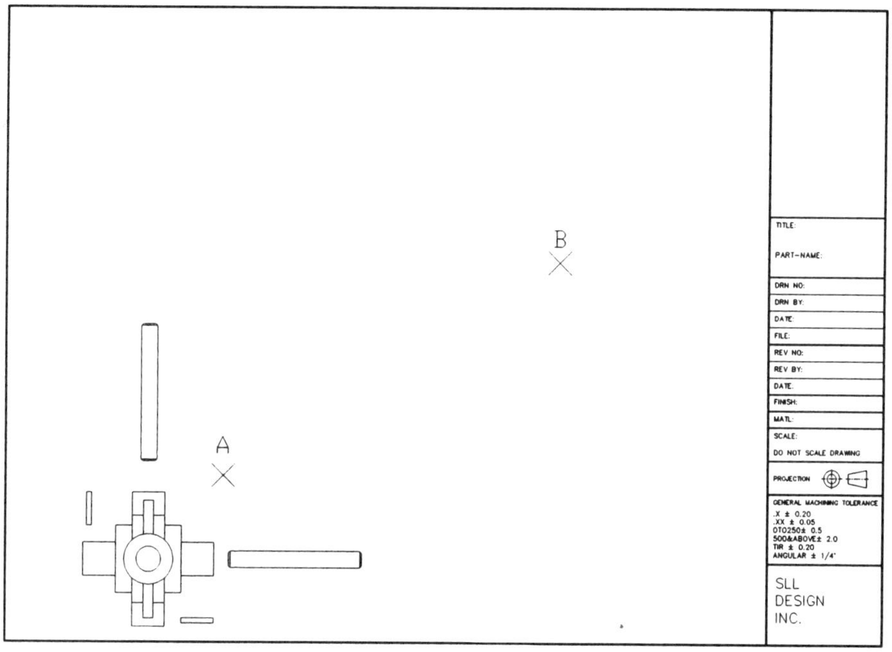

Figure 5.46 A top view of the U_JOINT1 scene created

Using the top view that you have created as the parent view, repeat the AMDWGVIEW command to create an isometric exploded view. See Figure 5.47.

<Drawings>   <Create View>

Command: **AMDWGVIEW**

[Type:	**Iso**
Hidden Lines	
Calculate hidden lines:	**YES**
Hide hidden lines:	**YES**
Display tangencies:	**NO**
Scale:	**1**
Relative to Parent:	**YES**
OK	]

Select parent view: **[Select A (Figure 5.46).]**
Location for isometric view: **[Select B (Figure 5.46).]**
Location for isometric view: **[Enter]**

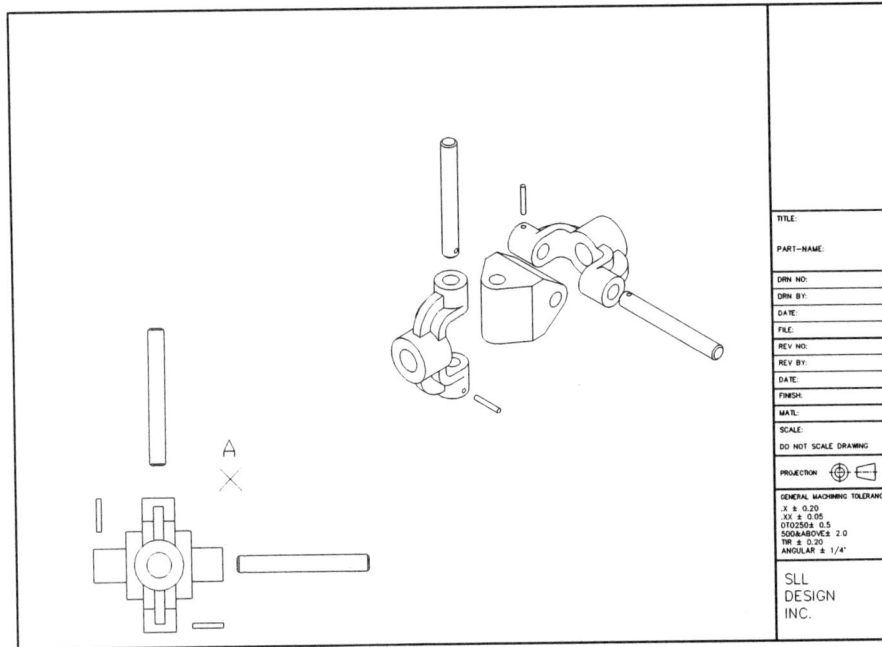

Figure 5.47 An isometric view of the U_JOINT1 scene created

You needed a parent view to create an isometric view, but now you may delete its parent view. Run the AMDELVIEW command to erase the top view of the exploded scene. Do not delete its dependent view. See Figure 5.48.

<Drawings>   **<Edit View>**   **<Delete>**

Command: **AMDELVIEW**
Select view to delete: **[Select A (Figure 5.47).]**
View has 1 dependent view. Delete it also? Yes/No/<Cancel>: **NO**

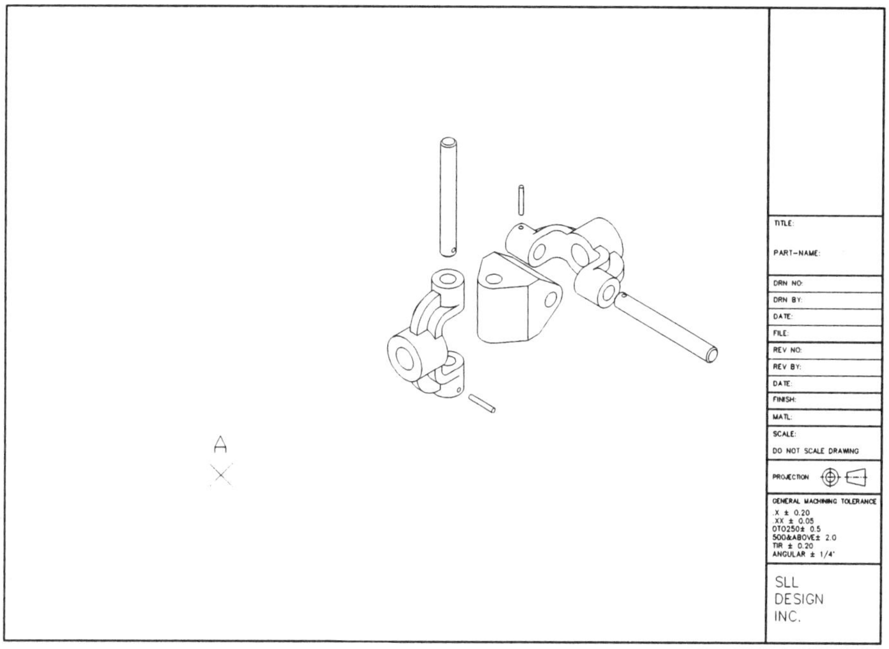

Figure 5.48 The top view deleted

After deleting the exploded top view and keeping the exploded isometric view, apply the AMDWGVIEW command again to make a new top view. This time, choose the scene without tweaking. See Figure 5.49.

<Drawings>   **<Create View>**

Command: **AMDWGVIEW**

[Type: **Base**
 Hidden Lines
     Calculate hidden lines: **YES**
     Hide hidden lines: **YES**
     Display tangencies: **NO**
 Data Set: **Assembly**
 Scale: **0.5**
OK   ]

[Select Scene: **U_JOINT2**
OK   ]

worldXy/worldYz/worldZx/Ucs/<Select work plane or edge>: **WORLDXY**
worldX/worldY/worldZ/<Select work axis or straight edge>: **WORLDY**
Rotate/Z-flip/<Accept>: **[Enter]**
Location for base view: **[Select A (Figure 5.48).]**
Location for base view: **[Enter]**

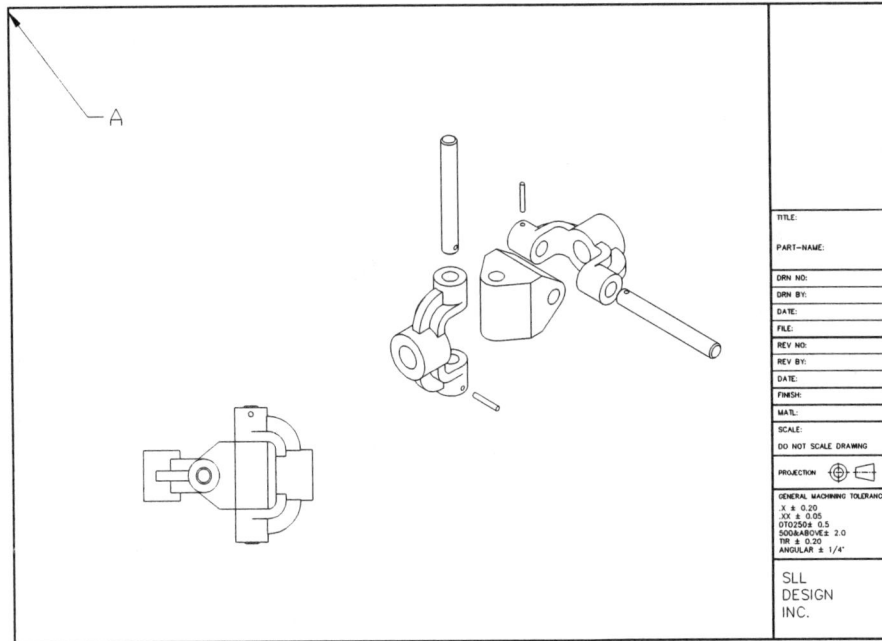

Figure 5.49 Top view of the U_JOINT2 scene created

Now you have two drawing views. The top view comes from a scene without any tweaking. The isometric view comes from the tweaked scene.

To continue, set the edit target with the AMTARGET command. Then run the AMASSIGN command to assign attributes to the component definitions. You will use these attributes for making a bill of materials.

```
<Assemblies>        <Instances>           <Edit Target...>

Command: AMTARGET

[Select Edit Target:      U_JOINT
 DOF:                     NO
OK                                    ]


<Assemblies>        <Component Definition>   <Assign Attributes...>

Command: AMASSIGN

[Component definitions:
    MAIN
    PIN
    LOCK
    YOKE
    SUB1
Add...
    [Attribute Name:    MATERIAL
     Attribute Value: ALUMINUM
     Column Data type:  STRING
     OK                            ]
DONE                              ]
```

Set the scene to U_JOINT1 with the AMSCENE command.

<Assemblies>   **<Scene>**   **<Manage...>**

Command: **AMSCENE**

[Select Scene To Activate: **U_JOINT1**
OK   ]

Run the AMBOMSETUP command to set up a bill of materials.

<Assemblies>   **<Scene>**   **<Bill of Materials>**   **<Setup...>**

Command: **AMBOMSETUP**

[Table definition
    Components to include: **All**
    Justification: **Left**
    Sort Order: **Down**
    Display Grid: **YES**
    File Out: **NO**
  Column Definition
    Add...
    [Column Name: **MATERIAL**
    Column Width: **10**
    Attribute Name: **MATERIAL**
    Column Date type: **String**
    OK   ]
  Balloon Definition
    Leader   **Straight**
    Balloon type   **Round**
OK   ]

After setting up a bill of materials, issue the AMBOM command to display it at the upper left corner of the drawing. See Figure 5.50.

<Assemblies>   **<Scene>**   **<Bill of Materials>**   **<Create Table>**

Command: **AMBOM**
Pick the base point for the BOM table: **END** of **[Select A (Figure 5.49).]**
Pick a point to indicate the BOM table direction and extend: **@100,-50**
Pick point to align BOM: **END** of **[Select A (Figure 5.49).]**

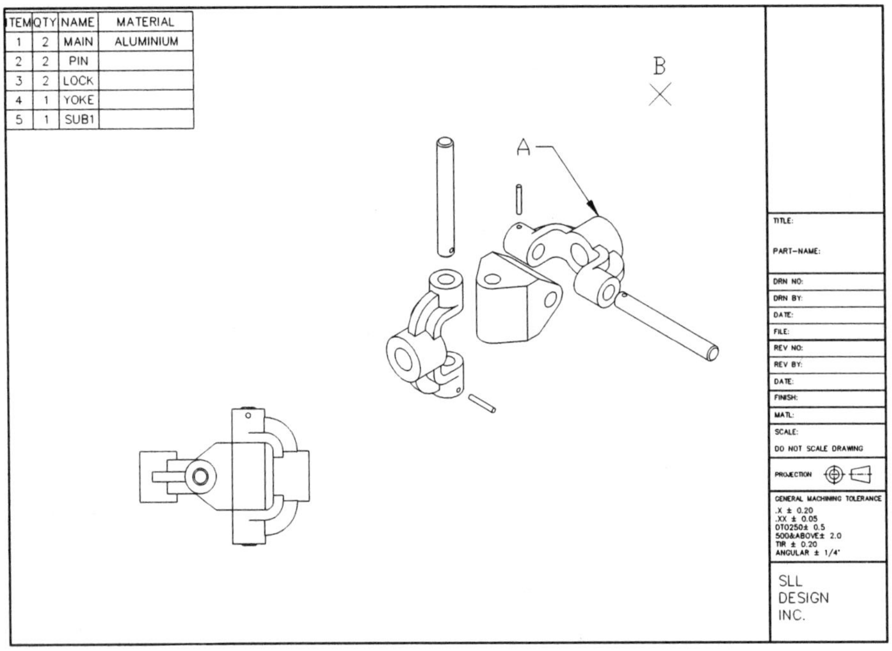

ITEM	QTY	NAME	MATERIAL
1	2	MAIN	ALUMINIUM
2	2	PIN	
3	2	LOCK	
4	1	YOKE	
5	1	SUB1	

Figure 5.50 A bill of materials created

The corresponding objects of a bill of materials are the callout balloons. Apply the AMBALLOON command to create a callout balloon. See Figure 5.51.

<Assemblies>   <Scene>   <Balloons>

Command: **AMBALLOON**
Select component to balloon [Return for Unassociated] **[Select A (Figure 5.50).]**
Select leader vertex: **[Select A (Figure 5.50).]**
Select leader vertex: **[Select B (Figure 5.50).]**

[Select Column to edit: **ITEM**
OK   ]

ITEM	QTY	NAME	MATERIAL
1	2	MAIN	ALUMINIUM
2	2	PIN	
3	2	LOCK	
4	1	YOKE	
5	1	SUB1	

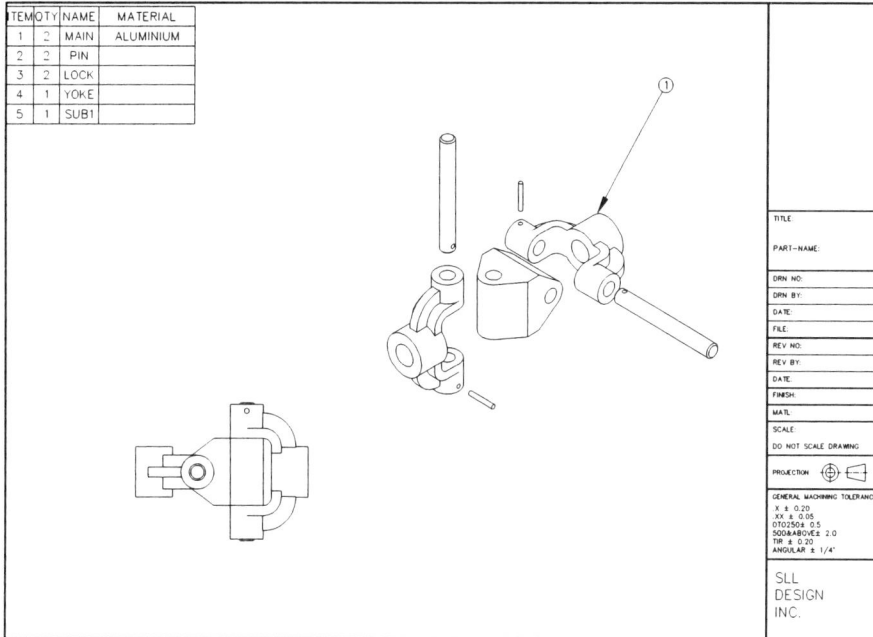

Figure 5.51 A balloon created

Refer to Figure 5.52. Repeat the AMBALLOON command to create callout balloons to the other instances.

\<Assemblies\>   \<Scene\>   \<Balloons\>

Command: **AMBALLOON**

ITEM	QTY	NAME	MATERIAL
1	2	MAIN	ALUMINIUM
2	2	PIN	
3	2	LOCK	
4	1	YOKE	
5	1	SUB1	

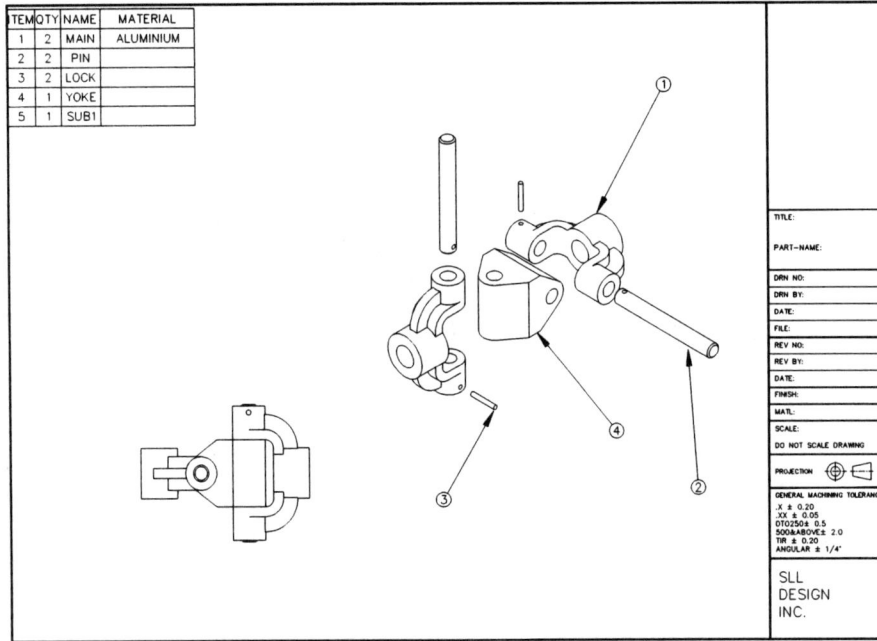

Figure 5.52 All balloons created

You may edit the bill of materials. Run the AMEDITBOM command. See Figure 5.53.

<Assemblies>   **<Scene>**   **<Bill of Materials>**   **<Edit Entry...>**

Command: **AMEDITBOM**

[Select BOM Entry: **1**
  Edit
     [Select Column to edit: **NAME**
      Data: **MAIN BODY**
      OK   ]
  Done   ]

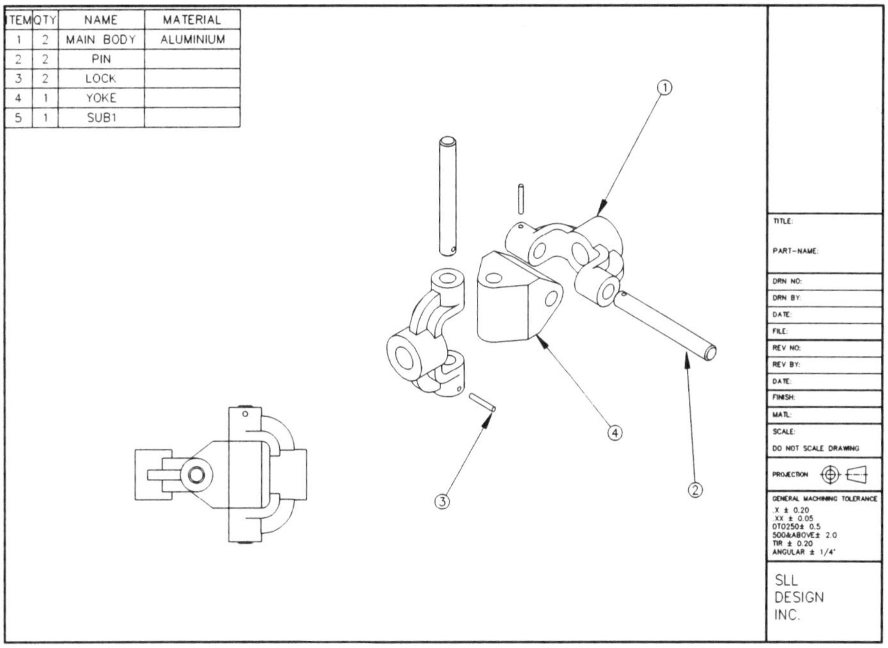

ITEM	QTY	NAME	MATERIAL
1	2	MAIN BODY	ALUMINIUM
2	2	PIN	
3	2	LOCK	
4	1	YOKE	
5	1	SUB1	

Figure 5.53 The bill of materials edited

You have completed an engineering drawing for the universal joint assembly. In the drawing, you created two scenes. You tweaked a scene and left another scene intact, untweaked. Using the two scenes, you created a top view of the un-tweaked scene and an isometric view of the tweaked scene. On the drawing, you have also created a bill of materials and corresponding callout balloons.

Save your drawing.

<File>   **<Save...>**

5.9   Sectional Assembly Drawing

Assembly drawing may include sectional views. To differentiate between various instances of an assembly in a sectional view, you need to assign a unique hatch pattern to each individual instance.

Here you will create an engineering drawing of the electric motor casing assembly that you created in Chapters 3 and 4. In this drawing, you will include an un-tweaked sectional view of the assembly and an exploded assembly.

Run the OPEN command to retrieve the drawing. See Figure 5.54.

<File>   **<Open...>**

Command: **OPEN**

[File name: **MOTOR.DWG**
OK   ]

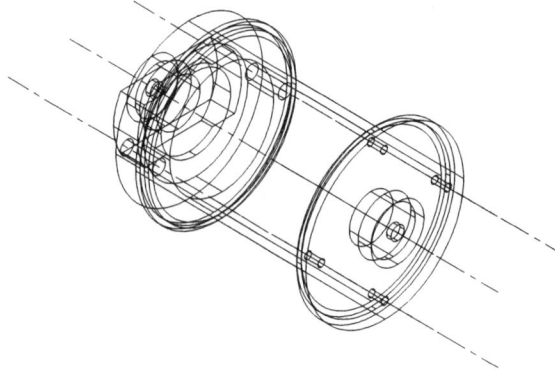

Figure 5.54 The electric motor casing assembly

To prepare the assembly for the subsequent making of a sectional view, apply the AMPATTERNDEF command to assign hatch pattern definitions to the three instances. Before you do that, issue the AMTARGET command to switch to edit mode.

<Assemblies>   <Instances>   <Edit Target...>

Command: **AMTARGET**

[Select Edit Target: **MOTOR**
 DOF: **NO**
OK   ]

<Assemblies>   <Component Definition>   <Hatch Patterns...>

Command: **AMPATTERNDEF**

[Component: **MOTOR_1**
Pattern: **ANSI31**
Scale: **20**
Angle: **0**
OK   ]

<Assemblies>   <Component Definition>   <Hatch Patterns...>

Command: **AMPATTERNDEF**

[Component: **MOTOR_2**
Pattern: **ANSI31**
Scale: **20**
Angle: **0**
OK   ]

<Assemblies>   <Component Definition>   <Hatch Patterns...>

Command: **AMPATTERNDEF**

[Component: **MOTOR_3**

```
Pattern:        ANSI31
Scale:          20
Angle:          90
OK                              ]
```

There are two ways to produce an exploded engineering assembly drawing. The first method is to use the AMTWEAK command to tweak the instances apart. The second method is to apply the explosion factor in a scene to create an exploded view automatically. The explosion factor controls the distance that instances will explode apart.

Apply the AMSCENE command to create two scenes. Set the explosion factor of one scene to 20 and that of the second to 0. Then select the scene with an explosion factor of 20 as the current scene. See Figure 5.55.

```
<Assemblies>    <Scene>        <Manage...>

Command: AMSCENE

[Explosion Factor:      20
 Automatic update:      YES
 Name:                  MOTOR1
Save
 Explosion Factor:      0
 Automatic update:      YES
 Name:                  MOTOR2
Save
 Select Scene To Activate:   MOTOR1
OK                                   ]
```

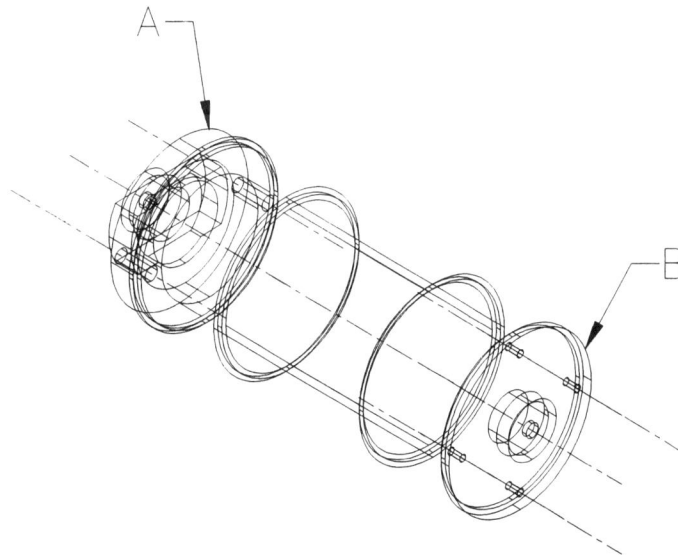

Figure 5.55 The MOTOR1 scene exploded automatically

As can be seen, the instances exploded apart automatically.

The explosion factor that affects the distances of explosion can be edited. Run the AMXFACTOR command to change the explosion factor of the instances in the assembly. See Figure 5.56.

<Assemblies>   **<Scene>**   **<Exploded Views>**   **<Explode Factor...>**

Command: **AMXFACTOR**
Select component: **[Select A (Figure 5.55).]**

[Explode Factor: **30**
OK   ]

<Assemblies>   **<Scene>**   **<Exploded Views>**   **<Explode Factor...>**

Command: **AMXFACTOR**
Select component: **[Select B (Figure 5.55).]**

[Explode Factor: **30**
OK   ]

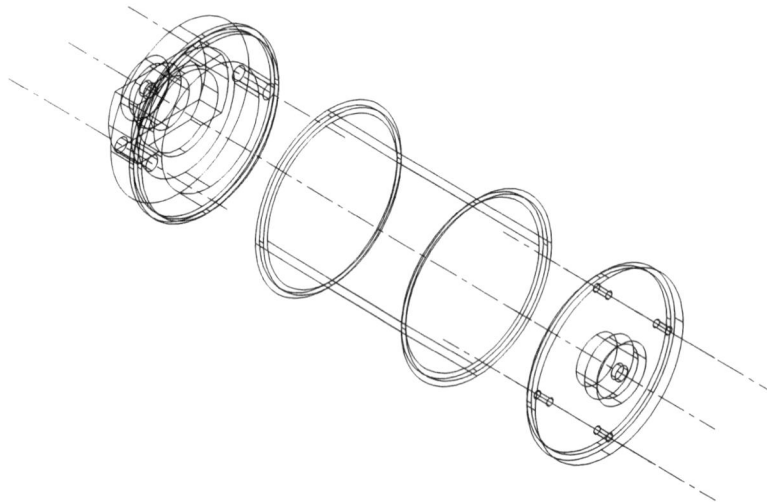

Figure 5.56 The explosion factor changed

After setting hatch pattern definitions and creating two scenes in model mode, you may work on the document. Apply the AMMODE command to switch to drawing mode.

<Drawings>   **<Drawing Mode>**

Command: **AMMODE**
Model/<Drawing>: **[Enter]**

Make a new layer with the LAYER command. Then insert a title block with the INSERT command. See Figure 5.57.

Command: **LAYER**
?/Make/Set/New/ON/OFF/Color/Ltype/Freeze/Thaw/LOck/Unlock: **MAKE**
New current layer: **TITLE**
?/Make/Set/New/ON/OFF/Color/Ltype/Freeze/Thaw/LOck/Unlock: **[Enter]**

Command: **INSERT**

[File name: **YOUR_TITLE_BLOCK**
OK   ]

Figure 5.57 Title block inserted in drawing mode

Set the line type scale to 15 with the LTSCALE command.

<Options>   <Linetypes>   <Global Linetype Scale>

Command: **LTSCALE**
New scale factor: **15**

Issue the AMDWGVARS command to set the variables that are involved in drawing creation. Then use the AMDWGVIEW command to create a base view. See Figure 5.58.

<Drawings>   <Preferences...>

Command: **AMDWGVARS**

<Drawings>   <Create View>

Command: **AMDWGVIEW**

[Type: **Base**
  Hidden Lines
      Calculate hidden lines: **YES**
      Hide hidden lines: **NO**
      Linetype of hidden lines: **HIDDEN**
      Display tangencies: **NO**
  Data Set: **Assembly**
  Scale: **1**
OK   ]

[Select Scene: **MOTOR2**
OK   ]

worldXy/worldYz/worldZx/Ucs/<Select work plane or edge>: **WORLDXY**
worldX/worldY/worldZ/<Select work axis or straight edge>: **WORLDX**
Rotate/Z-flip/<Accept>: **[Enter]**
Location for base view: **[Select A (Figure 5.57).]**
Location for base view: **[Enter]**

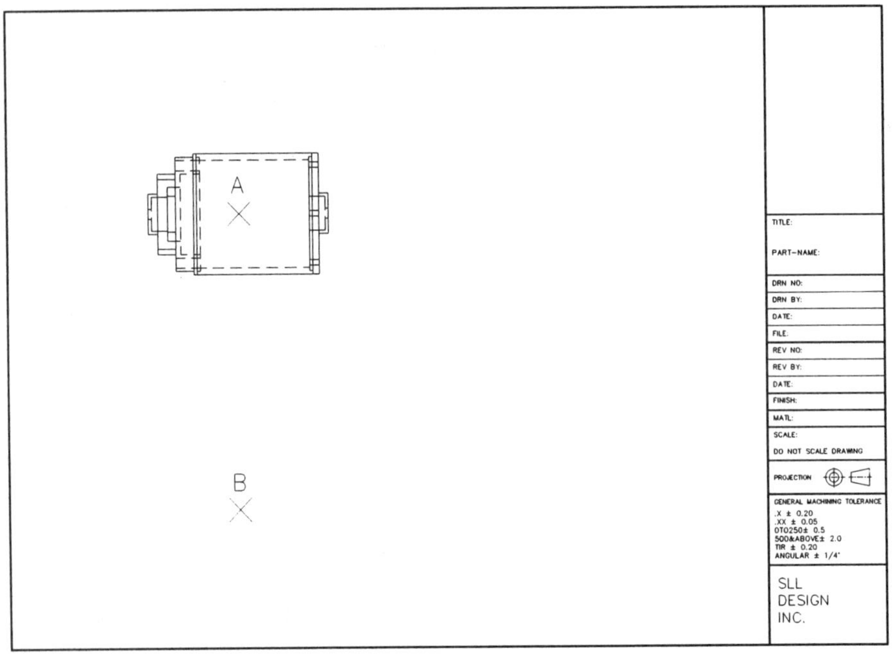

Figure 5.58 A top view created

Refer to Figure 5.58. This drawing view shows a scene with zero explosion factor and no tweaking. Using this view as the parent view, run the AMDWGVIEW command to create a sectional front view. See Figure 5.59.

<Drawings>   **<Create View>**

Command: **AMDWGVIEW**

[Type: **Ortho**
  Hidden Lines
      Calculate hidden lines: **YES**

Hide hidden lines:	**YES**
Display tangencies:	**NO**
Section View...	
[Type:	**Full**
Hatch:	**YES**
Pattern...	
[Pattern Properties:	
Pattern:	**ANSI31**
Scale:	**50**
Angle:	**0**
OK	]
Section Symbol:	**A**]
OK	]

Select parent view: **[Select A (Figure 5.58).]**
Location for orthographic view: **[Select B (Figure 5.58).]**
Location for orthographic view: **[Enter]**
Section through Point/Ucs/<Work plane>: **[Select the work plane in the top view.]**

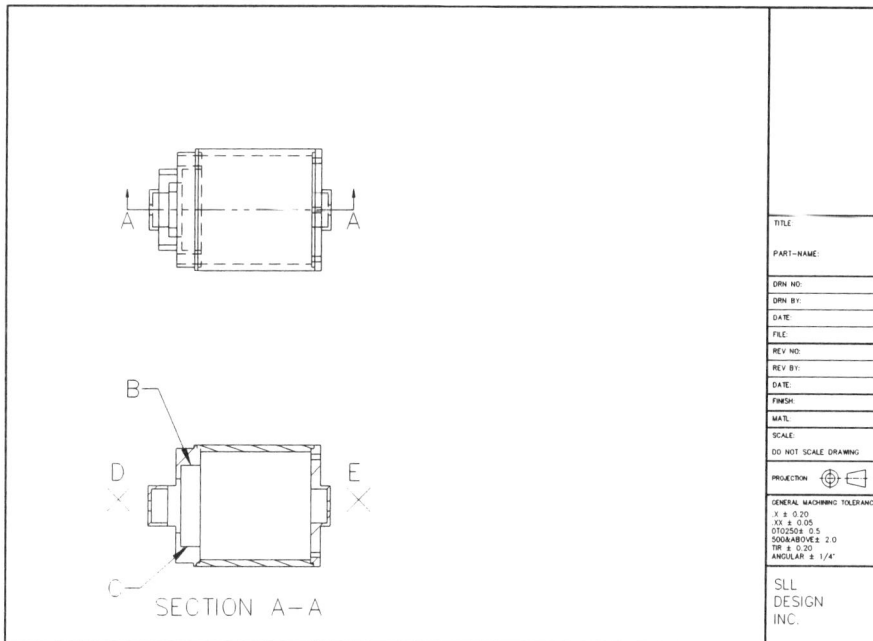

Figure 5.59 A sectional front view created

To complete the front view, run the AMCENLINE command to add a center line. See Figure 5.60.

   <Drawings>   **<Annotation>**   **<Centerline>**

Command: **AMCENLINE**
Select Edge: **[Select B (Figure 5.59).]**
Select mirrored edge or <RETURN>: **[Select C (Figure 5.59).]**
Select first trim point: **[Select D (Figure 5.59).]**
Select second trim point: **[Select E (Figure 5.59).]**

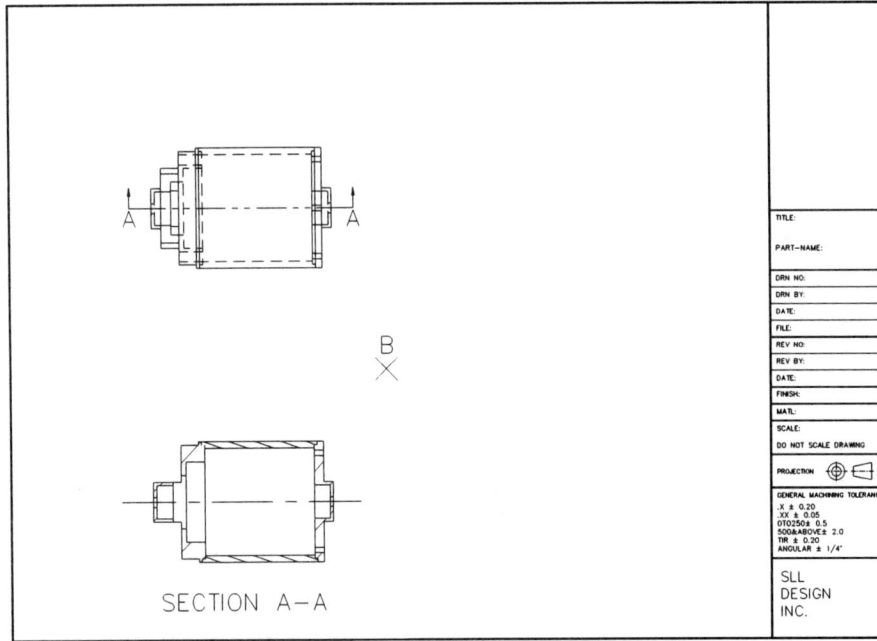

Figure 5.60 Center line created on the sectional front view

In the final drawing, you need one more drawing view. It is the isometric exploded view. To create this exploded view, you need to use the exploded scene. Because the two existing drawing views are derived from the scene of zero explosion, you cannot use them as parent view for the exploded isometric view. Therefore, you need to create a base view from the second scene to act as the parent view of the required isometric view.

Run the AMDWGVIEW command to create a top view from the exploded scene. See Figure 5.61.

<Drawings>   <Create View>

Command: **AMDWGVIEW**

[Type: **Base**
  Hidden Lines
    Calculate hidden lines: **YES**
    Hide hidden lines: **YES**
    Display tangencies: **NO**
  Data Set: **Assembly**
  Scale: **1**
OK   ]

[Select Scene: **MOTOR1**
OK   ]

worldXy/worldYz/worldZx/Ucs/<Select work plane or edge>: **WORLDXY**
worldX/worldY/worldZ/<Select work axis or straight edge>: **WORLDX**
Rotate/Z-flip/<Accept>: **[Enter]**
Location for base view: **[Select B (Figure 5.60).]**
Location for base view: **[Enter]**

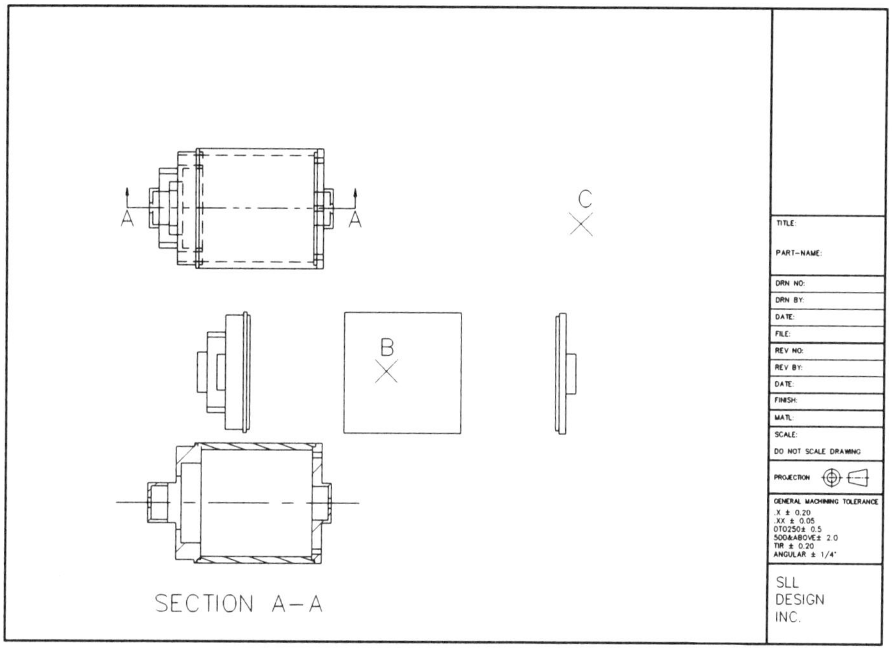

Figure 5.61 Parent view for the exploded isometric view created

Using the newly created base view as the parent view, run the AMDWGVIEW command to create an exploded isometric view. See Figure 5.62.

<Drawings>   <Create View>

Command: **AMDWGVIEW**

[Type:	**Iso**	
Hidden Lines		
Calculate hidden lines:	**YES**	
Hide hidden lines:	**YES**	
Display tangencies:	**NO**	
Scale		
Scale:	**1**	
Relative to Parent:	**YES**	
OK		]

Select parent view: **[Select B (Figure 5.61).]**
Location for isometric view: **[Select C (Figure 5.61).]**
Location for isometric view: **[Enter]**

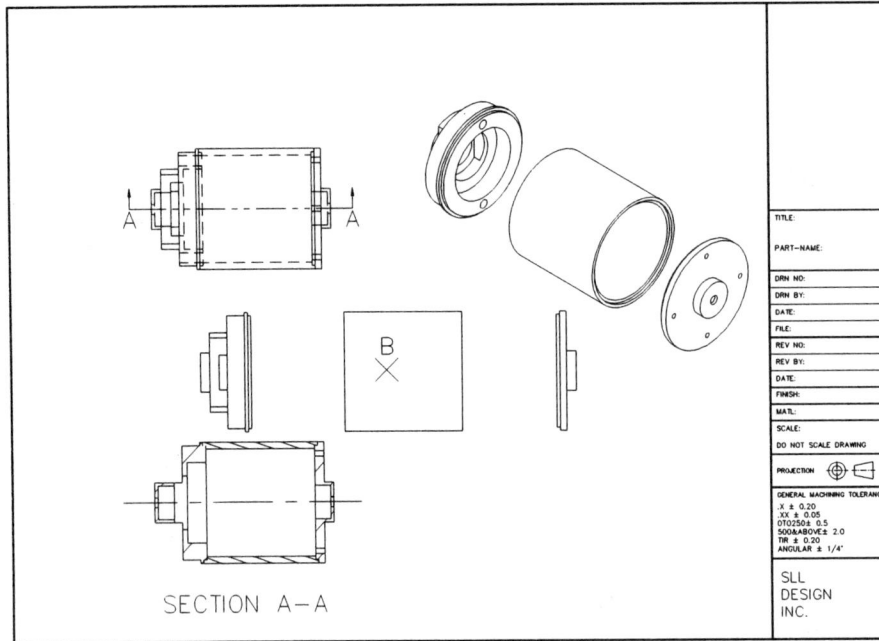

Figure 5.62 Exploded isometric view created

Having created the exploded isometric view, use the AMDELVIEW command to delete its parent view, which is not needed any more. Do not delete its dependent view. See Figure 5.63.

      <Drawings>   **<Edit View>**   **<Delete>**

Command: **AMDELVIEW**
Select view to delete: **[Select B (Figure 5.62).]**
View has 1 dependent view. Delete it also? Yes/No/<Cancel>: **NO**

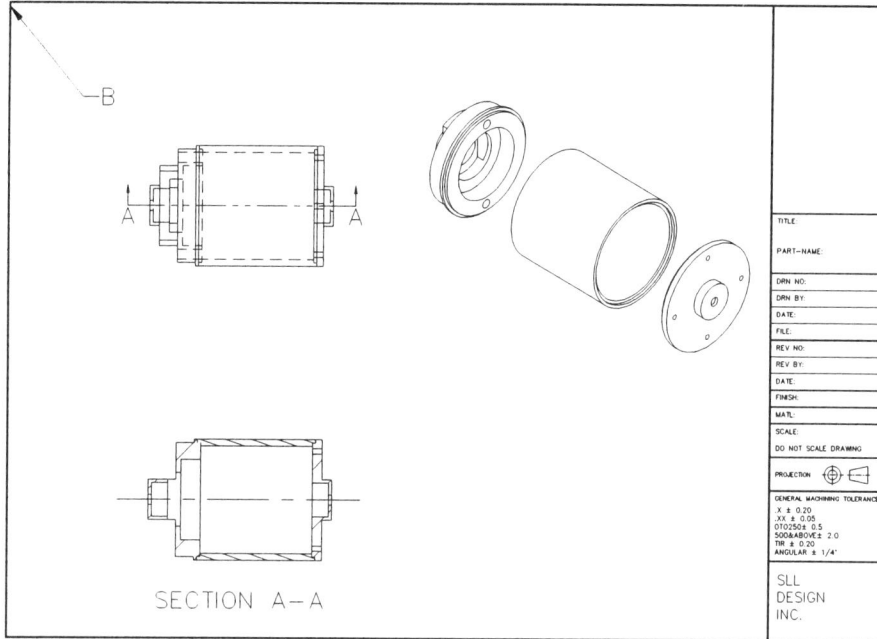

Figure 5.63 Parent view of the exploded isometric view deleted

The drawing views are completed. To complete the assembly drawing, run the AMBOMSETUP command to set up a bill of materials, apply the AMBOM command to create the bill of materials, and issue the AMBALLOON command to add callout balloons.

Run the AMBOMSETUP command.

\<Assemblies\>   \<Scene\>   \<Bill of Materials\>   \<Setup...\>

Command: **AMBOMSETUP**

```
[Table definition
     Components to include:     All
     Justification:            Left
     Sort Order:               Down
     Display Grid:             YES
     File Out:                 NO
Column Definition
     Add...
     [Column Name:            PART NO
      Column Width:           15
      Attribute Name:         PART NUMBER
      Column Date type:       String
     OK                                           ]
Balloon Definition
     Leader                   Straight
     Balloon type             Round
OK                                                 ]
```

Create the bill of materials with the AMBOM command. See Figure 5.64.

<Assemblies>   **<Scene>**   **<Bill of Materials>**   **<Create Table>**

Command: **AMBOM**
Pick the base point for the BOM table: **END** of **[Select B (Figure 5.63).]**
Pick a point to indicate the BOM table direction and extent: **@100<270**
Pick point to align BOM: **END** of **[Select B (Figure 5.63).]**

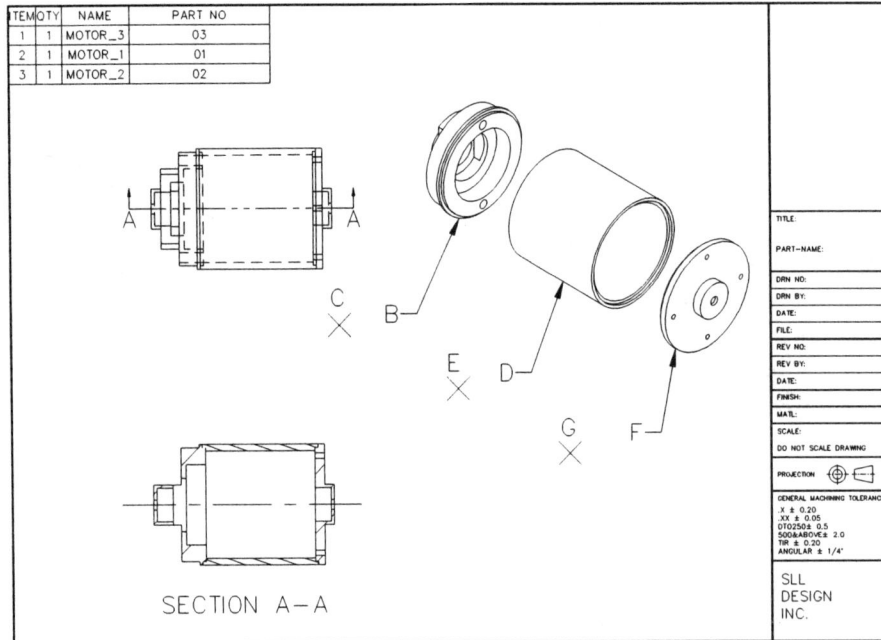

Figure 5.64 A bill of materials created

Add the callout balloons with the AMBALLOON command. See Figure 5.65.

<Assemblies>   **<Scene>**   **<Balloons>**

Command: **AMBALLOON**
Select component to balloon [Return for Unassociated] **[Select B (Figure 5.64).]**
Select leader vertex: **[Select B (Figure 5.64).]**
Select leader vertex: **[Select C (Figure 5.64).]**
Select leader vertex: **[Enter]**

[Select Column to edit: **ITEM**
OK   ]

<Assemblies>   **<Scene>**   **<Balloons>**

Command: **AMBALLOON**
Select component to balloon [Return for Unassociated] **[Select D (Figure 5.64).]**
Select leader vertex: **[Select D (Figure 5.64).]**
Select leader vertex: **[Select E (Figure 5.64).]**

Select leader vertex: **[Enter]**

[Select Column to edit: **ITEM**
OK   ]

<**Assemblies**>   <**Scene**>   <**Balloons**>

Command: **AMBALLOON**
Select component to balloon [Return for Unassociated] **[Select F (Figure 5.64).]**
Select leader vertex: **[Select F (Figure 5.64).]**
Select leader vertex: **[Select G (Figure 5.64).]**
Select leader vertex: **[Enter]**

[Select Column to edit: **ITEM**
OK   ]

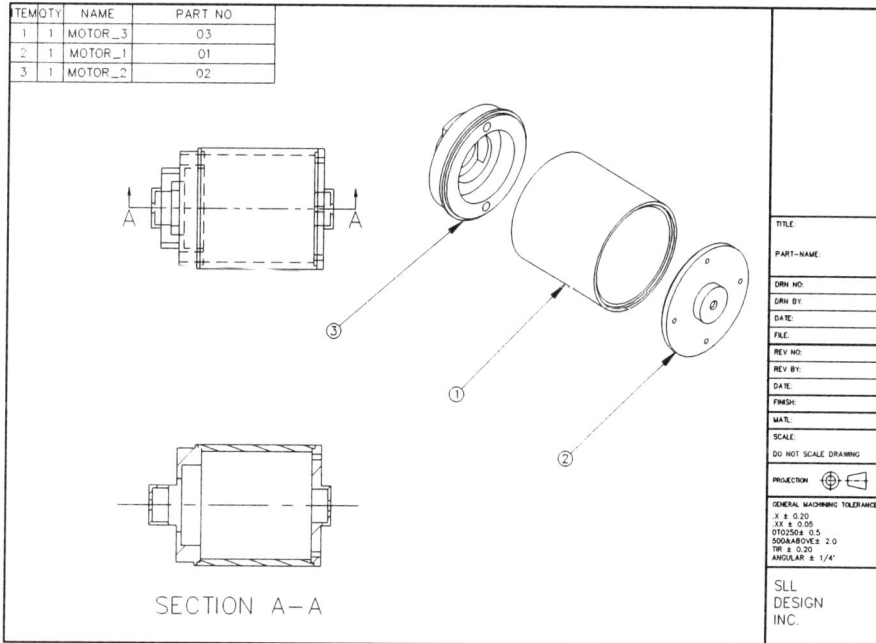

Figure 5.65 Callout balloons created

The assembly drawing is completed. Use the QSAVE command to save your drawing.

<**File**>   <**Save...**>

Command: **QSAVE**

[File name: **MOTOR.DWG**
OK   ]

5.10 Summary

In this chapter, you have applied the following AutoCAD Designer commands and variables in engineering drawing creation.

Drawing Views Commands:

AMCENLINE	AMCLDSP	AMDELVIEW
AMDWGOUT	AMDWGVARS	AMDWGVIEW
AMEDITVIEW	AMLISTDWG	AMMODE
AMMOVEVIEW		

Dimensions and Annotations Commands:

AMANNOTE	AMHIDEDIM	AMHOLENOTE
AMMOVEDIM	AMREFDIM	AMSHOWDIM
AMTEMPLATE		

Assembly Scene Commands:

AMSCENE	AMDELTRAIL	AMDELTWEAKS
AMEDITTRAIL	AMPATTERNDEF	AMTRAIL
AMTWEAK	AMSUPPRESS	AMUPDATESCENE
AMXFACTOR		

Bill of Materials Commands:

AMASSIGN	AMBALLOON	AMBOM
AMBOMSETUP	AMEDITBOM	

Variables:

AMCLCM	AMCLGAP	AMCLOSHT
AMCLPAR	AMCLTYPE	AMHIDLTYPE
AMLINETHICK	AMPROJTYPE	AMREUSEDIM
AMSECLTYPE	AMSTDDTL	AMSTDSCT
AMSTDTAP	AMVANISH	AMVPBORDER

For a brief explanation of these commands and variables, refer to the appendix of this book.

In this chapter, you created four engineering drawings. Two of these drawings were for the two solid parts you created in Chapter 2. The other two were assembly drawings for the two sets of solid parts you created in Chapter 3 and assembled in Chapter 4.

In an AutoCAD Designer drawing, there are two working modes, drawing mode and model mode. You created the solid parts in model mode and produced the engineering drawing in drawing mode. To create a drawing, you may choose an active part or an assembly. With an assembly, you may set up a number of scenes. In each scene, you may tweak or explode the instances apart. In an assembly engineering drawing, you may create drawing views from different scenes to illustrate the instances assembled together, and you may tweak or explode apart.

You may hide dimensions, and you may move dimensions within a drawing view and across drawing views. In addition to parametric dimensions, you may add reference dimensions to delineate better the solid part in drawing mode. An assembly drawing consists of a number of instances. In the assembly drawing, you may set up a bill of materials and callout balloons.

The parametric dimensions in an engineering drawing associate bidirectionally to the solid part. Change in the parametric dimensions in drawing mode modifies the solid part in model mode. Editing the solid part in model mode causes an automatic update of the parametric dimensions, as well as the reference dimensions, in drawing mode. As for the reference dimensions, they follow the change but cannot drive the change.

In the next chapter, you will create a solid part and inter-operate with NURBS surfaces and AutoCAD native solids.

5.11 Exercises

To enhance your knowledge further, you will create the documents of solid parts and assembly on your own.

Open the files LEVER.DWG, LINK.DWG, BODY.DWG, CLAMP.DWG, PIN1.DWG, and PIN2.DWG one by one. Change to drawing mode. Insert a proper title block. Make three drawing views. Position the dimensions properly. Hide those dimensions that are needed in model making but are irrelevant to manufacture. Then add reference dimensions to fully dimension the drawing for manufacture. Include an isometric view. Save each of the drawings again.

Open the file TOGGLE.DWG. Make two scenes from the assembly. Leave one scene as is, and tweak the other scene as shown in Figure 5.66.

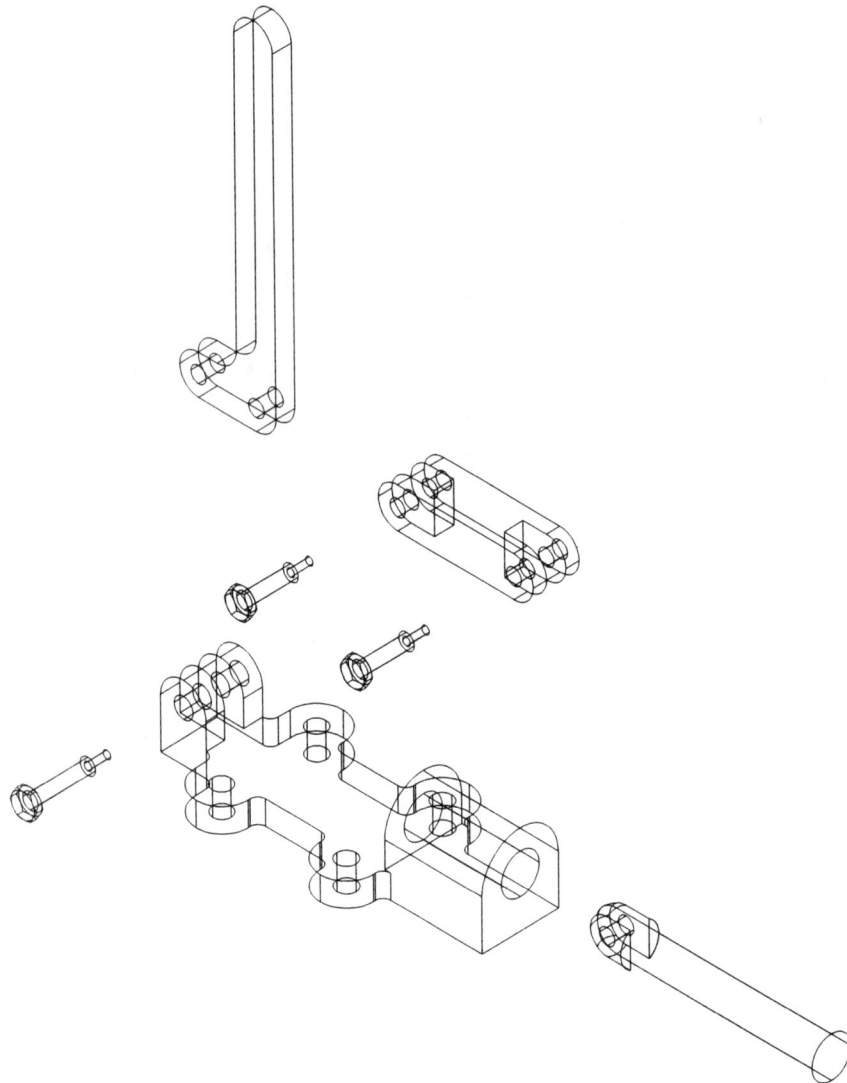

Figure 5.66 The second scene of the toggle clamp assembly tweaked

Change to drawing mode. Insert a proper title block.

Create an isometric drawing view of the tweaked scene and two orthographic views of the untweaked scene. See Figure 5.67. Save your drawing again.

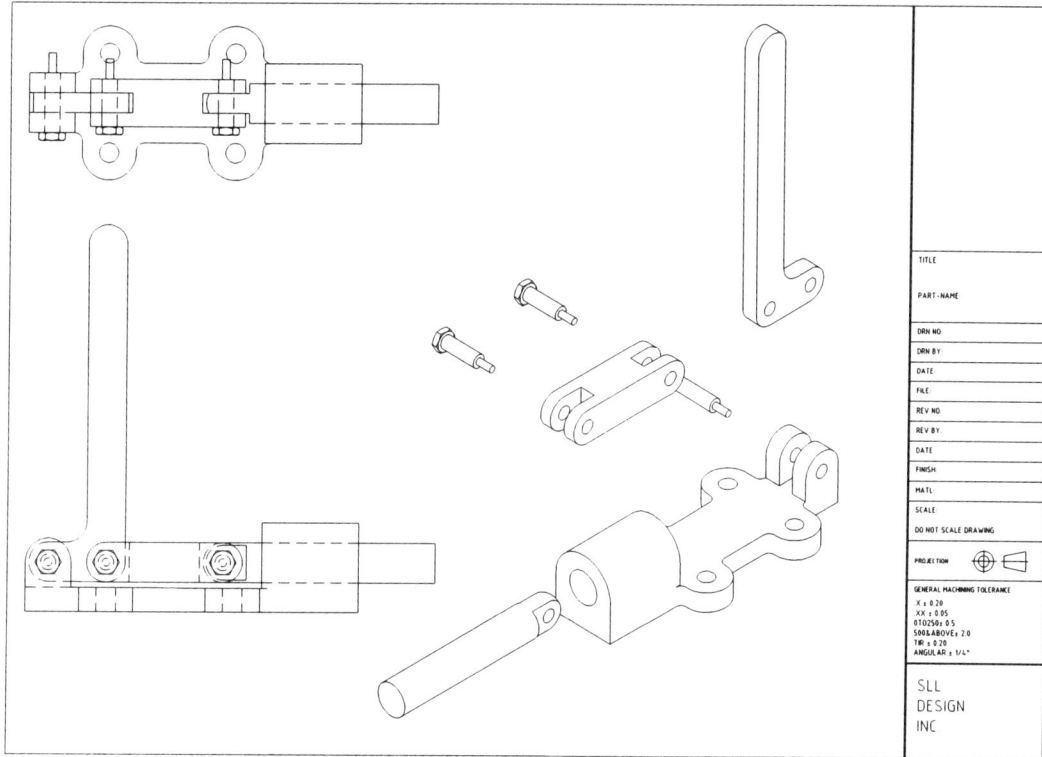

Figure 5.67 Assembly drawing of the toggle clamp

Chapter 6
Inter-Operation

You learned how to create parametric solid parts in Chapters 2 and 3, how to create assemblies from the solid parts in Chapter 4, and how to create engineering drawings for the solid parts and assemblies in Chapter 5.

After all this experience, you may find a number of limitations in using AutoCAD Designer alone in model making. One limitation is the absence of free-form surfaces. To overcome it, you may use AutoSurf to create a NURBS surface to form a surface feature to cut a parametric solid. Another limitation is the lack of variable fillets. If you want to have a variable fillet edge on your model, you may convert the model to a set of AutoSurf NURBS surfaces and then use AutoSurf to create the variable fillets. The third limitation is the restricted use of Boolean operations. In AutoCAD Designer, there can be only one active solid part. You cannot apply Boolean operations on two solid parts. In order to apply Boolean operations on two or more solid parts, you may convert the parametric solids to native solids before using Boolean operations. After that, you may convert the native solid back to a static base solid feature for subsequent adding of parametric solid features.

In this chapter, you will inter-operate AutoCAD Designer solids with NURBS surfaces and with native AutoCAD solids.

In order to inter-operate with AutoSurf NURBS surfaces, you need to have the AutoSurf R3 application properly installed in your computer. First, you will create a parametric solid part with AutoCAD Designer commands. Then you will create a NURBS surface feature using AutoSurf commands. Finally, you will use the NURBS surface feature to cut the solid part.

To inter-operate with an AutoCAD native solid, there is no extra software requirement.

6.1   Inter-Operation with AutoSurf

Figure 6.1 shows a parametric solid model with a free-form surface feature. In order to appreciate how a parametric solid part can inter-operate with AutoSurf NURBS surfaces, you will create a solid part with AutoCAD Designer; create a NURBS surface with AutoSurf; cut the solid part with the NURBS surface; and revert the solid part to a set of surfaces.

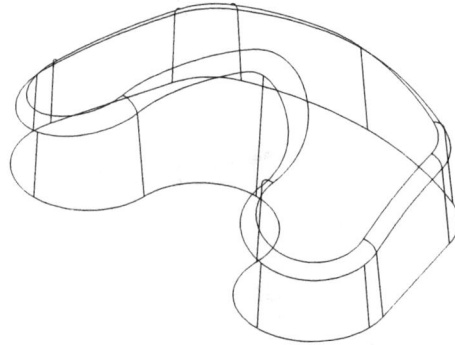

Figure 6.1 The parametric solid part with a NURBS surface feature

Start a new drawing with the NEW command.

<File>   <New...>

Command: **NEW**

Use the LIMITS command to set the drawing limit to 297 units times 210 units. Then apply the ZOOM command to zoom to this limit.

<Data>   <Drawing Limits>

Command: **LIMITS**
Reset Model space limits:
ON/OFF/<Lower left corner>: **0,0**
Upper right corner: **297,210**

[Standard Toolbar]   [Zoom All]

Command: **ZOOM**
All/Center/Dynamic/Extents/Left/Previous/Vmax/Window/<Scale(X/XP)>: **ALL**

Execute the DDLMODES command to create three additional layers, and set the current layer to SKETCH.

<Data>   <Layers...>

Command: **DDLMODES**

Layer name	Color
SKETCH	**cyan**
SURFACE	**green**
SOLID	**yellow**

Current layer: **SKETCH**

Set the UCS icon to display at its origin position by running the UCSICON command.

Command: **UCSICON**
ON/OFF/All/Noorigin/ORigin: **OR**

After making the necessary preparations, run the PLINE command to create a rough sketch as shown in Figure 6.2.

[**Draw**]   [**Polyline**]

Command: **PLINE**

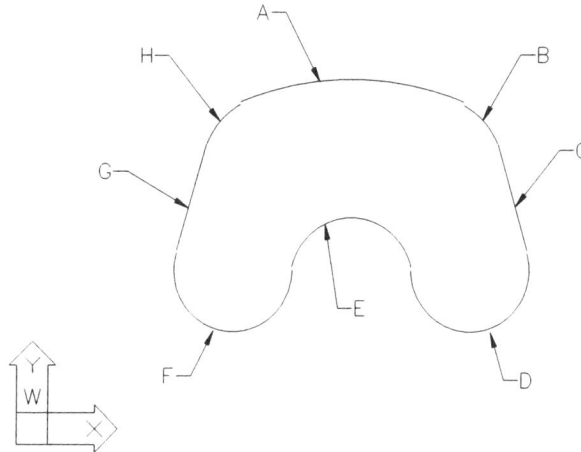

Figure 6.2 A rough sketch created

Execute the AMPROFILE command to resolve the rough sketch to form a profile.

<**Parts**>   <**Sketch**>   <**Profile**>

Command: **AMPROFILE**
Select objects for sketch:
Select objects: **LAST**
Select objects: **[Enter]**

Apply the AMADDCON command to add geometric constraints to the resolved sketch. See Figure 6.3.

<**Parts**>   <**Sketch**>   <**Constraints**>   <**Add**>

Command: **AMADDCON**

[X-Value constraint: **Apply to A/E (Figure 6.2).**
Y-Value constraint: **Apply to F/D, F/E, and H/B (Figure 6.2).**
 Radius constraint: **Apply to F/D, F/E, H/B, and H/F (Figure 3.5).**
 Tangent constraint: **Apply to all (Figure 6.2).**
Exit   ]

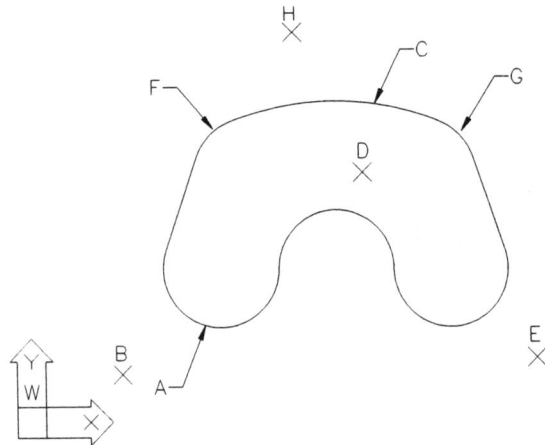

Figure 6.3 Geometric constraints applied

Run the AMDIMDSP command to set the display of parametric dimension to equation. Then issue the AMPARDIM command to add parametric dimensions to fully constrain the resolved sketch. See Figure 6.4.

<Parts>   **<Display>**   **<Dim Display>**

Command: **AMDIMDSP**
Parameters/Equations/<Numeric>: **E**

<Parts>   **<Sketch>**   **<Add Dimension>**

Command: **AMPARDIM**
Select first object: **[Select A (Figure 6.3).]**
Select second object or place dimension: **[Select B (Figure 6.3).]**
Undo/Enter Dimension value: **[Enter]**

Select first object: **[Select C (Figure 6.3).]**
Select second object or place dimension: **[Select D (Figure 6.3).]**
Undo/Enter Dimension value: **D0*5**

Select first object: **[Select A (Figure 6.3).]**
Select second object or place dimension: **[Select C (Figure 6.3).]**
Specify dimension placement: **[Select E (Figure 6.3).]**
Undo/Hor/Ver/Align/Par/Enter Dimension value: **D0*2**
Select first object: **[Select F (Figure 6.3).]**
Select second object or place dimension: **[Select G (Figure 6.3).]**
Specify dimension placement: **[Select H (Figure 6.3).]**
Undo/Hor/Ver/Align/Par/Enter Dimension value: **D0*3**

Solved fully constrained sketch.
Select first object: **[Enter]**

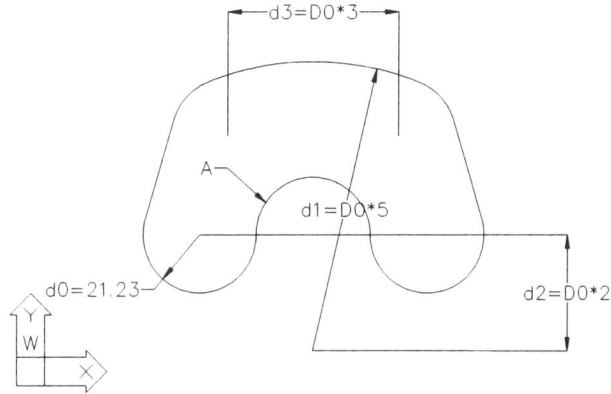

Figure 6.4 Fully constrained sketch

Set the fix point of the profile by running the AMFIXPT command. Apply the UCS command to set the origin to the fix point, and save the UCS so that you may restore to it later. Then set to an isometric view. See Figure 6.5.

<Parts>   <Sketch>   <Fix Point>

Command: **AMFIXPT**
Specify new fixed point for sketch: **[Select A (Figure 6.4).]**

[UCS]   **[Origin UCS]**

Command: **UCS**
Origin/ZAxis/3point/OBject/View/X/Y/Z/Prev/Restore/Save/Del/?/<World>: **OR**
Origin point <0,0,0>: **CEN** of **[Select A (Figure 6.4).]**

[UCS]   **[Save UCS]**

Command: **UCS**
Origin/ZAxis/3point/OBject/View/X/Y/Z/Prev/Restore/Save/Del/?/<World>: **SAVE**
?/Desired UCS name: **FIXPT**

Command: **8**

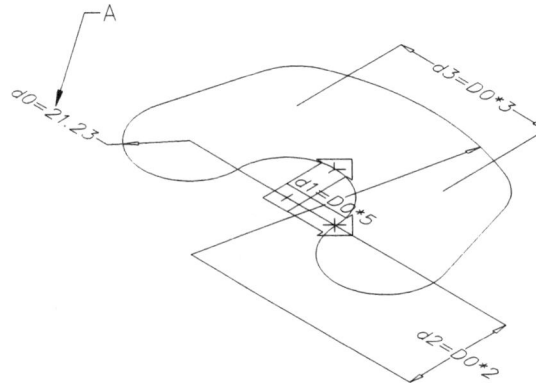

Figure 6.5 UCS origin set to the fix point of the sketch

Issue the AMMODDIM command to modify the dimension value of the D0 dimension to 20 units. Set the current layer to SOLID with the DDLMODES command. Then execute the AMEXTRUDE command to extrude the resolved sketch to form a sketched solid feature. See Figure 6.6.

<Parts>   **<Change Dimension>**

Command: **AMMODDIM**
Select dimension to change: **[Select A (Figure 6.5).]**
New value for dimension: **20**
Solved fully constrained sketch.

<Data>   **<Layers...>**

Command: **DDLMODES**
Current layer: **SOLID**

<Parts>   **<Feature>**   **<Extrude...>**

Command: **AMEXTRUDE**

[Termination: **Blind**
 Operation: **Base**
 Size:
    Distance: **D0*5**
    Draft angle: **-5**
OK   ]

Direction Flip/<Accept>: **[Accept, if the arrow is pointing upward. Otherwise, flip.]**

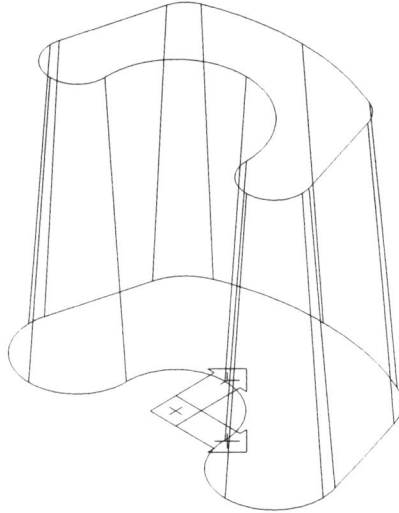

Figure 6.6 Base feature created

The base solid feature is completed. To continue, you will create a NURBS surface and use the surface as a feature to cut the solid feature.

In order to maintain a proper dimensional relationship between the solid part and the NURBS surface, you need to create the NURBS surface relative to the fix point of the solid part.

Earlier, you set the UCS origin to reside on the fix point. Now you will build the NURBS surface using the fix point as the origin point.

Set the current layer to SURFACE with the DDLMODES command. Then rotate the X axis of the UCS for 90° with the UCS command.

<Data>   **<Layers...>**

Command: **DDLMODES**
Current layer: **SURFACE**

[UCS]   **[X Axis Rotate UCS]**

Command: **UCS**
Origin/ZAxis/3point/OBject/View/X/Y/Z/Prev/Restore/Save/Del/?/<World>: **X**
Rotation angle about X axis: **90**

Run the SPLINE command to create a spline. See Figure 6.7.

[Polyline]   **[Spline]**

Command: **SPLINE**
Object/<Enter first point>: **-70,20**
Enter point: **0,32**
Close/Fit Tolerance/<Enter point>: **70,20**
Close/Fit Tolerance/<Enter point>: **[Enter]**
Enter start tangent: **[Enter]**
Enter end tangent: **[Enter]**

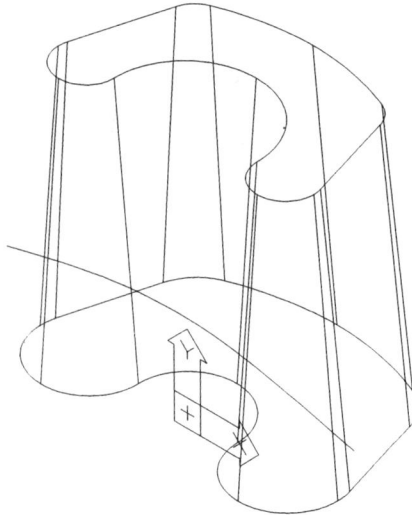

Figure 6.7 A spline created

Rotate the Y axis of the UCS 90° with the UCS command. Then use the SPLINE command to create another spline. See Figure 6.8.

[UCS]   **[Y Axis Rotate UCS]**

Command: **UCS**
Origin/ZAxis/3point/OBject/View/X/Y/Z/Prev/Restore/Save/Del/?/<World>: **Y**
Rotation angle about Y axis: **90**

[Polyline]   **[Spline]**

Command: **SPLINE**
Object/<Enter first point>: **-30,12**
Enter point: **20,20**
Close/Fit Tolerance/<Enter point>: **70,15**
Close/Fit Tolerance/<Enter point>: **[Enter]**
Enter start tangent: **[Enter]**
Enter end tangent: **[Enter]**

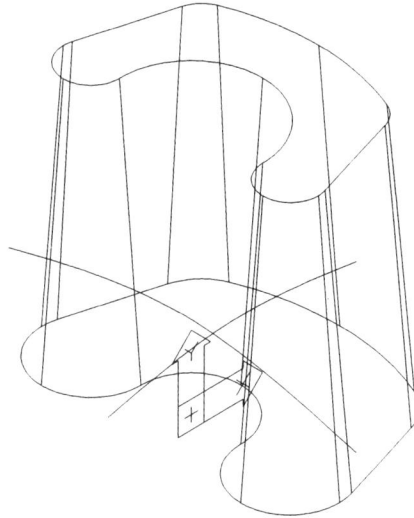

Figure 6.8 Another spline created

Translate the last spline with the MOVE command. Then set the current layer to SKETCH. See Figure 6.9.

[Modify]   **[Move]**

Command: **MOVE**
Select objects: **LAST**
Select objects: **[Enter]**
Base point or displacement: **0,0,-70**
Second point of displacement: **[Enter]**

<Data>   **<Layers...>**

Command: **DDLMODES**
Current layer: **SKETCH**

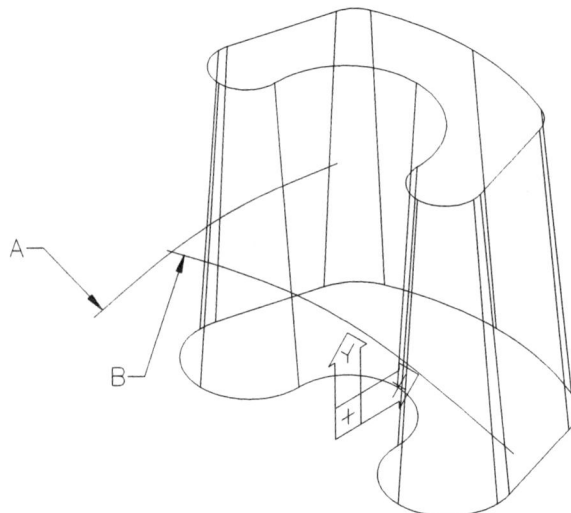

Figure 6.9 The second spline translated

Using the two splines as section and rail, respectively, execute the AMSWEEPSF command to create a swept NURBS surface. See Figure 6.10. The AMSWEEPSF command belongs to the AutoSurf application. You need to install the application properly in your computer before you can apply this command.

<Surfaces>   <Create Surface>   <Sweep>

Command: **AMSWEEPSF**
Select cross sections: **[Select A (Figure 6.9).]**
Select cross sections: **[Enter]**
Select rails: **[Select B (Figure 6.9).]**
Select rails: **[Enter]**

[Orientation: **NORMAL**
OK   ]

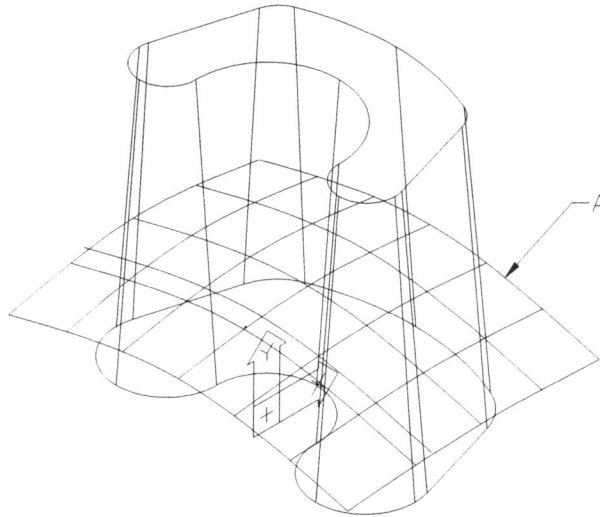

Figure 6.10 A swept surface created

Now you have a NURBS surface together with a solid part. Basically, you may use any kind of NURBS surface provided by AutoSurf to cut a solid part, provided that the surface is large enough to cut through the solid.

To use the NURBS surface to cut the solid, run the AMSURFCUT command.

   <Parts>   **<Feature>**   **<Surface Cut>**

Command: **AMSURFCUT**
Select surface: **[Select A (Figure 6.10).]**
Portion to remove: Flip/<Accept>: **[Accept, if the arrow is point upward. Otherwise, Flip.]**

After cutting the parametric solid with the NURBS surface, turn off the layer SURFACE with the DDLMODES command. See Figure 6.11.

   <Data>   **<Layers...>**

Command: **DDLMODES**
Layer off: **SURFACE**

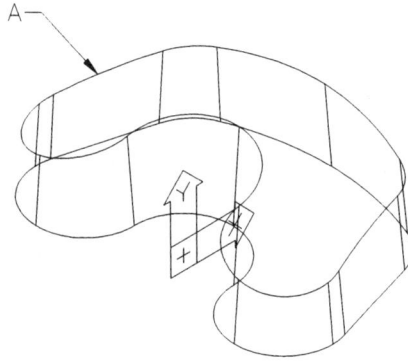

Figure 6.11 Solid part cut by the swept surface

To a solid part, a NURBS surface is a feature — a surface feature. You may continue to work on a solid that is cut by a surface. Run the AMFILLET command to fillet the upper edge of the solid part. See Figure 6.12.

<Parts>   **<Feature>**   **<Fillet>**

Command: **AMFILLET**
Pick the edge to fillet: **[Select A (Figure 6.11).]**
Pick the edge to fillet: **[Enter]**
Fillet radius: **D0/5**

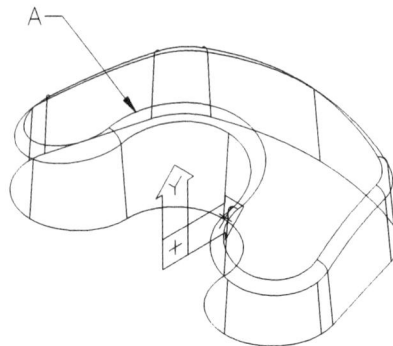

Figure 6.12 Upper edge filleted

Although the surface feature itself is not parametric, you may still modify its profile after it is used to cut a parametric solid. Run the AMEDITFEAT command to edit the surface feature. Pick the "surfCut" option. The original surface elicits. See Figure 6.13.

<Parts>   **<Edit Feature>**

Command: **AMEDITFEAT**
Sketch/surfCut/<select Feature>: **C**
Select surfcut feature: **[Select A (Figure 6.12).]**

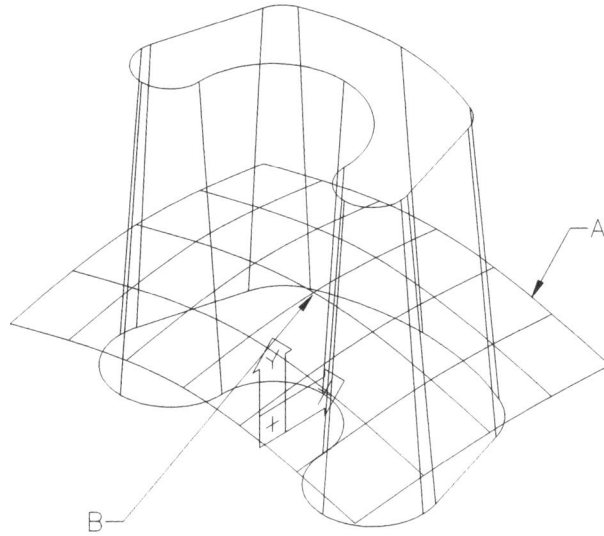

Figure 6.13 The original surface elicited

After you pick the "surfCut" option, the original NURBS surface appears again.

Before you edit the profile of the surface, run the AMEDITSF command to set the span of the surface. The AMEDITSF command is an AutoSurf command.

[**Surface Edit**]   [**Grip Point Placement**]

Command: **AMEDITSF**
Select surfaces: **[Select A (Figure 6.13).]**
Select surfaces: **[Enter]**

[Grips
          U: **7**
          V: **5**
    Span: **20**
OK   ]

The span that you have set defines a circular area with a radius of 20 units. When you pull a control point on the surface, you will deform such a circular area around that grip point.

Set the GRIPS variable to 1 to turn grips on. Then select the central point of the surface, and stretch it a distance of 10 units in the 90° direction. See Figure 6.14.

Command: **GRIPS**
New value for GRIPS: **1**

Command: **[Select B (Figure 6.13).]**

Command: ** STRETCH **
<Stretch to point>/Base point/Copy/Undo/eXit: **@10<90**

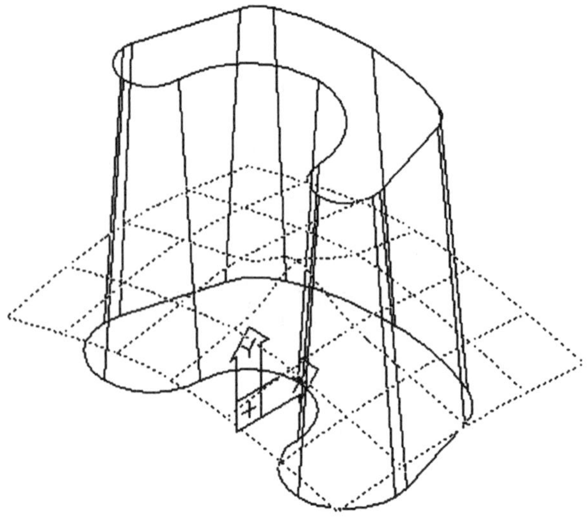

Figure 6.14 The surface stretched

As can be seen, the area of the surface affected by grip pulling is equal to the span that you defined earlier.

To update the change, run the AMUPDATE command. See Figure 6.15.

<Parts>   **<Update>**

Command: **AMUPDATE**

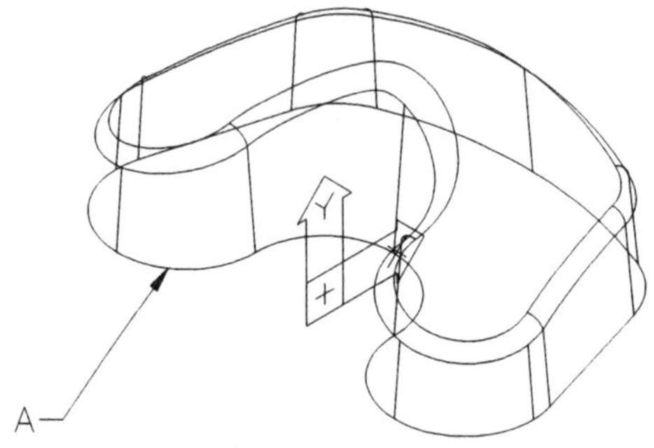

Figure 6.15 The solid part updated

You learned how to use a NURBS surface as a feature to cut a solid part. Run the SAVEAS command to save your file.

<File>   **<Save As...>**

Command: **SAVEAS**

[File name: **CONTROL1**
OK   ]

Sometimes, you may want to change a parametric solid part into a set of NURBS surfaces for further surface creation and editing. For example, you may want to have a variable fillet. To do this, you may run the AM2SF command. See Figure 6.16. Issue the SAVE command to save your file to another name.

<Surfaces>   <Create Surface>   <From ACAD>

Command: **AM2SF**
Face/<Objects>: **[Enter]**
Select objects: **[Select A (Figure 6.15).]**
Select objects: **[Enter]**

<File>   <Save As...>

Command: **SAVEAS**

[File name: **CONTROL2**
OK   ]

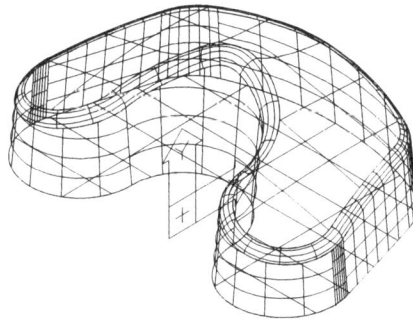

Figure 6.16 The solid part converted to a set of surfaces

To sum up, you may inter-operate between AutoCAD Designer and AutoSurf. To cut a solid part with an AutoSurf surface, you may use the AMSURFCUT command. To convert a solid part to a set of AutoSurf surfaces, you may use the AM2SF command. Of course, you need to install AutoSurf in your computer in order to do the inter-operation.

6.2 Inter-Operation with AutoCAD Native Solid

A solid part can also inter-operate with a native solid. Because native solid modeling is a part of the AutoCAD basic package, you do not need additional tools in order to inter-operate a solid part with a native solid.

Run the OPEN command to open the saved solid part file, CONTROL1.

<File>   <Open...>

Command: **OPEN**

[File name: **CONTROL1.DWG**
OK]

Issue the UCS command to restore to the saved UCS. The saved UCS locates at the fix point of the solid part.

[UCS] **[Restore UCS]**

Command: **UCS**
Origin/ZAxis/3point/OBject/View/X/Y/Z/Prev/Restore/Save/Del/?/<World>: **R**
?/Name of UCS to restore: **FIXPT**

Apply the CYLINDER command to create a native solid cylinder. See Figure 6.17.

[Solids] **[Cylinder]**

Command: **CYLINDER**
Elliptical/<center point>: **CEN** of **[Select A (Figure 6.15).]**
Diameter/<Radius>: **5**
Center of other end/<Height>: **50**

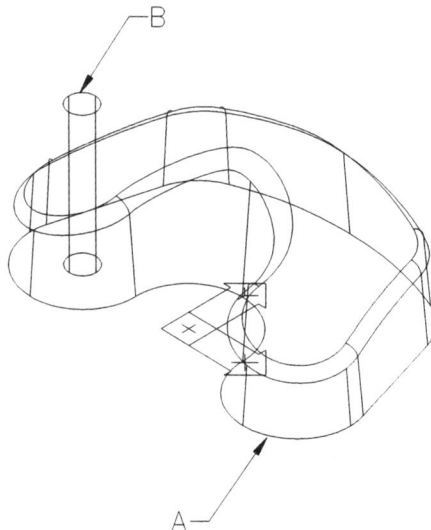

Figure 6.17 A native solid cylinder created

On your display, there are two distinctive types of solids, a parametric solid and a native solid. They are different objects. To inter-operate between them, you have to convert the parametric solid to a native solid. Run the EXPLODE command. Be very cautious when you run this command. If you run it on a parametric solid part, you will convert the parametric solid part down one level of complexity, the native solid. If you run it on a native solid, you will convert the native solid one level down, which is a set of faces and edges.

[Modify]   **[Explode]**

Command: **EXPLODE**
Select objects: **[Select A (Figure 6.17).]**
Select objects: **[Enter]**

After you run the EXPLODE command, there will not be any change on your screen. Do not run the command more than once on the solid part.

Now the parametric solid part becomes a native solid. The parametric parts history has been lost. You cannot modify its existing features any more.

Execute the SUBTRACT command to subtract the cylinder from the converted solid. See Figure 6.18.

[Modify]   **[Subtract]**

Command: **SUBTRACT**
Select solids and regions to subtract from...
Select objects: **[Select A (Figure 6.17).]**
Select objects: **[Enter]**
Select solids and regions to subtract...
Select objects: **[Select B (Figure 6.17).]**
Select objects: **[Enter]**

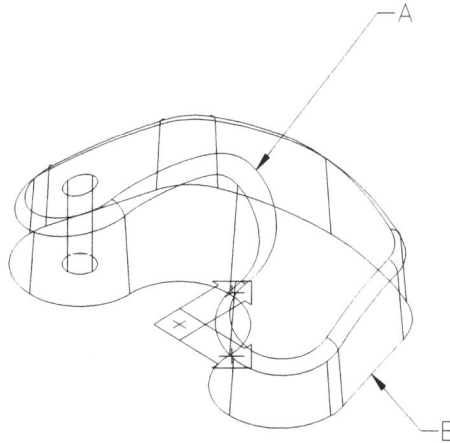

Figure 6.18 Cylinder subtracted from the converted solid

Just as you can convert a parametric solid part to a native solid, you can convert a native solid to a static solid part. Run the AMNEWPART command to convert the solid to a static base solid.

<Parts>   **<Part>**   **<New>**

Command: **AMNEWPART**
Select native solid or (RETURN) : **[Select A (Figure 6.18).]**
New part created.

The new solid part that you have created from a native solid is a static base solid. It has no history, because the native solid that it derives from does not have one. As a result, you may use it only as a base solid. You may add features to it but not edit it. The added features, however, are parametric and editable.

Try the AMEDITFEAT command on the top surface and the side of the static solid part. Notice that the command does not work on a static solid.

      <Parts>   **<Edit Feature>**

Command: **AMEDITFEAT**
Sketch/surfCut/<select Feature>: **C**
Select surfcut feature: **[Select A (Figure 6.18).]**
Operation cannot be performed on the selected feature.
Select surfcut feature: ***Cancel***

      <Parts>   **<Edit Feature>**

Command: **AMEDITFEAT**
Sketch/surfCut/<select Feature>: **[Select B (Figure 6.18).]**
Operation cannot be performed on the selected feature.
Bad selection. Please try again.
Sketch/surfCut/<select Feature>: ***Cancel***

You have converted the parametric solid part to a native solid, used a native solid to subtract the converted solid, and converted a native solid to a static solid part.

6.3 Summary

In this chapter, you applied the following AutoCAD Designer commands and AutoCAD commands to inter-operate AutoCAD three-dimensional objects.

AMNEW	AM2SF	AMEDITSF
AMSURFCUT	EXPLODE	SUBTRACT

The AMSURFCUT command, the AMEDITSF command, and the AM2SF command are part of the AutoSurf application; they are used here to illustrate how a parametric solid may inter-operate with a NURBS surface. For details about AutoSurf and AutoCAD native solids, please refer to textbooks on AutoSurf and AutoCAD native solids.

By now, you should be able to inter-operate between parametric AutoCAD Designer solid part with AutoSurf NURBS surfaces and AutoCAD native solids.

The appendix provides a brief explanation of all the AutoCAD Designer commands and variables.

6.4 Exercise

To enhance your knowledge of inter-operation, you will make the model that is shown in Figure 6.19.

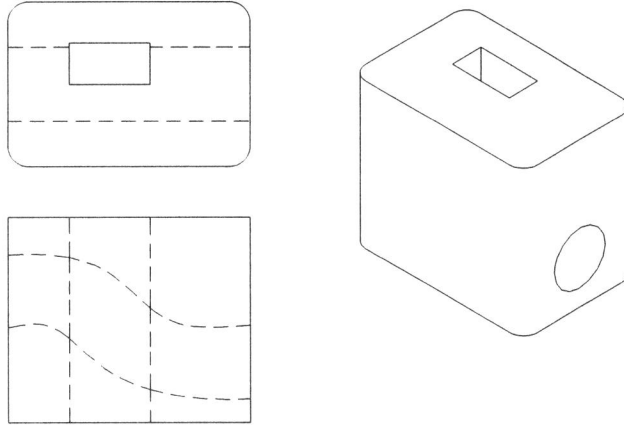

Figure 6.19 The completed model of the support pad

As shown in Figure 6.20, create a native solid model. First draw a rectangle. Then fillet the four corners. Finally, use the EXTRUDE command to extrude it to form a solid.

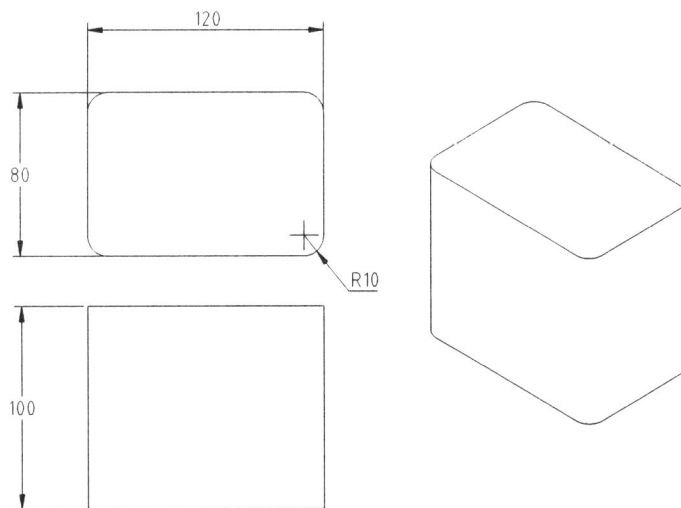

Figure 6.20 A native solid model created

Convert the native solid to a static base solid. As shown in Figure 6.21, make a sketch, resolve the sketch to form a profile, fully constrain the profile, extrude the profile, and cut the extruded solid from the base solid.

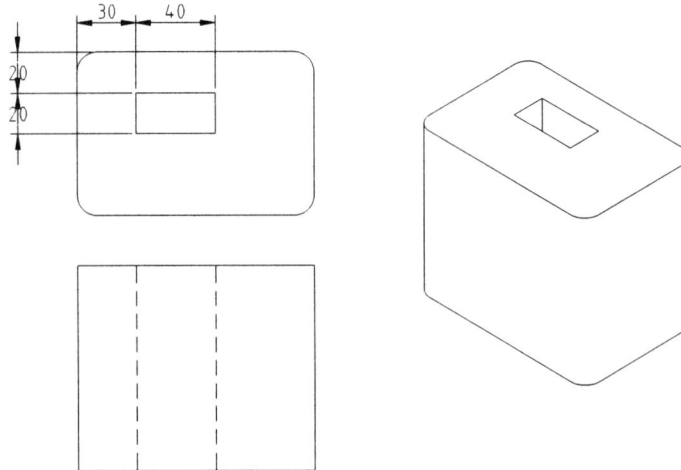

Figure 6.21 A sketched feature cut from the base solid feature

Draw a spline to pass through the points (-20,0,60), (35,0,60), (60,0,40), and (130,0,30). Create a circle with a diameter of 18 units at one end. See Figure 6.22.

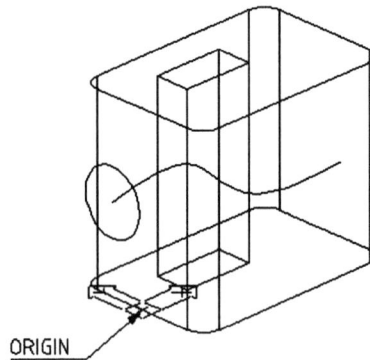

Figure 6.22 A spline and a circle created

Create a swept surface, using the circle as the cross section and the spline as the rail. See Figure 6.23.

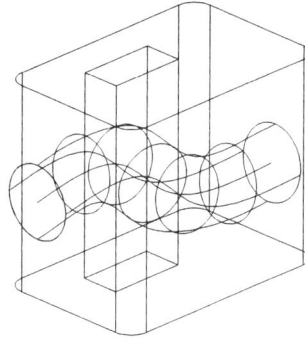

Figure 6.23 A swept surface created

Complete the model using the swept surface to cut the solid. See Figure 6.19. Save your drawing.

Appendix
Quick Reference

In the previous chapters, you have practiced how to create dimension-driven feature-based parametric solid parts, to create component definitions from solid parts, to instance component definitions, to apply assembly constraints to instances, to create two-dimensional engineering drawings, to produce an exploded view of an assembly, to apply utility commands on solid parts and assemblies, and to inter-operate parametric solid parts with AutoSurf NURBS surfaces and AutoCAD native solids.

This appendix provides a summary of the AutoCAD Designer Release 2 commands and variables, together with a table delineating the changes in command names and system variable names from AutoCAD Designer Release 1 to Release 2.

A.1   Pull-Down Menu and Windows Toolbar

There are four additional pull-down menu items and five additional toolbars.
The pull-down menus are

> Parts
> Assemblies
> Drawings
> Mtools

The toolbars are

> Part Create
> Part Edit
> Assembly
> Drawing
> View

A.2   Sketching and Resolution Commands

AMCOPYSKETCH	copies a sketch to the active sketch plane.
AMCUTLINE	resolves a sketch to form a parametric cutting line for subsequent preparation of an offset section in the drawing mode.
AMFIXPT	specifies a fix point on a sketch.
AMPATH	resolves a sketch to form a parametric path for subsequent sweeping of a profile.

AMPROFILE	resolves a sketch to form a parametric profile for subsequent extrusion, sweeping, or revolving.
AMSKPLN	sets the X and Y axes orientation of a sketch plane.

A.3   Geometric Constraints Commands

AMADDCON	adds the geometric constraints to a path, profile, or cutting line.
AMDELCON	deletes the geometric constraints from a path, profile, or cutting line.
AMSHOWCON	shows the geometric constraint symbols on a path, profile, or cutting line.

A.4   Parametric Dimensions Commands

AMDIMDSP	sets the parametric dimension display to parameter name, numeric value, or equation.
AMMODDIM	modifies the parametric dimensions of a path, profile, or cutting line.
AMPARAM	manages the global parameters for a set of solid parts in a drawing file or across a set of drawing files.
AMPARDIM	creates parametric dimensions interactively to a path, profile, or cutting line.
ERASE	deletes AutoCAD objects, including parametric dimensions.

A.5   Solid Feature Creation Commands

AMCHAMFER	creates chamfer edges on an active solid part.
AMEXTRUDE	creates a parametric sketched solid feature by extruding a profile.
AMFILLET	creates fillet edges on an active solid part.
AMHOLE	cuts a plain hole, countersinking hole, or counterboring hole in an active solid part.
AMNEWPART	starts a new solid part in a drawing, or converts an AutoCAD native solid to a static base solid feature.
AMREVOLVE	creates a parametric sketched solid feature by revolving a profile about an axis.
AMSWEEP	creates a parametric sketched solid feature by sweeping a profile along a path.

A.6   Solid Feature Modification Commands

AMACTPART	selects a solid part in a multi-part drawing to become the active part.

AMARRAY	creates multiple solid features by rectangular or polar arraying of solid features in a part.
AMDELFEAT	deletes a solid feature, and its dependent solid features, from an active part.
AMEDITFEAT	edits the solid features and sketches of an active solid part.
AMMAKEBASE	converts an active parametric solid part to a static base solid feature.
AMREPLAY	replays and truncates the parts history.
AMSHOWACT	highlights the active solid part or sketch plane.
AMSURFCUT	cuts an active solid part by using an AutoSurf surface feature.
AMUPDATE	updates an active solid part after editing its features or sketches.

A.7 Construction Features Commands

AMAXISDSP	controls the display of the work axes of an active part.
AMPLNDSP	controls the display of the work planes of an active solid part.
AMPTDSP	controls the display of the work points of an active solid part.
AMWORKAXIS	creates a parametric work axis on an active solid part.
AMWORKPLN	creates a parametric work plane on an active solid part.
AMWORKPT	creates a parametric work point on an active solid part.

A.8 Assembly Commands

AMALIGN	applies an alignment constraint to a pair of instances.
AMASSEMBLE	resolves the assembly constraints and assembles the instances together accordingly.
AMCONSTRAIN	applies assembly constraints to a pair of instances.
AMDELCONST	deletes the assembly constraints from a pair of instances.
AMEDITCONST	edits the assembly constraints of a pair of instances.
AMFLUSH	applies a parallelism constraint to a pair of instances.
AMINTERFERE	checks the inference between a pair of instances in an assembly.
AMMATE	applies a mating constraint to a pair of instances.
AMOPPOSE	applies an opposing alignment constraint to a pair of instances.

A.9 Component Definitions and Instances Commands

AMAUDIT	compares the time and date stamp of the externally referenced drawing files against the current assembly drawing, and determines whether you have to update the assembly.
AMBROWSE	manipulates the instances in an assembly.
AMCOMPIN	imports the component definitions from an external drawing file.

AMCOMPMAN	manages the component definitions in an assembly drawing.
AMCOMPOUT	outputs a component definition to an external drawing file.
AMDELCOMP	deletes an instance from an assembly drawing.
AMINSERT	inserts an instance to the assembly drawing.
AMNEW	creates a component definition or initializes a sub-assembly.
AMREFRESH	refreshes the external component definitions.
AMRENAME	renames an instance in an assembly drawing.
AMREPLACE	replaces an instance with another instance.
AMTARGET	chooses an assembly or a sub-assembly as the current edit target.
AMWHEREUSE	displays where an instance is used in an assembly drawing.

A.10 Drawing Views Commands

AMCENLINE	creates a parametric center line in drawing mode.
AMCLDSP	controls the display of the cutting line sketch on the active solid part.
AMDELVIEW	deletes a drawing view and, optionally, its dependent views.
AMDWGOUT	outputs a two-dimensional engineering drawing file from the drawing data of an AutoCAD Designer drawing file.
AMDWGVARS	manipulates the systems variables for drawing preparation.
AMDWGVIEW	creates a drawing view in drawing mode.
AMEDITVIEW	edits the zoom scale, the associated text, and the hidden line display of a drawing view.
AMLISTDWG	lists the information about a drawing view.
AMMODE	toggles between the part mode and the drawing mode.
AMMOVEVIEW	moves a drawing view and its dependent views.

A.11 Dimensions and Annotations Commands

AMANNOTE	manipulates the annotations in a drawing.
AMHIDEDIM	hides the dimensions in a drawing.
AMHOLENOTE	manipulates the hole notes in a drawing.
AMMOVEDIM	moves the dimensions from one view to another in a drawing.
AMREFDIM	adds reference dimensions to a drawing.
AMSHOWDIM	shows the hidden dimensions in a drawing.
AMTEMPLATE	manipulates the hole notes template.

A.12 Assembly Scene Commands

AMSCENE	sets to scene mode and creates, edits, and deletes scenes.
AMDELTRAIL	deletes the explosion trail path of an assembly scene.
AMDELTWEAKS	deletes the tweak of an instance in an exploded assembly scene.
AMEDITTRAIL	edits the explosion trail path of an assembly scene.

AMPATTERNDEF	sets the hatch pattern definition of the instances in an assembly.
AMTRAIL	creates an explosion trail path in an assembly scene.
AMTWEAK	tweaks the position of an instance in an assembly scene.
AMSUPPRESS	suppresses the visibility of an instance in scene mode.
AMUPDATESCENE	updates the scene.
AMXFACTOR	sets the explosion factor of an assembly scene.

A.13 Bill of Materials Commands

AMASSIGN	manipulates the component attributes.
AMBALLOON	creates the callout balloon.
AMBOM	creates a bill of materials.
AMBOMSETUP	sets up the callout balloons and a bill of materials.
AMEDITBOM	edits the bill of materials.

A.14 Utilities Commands

AMABOUT	displays the AutoCAD Designer version number and copyright notes.
AMASSMPROP	evaluates and displays the mass properties of an instance of an assembly.
AMASSMVARS	manipulates the assembly system variables.
AMASSMVIS	controls the visibility, the center-of-gravity symbol, and the degrees-of-freedom symbol of instances in an assembly.
AMLISTASSM	lists the information about an assembly.
AMLISTPART	lists information about parts and features.
AMPARTPROP	lists the mass properties of a part.
AMPARTVARS	sets AutoCAD Designer system variables.
AMVIEW	changes the view orientation in part mode.
AMVIEWRESTORE	restores the model space view of an edit target.

A.15 AutoCAD Designer Variables

AMAUTOASSEMBLE	controls whether the drawing is to be updated after the setting of an assembly constraint.
AMCLCM	controls the line length of the center line.
AMCLGAP	controls the gap length of the center line.
AMCLOSHT	controls the overshoot length of the center line.
AMCLPAR	controls whether the overshoot length of the center line changes parametrically.
AMCLTYPE	controls the center line type.
AMCOMPSV	controls whether compression is applied during saving.
AMCONDSPSZ	controls the constraint symbol display size.
AMHIDLTYPE	controls the hidden line type.

AMLINETHICK	controls the ISO and DIN thread thickness.
AMPROJTYPE	controls the projection type, first or third angle.
AMREUSEDIM	controls whether the parametric dimensions display automatically in the drawing view.
AMRULEMODE	controls whether the constraint rules are applied while resolving a sketch.
AMSECLTYPE	controls the cutting plane line type for a sectional view.
AMSKANGTOL	controls the angular tolerance while resolving a sketch.
AMSKMODE	controls whether to treat the sketch as precise or as rough while resolving a sketch.
AMSKSTYLE	controls the sketch line type.
AMSTDDTL	controls the detail callout standard.
AMSTDSCT	controls the sectional view cutting plane standard.
AMSTDTAP	controls the tapped hole standard.
AMVANISH	toggles on and off the display of tapped hole vanishes (also known as thread runout).
AMVIEWRESTORE	controls whether the subassembly view is restored while switching between edit targets.
AMVPBORDER	toggles on and off the display of the viewport borders.

A.16 Related AutoCAD Variable

CMDDIA	toggles between dialog box display and command line prompt for command interaction.
DISPSILH	toggles on and off the display of silhouette edges.
ISOLINES	controls the number of isolines for the display of curved surfaces.
PICKBOX	sets the size of the pick box at the cross hairs. It controls the distance tolerance while resolving a sketch.

A.17 Related Short Cut Keys

F	fits all the entities to the screen display.
S	starts the SPLINE command.
W	toggles between drawing mode and model mode.
QQ	edits drawing view with the AMEDITVIEW command.
UU	sets the UCS to the current view.
VV	hides and unhides objects.
1	sets the display to a single viewport.
2	sets the display to two viewports.
3	sets the display to three viewports.
4	sets the display to four viewports.
5	sets the display to the top view.
6	sets the display to the front view.
7	sets the display to the right side view.

8	sets the display to the isometric view.
9	sets the display to the plan view of the current UCS.
]	rotates the display view to the right.
[	rotates the display view to the left.
=	rotates the display view upward.
-	rotates the display view downward.

A.18 Command Name Changes Related to Previous Release

If you have been a user of AutoCAD Designer Release 1, you may find that the AutoCAD Designer command names have changed significantly. The following table gives the changes in the command names.

Designer R1	Designer R2	AutoSurf R3	AutoCAD
ADACTPART	AMACTPART		
ADADDCON	AMADDCON		
ADANNOTE	AMANNOTE		
ADASFCONV	——	AM2SF	
ADAXISDAP	AMAXISDSP		
ADCHAMFER	AMCHAMFER		
ADDELCON	AMDELCON		
ADDELFEAT	AMDELFEAT		
ADDELREF	——	——	ERASE
ADDELVIEW	AMDELVIEW		
ADDIMATT	——	——	DIMOVERRIDE
ADDIMDSP	AMDIMDSP		
ADEDITFEAT	AMEDITFEAT		
ADEDITVIEW	AMEDITVIEW		
ADEXTRUDE	AMEXTRUDE		
ADFILLET	AMFILLET		
ADFIXPT	AMFIXPT		
ADFRZDIM	AMHIDEDIM		
ADHOLE	AMHOLE		
ADHOLENOTE	AMHOLENOTE		
ADISOLINES	——	——	ISOLINES
ADLIST	AMLISTPART & AMLISTDWG		
ADMAKEBASE	AMMAKEBASE		
ADMASSPROP	AMPARTPROP		
AMMESH	——	——	HIDE, SHADE & RENDER
ADMODDIM	AMMODDIM		
ADMODE	AMMODE		
ADMOVEDIM	AMMOVEDIM		
ADMOVELDR	——	——	Grip manipulation
ADMOVEVIEW	AMMOVEVIEW		
ADNEWPART	AMNEWPART		

Designer R1	Designer R2	AutoSurf R3	AutoCAD
ADPARAM	AMPARAM		
ADPARDIM	AMPARDIM		
ADPARTIN	——	——	INSERT
ADPARTOUT	——	——	WBLOCK
ADPARTVIEW	AMVIEW		
ADPATH	AMPATH		
ADPLNDSP	AMPLNDSP		
ADPROFILE	AMPROFILE		
ADPTDSP	AMPTDSP		
ADREFDIM	AMREFDIM		
ADREVOLVE	AMREVOLVE		
ADSATIN	——	——	ACISIN
ADSATOUT	——	——	ACISOUT
ADSETTINGS	AMPARTVARS & AMDWGVARS		
ADSHOWACT	AMSHOWACT		
ADSHOWCON	AMSHOWCON		
ADSKPLN	AMSKPLN		
ADSWEEP	AMSWEEP		
ADTHAWDIM	AMSHOWDIM		
ADUPDATE	AMUPDATE		
ADVER	AMVER		
ADVIEW	AMDWGVIEW		
ADWORKAXIS	AMWORKAXIS		
ADWORKPLN	AMWORKPLN		
ADWORKPT	AMWORKPT		

The following is a table of the changes in the system variable names.

Designer R1	Designer R2	AutoCAD
ADBORDER	AMVPBORDER	
ADCONDSPSZ	AMCONDSPSZ	
ADHIDLTYPE	AMHIDLTYPE	
ADISOCYL	——	DISPSILH
ADISONURB	——	DISPSILH
ADPROJTYPE	AMPROJTYPE	
ADREUSEDIM	AMREUSEDIM	
ADRULEMODE	AMRULEMODE	
ADSECLTYPE	AMSECLTYPE	
ADSKANGTOL	AMSKANGTOL	
ADSKMODE	AMSKMODE	
ADSKSTYLE	AMSKSTYLE	

Index